1986

Foundations of
Psychobiology

Foundations of
Psychobiology

Daniel N. Robinson
Georgetown University

William R. Uttal
University of Michigan

Macmillan Publishing Co., Inc.
New York

Collier Macmillan Publishers
London

Macmillan Publishing Co., Inc.
866 Third Avenue, New York, New York 10022

Collier Macmillan Canada, Inc.

Library of Congress Cataloging in Publication Data

Robinson, Daniel N., Date:
  Foundations of psychobiology.

  Includes bibliographies and index.
  1. Psychology, Physiological. I. Uttal,
William R. II. Title. [DNLM: 1. Psychophysiology.
WL 102 R659f]
QP360.R613   152   82-6564
ISBN 0-02-402460-0   AACR2

Printing: 1 2 3 4 5 6 7 8   Year: 3 4 5 6 7 8 9 0

ISBN   0-02-402460-0

For Francine and Mit-chan

Preface

Another text in psychobiology!

Well, yes and no. A common complaint among those who take the responsibilities of teaching seriously is that none of the available texts in psychobiology really satisfies the objectives of the course. And, of course, as long as this remains the ageless lament of professors, there will always be room for still another text and for writers who allow hope to triumph over reality.

We did not undertake the present work merely for our own courses, and we certainly do not offer it as the answer for all courses. If, as Aristotle taught, virtue is the midpoint between two vices, our virtue here is to be found between selfishness and grandiosity. But if virtue carried no burden it wouldn't be virtue, and so we should say a few words about the burdens of sticking to the middle course.

First, and most obvious, is the burden of *selection.* The author who would please everyone—or at least displease the fewest—must leave no stone unturned, no topic uncovered, no fact or hypothesis slighted. Such an author has the luxury of writing a very thick *handbook,* an enlarged glossary with pictures. The strategy behind such estimable works is to say very nearly everything, thereby permitting the professor to choose this and jettison that. That such tomes have an important function cannot be denied, but it is not at all clear that the uninitiated undergraduate gains much from them. Courses tend to be organized around assigned texts. Where the latter are oppressive, the former are likely to be incoherent.

Our own effort is a modest one. The discipline itself is bloated with extremely technical information which the novice routinely finds forbidding. In our own experience, 400 pages of such material are about as many as a bright and motivated undergraduate is likely to manage in a single term. We have no evidence to suggest that the student, in just this one term, can become a competent neuroanatomist, neurochemist, neurophysiologist, psychobiologist, and clinical neurologist. We have been content, therefore, to provide critical appraisals of those methods and findings that stand at the foundation of modern psychobiology, and to do so within a small number of traditional psychological contexts. We offer as much anatomy and physiology as these contexts require, no more and no less. The contexts themselves—perception, learning, memory, personality, emotion, and so on—are, as we say, traditional, though our approach is occasionally unconventional. We have not selected our material in such a way as to celebrate the genius of our contemporaries. Rather, we have attempted to alert the student to any number of conceptual and methodological problems that continue to vex the discipline. Thus, the text is not a review of a settled body of knowledge and opinion but an introduction to the assets *and* the liabilities of a relatively new realm of inquiry that is not fully defined.

In matters of this kind, selection entails a perspective. What we offer in this book is our perspective on the first course in psychobiology. We recognize this course as one among many the undergraduate will complete; one among many striving to honor the purposes of a broad education in the liberal arts and sciences. Accordingly, we attempt to make contact, where appropriate, with the balance of the student's education—an education that includes philosophy, history, the natural sciences. In the most fundamental respect, all of these courses are courses in *epistemology*, courses addressed as much to the issue of *how* we know as to the purely factual matter of *what* we know. The specialty of psychobiology, more than most, actually does make direct contact with problems historically treated in philosophy, ethics, biology, medicine, and their offshoots. In light of this, it seems to make no sense to avoid discussions of this contact in a text intended to introduce the student to the subject. Philosophy of Mind is alive and well today, and it routinely avails itself of the discoveries emanating from the psychobiologist's laboratory. Medical ethics, too, commands keen attention as it examines "psychosurgery," concepts of persons, "brain death," and any number of issues at least partly illuminated by psychobiological findings and methods. We do not consider such cross-disciplinary concerns to be digressions in the inroductory course even if they do not crop up in the day-to-day activities of most psychobiologists. Rather, we take them to be central to the contribution our specialty might make to undergraduate education. Such concerns cannot, of course, dominate a book such as this, but we alert the reader to the fact that they have not been "officially" ignored.

In addition to the burdens of selection and perspective there is that of *organization*. Were psychobiology a highly developed subject—organized around tried and true theories and now awaiting the results of just a few "crucial experiments"—the task of organization would amount to no more than the telling of a story. Our colleagues recognize, however, that this is now scarcely the state of affairs. New methods and the burgeoning of fact race on far faster than our attempted integrations. Texts intended for fellow-specialists must strive to be current and exhaustive even as this race goes on, but a text intended for undergraduates can and (in our view) must "leave the field." The undergraduate need not know what was discovered last Tuesday in order to have an instructed sense of the aims and character of psychobiology. We have organized the present text, therefore, around but a handful of issues and psychological processes likely to engage the energies of psychobiology for the indefinite future. Necessarily, we have left much unsaid. But there will always be "another text in psychobiology."

D. N. R.
W. R. U.

Contents

xi

3 Basic Anatomy and Physiological Principles of the Nervous System   87

4 Sensory, Perceptual, and Elementary Cognitive Processes   133

5 Mechanisms of Behavioral Adjustment   197

9 Twenty Questions for an Evolving Psychobiology

Glossary

Index

Foundations of
Psychobiology

1 The Province of Psychobiology

What Is Psychobiology?

The central aim of this text goes beyond equipping the reader with a knowledge of the ever-increasing facts and the ever-changing methods of a scientific specialty. The all too common tendency among writers of scientific books is to flood the nonspecialist reader with waves of detail without pausing to assist in the far more important matter of *perspective*. As with all texts in psychobiology, this one too is crammed with technical material, with terms that must seem strange to the uninitiated, and with figures and graphs that can be deciphered only with practice. But even having mastered this material, the reader could very well remain largely in the dark regarding the essential character of psychobiology; just as someone who has committed to memory the Periodic Table might have less than a useful acquaintance with the actual material world.

As with all fields of science and scholarship, psychobiology can be conveniently and economically defined in a sentence or two. The commonest definitions are of the following sort.

1. Psychobiology is the scientific specialty concerned with the relationship between neural and behavioral processes.
2. Psychobiology is that field of research which examines the biological basis of perception and behavior.
3. Psychobiology aims to explain psychological phenomena by reducing them to their underlying physiological causes.

These definitions are, after a fashion, true but as incomplete and ultimately uninforming as most attempts to capture something complex with no more than a handful of words. It is, for example, equally true that *physics is the science of radiation and*

1

matter, but it is doubtful that one would know much about the nature of physics having learned only this catchy phrase.

When we refer to the *essential character* of psychobiology we have in mind attributes similar to those we would have to know about before we could say that we knew a person very well. We generally regard as quite incomplete our knowledge of persons about whom we have no facts beyond their names, occupations, and addresses. But this is just the sort of knowledge conveyed by the three definitions offered above. What they give us is a name (psychobiology), an occupation (concern with brain-behavior relations), and an address (it goes on in laboratories).

To know persons well we must inquire into their background, education, aspirations, the source of these, the things they value, their beliefs, and so on. And to know a discipline well it is necessary also to know something about its history, what it has learned or borrowed from other disciplines, what it strives to accomplish, what it accepts, and what it rejects. Those who know persons very well can usually offer a reasonably good explanation for their behavior. That is, aware of their "personality," convictions, and goals, friends are not at a loss to account for their actions. Today there are thousands of specialists working on problems in psychobiology. To one who is unfamiliar with the roots and aims of the discipline, these activities are not likely to form a coherent pattern. The honest if innocent observer might wonder, for example, why all the activity is occurring in laboratories. To explain this with a wave of the hand by saying "Psychobiology is a science, and science is done in laboratories" is to be less than instructive. After all, astronomy is a science and it is not done in a laboratory; nor is theoretical physics.

In such matters it is advisable to be systematic, even at the risk of being a bit tedious. It took the world of thought many centuries to decide that the laboratory was the proper place for answering certain kinds of questions. It took this same world an additional several centuries to decide that certain *psychological* questions could be answered in the same setting. Accordingly, one who would know the *essential character* of psychobiology must begin the study with a review of the kinds of issues and obstacles that had to be dealt with for this science to come into being.

Psychobiology: Its Formal Properties

With most hybrid sciences (for example, *bio*chemistry or *neuro*anatomy), the compound name consists of easily defined elements. Biochemistry is the science devoted to the chemical laws and processes of living things, and neuroanatomy is the study of the structures of the nervous system. Perhaps the first problem faced by those beginning a study of psychobiology is created by the wide variety of meanings associated with "psychology." The student who has completed a course in General Psychology may, in this matter, be nearly as confused as one who has not. Is psychology "the science of behavior?" Is it "the science of the mind?" Is it "the study of individual and social processes?" Is it "the study of mental health and illness?" Each of these definitions of "psychology" can be found in textbooks, and all of them can be defended with greater or lesser conviction. From the perspective of the psychobiologist, however, how psychology is defined is of less importance than is the *empirical* standing of the alleged subjects.

The *empirical* standing refers to the extent to which the alleged subject of psychology can be directly observed or validly inferred from what is directly observed. Thus, if one defines psychology as, "the study of mental health and disease," then psychobiology demands only that these descriptions be refined to the point at which something *observable* is involved. Mental disease, for example, may be said to include hallucinations, and these may be defined as "reports of perceptions in the absence of any relevant external stimulus." It is at this point, and not before,that the psychobiologist may begin to study the *physiological* events associated with, in this case, hallucinations.

However, in psychobiology, as in all sciences, not every event worthy of study is directly observable. In some cases, one knows of such events only in terms of the effects they have on other (and observable) events. A physicist may not be able to measure directly the mass of a body, but will be able to *infer* its mass from its acceleration during free fall. Similarly, the population geneticist may not be able to observe directly the changes in chromsomes caused by radiation, but will be able to *infer* such changes from effects observable in the offspring-generation. So, too, in psychobiology: the experimenter is not able to observe directly the hunger of an animal, but is able to infer it from, for example, the rate at which the animal consumes food when it is available, or even from the amount of weight the animal has lost since the last feeding.

Note, however, that the foregoing examples are fundamentally different. The physicist is able to determine the mass of an object, given its acceleration, because the relationship is governed by a fundamental law, in this case, $F = m \times a$, which establishes the interrelationship among force, mass, and acceleration. Actually, what is involved here is not an inference at all, but a *deduction: If* $F = m \times a$, and *if* one knows the values of F and of a, *then* m is completely determined. But conclusions of this sort are only possible when well-established laws are available, and such laws are simply not now available in psychology. Instead, the psychologist must traffic in the type of inference illustrated by the case of the hungry animal. It is known, for example, that all animals—including human animals—nearly invariably eat when hungry and that both the rate and amount of consumption roughly reflect the degree of hunger. Thus, when *this* animal eats at such a rate and in such amounts, it is plausible to conclude that it is hungry. In such cases, what is involved is not a *deduction* from a universal law, but a *generalization* based upon a number of previous observations. This is an *inductive* process and it is common to all experimental sciences lacking well-established and valid universal laws.

In light of these considerations, it is possible to give an approximate definition of psychobiology: psychobiology is an *inductive science.* Moreover, it is an inductive science addressed to the *empirically* established features of human and animal psychology. What is lacking in this approximate definition is, of course, a statement as to the "empirically established features of human and animal psychology." Again, it is instructive to look to the developed sciences in order to appreciate how difficult it is to find an exhaustive list of psychological facts, events, and processes. Physics, for example, is exhaustively defined as "the study of radiation and matter" since there is nothing in the material universe that does not manifest itself in the form of material or radiational effects. Biology cannot, perhaps, be defined as sharply, but a nearly exhaustive definition is conveyed by the processes of growth, nutrition, and reproduction. And, like radiation and matter, the processes of growth, nutrition, and reproduction can be illustrated by observable and physical events taking place in living organisms.

When we turn to the traditional concerns of psychology, however, matters are not nearly as clear. The process of perception is illustrative. To what observable and physical event does one refer when one says, "Smith perceives his uncle in the crowd." Or when one says, "Smith perceived a trace of doubt on the face of his professor?" The same problem occurs in the study of motivation, another field that has a long history of interest to psychologists. What is the physical and observable element in the statement "Smith is highly motivated to improve his character?" Finally, take such entities as "thoughts" and "hopes." What is the observable and physical reference in such sentences as "Smith hopes it will rain on Friday," "Smith thought often of his days in the country," and "Smith desperately desires a just world"?

One way of getting around (though not solving) such problems is legislative! One simply declares that the exhaustive subject matter of psychology is *behavior* and that any state or event or process not directly evident in the behavior of man or beast is simply to be ignored. This is the legislative remedy proposed by those who subscribe to "radical behaviorism," and it has had a considerable influence in modern psychology. To accept the legislation is to put psychology on the same firm footing shared by the physical and biological sciences, and to guarantee that psychology will confine itself only to directly observable and measurable phenomena. The desired effect sought by those who promoted this approach was to free psychology of the burden of having to speak *scientifically* about things that were utterly beyond the realm of observables—things like perceptions, desires, motives, and thoughts.

To some extent, psychobiology reflects the early influence of behavioristic approaches. There is general agreement among contemporary psychobiologists that, when possible, the actual *behavior* of animals be used as the criterion of psychological processes. But from the perspective of the psychobiologist, behavior is only one more event to be understood in terms of physiological functions; it is not the *only* event. Thus, psychobiologists are at least as interested in, for example, those activities in the chess player's brain as a strategy is being formed as they are in the activities connected to the movement of one of the pieces. The point here is that the psychobiologist does not rule out a priori any reliable phenomenon proceeding from the "psychological" side of animals and human beings. If persons reliably claim to have "hopes," "desires," "thoughts," "feelings," "dreams," and many other states or mental conditions, the psychobiologist does not dismiss them merely because they may not lead to observable behavior. Instead, these states and conditions are taken to be genuine, and the task then becomes one of discovering those physiological processes on which they depend or with which they are reliably correlated. The assumption in all of this is (if only implicitly) that each and every genuine psychological event or process is the expression of an underlying biological event or process. Every science proceeds from certain assumptions which the science itself cannot validate. Psychobiology is no exception. Its fundamental assumption is that there is no psychological occurrence where there is no physiological cause. The discipline may be defined, therefore, as *the experimental investigation of the biological foundations of psychological processes.*

This definition accurately expresses the professional activities of most psychobiologists, but it does not sufficiently convey the broadest aims of the discipline. Although something can be said for the gathering of facts "for their own sake," the aims of science usually go beyond the ritual filling of handbooks. What is at the very heart of science is the universal desire to understand the world, and this desire finds partial satisfaction when we are able to explain the causes of things. Scientific explanations provide one form of understanding. In their most developed state, these explanations appear as *general laws* (for example, $F = m \times a$); in a less developed state, as *redescriptions*. Thus, the striking and frightening phenomenon of lightning becomes less ominous and less intimidating when science redescribes it in terms of ionic motion. And, though no less beautiful, the flight of the bird becomes understandable through the principles of aerodynamics.

Psychobiology shares the general aim of all the sciences—that is, to enhance our understanding of the world by explaining things through general laws or redescriptions. The ultimate goal, then, is not simply the collecting of facts for their own sake, but the collecting of facts for the purpose of discovering those general laws governing the relationship between biological and psychological processes. Thus, a more complete definition of psychobiology is *the experimental investigation of the general laws governing the relationship between biological and psychological processes.*

Minds and Bodies

In the foregoing definition, the term *relationship*, is properly neutral, but it is not long after the student has begun to study psychobiology that interesting questions arise concerning the sort of "relationship" that exists between biological and psychological processes. Historically, a number of possibilities have been proposed. Some have argued, for example, that the essential quality of mental events is so unike anything found in the purely physical world that the two realms—the mental and the physical—are utterly distinct and that neither is reducible to the other. The point here is that, although it makes sense to speak of large, round, blue objects, it makes no sense to speak of *thoughts* in such terms. Indeed, it makes no sense even to speak of thoughts as occupying a space or having a location, let alone having mass or color. When one has the idea of a blue sky, the argument continues, one is surely not having a "blue idea."

This position is the one adopted by the classical *dualist*, so-called because of the commitment to divide the contents of the universe into two classes; the physical and the mental. This, however, is a very broad category and it fails to distinguish among several different forms of dualism. One may concur, for example, that the universe contains two kinds of "stuff"—mental and physical—but may also insist that one arises out of the other or is somehow controlled or caused by the other. The renowned French philospher and mathematician, René Descartes (1596–1650) proposed just this sort of interaction. It was his thesis that the mind (soul) controlled the body in all actions that proceeded from the actor's intentions, but that the material body had no effect on the mind (soul). Descartes, of course, was not unaware of the effects of disease and injury on, for example, perception, memory, movement, and speech. But these functions did not figure in Descartes' conception of *mind*. For him, "mind" referred to those abstract features of thought by which persons framed courses of action and executed their rational designs. To Descartes, the "mind" was involved primarily with what might be called the highest cognitive and moral sides of life, and not with such rudimentary operations as perception and movement. The label assigned to Descartes' "solution" to the mind/body problem is *one-way interactionism*, with the causal chain starting in the mental realm and culminating in the behavioral (physical) realm.

Those who most immediately found fault with Descartes' positon argued that, on whatever basis the mental makes contact with the physical, the same basis exists for the physical to make contact with the mental. The criticism took this form: If Descartes wants to insist that the mind is so unlike anything physical that it cannot be affected by physical things, then he must also conclude that it cannot, itself, affect anything physical. On this account, two alternative theories become possible. First, it may be proposed that mind and body affect each other. This is the theory of *two-way* or *reciprocal interactionism*. The other alternative arises out of the conviction that Descartes' critics were quite correct: *Since* mind and matter are entirely unlike each other, it follows that neither can have any effect on the other. Rather, each proceeds according to its own nature, following the dictates of its own causal laws. One set of "mental" laws governs the operation of psychological processes and another set of physical laws governs the operation of physical bodies. The two sets of laws, however, operate in parallel, which is why there is an *apparently* causal connection between mental and physical events. In fact, however, there is only a parallel relationship, a mere correlation. This thesis, compellingly defended by the philosopher Gottfried von Leibniz (1646–1716), has been dubbed *psychophysical parallelism*.

On still another account, it has been argued that every mental event or state must have a cause, and that the only causes in the universe are physical. Thus, mental events come into being as a result of preceding biological events, which, typically, are events in the brain. This is the argument behind claims of the sort, "The brain is the *organ* of mind", and it has been labeled *epiphenomenalism.* The prefix "epi" in this case refers to that which *depends upon* something else and which would not exist were it not for this other thing. According to epiphenomenalism, then, the mental realm contains phenomena which could not occur were it not for the physical processes of the brain.

All of these theories are *dualistic* in that they all accept at least the existence of mind and mental events. There is, however, a more radical theory—one often designated as *monistic materialism*—which denies that there is anything in the universe other than physical things. On this view, the so-called "mental" realm is but the legacy of ages of witchcraft, superstition, and scientific ignorance, a legacy that exists now in the form of mentalistic language and mentalistic explanations. Properly understood, there is no mind as such; only a collection of biological processes giving rise to certain events and states which we call mental only because we do not yet understand them at a scientific level. Like older generations ignorant of the causes of lightning, we still speak of "thoughts," "perceptions," "motives," and so on. We know now that lightning is simply an old word for what in fact are *electrical discharges.* Similarly, as science develops, words like thought, perception, and motive will be replaced by statements of what is occuring in the brain. The thesis advanced by monistic materialists is sometimes called the *identity thesis,* for it asserts that so-called mental events are not caused by events in the brain, but that, in fact, they *are* these very events. In other words, mind-talk *is* brain-talk, but we have not yet learned enough to achieve a complete translation.

Although during the earlier stages of its development psychobiology was completely bound up with this issue, the contemporary psychobiologist no longer seeks to settle it, or (typically) even address it. What has become clearer over the decades and centuries is that the issue, at the root, is a metaphysical one, perhaps forever beyond the reach of experimental science. How one settles the issue may, that is, depend far less on the available facts and much more on the meaning we choose to assign to such words as "mental," "mind," "consciousness," and the like. More than one philosopher has concluded, at least provisionally, that the entire mind/body problem is only a reflection of how we have chosen to talk about the issue. Therefore, no amount of scientific information, in itself, will require us to *talk* differently. A parallel is sometimes drawn between issues like the mind/body problem and, for example, the issue between creationists and evolutionists. In the latter case, both have access to the same facts and both have adopted theoretical positions quite able to absorb the available facts and the likely findings of the future. This is the sense in which the issue may be called *metaphysical* rather than scientific or merely scientific.

The scientist's position on such matters is practical and resolute, but not dogmatic. As a working hypothesis, the scientist takes for granted that events come into being by virtue of other events, and that the connections may be taken as causal when one class of events reliably precedes the other. The working hypothesis of the psychobiologist is that psychological events are, in this sense, caused by biological events, and the purpose of research is to identify specifically the causal elements. But this hypothesis did not simply spring up out of the blue. It took many centuries for there to be sufficient data and good enough methods for this perspective to seem to be warranted. It is instructive to examine some of the highlights of this history.

Historical Foundations—The Pre-Modern Period

Long before any proposed official theories of mind there were well-established religious and social practices that rested on what may be called implicit theories. Let us recall, for example the ancient Egyptian techniques of embalming and mummification. The notion behind these was that each person has both a corporeal soul and a spiritual soul; the former giving life to the body and the latter somehow surviving the body. This is one way of explaining the practice of leaving the mouth of the embalmed corpse open. It was through this opening that the spiritual soul could exit and present itself for judgment.

Although it is possible to reconstruct what must have been the theoretical foundations of such ancient rituals, the first unequivocally theoretical attempts to arrive at a *scientific* understanding of the mind were made in ancient Greece. These attempts came from two distinct quarters; the practical quarter of Greek medicine and the speculative quarter of Greek philosophy. Hippocrates, who flourished at about 400 B.C., was the founder of the most influential school of Greek medicine, and his teachings included theories about and treatments for diseases we would not now call "psychological." Central to Hippocratic thought was the theory of *humors*—substances distributed throughout the body and responsible for a wide range of symptoms including fevers, palsies, terrifying dreams, fits of depression, and mental incompetence. It was assumed that nearly all mental ills resulted from an imbalance or a lack of harmony in the body's humors, and that the aim of therapy must be to restore equilibrium.

In the speculative arena, it was Aristotle (385–322 B.C.) who most directly addressed mental science, reserving a full essay (*De Anima*) for this topic. This work, usually translated as "On the Soul", actually considers the broad question of the biological principles underlying life itself. It is in this essay that the soul (*psyche*) is defined as the "first principle of living things" (*arche zoön*) and is analyzed in terms of its several different functions. The general thesis is that "life" is to be understood as an ensemble of specific processes which become more numerous as animals become more advanced. Thus, the simplest forms of life are "animated" by no more than the processes of nutrition and reproduction, whereas higher forms of life also possess the capacity to sense and to move.

There is no question but that Aristotle was convinced that all of these "faculties" were completely determined by the material organization of the animal—that is, by biology. Nothing other than physical processes was responsible for nutrition, reproduction, sensation, and locomotion. Similarly, the *emotions* of animals were explained in terms of various kinds of agitation and disorder; this thought led to Aristotle's theory that the very young are difficult to educate because of the "turbulence" occurring in their minds. It seems also to have been Aristotle's view that the motion of the blood was central to such processes and that, therefore, the heart was chiefly responsible for them. In some of his writing, he suggests that the brain's principal function is to regulate the temperature of the blood. (Note that a beheaded chicken will continue to run, but a chicken whose heart has stopped beating will not. The conclusions are obvious!)

However, when Aristotle turned from such basic processes as nutrition and locomotion to the complex processes of *thought*, his theory became more difficult to state. He grants to the advanced (but nonhuman) species a form of intelligence and he anchors this intellectual faculty to the same physiological processes as those governing other functions of the soul. But man, according to Aristotle, has more than an intellectual faculty; he has, too, a purely *rational* faculty by which he comes to know universal principles. A merely intelligent animal may know that, for example, the sum of the squared sides of *this* right triangle equals the square of the hypotenuse, but this mere intelligence will never permit a knowledge of the universal theorem $a^2 + b^2 = c^2$. Even the intelligent being who calculated this relationship with a great many right triangles could only conclude that it is *probable* that $a^2 + b^2 = c^2$, since any generalization from specific cases can only be assigned a probability. But the Pythagorean theorem is recognized not as probably true. It is known to be certainly true and necessarily true in all cases. This form of knowledge cannot be based on the senses, but must proceed from some higher faculty, from the faculty of *reason*. And it was just this faculty that Aristotle found he could not explain in purely physiological terms.

Although a number of ancient Greeks may be credited with significant observations in medicine and in nature, the ancient Greek world was not especially active in experimental science, at least in the realms of psychology and physiology. The different schools of medicine certainly employed trial-and-error methods of experiments in an effort to discover reliable treatments, and Aristotle himself was one of history's most active naturalists. But what we do not find in this otherwise distinguished epoch is the clear recognition that matters of biological fact are to be settled by controlled experiments.

The experimental approach did not suddenly dawn on the world. By the second century A.D. some genuinely experimental activity can be documented; for example, in the works of Galen (*c.* 130–200 A.D.). More than anyone earlier, it was Galen who built on the excellent anatomical observations of the ancient Greeks and who corrected their theories through experimentation. One example is sufficient here. The ancients had reasoned that, since words are produced in the throat, and since thought is expressed in speech, the mechanisms of thought must be located in the chest—the heart, again, the preferred site. Galen, however, in studying the cranial anatomy of pigs, discovered the laryngeal nerve and observed that it originated in the brain. He proceeded to cut both laryngeal nerves in the living pig and thereby demonstrated (a) that respiration remained normal and (b) that the animal's vocalizations were nearly completely eliminated.

For many centuries following Galen's remarkable efforts, scientific and speculative activities were all but silenced. The aptly named "Dark Ages" filled the period from the seventh to the ninth centuries; the period when Western communities were often nomadic, when barbarian assaults were the rule, and when even the tools of scholarship (for example, papyrus from Syria) were unavailable in the non-Islamic world. But with strength came peace and, by the eleventh century, the now settled communities of Europe and England hosted a revival of systematic thought and learning. Soon, the Abbey schools of the Middle Ages were transformed into the great Medieval universities and it was within their walls that scientific explorations were begun anew. In the so-called Renaissance of the thirteenth century we discover genuinely experimental studies undertaken at the University of Oxford by such clergymen as Roger Bacon and Robert Grosseteste. But the return to biological research—and particularly to that type which is at the center of psychobiology—occurred much more gradually, and only during the Italian Renaissance of the fifteenth and sixteenth centuries. It was in this latter period, often as a result of artistic needs and inspirations, that anatomical research again prospered and that the desire to recapture the classical way of life gave rise to scientific speculation and studies devoted to *man*. Since that time and for the five hundred years separating that epoch from our own, there has never been a single decade in which there has not been an *experimental* contribution relevant to the history of psychobiology. A few words are in order concerning these early modern contributions.

Historical Foundations—The Modern Period

With rise of the Medieval universities there occurred a renewed interest in professional education, particularly in law and medicine, although religious considerations continued to hamper studies of human anatomy. Though the very practice of medicine increased the knowledge of anatomy, it was not until the sixteenth century that this division of science began to be liberated from the authority of Galen. The modern period of anatomical research, then, may be said to have begun with Andreas Vesalius (1514–1564) whose *De fabrica corporis humani* (1543) is a landmark in the history of science. William Harvey's (1578–1657) pioneering research on the circulation of blood, and Anton von Leeuwenhoeck's (1632–1723) development of the microscope are but two of the many individual achievements which led to modern physiology. Through ever more accurate anatomical studies and through the application of experimental methods to problems in physiology, the eighteenth and nineteenth centuries built on these earlier accomplishments, and soon created the distinct specialties of neuroanatomy and neurophysiology. Sir Charles Bell (1774–1842) and Francois Magendie (1783–1855) independently discovered that the sensory and motor functions of the spinal cord are anatomically separated—the so-called Bell-Magendie Law. Louigi Galvani, in the last decade of the eighteenth century, demonstrated that muscles were activated by *electrical* forces, and thereby laid the foundations of later theories of neural function. A number of investigators, especially Robert Whytt (1714–1766), completed experiments on involuntary (reflex) behavior, and distinguished between those actions requiring the participation of the brain and those that could be elicited by stimulation of the spinal cord. Research of this kind not only paved the way for Ivan Pavlov's (1849–1936) celebrated studies of the *conditioned reflex*, but also drew attention to the possibility that different psychological processes might be controlled by specific neuroanatomical regions.

This latter possiblity was contended hotly throughout the latter years of the eighteenth century and the first half of the nineteenth. The case for strict "localization of function" was made most thoroughly by the distinguished anatomist, Franz Gall (1758–1828), who insisted that each specific mental or moral faculty existed through the activity of a specific region of the brain. He was a pioneer in the fields of comparative anatomy and fetal neuroanatomy and was the founder of the earliest system of Psychobiology, that is, "phrenology," a study of the shapes and protuberances of the skull. When Gall examined the brains and the craniums of many deceased persons—primitive people, men of genius, criminals, and children—and compared their skulls and brains with those common among various species of animals, he arrived at the conclusion that the total amount of a given brain devoted to a specific faculty determined how much of that faculty the person or animal had. He hypothesized further that there were some three dozen such faculties, and that these accounted for all of the intellectual, emotional, perceptual, memorial, motivational, and social aspects of mental life. The task, as he saw it, was to study the anatomy of the brains of all the advanced species, of the various human races and cultures, and of those who, in life, had distinguished themselves through works both good and evil, and in this way to develop a natural science, a *neural* science of the animal kingdom.

Because of the rough correspondence between the shape of the skull and the shape of the surface of the brain beneath it, Gall proposed that we may discover a person's basic mental and emotional nature by examining the cranial bumps and grooves—hence, the name phrenology from the Greek *phrenes* (brain or mind) and *logos* (science). This part of Gall's program, though influential for a short time, was ultimately ridiculed and survives now only as one of several bad jokes in the history of science. But the major part of the program—the part that recommends correlational studies of brain function and psychological function—is at the very foundation of contemporary psychobiology.

Those who disagreed with Gall's theory attempted to test its implications experimentally. Thus, early in the nineteenth century the field of *experimental neurosurgery* began, largely through the efforts of Pierre Flourens (1794–1867). The technique Flourens applied to Gall's theoretical assertions was that of *ablation*, which is the surgical destruction or removal of a specific portion of the brain in order to determine whether a given faculty or ability is thereby eliminated. Flourens was not the first to employ this method, but he was among the first to direct it toward the predictions of a well-developed theory and to do so in such a way as to reveal both the power and the limitations of the method.

As these developments were taking place in the scientific communities of the Western world, the medical specialty of neurology was also prospering. Improved techniques in surgery and in microscopy permitted clinicians to specify ever more precisely the relationship between diseases of the brain and psychological disorders. Thus, by the first decades of the nineteenth century, there was already a thick handbook of reliable findings which connected specific regions of the brain to such psychological functions as perception and behavior. It was, however, not until the 1860s that such complex functions as *language* were identified with specific areas of the brain, and not until the twentieth century that the neuroanatomical foundations of specific cognitive and emotional disturbances were uncovered.

The major methods of psychobiology and their historical points of origin will be discussed throughout this text within the context of specific issues. In most instances, the current techniques are improvements and refinements of earlier ones. But in many instances, it has been just such refinements that have brought into question theories that prevailed when methods were more primitive and not well understood.

Psychobiology and the Interdependence of the Sciences

Even the sketchy historical review just given conveys the debt psychobiology owes to anatomy, physiology, medicine, and optics. Today, too, the psychobiologist depends heavily on methods developed in these and in entirely different branches of science, for example, in engineering, mathematics, physics, chemistry, genetics, anthropology, statistics, and pharmacology. And, of course, as a branch of modern psychology, the specialty also depends on other areas of psychology devoted to studies of perception, learning and memory, motivation and emotion, language and thought, mental illness, and so on. What is unique about psychobiology, therefore, is neither its methods nor its choice of topics, for the same methods abound in the biological and physical sciences, and the same topics engage the interests of many psychologists who are not trained in or even particularly interested in psychobiology. Rather, what is unique about it can be stated in this sentence: Its interest in physiology is confined to those physiological processes of *psychological* importance, and its interest in psychology is confined to those events and functions which are interpretable in the language of the biological sciences.

In recent decades, psychobiology has, as it were, begun to pay back its historic debts to the sciences and to other branches of psychology. The discoveries of the psychobiologist have, for example, thrown new light on basic physiological mechanisms, on principles of neuranatomical organization, and on the manner in which organism and environment interact in settings described as "perceptual" or "motivational" or (even) "social." These developments now make it somewhat arbitrary to classify experiments rigidly. When, for example, we study the effects of morphine on pain perception, is this a study in pharmacoloy or in perception or in neurophysiology or in neurochemistry? When the effects of brain lesions on memory are examined, is this a branch of neurology or psychology? And when different strains of a given species are inbred successively to determine the hereditary foundations of "emotionality," is the research best viewed as part of genetics or psychiatry?

The point, of course, is that even the simplest form of life is far too complex to be completely understood by one branch of science, let alone by one specialty within a branch of science. The behaving organism is a chemical system, a neurological system, a psychological system, a physical system, and the member of a social system. The question, therefore, is not "Which science is best equipped to explain this behavior?" but "Which methods and perspective are best suited to address certain issues arising out of such behavior?" The rat pressing a bar and eating the pellets of food resulting from this behavior can be understood in the different languages of physics, biology, psychology, and ethology. As a system in motion, the rat can be described according to the language and laws of dynamics. As a system engaged in metabolic processes, the rat can be described according to the language and the laws of biochemistry and nutrition. And as a system engaged in adaptive reactions to a perceived environment, the rat can be described in the language of psychology or by the laws of conditioning.

What one takes to be a "good" explanation depends, in part, one what one finds puzzling about the event he seeks to explain. If one finds it odd that all five of Smith's children have blue eyes, the question "Why are all the Smith chidren blue-eyed?" might be answered "Because Mr. and Mrs. Smith and both of their parents are blue-eyed." But suppose this simply raises the question "Yes, but why are the children of blue-eyed parents blue-eyed?" At this point, it may be necessary to discuss the principles of Mendelian inheritance, and to note that certain genes, associated with the degree of pigmentation of the iris of the eye, are passed on from parents to children. Yet, the questioner may persist "Why do genes of a certain kind cause the iris to appear blue?" This then drives the issue out to the frontiers of molecular biology and ultimately to that realm of particle interactions in which the modern physicist labors. We see, then, psychobiology is not alone in its dependence on other branches of science, and that the explanations it provides are no less immune to probing questions than are the explanations provided by other disciplines. In light of this, it will be instructive to review briefly the level of explanation sought by psychobiologists as they approach various problems.

Explanation—"Molecular and Molar" and "Casual and Rational"

Physics has not yet isolated the ultimate units of matter—though there are several candidates—nor has it yet been able to translate its own general laws of the *macrocosm* (for example, planetary motion) into the language of the *microcosm* (for example, energy exchanges during the orbital transitions of electrons). Indeed, it is far from clear that the *same* laws operate at both levels, or that any experiment could confirm that they do if, in fact, they do. This problem exists in one or another form in every science. Scientists working in animal husbandry know what to do if someone wants taller sheep or heavier cattle or terriers with long noses, but it is not now possible to go from the facts of husbandry or population genetics to the principles of the molecular biology of the gene.

    The distinction between so-called molar laws and molecular laws pertains to the level of *observation* at which phenomena are studied, measured, and explained. There is no sharp boundary that separates the two laws: What botanists may call a "molecular" level of explanation, particle physicists may judge to be "molar." The psychobiologist generally confines observation to nothing smaller than a single neuron and frames explanations according to the characteristics of relatively large populations of such neurons. Similarly, the psychological processes and events are generally of the molar variety—perceptual reports, observable behavior, problem solving, goal seeking, mating, expressions of emotionality. In these cases, where the psychological features are displayed by the total organism, the search is for those mechanisms and processes capable of giving rise to complex patterns of behavior. Such mechanisms and processes, although themselves based upon molecular or even subatomic events, cannot be meaningfully interpreted at any but the molar level, at least at present. Therefore, in most research and theories within psychobiology, the experimental methods and explanatory principles are of the molar variety. There are, of course, important exceptions, as will be noted in the later chapters—for example, studies of what are called "microneural" activity, studies of single neuronal units in an attempt to uncover the basic principles on which sensation, learning, memory, and adaptation are based. Nevertheless, the vast majority of findings that shape psychobiology come from research into the functions of relatively large structures and subsystems of the nervous system.

Psychobiology's Modern Founders

We began this chapter by expressing the judgment that an understanding of the essential character of psychobiology required a knowledge of its history, its relationship with other disciplines, and its goals and basic assumptions. We have therefore devoted more than the usual amount of space to the historical and the formal aspects of the subject, even to the point of including philosophers in a technical and scientific text!

But a discipline is more than its past and is also more dynamic and lively than one would guess merely from a knowledge of its formal properties. Apart from these considerations, modern psychobiology has arisen from the actual experimental labors and theoretical writings of the scientists themselves. At least in a weak sense, *psychobiology is what psychobiologists do*. What most of today's psychobiologists do was made possible by the contributions of a relatively small number of outstanding scientists, some of whom are still active and all of whom lived into our own century. Their pioneering efforts are, as it were, written between the lines of all the following chapters of this book. Space is set aside for them in this chapter to acknowledge the special part they have played in determining how today's psychobiologists understand and approach the problems of psychobiology. The importance of their contributions will only become appreciated by the reader within the context of later chapters. Here it is sufficient to sketch these varied contributions and to provide biographical outlines of those who made them. The scientific fields of the several contributors fall under four overlapping categories: anatomy, neurophysiology, experimental neurosurgery, and theory.

Anatomy

As is now well known, the structural unit of the nervous system is the *neuron,* a specialized cell in chemical communication with its neighbors (Chapter 3). But before the twentieth century the prevailing view was that the entire nervous system was a physically interconnected web with no separate "parts." We owe it to the brilliant anatomical studies of *Santiago Ramon y Cajal* that we now appreciate the structural integrity of independent neural cells. The importance of his work cannot be overestimated in the modern history of the "neural sciences," including psychobiology. To think of the nervous system as a continuous network—a spider's web—of tubes or filaments of various sizes is to look for mechanisms of an essentially hydraulic or mechanical nature. It is, in a word, to have no more than a *Cartesian* view of the nervous system. Once, however, the fact of individual neural cells is accepted, an entirely new and fruitful line of inquiry emerges. It now becomes necessary to determine how the individual cell reacts to stimulation; how its reactions are transmitted to neighbors; whether or not there are different *types* of such cells.

Ramon y Cajal was, of course, not the only scientist who defended what we now call the *neuron doctrine.* He was, however, the most productive and discerning of the early twentieth century anatomists and his work quickly became a guide to others and a standard of excellence. Developments in microscopic neuroanatomy since his time have been rapid and extensive (Chapter 2). The indebtedness of these anatomists to Cajal is deep and widely acknowledged.

Neurophysiology

The most important contributions to neurophysiology have taken two forms. There are those that explain the basic mechanisms controlling individual neural cells, and those that explain the interactions among neighboring cells or cells comprising a specific system. British scientists have taken the lead in both.

In 1906 there appeared *Sir Charles Sherrington's The Integrative Action of the Nervous System,* a book based on his Silliman Lectures at Yale in 1904. More than any other work, this book may be said to have introduced the modern era functional neurophysiology. Sherrington's research on reflex mechanisms in the spinal cord—his isolation of mechanisms of excitation and inhibition—established the basic principles of information flow and control in the reflex pathways. Together with Ramon y Cajal, he defended the *neuron doctrine* late in the nineteenth century. He developed his own techniques for stimulating small clusters of cells and observing the effects on muscle activity. He showed that the latter effects were typically the result of competing excitatory and inhibitory influences, the motor response to these being a kind of "algebraic sum."

Of Sherrington's many distinguished students, surely the most celebrated is *Sir John Eccles* who, like his teacher, has remained fully mindful of the philosophical and the moral dimensions of science. Eccles has extended the work on inhibitory and excitatory mechanisms and has done much to work out the principles of *synaptic* physiology and biochemistry (Chapter 3) as well as the mechanisms of control in such complex structures as the cerebellum.

Where Sherrington and Eccles clarified the *integrative* properties of neural networks, *Sir Alan Hodgkin* and *Sir Andrew Huxley* have discovered the microchemistry of those neuronal events that culminate in the *neural impulse* (Chapter 3). Their research has established the ionic and electrochemical basis of neural activity and the manner in which individual neural cells can "code" properties of stimulation (Chapters 3 and 4).

Experimental Neurosurgery

The anatomists and neurophysiologists have provided the maps and the mechanisms by which we might begin to understand the operating principles of the nervous system. But the science of psychobiology must address the broad *psychological* consequences resulting from these principles. One of the more direct approaches to this issue involves the selective destruction or stimulation of specific regions of the brain and the observation of resulting effects on the perception and behavior of the experimental animal. As we have noted, this approach dates from early in the nineteenth century. But it was not until the present century that the necessary care and controls were exercised in measuring the psychological side of the brain-behavior equation. The most important work in the first half of this century was done by *Karl Lashley* who did much to establish the functional dependence of perception and behavior on specific portions of the cerebral cortex. Subsequent research has begun to modify both Lashley's findings and his conclusions, but he remains the pioneering figure in that division of psychobiology that studies the psychological functions served by the major "centers" of the brain.

The term "experimental neurosurgery" must be used advisedly when discussing those findings arising out of studies of the human brain. Surgeons, after all, do not drag citizens in off the street in order to do experiments on their brains! But the surgeons do perform necessary operations on diseased brains and, in the course of these operations, it is often necessary to stimulate or record from regions near the diseased region. The American neurosurgeon *Wilder Penfield* has been the pioneer in this approach. Over a long and distinguished career he was able to observe the effects of electrically stimulating various regions of the brains of thousands of human patients and thereby map any number of significant psychological functions, such as perception, memory, and language.

Theory

All the scientists cited here have made at least implicit conributions to theory. But two figures stand out for theoretical contributions that uniquely influenced the modern evolution of psychobiology. We refer here to the Russian physiologist *Ivan Pavlov* and the Canadian psychologist *Donald O. Hebb*. Of the first we should say that his work on *conditioned reflexes* (Chapter 5) is less important than his persistent and often strident defense of the biological approach to psychological issues. His deserved fame as an experimental scientist gave him an instant audience in America and elsewhere during the early decades of the twentieth century. It was to this audience that he spoke in the language of naturalism and psychological materialism, insisting that nothing in principle prevents an explanation of psychological phenomena in terms of the laws and mechanisms of physiology.

Hebb, too, but in a psychologically more informed and systematic manner, has kept this tradition alive. His influential *Organization of Behavior* (1949) attempted to provide a theoretical account of learning and memory framed entirely in physiological terms. His other books and many articles have inspired confidence in the psychobiological approach.

Finally, we must refer to the numerous contributions to modern psychobiology made by *Roger Sperry*, contributions going beyond his insightful and suggestive experimentation and entering the less populated realm of psychological theory. Some forty years ago Sperry alerted the scientific community to the subtlety of the *plasticity* of developing nervous systems, to the nature of those *critical periods* during which undifferentiated tissue now becomes fixed in its functions. His now classic research on the newt, in which Sperry rotated the eyes 180° in this developing organism, demonstrated the inability of conditioning to overcome those fixed modes of information processing laid down genetically. More recently, his pioneering studies of the effects of sectioning the neural connections (*commissures*) joining the two cerebral hemispheres, have led to the current debates on "split-brain man" and the psychological unity or duality of one's self. As with Sherrington, Eccles, and Penfield, Roger Sperry has addressed the problem of consciousness and has attempted to set the boundaries within which science can explore and explain the facts of mental life. Dr. Sperry received the Nobel prize in 1981.

As we have indicated, this is an all too contracted list of notables. As early as 1906, Sherrington found it necessary to cite *hundreds* of fellow scientists in *The Integrative Action of the Nervous System.* Now, nearly eighty years later, one would have to cite thousands just to summarize the more important contributions to the recent history of psychobiology. Those we have chosen to mention are unarguably among the leaders of research and theory, but our list is scarcely exhaustive. Other names are added throughout the following chapters and in the "Suggested Readings," but we have not really scratched the surface of the long and constantly growing list of "Who's Who."

Santiago Ramon y Cajal
1852–1934

(*Reprinted with the permission of the National Library of Medicine.*)

Ramon y Cajal received his medical degree from the University of Zaragoza (1873) after years of resisting his father's pressures in that direction and after an aimless period as an apprentice to a barber and a shoemaker. His earliest interests in art, which his father thought to be pointless, would later serve him as he constructed his anatomical sketches. With his doctorate in 1875 came the opportunity for university life which he lived nearly without interruption as chairman of the departments at Valencia (1883), Barcelona (1887), and Madrid (1892–1922). His achievements were internationally recognized and by 1894 they would lead to his invitation by the Royal Society to give the prestigious Croonian Lecture. In 1906 he and C. Golgi shared the Nobel prize in medicine and physiology for their contributions to microscopic anatomy.

It is chiefly to Ramon y Cajal and to Sherrington that the credit must go for establishing the *neuron doctrine* in neurophysiology—the doctrine according to which each neuron is an anatomically distinct structure. Using Golgi's recently developed stain (potassium dichromate and silver nitrate), Ramon y Cajal traced individual sensory and motor neurons in the embryonic spinal cord. His work provided the first convincing demonstration of the physical separation between neurons in the given pathway. Before this work such notions were entirely speculative and not shared widely. Over the course of his career Cajal extended his studies from spinal cord to brain and did much to establish the cytoarchitectonics—the distributions of various cell types in the architecture of the brain—of the cerebral cortex and the cerebellum. In the wake of these latter achievements, others such as Brodman would construct ever more precise cortical "maps" of various functions, such as sensory, motor, linguistic, and so on. Thus, the emerging psychobiology would receive the problem of *localization of function* in a way that respected the actual cellular anatomy of the cerebral cortex. This problem, as we shall see in later chapters, has been central to the development of psychobiology.

Sir Charles Scott Sherrington
1857–1952

(The P.A. Woodward Library's portrait of Sir Charles Scott Sherrington, O.M.P.R.S., at the University of British Columbia.)

Charles Sherrington was born in Islington, England, and raised in Ipswitch. His early education in classics and literature created a pattern of interests that would endure throughout his long scientific career. His devoted stepfather, Dr. Caleb Rose, was no doubt largely responsible for his decision to enter medicine. Sherrington was awarded his medical degree from Cambridge in 1855, having distinguished himself in his studies at that University. He thereupon journied widely, first in connection with medical interests, but then and increasingly in the interest of basic research. His academic appointments included professorships at Liverpool (1895–1913) and Oxford (1914–1935), retiring from the latter as Waynflete Professor of Physiology. But even until the final days of his life, his "retirement" found him busy, productive, and original.

His Gifford Lectures, published in 1940 under the title *Man on His Nature,* remain the best source of Sherrington's scientific perspective and his metaphysical and religious convictions. They do much also to account for the extraordinary effect he had on his extraordinary students such as Eccles, Penfield, Granit, Fulton, and many others.

Sherrington held honorary degrees from over a score of universities on the continent, in Great Britain, in America and Canada. He served as President of the Royal Society, was Trustee of the British Museum, and was a Fellow of many prestigious scientific societies and academies all over the world. He was awarded the Nobel Prize in 1932. An informative and often quite moving account of Sherrington and his place in contemporary science has been written by Sir John Eccles and Professor William Gibson: *Sherrington: His Life and Thought* (Springer International, 1979).

Sir John Carew Eccles

1903–

Sherrington's most famous student and the premier neurophysiologist of our time, Sir John Eccles was born in Australia and educated at the University of Melbourne. He was brought to Oxford, and thus to Sherrington, as a Victoria Rhodes Scholar in 1925 and was awarded the M. A. (1929) and Ph.D. (1929) by that University. The work begun under Sherrington's direction has now been continued and expanded for more than a half-century. It is best viewed as "variations on a constant theme," the theme being the functional organization of neural systems. In recognition of his scientific achievements, Sir John was knighted in 1958 and awarded the Nobel prize in 1963. He is a Fellow of the Royal Society and of both Exeter and Magdalen Colleges, Oxford. He has held professorships in Great Britain, Australia, New Zealand, and the United States and has been invited to give any number of endowed addresses: the *Gifford* Lectures (Edinburgh), the *Waynflete*Lectures (Oxford), the *Ferrier* Lectures (Royal Society), and, of course, the *Sherrington* Lectures (Liverpool).

The high standing enjoyed by Sir John within the world's scientific community has been earned chiefly by his pioneering research in synaptic physiology and spinal reflex mechanisms. But his contributions go beyond these and have come to include original essays and books on philosophy of mind, philosophical psychology, and metaphysics. This dimension of this thought appears as early as 1953 in *Neurophysiological Basis of Mind* and has been fully developed in *Facing Reality* (1970) and in his published Gifford Lectures, *The Human Mystery* (1978) and *The Human Psyche* (1979). *The Self and Its Brain* (1977), written with Sir Karl Popper, has inspired much controversy and productive analysis through its systematic critique of psychological materialism. As with Sherrington, Sir John concludes from a lifelong study of the nervous system that the full measure of human psychology cannot be reduced to the value-free and the culture-free mechanisms of neural function.

Sir Alan Lloyd Hodgkin
1914–
Sir Andrew Fielding Huxley
1917–

We present these scientists together because their years of fruitful collaboration led them, together with Sir John Eccles, to share the Nobel prize in 1963. Both were educated at Cambridge and both are Fellows of Trinity College.

The theory that nervous functions are of an electrical nature is, as we have noted in this chapter, an old one, receiving its scientific standing from the research of Galvani toward the end of the eighteenth century. Not until the end of the nineteenth century, however, was any significant advance made toward an understanding of the basic mechanism by which neural signals are generated and conducted. Even before the end of the last century there was mounting evidence that the mechanism was chemical in origin and ionic in nature, a proposal developed and defended by, among others, Rene Du Bois-Reymond.

The major accomplishment of Hodgkin and Huxley, in a series of extraordinary experiments—some of them requiring what may properly be called the *invention* of new research methods and equipment—was the demonstration of the actual ionic events underlying the formation and propagation of the neural impulse (Chapter 3). They established further a strikingly complete mathematical model of the entire process, the most complete scientific model of neural function to date. Sir Alan Hodgkin's *The Conduction of the Nervous Impulse* (1963) remains the premier treatise on that subject.

The name "Huxley" will, of course, have a familiar ring to students of the history of science. Grandson of Thomas Henry Huxley, Darwin's most devoted and effective disciple and a great scientist in his own right, Sir Andrew has served as President of the British Association and Jodrell Professor of Physiology, University of London.

25

Karl Spencer Lashley
1890–1958

(Reprinted by permission of the Harvard University Archives.)

Karl Lashley was born in Davis, West Virginia, where his father was alternately postmaster and mayor. His mother was a bibliophile whose personal library displayed tastes both eclectic and deep.

Lashley's undergraduate degree was earned at the University of West Virginia (1910) but it was during his doctoral studies at Johns Hopkins (1911–1914) that he formed his lifelong interests in animal behavior and its biological basis. One of his chief mentors at Johns Hopkins was H. S. Jennings, a pioneer in the field of invertebrate learning. Lashley's academic and scientific career passed at the University of Minnesota (1917–1926), the University of Chicago (1926–1935), and at Harvard University (1935–1955), though all but seven of these last years were spent as Director of the Yerkes Laboratories of Primate Biology.

It was in the decade beginning in 1919 that Lashley's research on the functional organization of the rat's brain reached scientific maturity. His use of the ablation technique (Chapter 2) was combined with methods of behavioral analysis in a manner that was nearly without precedent at the time. In numerous and programmatic studies, Lashley worked out the effects of cortical lesions on any number of basic sensory, motor, and learning functions. His results led him to his famous *principle of equipotentiality* and *principle of mass action*. The first of these emphasizes the ability of the cerebral cortex to compensate for the deficits produced by lesions. One must not exaggerate the "equi-" part of the first principle, but Lashley did show the surprising degree to which the cortex as-a-whole can continue to mediate complex processes even after one of the primary cortical areas has been destroyed. By *mass action* Lashley sought to stress this *cortex-as-a-whole* nature of cerebral function.

Although he once published with John B. Watson (on the subject of migratory behavior in birds) and although he was very much the "behavioral scientist," Lashley was never persuaded by the radical behavioristic theses dominant within experimental psychology. His criticisms of Pavlov were relentless and successful. His attention to cognitive functions virtually created the current perspective in psychobiology.

Wilder Graves Penfield
1891–1979

(Reprinted by permission of Director, MNI, Montreal Neurological Institute.)

Wilder Penfield was born in the then-hinterland of Spokane, Washington, and completed his undergraduate studies at Princeton (1913). Through a Rhodes scholarship, he was able to study at Oxford with Sherrington in 1914–1916 and 1919–1920, earning B.A. (1916), M. A. and B. Sc. (1919), and D. Sc. (1935) degrees from Oxford. His medical degree was awarded by Johns Hopkins in 1918.

Although he held medical and research positions in the United States, Penfield became a naturalized citizen of Canada and the director of the famed Montreal Neurological Institute where most of his important contributions to science were made. His many books are wideranging in their discussions of human brain function and its implications: *Epilepsy and Cerebral Localization* (1941), *Cerebral Cortex of Man* (1950), *No Other Gods* (1954), *Excitable Cortex in Conscious Man* (1958), *Speech and Brain Mechanisms* (1959), and *Man and His Family* (1967). These are only some of his works suggesting the breadth of his concerns.

Penfield is best known perhaps for his studies of the human brain, directly stimulated in his conscious (locally anesthetized) neurosurgical patients. From many hundreds of such studies Penfield was able to map cortical regions associated with thought, language, and memory, as well as more limited sensory and motor functions. On the purely therapeutic level, these same operations relieved countless patients of their epileptic seizures and paved the way to a full appreciation of the electrocortical mechanisms of neuropathology. In discovering that cortical stimulation could revive the patient's vivid recollections of past occurrences Penfield also encouraged further research and theory into the cortical mechanisms of memory and memory consolidation (Chapter 6).

Ivan Petrovich Pavlov
1849–1936

(Photograph by United Press International.)

The son of an Orthodox priest, Ivan Pavlov was born in Ryazan, Russia, and educated in science and medicine at the University of St. Petersburg (now Leningrad). Soon after graduation (1883) he left Russia to spend two years in Germany in the laboratory of the famous Carl Ludwig who had been one of the many outstanding German scientists trained by the great Johannes Müller. (Others included Ernst Brücke, Emil Du Bois-Reymond, and Hermann von Helmholtz.)

Not long after his return to Russia, Pavlov was appointed as the head of St. Petersburg's Physiology Department in the Institute for Experimental Medicine (1890). It was then that he began his research in gastric physiology for which he was to become famous. Published in German in 1897 and then in English in 1902, his *The Work of the Digestive Glands* provided a new and modern understanding of the biochemistry and physiology of digestion. He was honored for this work by the award of the Nobel prize in 1904.

Today, of course, Pavlov is most widely recognized for his theory and research on *conditioned reflexes.* He had introduced the international scientific community to this work as early as his Nobel Prize address but its greatest influence awaited the English edition of *Conditioned Reflexes: An Investigation of the Physiological Activities of the Cerebral Cortex* (Oxford, 1927). In this work, and in the written debates he carried on with his critics, Pavlov did much to impose a rigorously biological perspective on what had traditionally been taken to be a purely "mental science." His authority was routinely invoked by the early defenders of *behavioristic* psychology (for example, John B. Watson) and by others who attempted to fashion a scientific psychology out of mechanistic and associationistic principles.

Although a public sceptic regarding the virtues of the great Soviet experiment, Pavlov would ultimately be used as the father of an official Soviet psychology. Only quite recently has the scientific community within the Soviet Union been liberated from the Pavlovian perspective, which was incomplete from the first.

Donald Olding Hebb
1904–

Donald Hebb was born in Nova Scotia, Canada, and received his B.A. from Dalhousie University in 1925. He has said in an autobiographical note that his undergraduate performance was far from admirable, a fact not all that uncommon when the lives of consequential persons are studied.

After taking an M.A. at McGill (1932) he proceeded to the doctoral program at Harvard, earning his Ph. D. in 1936, strongly influenced by Karl Lashley first at the University of Chicago (1934) and then at Harvard.

Although Hebb has published many experimental articles in the areas of learning, brain function, perception, and so on, he is best known for his theoretical and integrative writings and especially for *The Organization of Behavior*. In this book he attempted to restore connectionistic theory to psychobiology after the work of Lashley and the Gestalt psychologists seemed to doom such theories to scientific oblivion. The central argument of the book is that learning and memory are to be understood as the result of the formation of functional networks able to create electrical codes maintained by "reverberatory circuits." The interesting and subsequently partially confirmed theory of *structural* changes in neurons as a corollary of learning was another important feature of Hebb's thesis.

Hebb has been honored by the major psychological and scientific societies of Canada and the United States, winning the Coronation Medal in his native land (1953) and the Warren Medal awarded by our Society for Experimental Psychology. He is past President of both the Canadian and the American Psychological Associations and the retired Chancellor of McGill University.

Roger Wolcott Sperry
1913–

Roger Sperry was born in Hartford, Connecticut. He earned both B.A. (1935) and M. A. (1937) at Oberline College. He then went to the University of Chicago, to the laboratory of the famous Paul Weiss, receiving the Ph. D. from there in 1940. His earliest research did much to correct Weiss's own theories regarding the plasticity of neural tissue. Sperry showed, with better methods and more systematic experiments, that transplanted neural tissue, functionally organized in the donor-specimen, retains its organization in the host-specimen. His careful anatomical studies also revised thinking in the area of developmental neurobiology. He demonstrated, for example, that retinal fibers grow and proceed toward specific brain regions and that their organization is largely independent of external conditions of stimulation. Surgically "scrambled" nerves subsequently "unravel" themselves in the course of development and proceed toward the same target areas as do normal fibers.

It was chiefly in the 1950s that Sperry's now famous work on the cerebral commissures came to dominate his energies. By surgically severing the commissural connections between left and right hemispheres, Sperry was able to study the functions localized in each hemisphere and, indirectly, to determine the importance of interhemispheric influences in the normal animal. His research was the first to establish the degree of functional independence possessed by each hemisphere when removed from the influences of its neighbor, a degree of functional independence that suggested a "two-brain" animal and, in time, a "two-self" person. Controversy still surrounds the entire question of "split-brain man", as we shall note in later chapters, but Sperry's experimental methods and data remain the foundation for the most current thinking in the area of cerebral functions. Joining Sherrington, Eccles, Penfield and others, Sperry has kept the philosophical aspects of the psychobiological issues alive by contributing a number of thoughtful essays on the subject of consciousness and mental life.

Organization of the Text

We hope, to this point, to have acquainted the reader with the gradual evolution of the psychobiological perspective and with the discipline's relatively rapid development in the twentieth century. We are now ready to move into the technical aspects of modern psychobiology, a move that will perhaps be less jarring now that the broad historical and philosophical contexts have been briefly outlined. A few words are in order as to how we have chosen to organize the balance of the book.

As with all scientific fields not yet in possession of established theories, psychobiology presents the student with the burden of mastering a very large number of facts that cannot be easily summarized and integrated. In physics, by comparison, once one knows Ohm's law or the gravitational laws, it is easy to describe and keep track of an immense number of experimental or observational data. Without laws and theories, such data pretty much have to be taken one at a time. Again taking physics as an example, a book bearing the title, *Quantum Mechanics,* is able to present an extraordinary number and variety of events, ranging from particle interactions to atmospherics, and to discuss all of them within the context of a small number of fundamental principles.

In psychology, however—and psychobiology is no exception—the relative absence of such principles makes it necessary to divide the subject into many small categories and attempt to explain the principles operating within them. There is no equivalent of quantum mechanics or the theory of relativity in psychology. Thus, the facts and "laws" of, for example, learning and memory cannot be readily applied to perception or emotion or language or personality. Indeed, when principles are found that apply as much to any one of these processes as to all the rest, they are invariably not psychological principles, but the established laws and principles of physiology.

Because of this, the sequence of topics in an introductory treatment of the subject is always somewhat arbitrary. Moreover, the transitions from chapter to chapter are often abrupt. Authors may strive to make them smoother, but in a sense to succeed in this is to fail to convey the actual state of the discipline. Accordingly, the best approach is simply to admit the problem exists and to beg the reader's pardon for the inescapably choppy organization.

Our acknowledgment that the chosen organization is arbitrary, however, does not suggest that it is *capricious.* There is a general conviction among psychobiologists that the more complex psychological functions arise from the interaction of simpler ones, and that all psychological functions (probably) are grounded in a surprisingly small number of basic processes. Note that this is a *conviction*, not an established fact. But even as no more than a conviction, it presents a compelling challenge: To wit, one should be able to move steadily from the level of elementary processes to those of ever greater complexity in attempting to establish the physiological foundations of psychological processes. Called by a more neutral term, this conviction is a "working hypothesis" shared by most contemporary psychobiologists and one that has dictated the orientation of this text.

In Chapter 2, the reader is introduced to the experimental and clinical techniques employed to study the functions of the nervous system and the manner in which these techniques make various psychological processes possible. Psychobiology now depends upon any number of complex devices and methods used throughout the biological and physical sciences, and it is important for the student to comprehend, at least in general terms, how these apply to basic scientific questions. Very nearly all of the findings presented in the balance of the book came about as a result of these instruments and methods. It is thus necessary to appreciate their assets as well as their limitations.

Chapter 3 summarizes the basic anatomy and general physiology of the nervous system. Entire volumes are devoted to this subject, so no single chapter can even pretend to be exhaustive. The chapter focuses on those features of neuroanatomy and neurophysiology that have come to figure importantly in psychobiology. The reader should not be disappointed, therefore, if little or no attention is given to the nervous supply to the teeth or the toes or (even) the scalp! Included in the chapter is what will be taken for granted as specific psychological processes are examined in later chapters.

Within the context of the neurophysiological principles and the anatomical organization presented in Chapter 3, the findings in the areas of *sensation, perception,* and elementary *cognition* are set forth in Chapter 4. The focus of the chapter is on the means by which the detection and organization of environmental events are achieved. The chapter includes such complex functions as *pattern perception* and *color vision,* but these functions are explained according to the most basic principles operating in the early stages of information processing.

Chapter 5, "Mechanisms of Behavioral Adjustment," explores a wide range of responses made by organisms facing various environmental challenges. *Instinctual, reflexive,* and *learned* modes of adjustment and how each mode is mediated by various physiological processes are discussed. Genetic and biochemical considerations are explored within a loosely Darwinian context. The behaviors examined are those that can be explained without reference to such higher functions as "thought" or "cognition." This is not to say that the behaving animals do not "think"—only that their actions can be predicted and controlled almost entirely by manipulations of relatively simple features of the external environment and of the organism's own motivational systems.

The psychobiology of memory is a maze of confusion and theoretical conflict. There are problems of definition, problems of measurement, and awesome problems of interpretation. Variations among species, the baffling nature of human memory, and surprises from the Neurology clinic promise to keep this subject alive for many years. Chapter 6 presents those (few) findings that are now quite secure and those (few) theoretical integrations that honor the facts. It then proceeds to the relative chaos that abounds when *memory* is not confined to left and right turns in a runway or key pecks directed at one of two lights. The chaos is not the result of insufficient data but the resistance of these data to orderly organization.

In the following chapters processes even more complex than memory are then examined, for example, emotion, personality, psychopathology, language, consciousness, and thought. These are the topics the nonspecialist takes to be "real psychology", that is, the topics that are closest to everyone in the most personal respects. Again, contemporary psychobiology has enriched the fund of basic *factual* information regarding these processes but has not been able to absorb the facts into a coherent theoretical framework. In each of these chapters, the facts from research on animals is first reviewed. Clinical research is examined to discover points of similarity and departure in comparisons of animal and human processes. Various theoretical proposals are presented and critically assessed.

In the final chapter the authors review the methods, findings, and hypotheses and attempt to anticipate the more fruitful turns psychobiology might take. Some dead ends are already visible, even though more than one persistent soul continues down their paths. In this same chapter, several of the issues raised in Chapter 1 are freshly engaged in order to determine what might be called the limits of psychobiology. It is hoped that by this time the reader will have arrived at a provisionally settled position on such matters and will weigh the last chapter less as a student than as a critic.

Suggested Readings

In this and the subsequent lists of books and published articles, we have attempted to provide a useful combination of more or less "classic" works, standard works, and current works. Additionally, where appropriate, we have included published experimental papers that tend to convey the methods and strategies adopted by researchers in the neural sciences. It would be very useful to the reader to examine at least one such paper in each section in order to appreciate the complexities and difficulties behind each of the general findings reported in the text.

In some cases, it has been proper to include very recent references, but by and large those chosen for inclusion contain the relatively settled facts and principles of each of the major areas. Psychobiology is a discipline whose factual base broadens daily. Because of the rapid accumulation of data and methods, one would be on firmer ground by consulting works that have had enough time to undergo criticism and full assessment.

Historical Foundations
1. R.M. Young, *Mind, Brain, and Adaptation in the Nineteenth Century*, Clarendon Press, Oxford, 1970.
2. D.N. Robinson, *An Intellectural History of Psychology*, revised edition, Macmillan, New York, 1981, chs. 9–13.
3. W.R. Uttal, *The Psychobiology of Mind*, Earlbaum, Hillsdale, NJ, 1978, ch. 2.
4. J.R. Kantor, *The Scientific Evolution of Psychology* (2 vols.), Principia Press, Chicago, 1963.
5. D.B. Klein, *A History of Scientific Psychology*, Basic Books, New York, 1978.

Philosophy of Mind
1. G. Ryle, *The Concept of Mind*, Barnes & Noble, New York, 1949.
2. C.V. Borst (ed.), *The Mind/Brain Identity Theory*, Macmillan, London, 1970.
3. D.N. Robinson, *Systems of Modern Psychology: A Critical Sketch*, Columbia, New York, 1979, chs. 1, 2.
4. K. Popper and J. Eccles, *The Self and Its Brain*, Springer—Verlag, Heidelberg, 1977.

2 Methods of Psychobiological Investigation

Introduction

In this chapter we consider some far more mundane and practical matters than those esoteric, philosophical and historical ones discussed in Chapter 1. But mundane and practical as they may be, the methods used by neuroscientists and psychobiologists are the meat and potatoes of this science. Without the new techniques of the last half-century, our knowledge of the relationship between brain and mind would have remained speculative, argumentative, and moot. The fundamental breakthroughs in the study of this age-old problem that have occurred in the last century certainly must be attributable largely to the extraordinary developments in methodology. It is not an exaggeration to say that the revolution in the conceptual foundations of psychobiology itself is also based on the revolution in technique. There is nothing as difficult as attempting to understand the principles of function or structure when they are invisible. Methodological innovation makes the invisible visible, and thus new methods lead to new ideas, while clarifying others that have been around for many centuries.

This conceptual revolution, based as it is on new observational procedures, continues. Almost every year a major new technique for studying some microscopic or macroscopic aspect of the anatomy or physiology of the brain is announced. More often than not these new developments depend upon electronic, nuclear, chemical, or computational manipulations that would have not been imaginable only a few years earlier. For example

35

the CAT (computerized axial tomography) scanner, of which we will have more to say later, depends on the ingenious linking of a computer to an X-ray detector in such a way that the computer is able to produce a picture far superior to ordinary X-rays. Though expensive (a considerable amount of controversy surrounds the cost-benefit ratio of such complex instruments) one has only to look at a sample display from such a device to appreciate the profound accomplishment this piece of technology represents in human terms. Not too many years ago the information contained in a CAT scan had to be obtained by means of exploratory surgery, or in some cases was simply not obtained, to the lethal detriment of the patient.

microelectrodes

If the CAT scanner represents a breakthrough in the clinical study of the macroscopic (large scale) portions of the human brain, it is clear that the capillary microelectrode serves as a similar breakthrough at the microscopic (small-scale) level. These tiny glass or metal electrodes can be inserted into a single neuron, which itself may be only a few microns (millionths of a meter) in diameter. Detailed analysis of the electrical activity of the individual neuron using this powerful miniature tool, since its first application to muscle fibers by Gerard, Ling, and Graham in 1946, has been the cornerstone of the magnificent accomplishments of the neuroscience laboratory.

The purpose of this chapter is a straightforward one. It is to examine the methodological basis of psychobiology. Here we introduce techniques used to study the nervous system and behavior. Our purpose is to prepare the reader for the subject matter of psychobiology discussed in later chapters that has actually been obtained with these methods. Because we wish to paint with a broad brush and at least mention a wide variety of techniques, we have chosen to limit our discussion to a qualitative level. More specific quantitative or technical details can easily be obtained elsewhere, once the reader knows what to look for.

We begin this survey of instruments and techniques with a relevant conceptual point. It may surprise some students of psychobiology that controversy surrounds questions of neural structure and function as well as the more abstract psychobiological relationships. Even the nature of the anatomy of the brain is not as clear-cut as a neophyte entering the field might think. Not all of the different methods that approach such an easily asked question as "Where are the visual regions of the brain?" necessarily produce the same answer. One could try to answer this question by means of ablative surgery in which brain tissue is removed, by means of evoked potentials elicited in the brain by visual stimulation, or by determining the distribution of various structural or functional classes of neurons in the brain. More often than not, however, these techniques (and others as well) give different answers to the same question. Each suggests a different extent of the "visual" regions. Which technique is providing the "correct" answer (or even if there is a correct answer) is not always so easy to determine. It is at this point that the interpretative and speculative skills of the neuroscientist must be called into play to provide the most useful and fruitful conception of visual localization.

Thus in this context, what first seemed to be noncontroversial—neuroanatomy—must be recognized as a dynamic and often even contentious field. Furthermore, many kinds of theories of classification are under review at present; there are not only disagreements about the choice of methods, but also disagreement among neuroanatomists as to what the results of a particular method actually mean.

All of the methods examined in this chapter provide a view of the nervous system that is indirect; for example, the trace on an oscilloscope is *not* a neuronal impulse but a *representation* of that response. There are usually many sources of potential artifact between the actual event and what may be a wildly distorted representation of it. Similarly, stained dead tissue reflects the organization of the living brain, but is *not* living brain. We must extrapolate from such clues to theories of anatomy that may be as controversial as purely psychological theories.

These conceptual concerns aside, there is an identifiable constellation of basic research questions that guides the work of contemporary neuroanatomists and neurophysiologists. The answers to research questions provide the technical foundation for psychobiological issues which themselves are quite distinct. For example, neuroanatomists, who are interested mainly in the structure of the nervous system, seek to answer the following general questions:

1. What are the major macroscopic subdivisions of the nervous system?
2. How are these major regions interconnected?
3. What are the shapes and structures of the microscopic (cellular) components (neurons) of the nervous system that are the functionally significant building blocks of the major subdivisions?
4. How do the shapes of neurons differ from region to region or layer to layer?
5. How are these neurons interconnected?
6. What are the rules of classification used to provide coherent answers to these anatomical questions?

A comparable set of fundamental questions guides the research activities of neurophysiologists who are primarily interested in the *functional* processes that occur within the nervous system and its elements, rather than with the structure of the parts of that system. The questions they ask, therefore, are somewhat different and require different methods. In brief, neurophysiologists are concerned with the following issues.

7. How do different major areas of the nervous system interact? (Note that this question is different from the anatomical question concerning the pathways by which they are interconnected). This question is concerned with processes such as excitation and inhibition within and between major regions rather than with the pathways over which these processes occur.
8. What regions of the brain seem to be associated with which psychological functions? (This is *the great issue* of localization.)
9. How is physical energy transduced at receptors?
10. How does a neuron convey information from point to point within the neuron?
11. How is information transmitted across the gap between different neurons?
12. How is sensory and motor information encoded by neuronal activity? (This is *the great issue* of representation.)

To neurophysiologists and neuroanatomists these are the central problems to be solved. They are not, however, psychobiological issues per se. Psychobiologists are concerned with how the various parts of the brain are associated with mental and behavioral processes. It is this overarching issue that is dealt with in subsequent chapters of this book. In the following sections of this chapter we consider in detail some of the methods which are used in attempts to settle this issue.

Some Basic Electronics

voltage

Because psychobiology today is so heavily dependent on electronic instrumentation, it is essential that the reader understand certain fundamental facts concerning basic electrical measurements and displays. Perhaps the most basic concept of all is *voltage* or *electrical potential*. To understand voltage we have to appreciate that a basic property of matter is *charge*. For our purposes we can consider charge to be an irreducible characteristic of elementary physical particles. Some particles are negatively charged (for example, electrons and antiprotons) and some are positively charged (for example, protons and positrons). Actually a fairly complete description of *charge interaction* can be given in terms of the electron. A surplus of electrons produces a net negative charge and a deficiency produces a net positive charge. The region deficient in electrons will be more positive than a "neutral" region. Though the charge on each electron is very small and indivisible, at the aggregate, macroscopic level at which we deal with matter, charges can be relatively large and quite variable—sometimes capable of throwing electric sparks for a considerable distance and sometimes so slight as to be barely detectable with all but the most precise laboratory equipment.

In normal matter, most of the time, the net charge on any object is zero because any momentary deficiencies or surpluses of electrons are quickly neutralized by the many free electrons available in the environment. In some situations, (for example, in materials that display a very poor electrical conductance) a surplus or deficiency of electrons can be maintained for a considerable period of time. Electrons in this case are not easily acquired and do not easily leak away, and the object will exhibit a net nonzero charge. Similarly, and this is germane to the discussion in Chapter 3, if *ions*—atoms which either possess one or more electrons too many or too few—are unequally distributed on either side of a membrane, a charge difference will be produced across that membrane. The charge will be proportional to the concentration difference of the charged ions. If two such charged objects are brought near each other, mechanical force will be exerted between the two, as shown in Figure 2–1. If the two objects are both positive or both negative, then they will tend to repel each other. If, on the other hand, one is positive and one is negative, they will tend to attract each other.

ions

If the two objects are rigidly held apart (or together), there will be no actual physical movement; however, a delicate scale can measure the mechanical force exerted between them. If a conducting pathway is placed between the two charged objects, an electrical current consisting of surplus electrons will flow from one object to the other as shown in Figure 2–2. The

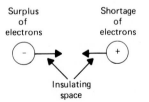

Figure 2–1 A mechanical force being exerted between two charged objects.

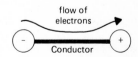

Figure 2–2 An electrical current flowing between two charged objects.

magnitude (amperage) of this current will be proportional to the charge difference between the two objects; the magnitude of this charge difference in turn depends on the relative number of electrons on the two objects. The magnitude of the charge difference is measured by an instrument called a *voltmeter*. Most practical *voltmeters* are, in fact, current meters, but the two measures (current in amperes and electrical potential in volts) are linearly related to each other by a relationship known as Ohm's law.

Ohm's law

$$I = \frac{E}{R}$$

(Eq. 1)

where E = voltage in volts, I = current in amperes, and R = resistance of the current pathway to the flow of electrons in ohms.

The two important points for our present purposes are

1. Voltage is a measure of the electrical force that either impels currents of electrons or produces physical motion.
2. This voltage is a result of the charge difference between *two* points.

Voltage cannot be measured with a single contact, but must always be measured between two points (two objects with different net charges, or the two sides of a membrane dividing two different ionic concentrations, or the two poles of a battery). It is *impossible* to measure voltage with a single contact!

Voltmeters of the galvanometric (current) type just discussed are actually little motors driven by the current produced when differently charged regions tend to equalize the distribution of electrons. The problem with voltmeters of this sort for neurophysiological research is that they respond much too slowly. To point out a particularly relevant example, they are much too slow to follow the course of a neuronal event which may last only a few milliseconds. In 1920 two neurophysiologists, J. Erlanger and H. Gasser, first applied another kind of

oscilloscope

voltmeter—the *oscilloscope*—to the study of nervous action. A diagram of a typical oscilloscope is shown in Figure 2–3. Such a device does not depend on the movement of a mechanical pointer, as does the galvanometric type voltmeter, but uses a beam of electrons that can be moved from point to point on the surface of a fluorescent screen at very high speeds. Indeed, the speed of movement of the beam of electrons is virtually that of the speed of light and is in fact constrained more by the ability of the electronic amplifiers to pass rapidly varying signals than by the negligible inertia of the electrons themselves.

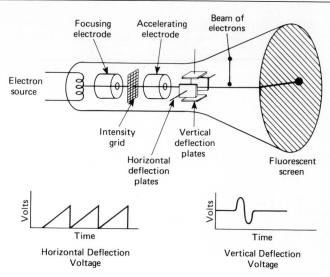

Figure 2–3   A typical electrostatic oscilloscope.

In a typical *electrostatic* oscilloscope (there are also *electromagnetic* types which operate on a slightly different principle), the height of the beam of electrons is controlled by the vertical deflection plates, as indicated in Figure 2–3. It is the repulsive force between a negatively charged deflection plate and a negatively charged beam of electrons (or the attraction between a positive plate and a negative electron) that is responsible for the point on the screen that is bombarded by the beam of electrons. The position of the spot of light, therefore, above or below some neutral point, represents the magnitude of the voltage applied to those plates, and in the situation we are considering here, this magnitude may be the amplified signal produced by a neuron as a function of time. How then do we provide for the horizontal deflection to complete this two-dimensional graph? If a triangular shaped voltage, also shown in Figure 2–3, is applied to the horizontal plates, the point of light produced by the beam of electrons impinging on the phosphor will be moved horizontally in direct proportion to the passage of time. Thus a two-dimensional graph of *voltage as a function of time* is produced on the oscilloscope screen. This trace can be photographed for subsequent measurement. Figure 2–4 shows the output of such a system. Here the spike action potentials of a single neuron have been plotted following the presentation of a stimulus.

This brief discussion of charge, voltage, and the basic neurophysiological measuring instrument—the cathode ray tube (CRT) oscilloscope—is a very modest introduction to the complex electronic instrumentation now commonly used in neuro-

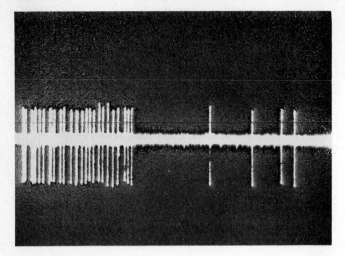

Figure 2–4 A typical oscilloscopic plot from an electrophysiological experiment. Vertical lines are spike action potentials. (Courtesy of Professor Daniel Green of the University of Michigan.)

physiological research. Each aspect of the system has become an art-form unto itself. An elaborate technology, for example, has grown up around the high-gain amplifiers used to magnify the very tiny voltages generated by individual neurons. Another set of special techniques is required to shape and to time the electrical stimuli which are so useful in this kind of research. Furthermore, in some cases digital computers must be made a part of the system in order to display complex signals and to extract exceedingly small responses from the electrical (both electronic and physiologic) noise in which they are often embedded. However incomplete, this brief introduction should help the reader to follow later discussions of those psychobiological findings arising from these research techniques. Figure 2–5 shows a diagram of an entire modern electrophysiological research laboratory.

Major Methods of Study

In the following sections of this chapter we have organized the material according to a plan that is based upon the particular task at hand. Some methods are best suited for studying the macroscopic structure of the nervous system. For example, it would be virtually useless to try to study the electrophysiology of a single neuron with a very large electrode (unless the neuron could be isolated by dissection). But large electrodes are superb for measuring compound evoked potentials obtained from large numbers of neurons and, therefore, can be profitably used at that macroscopic level. On the other hand, too small an electrode would make the search for a particular functional unit of the brain tedious and ultimately self-defeating. Similarly,

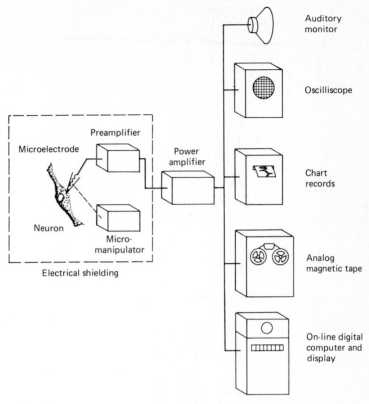

Figure 2–5 A complete neurophysiological laboratory.

some methods that are excellent for the study of anatomy are poor if one's goal is to study function, and vice versa. Our discussion of methods is therefore organized into categories on the basis of the goals of the neuroscientist, as follows.

1. Macroanatomical methods.
2. Microanatomical methods.
3. Methods for the study of macroscopic function.
4. Methods for the study of microscopic (neuronal) function.
5. Methods for the study of cellular chemistry.
6. Methods for the study of behavior.

Macroanatomical Methods

The description of the structure of the larger centers, nuclei, nerves, and tracts of the brain and the other parts of the central and peripheral nervous systems and the interconnections among those regions have long been a matter of concern to neuroscientists. However, for centuries, as we mentioned in Chapter 1, religious or other cultural prohibitions against the dissection of the human body restricted progress in this field. It was no small step, therefore, when, among others, Andreas Vesalius (1514–1564), Leonardo Da Vinci (1452–1519), and Jean Fernel (1497–1558), and their contemporaries in the sixteenth century began to dissect and study the human nervous system along with other parts of the body. It is also interesting to note in retrospect that the original participants in this kind of study were often savants like Vesalius and Leonardo who were talented artists as well as scientists. We know that Leonardo's efforts to picture the human body had drawn him to detailed anatomical studies to which he applied standard artistic techniques. For example, he determined the shape of the hollow ventricles within the human brain by filling them with wax and then dissecting away the nervous tissue surrounding the *endocast* formed by the wax, an obvious modification of the lost wax technique for making jewelry. Vesalius was a trained physician, but it takes no great artistic insight to appreciate the enormous graphic talents exemplified in Figure 2–6.

Other contemporaries of these giants contributed to what was an astonishingly complete, accurate, and essentially modern view of the gross anatomy of the nervous system by the end of the sixteenth century. These early artist-neuroanatomists may not have known how the brain worked, but they certainly had a good idea of what it looked like! They were able to identify the cranial and spinal nerves. They developed the concept of sensory and motor nerves and incorporated the idea of a central integrating brain into their discussions. They also were able to discern the differences in internal structure and appreciate that the brain was composed of two kinds of tissue—gray matter (now known to consist mainly of unmyelinated, that is, unsheathed, cell bodies and short fibers)—and *white matter* (now known to be composed chiefly of great tracts of long fibers covered with fatty myelin sheaths). Unfortunately, without special preparation the gray matter all looks alike, and there were few structural clues to suggest to these early workers that there was any degree of differentiation of the various brain regions (other than behavioral observations that had hinted at specialized localization for centuries). The overall shape of the brain and its major structural components, nevertheless, were almost as well understood then as they are now as a result of the application of techniques of gross dissection. Students of gross anatomy still use the blunt probe, the scalpel, and the dissecting needle in much the same way as their predecessors did in the Renaissance.

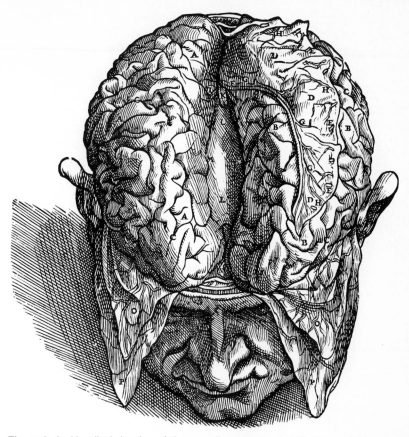

Figure 2–6 Vesalius' drawing of the overall appearance of the human brain.

In recent years, however, a great deal of attention has been directed at the determination of the subtle subdivisions of the various lobes and bulges on the brain, brain stem, and spinal cord. One of the great persisting ideas of psychobiology is that the brain is not homogeneous in its function. The suggestion that it is also not homogeneous in its structure follows directly from this idea and as a result the search for structural and functional specializations of the brain has been continuous for centuries. Figure 2–7A shows a photograph of an unprepared brain slice. Figure 2–7B shows the same section now enhanced by the application of an appropriate stain.

One means of studying the gross arrangement and organization of the major subdivisions of the brain is to make some kind of surgical insert at one point and to observe how the resulting degeneration that inevitably occurs is projected to other portions of the brain. Degeneration methods depend upon the fact that if a neuron is cut there may be substantial changes in the separated parts. Typically there is a massive decay in the

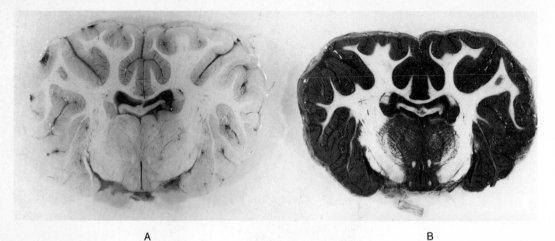

Figure 2–7 *A.* A slice of unprepared sheep brain tissue. *B.* A slice of stained sheep brain tissue. Note the clarity of the stained section compared with the unstained (Courtesy of Professor R.G. Northcutt of the University of Michigan.)

degeneration technique

portion of the neuron that is cut off from the metabolically active regions in the cell body. This massive decay of the portion distal to the cut is called *anterograde degeneration*. But *retrograde degeneration* can also occur. That is, there may also be disruptions of the structure and function of the portion of the neuron between the cut and the cell body or even of the cell body itself. Sometimes these degenerative processes are so extensive that they can be detected with a simple magnifying glass. Higher magnification is required, however, to distinguish more subtle changes. In some instances special stains must be used to mark selectively less obviously degenerated regions that would otherwise be indistinguishable from their surroundings. One particular technique—the *Fink-Heimer stain*—has proven to be especially useful as a means of tracking fibers undergoing anterograde degeneration. It is a silver stain that acts specifically on axons that are actually in the process of decomposing; however it does not act on the entire fiber—only on those portions that are literally falling apart at the moment of application. Only part of the degenerating neurons thus become visible. Figure 2–8 is a good example of such a preparation.

Both gross dissection and degeneration techniques require that the nervous system be that of a dead or dying organism. Obvious ethical principles make it impossible to apply these techniques casually to a human, other than in the most extreme therapeutic situations or after the patient has succumbed to whatever ailment was afflicting him or her. How much more desirable it would be in a clinical setting if the investigator

Figure 2–8 Frontal section of the medulla of an experimental rat to show the cortico-spinal (pyramidal) tract of nerve fibers. One motor cortex was surgically removed at birth, then the other was removed when the animal matured. The rat was then killed and sections of its brain stained by the Fink-Heimer-Nauta method. The fibers of the cotricospinal tract are blackened. (Courtesy of Professor Samuel Hicks of the University of Michigan).

could study the anatomy of the brain in the intact living human being. The investigator could help in many instances to alleviate the pain and suffering that some abnormal neuroanatomical condition might be causing, and could also survey a much larger number of brains under more normal conditions to determine the normal range of anatomic variation. This latter possibility is an especially important one. It is not always appreciated that the development of new measuring instruments sometimes places us in the undesirable position of being able to observe some aspect of brain anatomy and yet not know whether it is within the limits of normal variation. For example, some shrinkage of the brain is normal in older people, and fluids must fill in the spaces that develop between the brain and the skull. But, to what extent is this accumulation of fluid normal and to what extent is it pathological? Large groups must be sampled to make any particular observation of brain shrinkage meaningful.

In the past century various noninvasive technologies to examine gross brain anatomy have been developed starting, of course, with the standard X-ray. But the usual X-ray of the brain within the bony vault of a human head is a vague and two-dimensional shadowgraph that is obscure and difficult to interpret under the best of conditions.

New techniques overcome this fundamental limitation of the conventional X-ray technique. One of these remarkable new

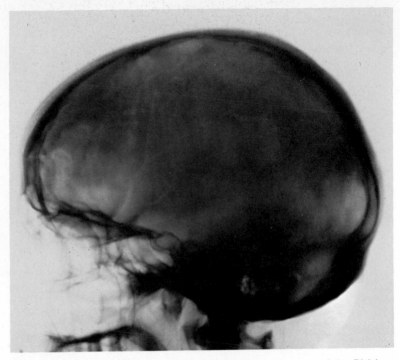

Figure 2–9 A standard X-ray radiograph of the brain. (Courtesy of the Division of Neuroradiology, Department of Radiology, University of Michigan.)

CAT scan

techniques for inspecting the anatomy of the normal human brain as well as other internal structures is computerized axial transverse tomography or CAT scan. A CAT scanner greatly enhances both the nature of the representation and the discriminability of tissues of different density. Consider for a moment the output of a conventional X-ray examination of the brain. A typical radiogram is shown in Figure 2–9. This display is a simple shadowgram taken by placing an X-ray emitter on one side of the brain and a photographic plate on the other. The X-rays pass through all of the intervening tissues; the image density on the plate is inversely proportional to the total density of all of the points in the pathway from the X-ray emitter to the plate. With such a conventional radiogram it takes a density difference of greater than 20 percent to produce a differential shading on the radiogram.

The CAT scan is a quite different system. First, it does not produce a simple shadowgram of the same sort as the conventional X-ray. Its output is a plot of a cross section of a part of the body. To make this point clear consider the sample CAT scan shown in Figure 2–10. In this figure a map of a cross-sectional slice of the head is produced. Second, the CAT scanner is much

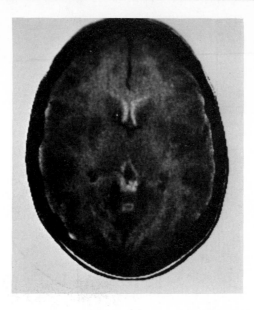

Figure 2-10 A sample CAT scan of the brain. (Courtesy of the Division of Neuroradiology, Department of Radiology, University of Michigan.)

more sensitive than ordinary X radiogram. Density differences as small as 0.5–1 percent routinely show up as differentially shaded on the CAT scan display. (The CAT scan is not technically a radiogram because it is only indirectly the result of the X-rays. The actual CAT scan picture is photographed from the output of a computer which processes the output of an electronic detector of X-rays.)

It is important to appreciate that the CAT scan is not the result of a single view, but rather is the computed output of a very large number of X-ray measurements made with a system which actually rotates around the body of the patient. Figure 2–11 shows this arrangement. The X-ray emitter in this case is designed to emit a fine beam of X-rays which are picked up, following passage through the patient, by a relatively small and sensitive detector on the opposite side of the U-shaped arm. The intensities of the X-rays passing through the tissue on all of the

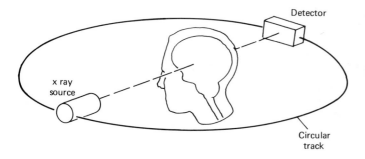

Figure 2-11 The arrangement of the detector and X-ray source in a CAT scanning apparatus. The two units rotate about the subject taking measurements along various axes through the head.

various radial pathways are stored in the computer memory. By a series of mathematical operations, this information is used to reconstruct the X-ray density at each and every internal point on the slice of tissue shown in Figure 2–10. The CAT scan is thus a cross-sectional slice transverse to the long axis of the patient. In order to obtain a full three-dimensional reconstruction, the neuroanatomist has only to move the patient slightly. A sequence of scans taken along the body would thus recreate the shape of the internal structure.

The immense value of the CAT scan device in the present context is that it allows a very detailed mapping of the structure of the brain in situations in which it might be otherwise necessary to do exploratory surgery. Even though the device and its use are expensive, clearly it is serving a medical and scientific role of great importance.

The CAT scan, however, operates at a rather gross level. Although it can show where, for example, the brain may be compacted by an accumulation of fluid, or the presence of a tumor, or the normal or abnormal appearance of the ventricles of the brain, this device is not very good at separating equal density portions of the solid matter of the brain or tracing out the interconnections between various nuclei within the brain. It is a convenient and powerful means of examining gross anatomy without opening the skull, but is not an analytic tool since it cannot effectively distinguish various structures with very different organization if they have the same X-ray densities.

Other techniques must, therefore, necessarily be utilized to trace out these regions and interconnections. One alternative takes advantage of some newly discovered enzymes that have unusual transport characteristics. Horseradish peroxidase (HRP), for example, has the curious property of being unable to pass through the axonal membrane even though it can pass freely along axons and move easily through the membrane of the neuron's cell body or at axonal and dendritic terminations. Thus to mark a tract, the neuroscientist may perfuse HRP into one region of the brain containing cell bodies and observe (by means of appropriate staining or autoradiographic techniques) the points to which HRP is transported. The two regions of the brain must, therefore, be connected by fibers and can be considered to be anatomically as well as functionally interconnected. HRP has the additional property of flowing both backward and forward in a neuron (in the sense that it may flow counter to the flow of nutrients from the cell body to the axonal terminations). Therefore it is not always certain in which direction the fibers would normally conduct information.

These then are some ways in which macroanatomical structures can be analyzed. We now turn to methods better suited for the study of the microscopic structure of the neuron system.*

Microanatomical Methods

In the previous section we discussed the various techniques that can be used to study the gross anatomy of the nervous system. As we have noted, the general structure of the brain has been known for hundreds of years even though some of the newer procedures have only been available for less than a decade. The main frontier at this macroscopic level lies in the twin tasks of identifying the brain nuclei (clusters of cell bodies) and tracing out the various tracts (clusters of axons) and interconnections between those nuclei. Considerable progress has been made and continues to be made in macroscopic studies. However, much of the energy in neuroanatomy in recent years has been directed toward the determination of the microstructure of the nervous system and, in particular, of the form and organization of the individual neurons and those subneuronal processes that are the basic cellular building blocks.

The classic tool for the study of microstructure, of course, is the optical microscope. This device, invented almost 400 years ago first by Zacharias Janssen (1580–1638) and then again by several natural scientists including Antonie van Leeuwenhoek (1632–1723), and Robert Hooke (1635–1703), has undergone a progressive evolution up to the high level of development shown in Figure 2–12. Very important discoveries in neuroanatomy continue to be made using optical microscopy. The Hungarian neuroanatomist Janos Szentágothai, for example, has developed extremely important conceptual models of neuronal organization in various parts of the brain based mainly on optical micrographs. A sample of one of his drawings of the visual cortex (and the optical micrograph on which it based) is shown in Figure 2–13(A and B).

However, the conventional optical microscope is but one part of what is now turning out also to be a complex system, and other tools must be utilized in conjunction with it to make full use of its power. One problem with the study of neurons is that these cells are virtually transparent and are very hard to see under normal, unprepared conditions. The major procedure

---

*The reader may wish to consult the next chapter to become familiar with the basic anatomy of neurons.

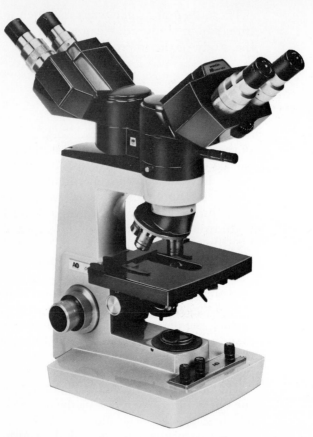

Figure 2–12 A modern optical microscope. (Courtesy of the American Optical Cooperation.)

staining

used in optical microscopy over the years to overcome this difficulty has been to stain neural tissue with some sort of a colored or opaque marker that distinguishes it from surrounding tissues. It is not necessary to mention all existing stains here (entire volumes are devoted to this complex topic) or to describe in detail the particular parts of a neuron that are selectively stained by any given agent. The critical conditions under which a stain is taken up by a cell are not always well understood, and in themselves represent formidable biochemical research challenges. Indeed, in some cases staining seems to be only fortuitous and not to follow any deterministic rules. For example, Golgi silver stains seems to act almost randomly; only a small percentage of neurons exposed to this stain are affected. However, when a neuron is affected at all, the entire cell is stained and stands out under optical microscopic examination just as if it has been isolated from its neighbors. Figure 2–14(A) shows such a Golgi stained neuron.

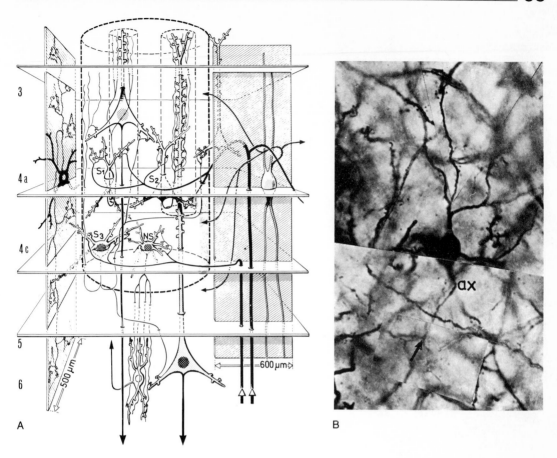

Figure 2–13 *A.* One of Szentágothai's drawings of the organization of the neurons of the cerebral cortex. *B.* A sample of the kind of optical micrograph that led to the drawing shown in *A.* (Reproduced with the permission of Elsevier Scientific Publishing Company, Amsterdam, from *Brain Research*, 1975, 95: 475–496.)

Nissl stains, on the other hand, act selectively on cell bodies and do not stain other parts of the neuron. But they do seem to work on much larger proportions of the population of neurons than do Golgi stains. Therefore, they are particularly useful for examining the distribution of various types of neurons in different layers of the cerebral cortex for example. Figure 2–14(B) shows a Nissl stained preparation of a slab of cortex. Other stains, such as the Bodian stain, act unselectively on myelinated axons as well as cell bodies, and thus are very useful for tracking those elongated fibers or for looking at their spatial arrangement in nerves and tracts. Figure 2–14(C) shows one effect of using this particular type of stain.

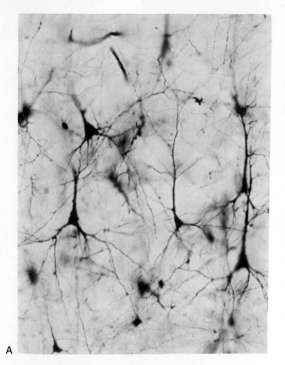

A

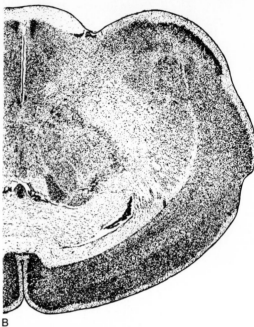

B

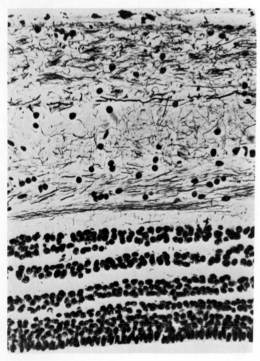

C

Figure 2–14 *A.* Neurons in the sensory cerebral
cortex of an 82 year-old man studied at autopsy
and stained by the Golgi method. It selectively
blackens only a few of all the nerve cells, making
it possible to see details of their structure. The
bodies of these neurons are pyramidal in shape,
snf about 30 to 50 microns wide, about a twentieth
or a thirtieth of a millimeter. The microscopic section is thick and only some of the stained neurons
are in focus. (Courtesy of Professor Samule Hicks
of the University of Michigan.) *B.* A sample of Nissl
stained tissue. This is a cross section of the brain
of a hamster. Note that only the cell bodies are
stained with this method. (Courtesy of Professor
R.G. Northcutt of the University of Michigan.) *C.* A
sample of a Bodian stained slab of neural tissue
from the optic tecum of the Longnose Gar. The
numbers and letters refer to various neuronal
levels. Note that both axons and cell bodies are
stained with this silver stain. (Courtesy of Professor
R.G. Northcutt of the University of Michigan.

Even though the detailed chemistry behind the effectiveness of any particular stain is extremely complex, we often do know the nature of the target substance on which the stain works. Nissl stains specifically combine with the genetic molecules DNA and RNA. Golgi stain become associated with the cell membranes of selected neurons. The Loyez stain has an affinity for myelin.

phase-contrast microscopy

Unfortunately, stains of the type just mentioned scarcely solve all of the microanatomic problems that one may encounter. Sometimes stains cannot be applied. If, for example, one wants to examine the living cell, staining is not the general method of choice. Only a few stains can be applied directly to unprepared and metabolically active tissue. The disruptions caused by the usual microscopic preparation procedures, which may require freezing, slicing, staining, and mounting, are not conducive to the continuity of life! Special *phase contrast microscopes*, therefore, have been developed. These take advantage of slight difference in the refractive index of living cells to visualize such exciting processes as cell division by living neurons. Figure 2–15 shows a phase contrast display. Furthermore, some fluorescent dyes (for example, Procion yellow) have the advantage of being innocuous to living cells. They can be injected into a single neuron without interfering with its normal life. Procion yellow has the additional advantage of migrating to all portions

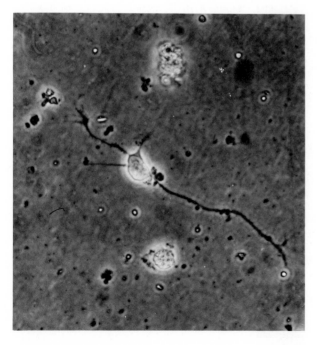

Figure 2–15 A sample of a phase contrast optical micrograph of a goldfish retinal ganglion cell. (Courtesy of Professor Bernard Agranoff of the University of Michigan.)

of the cell—even into very small ramifications that are quite distant from the cell body—but yet will not pass out of the cell since the plasma membrane is impermeable to Procion yellow. A neuron prepared in this manner can be examined with an optical microscope under a bluish light. Under these conditions it will fluoresce with a bright yellow light in all of its three-dimensional splendor. Accurate information of the micro-anatomy of the neuron can be obtained in this manner. Figure 2–16 shows a neuron fluorescing with a dye called diI.

As powerful as it is and as useful as it has been, the optical microscope is not capable of examining the *ultramicroscopic* structure of a neuron simply because it can not magnify the tissue sufficiently to bring subcellular organnelles, tubules, and membranes to visibility. This limited magnification is due not to any technological underdevelopment of the instrument. Rather, it is the result of a fundamental constraint imposed by the wavelength of light. Theoretically, the resolving power of a microscope is limited to about half the wavelength of the light that is used. Beyond that limit, diffraction effects produce blur and obscure the microstructural details. It is possible to improve optical equipment to some degree by using shorter (ultraviolet) wavelengths instead of visible light, but ultraviolet light does not readily pass through glass and thus expensive

Figure 2–16 A goldfish retinal ganglion cell fluorescing with diI. (Courtesy of Professor Bernard Argranoff of the University of Michigan.)

quartz lenses must be used. Even then the magnification is not sufficient to allow viewing of the small details of neural structure.

The ultimate solution to the problem of the magnification limits of optical microscopy has been to abandon glass lenses and visible and ultraviolet light altogether and to turn to beams of electrons and magnetic focusing—techniques used in the *electron microscope* (EM). Electrons, though conceptualized as particles, also have wavelengths associated with them, and these wave-like particles can thus be refracted and focused just as light. The focusing "lenses" in this case, however, are not made of glass or quartz, but are magnetic fields produced by passing electrical currents through coils of wire. Electron microscopes may have very high magnification power—in some extreme cases up to several hundred thousand times the size of the original material. At this level of magnification structures just above the molecular dimension can actually be visualized or photographed from luminescent displays onto which the magnified beam of electrons is projected.

electron microscopy

Two kinds of electron microscope exist, each of which has advantages for cerain applications. One type, the transmission EM, works very much like the conventional optical microscope, though with far greater magnification. A beam of electrons is passed through the material to be examined and minute differences in electron absorption density produce pictures that are accurate shadowgraphs of the material being examined. A transmission EM produces a two-dimensional appearing picture, one of which is shown in Figure 2–17, of very thinly sliced tissues. It is vitally important that very thin tissue be used in such a device since electrons are easily absorbed. Therefore, special *microtomes*, typically using glass shards as cutting knives, have been designed to make such ultrathin sections. By stacking up several electron micrographs taken at different depths in the tissue, a three-dimensional reconstruction can be made of the spatial arrangement of the smallest components of neural tissue.

A far more realistic three-dimensional image can be produced, however, by what is referred to as a *scanning EM*. This device does not pass a beam of electrons through the tissue, as does the transmission EM, but rather depends on secondary emission of electrons from what is often a metallic replica of some biological tissue. The replica is bombarded with electrons focused in a relatively fine beam by the scanning EM. Replicas for the scanning EM are produced by evaporating an appropriate metal (such as osmium) on to a biological specimen. Scanning EMs produce magnificent pictures with a three-dimensional realism that can be quite astonishing. For example,

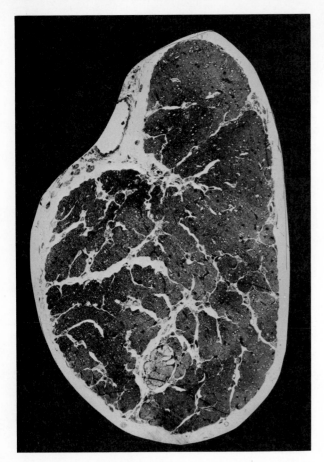

Figure 2-17 A two dimensional transmission electron micrograph of the goldfish optic nerve. (Courtesy of Professor Stephen S. Easter of the University of Michigan.)

consider the scanning electron microphotograph shown in Figure 2-18.

Sometimes the microstructure of a neuron is so delicate or subtle that ordinary techniques simply do not work. For example, we know that even the delicate cell or plasma membrane of a neuron is not a simple structure, but itself may have a complicated inner structure. How does one tease apart the constituents of a structure only two molecules thick? The parts of neurons may be disassociated by centrifugation, detergents, or even ultrasonic oscillation, but the most effective way of disassembling the delicate membrane itself is by means of a process called *freeze fracturing*. Freeze fracturing the plasma membrane of a neuron is accomplished by suddenly immersing tissue in liquid freon, a substance that has a temperature of about $-150°$ C. If the tissue is subsequently placed in a vacuum at a temperature of about $-100°$ C, the two sides of the membrane will spontaneously separate from each other. Rep-

freeze fracturing

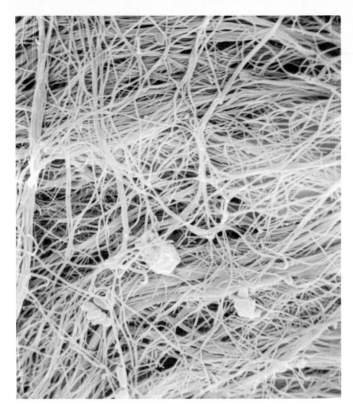

Figure 2–18 A sample of a three dimensional appearing scanning electron micrograph of the optic nerve of the goldfish. (Courtesy of Professor Bernard Agranoff of the University of Michigan.)

licas can then be made of the separated sides of the membrane and scanning electron micrographs can be taken at some later time. The final effect can be quite striking as shown Figure 2–19.

Incidentally, it should be appreciated that it is possible to contribute to knowledge of the *macro*anatomy of the brain by means of *micro*anatomic techniques. The classic subdivisions of the brain (the Broadman areas shown in Figure 2–20) were based on microscopic examination of anatomical types of neurons—a subscience of neuroanatomy known as *cytoarchitectonics*. It is not always the case that the divisions of the brain in such cytoarchitectonically defined areas are the same as those defined by evoked potential or degeneration techniques. Different techniques often give different answers to the problem of regional subdivisions in the brain.

At the present time, various microanatomical methods have allowed us to analyze neuroanatomy down to the level of membrane structure and intracellular organnelles of comparable size. It is becoming increasingly clear that the neuron is a vastly more complicated structure than had previously been suspected. We now know that there are a wide variety of

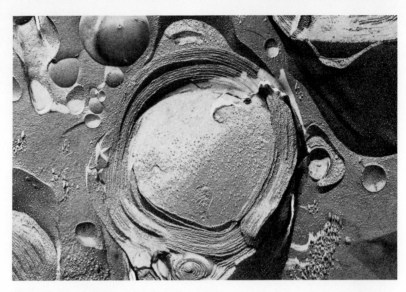

Figure 2–19 A freeze fractured micrograph of myelinated cochlear nerve fibers and some surrounding cells. Note particularly the separation of the myelin layers. (Courtesy of Dr. Kyle E. Rarey of the Department of Otorhinolaryngology of the University of Michigan.)

intracellular processes that carry out a variety of genetic, metabolic, and transport functions within the body. Even the interior of an axon is now known to include many fine microtubules and reticular frameworks either for transporting or for storing the secretions produced within the neuron. Thus, even though the neuron is specialized in structure and function for the transmission and integration of information, it is truly as much a cell as any other cell of the body, with all of the attendant properties present at least to some degree. We shall return to consider the general anatomy of the neuron in the next chapter. Now let us turn to matters of neural function.

Methods for the Study of Macroscopic Function

Just as some methods are best for studying the macroanatomy of the brain and some are best for studying microscructure, there are some procedures that are best suited for studying the function of the larger portions of the brain and some that are best suited for studying the function of the individual microscopic neurons. At the macroscopic level, psychobiologists have been interested for years in finding out which parts of the brain are associated with which psychological functions. This, as we have noted, is the grand problem of the *localization of function*.

localization of function

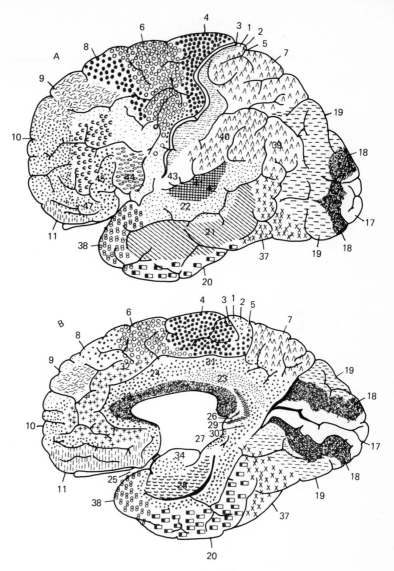

Figure 2-20 The Broadman areas of the brain.

On the other hand, when we approach the problem of microscopic function, we are more concerned with finding out how the individual neuron *encodes* or *symbolizes* information passing through it. This is the grand problem of the *representation of information*. In later chapters of this book we shall examine some of the findings that have resulted from both of these lines of research, but in this chapter our attention is turned exclusively to methodology. Let us, then, consider those methods developed to answer the functional question "What regions of the brain are associated with specific psychological functions?"

or "Where are particular psychological functions localized in the brain?"

One of the traditional procedures for answering this question of localization of function involves the evocation of electrical responses from the brain. One region of the brain may be stimulated and responses detected in others. Stimuli applied to the receptor organs also typically produce relatively well-localized electrical evoked responses in the various regions of the brain associated with that modality. The conceptual anchor provided by the well-defined nature of these stimuli has made it a relatively straightforward task to identify these regions.

evoked potentials

The evoked potential technique, applied to the exposed brain, involves direct stimulation of the brain with electrical or chemical agents or the application of a natural sensory stimulus and the recording of neuroelectrical responses evoked at distant points on the surface or in the depths of the brain. Thus, for example, electrical stimuli applied to the occipital cortex may evoke responses in the lower portion of the temporal lobe of the cerebral hemisphere. The implication of such an outcome is that there are functional as well as structural interconnections between these two brain regions.

Figure 2–21, for example, shows the evoked potentials produced by acoustic stimulation on the parietal lobe of the brain of a dog. The great advantage of this technique is that it involves the normal receptors, and thus the normal neural coding scheme, in the process. Direct electrical stimulation, on the other hand, is always beset with the potential artifact of abnormal activation—that is, the activation of areas additional to those under examination as well as unusual patterns of activity within the region of interest.

Evoked potentials may also be recorded from the surface of the scalp—a technique that is of particular interest and value to psychologists who, not being physicians, are prohibited from using any technique that involves penetration of the skin. Evoked brain potentials recorded from the surface of the scalp, however, are extremely low-level signals (often less than 100 microvolts) compared to the corresponding signals obtained directly from the surface of the brain (often tens of millivolts in amplitude). Therefore computer techniques must be used to average a large number of scalp responses in order to extract the evoked neural response from the various kinds of electronic and physiological noise in which they are embedded. The general technique is, however, otherwise the same. A stimulus is applied to one of the normal sensory receptor systems and the potential produced by that signal is detected. Evoked brain potentials recorded from the surface of the scalp are less easy to localize in particular regions of the cortex than those recorded directly

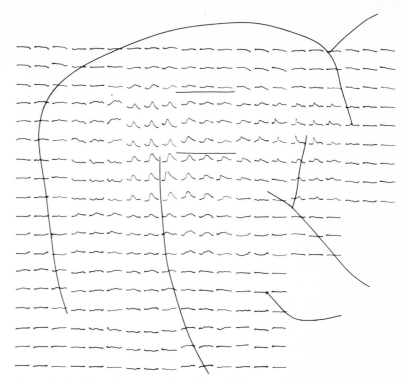

Figure 2–21 Evoked potentials from the parietal area of the cat's brain produced by a tone burst. (Courtesy of Professor Clinton N. Woolsey of the University of Wisconsin.)

from the brain because of the shunting properties of the intervening tissue. Furthermore, the signals from the surface of the skull are not exact replicas in shape or site of origin of those directly obtained from the brain. Rather, they probably represent a composite of the outputs of a number of brain locations. Indeed, some components of the evoked potential can be detected over the entire skull.

EEG There also exists the familiar electroencephalogram (EEG), which is easily detected without computer processing and often with less sensitive amplifiers than those that must be used to study evoked potentials. The spontaneously occurring EEG has been studied for years; unfortunately, the exact significance of this signal still remains a matter of some speculation. A typical evoked brain potential and one of the many different kinds of electroencephalograms are shown in Figure 2–22.

In a similar way electrical or chemical stimuli can be applied to the cortex to determine which parts are involved in its motor output. For over a century it has been traditional to stimulate the brains of both humans and lower animals in this way to

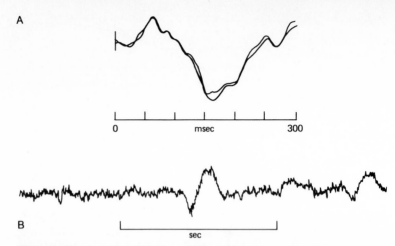

Figure 2–22 *A.* An evoked brain potential from the human visual cortex. (Courtesy of Professor Kenneth Kooi of the University of Michigan.) *B.* A typical electroencephalogram from an awake subject. The large excursion in the middle is an artifact produced by eye movements. (Courtesy of Dr. Michael Feinberg of the University of Michigan.)

determine which regions produced motor responses and the way in which these regions are organized. The precentral motor area (in front of the great central fissure) has been precisely mapped in this manner for many species, and these maps of the motor system are one of the great successes of modern psychobiology. Unfortunately, the specific antecedent conditions and the neural correlates of other more central and integrative processes, such as memory and cognition, are less well linked, and it has proved extremely difficult to study the neural locus of mental processes of this kind. It is, indeed, possible that they do not occur within any localized structure in the way that motor and sensory functions do.

In the last decade there has been a wave of new developments in technique that have made a wide variety of additional functional localization studies possible. Most of these novel

radioactive tracers

developments in methodology involve the use of a tracer or chemical that plays some role in normal brain processes or has an affinity for some other substance that is normally present in certain parts of the brain. For example, the metabolism of the substance deoxyglucose is now definitely known to be intimately and generally related to the amount of neural activity going on in any part of the brain. Deoxyglucose is broken down in regions of high neural activity and its component parts then become incorporated into the cellular substance in those regions. If the deoxyglucose is *radioactively tagged* (that is, if a chemical substitution is made of a radioactive carbon atom, usually carbon-14, for one of the nonradioactive normal carbon atoms), these radioactive atoms will illuminate the point of high activity when a radiogram is made of the brain tissue.

The procedure is relatively straightforward. Radioactively tagged deoxyglucose is injected into the circulatory system of the experimental animal. Neural activity in a particular location is aroused either by electrical or natural stimulation or by some behavioral task. Larger amounts of radioactive carbon are taken up by active brain regions than by inactive ones. Afterward the animal is quickly sacrificed, the brain sliced into relatively large sections, and the slices placed on a photographic plate. The regions in which deoxyglucose had been utilized most heavily, and in which its breakdown products are most prevalent, will be most highly radioactive. They will, therefore, expose more silver salts in films and show up as darker regions on the plate, as shown in Figure 2–23. Depending on what the behavioral task or stimulus was (in this case an acoustic stimulus), it is safe to bet that the most heavily radioactive regions were associated with the most active regions of neural activity (in this case an auditory nucleus). One may then draw conclusions concerning the relationship between the behavioral task and the brain location.

In this type of experiment the animal must be sacrificed and the brain dissected, sliced, and autoradiographed. Therefore, this procedure is also not one that a psychobiologist is likely to apply to humans! Something far less draconian is required for the study of localization and function in humans. One new technique suitable for human experimentation takes advantage of the fact that not only is neural metabolism higher in those regions of the brain that are most active, but the blood supply to such a region also is enhanced. Indeed it has now been shown that the blood flow to a region of the brain and the level of activity in that region are highly correlated. Therefore to measure regional activity one must find some way to measure the differential flow of blood during various kinds of mental

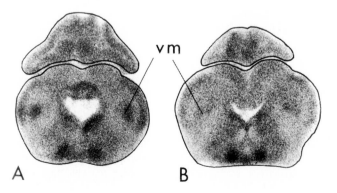

A   B

Figure 2–23 A radioautograph produced by varying the regional metabolism of deoxyglucose. *A.* The autoradiograph of the brain of a Guitarfish produced when noisy acoustical stimuli were applied for a prolonged period. *B.* The autoradiograph produced when another animal was kept in a quiet environment. Note the particular region (vm) that is selectively activated by the noise. This is the ventromedial auditory nucleus. (Courtesy of Professor R.G. Northcutt of the University of Michigan.)

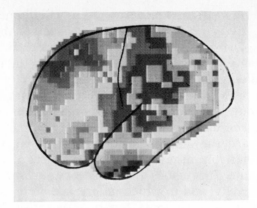

Figure 2–24 A computer processed picture of resting brain activity as indicated by the distribution of radioactivity in the blood supply. (Courtesy of Dr. Neils A. Lassen of the Bispebjerg Hospital, Copenhagen.)

tasks. One solution to this problem also depends on radioactive tracers. In this procedure a small amount of saline solution containing xenon 133—a gamma-ray emitting substance—is injected into the blood supply. The person's head is positioned in front of an array of about 250 gamma-ray detectors, which individually detect the amount of radioactivity being emitted from the various portions of the head beneath each detector. Because the radioactive saline is quickly and evenly distributed throughout the blood, the amount of radioactivity coming from various regions of the brain reflects the amount of blood being sent to that region. The output of the array of detectors is then processed by a computer, the main task of which is to plot a topographic display similar to the one shown in Figure 2–24. The results of studies using these methods are striking. The pattern of blood supply changes even when the subject does something as subtle as changing what he or she is thinking about. In Figure 2–25, for example, are shown the different distributions of blood for three different kinds of mental activities.

Radioactive materials that are specifically taken up by abnormal tissue can also be used as tracers in conjunction with techniques that are similar to the CAT scan described earlier. Cesium, for example, has an affinity for the heart, as does iodine for the thyroid. Similarly, some technetium and nitrogen compounds tend to be specific for certain normal and pathological brain tissues. Deoxyglucose, with its ability to distinguish brain areas with different degrees of metabolic activity, can also be used in this procedure.

If radioactively tagged versions of any of these substances are injected into the bloodstream, they will accumulate in target tissues, and this radioactivity can be detected with devices sensitive to the emitted radiations. Then, by applying appropriate computer techniques, a cross-sectional picture similar to a

PET scan

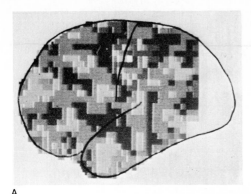

A

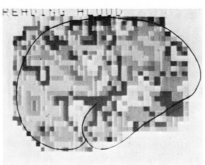

B

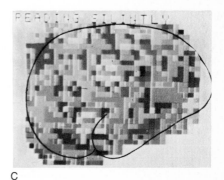

C

Figure 2–25 *A.* The change in blood distribution in the brain during rhythmic movement of the right hand. *B.* The change in blood distribution in the brain during reading aloud. *C.* The change in blood distribution in the brain during silent reading. Note that In each case it is the difference between the indicated brain activity and the resting activity shown in Figure 2–24 that has been plotted. (Courtesy of Dr. Neils A. Lassen.)

CAT scan can be produced. In this case, however, the significant radiation is emitted by the radioisotope within the brain. This system is therefore referred to as emission computed tomography (ECT) or, depending upon the specific radioactivity, positron emission tomography (PET), among others. PET scans work indirectly; positrons emitted by the radioactive material interact with electrons in the matter of the brain to produce two gamma-ray photons, which are then detected with appropriate detectors. Since there are many stray gamma-rays always passing through the space in which the patient is placed, the system is set up to respond only to the simultaneous ejection of two gamma-rays in exactly opposite directions. This dictates a particular type of device—a circular array of gamma-ray detectors. A typical PET system of this sort is shown in Figure 2–26.

Important functional differences exist between ECT and CAT scanners. Because the CAT scan is based upon a very fine beam of X-rays and the ECT scan depends upon a rather diffuse emission, the ECT image is usually less sharp than the CAT image. Thus, one pays a substantial price with an ECT scan in terms of image resolution. This is illustrated by comparing Figure 2–27, which shows a display from an ECT device, with the CAT scan in Figure 2–10. However, there is something to be

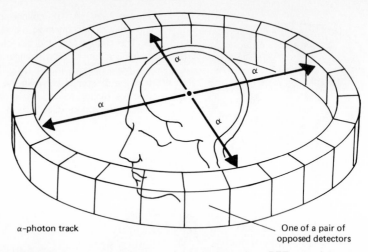

α-photon track

One of a pair of
opposed detectors

Figure 2-26 The arrangement of the detectors in a PET scanning apparatus. Simultaneous activation of detector pairs on opposite sides signals emission (as opposed to spurious) photons.

gained from the use of the ECT device. CAT scans, for all their precision and resolution, are records of structure only. The various regions of the brain can be discriminated only if they differ in density to X-rays. The ECT scan, however, depends upon the uptake of radioactive substances by areas of the brain that may differ in metabolism. Thus localized analysis of brain function is possible—areas that differ in their function may be discriminated even if they are equal in density. Often a metabolic abnormality can be detected long before it produces structural signs.

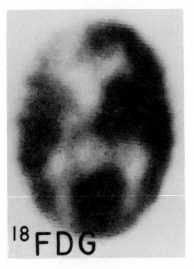

^{18}FDG

Figure 2-27 The display from a modern PET scanning device. ^{18}FDG refers to the radioactive material used—a positron emitting sugar. (Courtesy of Dr. David Kuhl, UCLA School of Medicine.)

In spite of the effectiveness and popularity of these new computer and radioisotope techniques, some older well-tested procedures also continue to provide insights into the localization of function in the nervous system. We refer here to the techniques of experimental brain surgery and the associated behavioral assays that have long been a rich source of understanding of mind/brain relationships. In the main these techniques have been applied mainly to experimental animals; only in the most extraordinary circumstances—in accidents or as adjuncts to some therapeutic brain surgery—would such a procedure be applicable to humans. In principle, however, the surgical techniques that might be used on humans are roughly the same as those used on lower animals. Furthermore, there is little reason to expect that the findings from monkeys, for example, would differ in any fundamental way from those that might be obtained using humans, at least where there is a comparability of behavioral functions in the two species.

ablation

The general paradigm in ablative (or extirpative) psycho-surgery is to destroy or produce a *lesion* (either permanently or temporarily) in a localized region of the brain and then to observe the effect on behavior. This sentence, though easy enough to phrase as a sequence of words, hides a wealth of technical difficulties. For example, to produce a lesion in a "localized region" of a small brain like that of a rat is no easy task. Extreme precision is required even to localize the region of interest. Yet as good as the *stereotaxic* instrument (the device for

stereotaxic instrument

locating brain regions) may be (and a good one is shown in Figure 2–28) the scalpel, suction machine, or electrolytic spark that has to be used to remove the tissue is rarely as precise when it comes to the actual destruction of tissue; nor, for that matter, are the brains of individual animals all identical. It is always necessary, therefore, in this type of experiment to carry out a postoperative microscopic examination of the brain to determine exactly the extent of tissue destroyed for each and every preparation.

It is also possible to produce reversible lesions. Certain chemicals as well as cooling can temporarily deactivate a relatively sharply demarcated region of the brain. At some subsequent time, as the effects of the chemical wear off or as the brain is warmed by natural circulation, the normal function of that area often returns. Such a procedure is highly useful in that a comparison may be made not only between preoperative and postoperative responses, but between normal function before and after recovery.

Reversible and irreversible lesions become meaningful in psychobiological terms only when associated with some kind of test to assay the behavioral deficit that is putatively produced

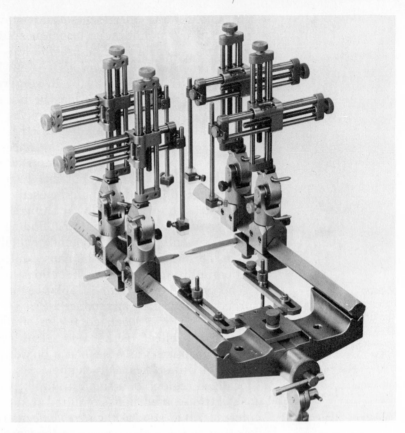

Figure 2–28 A modern stereotaxic instrument. (Courtesy of David Kopf, Inc., Tujunga, California.)

by the destruction of the brain tissue. In some cases, animals with lesions become grossly different in their overall behavior. Extreme docility or extreme "touchiness" may be produced by relatively minor surgical interventions. The animal may eat prodigious amounts of food or drink inadequate amounts of water. The animal may no longer display certain sensory function or may be paralyzed or weak. Whatever the outcome of the lesion may be, great caution must be exercised in linking the behavioral change to the particular surgery. It is not unknown for an animal to lose some skill or sensitivity following an operation, and then to have that skill recover *when some other region is removed*!

sham procedures

Great care must also be taken to assure that the trauma of the surgery itself, rather than the specific localized lesion, is not producing the behavioral change. Some sort of *sham operation* is usually desirable as a control in well-planned experiments. A sham operation replicates all of the surgical steps except the final removal of the neural tissue. Alternatively, the investigator may substitute some other area thought to be unrelated to the function under consideration. Only after such sham controls, histological examination, and careful consideration of the possible alternative explanations have been taken into account is the psychobiologist warranted in claiming that the *behavior* may have been modified by an experimentally produced brain lesion. As we shall see in later chapters, it now appears that there may be no single *center* for any psychological function, but rather a complicated *network* of nuclei instead.

The continued application of the well-established old ablative and new radioisotope techniques is having a profound effect on our understanding of brain localization. Some of the new techniques have allowed us for the first time to test historic theories of brain organization. But studies of relatively large regions of the brain obscure a finer level of activity that requires quite a different technology for their elucidation. The topic to which we now turn concerns methods appropriate for the study of microscopic function.

Methods for the Study of Microscopic Functions

microelectrode recording

Though there have also been many new developments in the study of the function of individual neurons, the method most often chosen remains the *intracellular microelectrode*. The basic problem with the study of neuronal function (and this, in large part, means function as signaled by membrane electrical activity) is the small size of most neurons. Though there are a few animals (for example, the squid) in which unusually large (1 mm in diameter) neurons exists, the neurons of mammals are at best only a few tens of micra in diameter. The classic technical problem in studying neuronal responses, therefore, has been how to make contact with the interior of these tiny cells. It is important to have one electrode inside the cell because, as has been known for almost seventy years, it is the dynamics of the membrane permeability and ion concentrations on either side of the membrane that makes possible the action of neurons. (We will discuss membrane function in more detail in Chapter 3.)

It was not until 1949, however, that the first microelectrodes small enough to be inserted inside mammalian neurons were developed. It took one of the terribly insightful "tricks" that sometimes can revolutionize an entire science to accomplish this tour de force. The distinguished neurophysiologist Ralph Gerard and some of his coworkers appreciated that glass flowed beautifully when it was heated to a liquid state. They therefore took a small (1 millimeter thick) glass pipette and heated it at a single point while pulling on each end. As the glass in the tube became less viscous it stretched and thinned, but in doing so it almost perfectly maintained its original tubular shape. Finally when it was thin enough, the tube broke into two tapering pipettes, maintaining in a reduced form the cross-sectional shape of the original tube. The fine opening at the point where the pipette broke could be as small as a couple of microns. In new automated systems for "pulling" micropipettes the opening at the tip can be as small as a fraction of a micron.* Such a micropipette is fine enough to be pushed into even a small mammalian neuron without destroying it. In fact, the surface tension of the cell membrane is usually strong enough so that the membrane actually closes up around the microelectrode like a self-sealing tire thus preventing the intracellular contents from spilling out.

Because they are so small, glass microelectrodes act as capillary tubes and it is sometimes hard to fill them with the conducting salt solutions that are the actual electrical contacts with the intracellular fluids. Glass, of course, is a very good insulator; the electrode would not be electrically active unless the salt solution within it was in contact with the salt solution inside the cell. Special techniques for filling microelectrodes have been developed along with these special techniques for producing them. For example, the microelectrodes must often be boiled in the salt solution to be properly filled. Sometimes microelectrodes are made from finely etched metals such as tungsten; in that case they must be insulated (except at the tip) with glass or special varnishes. Metal microelectrodes are best suited for extracellular recording rather than for obtaining signals from within the neuron.

As tiny as the tip of a well-manufactured glass or metal microelectrode may be, it is figuratively only the tip of a instrumentation iceberg. The electrode could not perform its function unless the signals it receives from the neuron are detected, amplified, and displayed in a usable form. The electrode must also be mechanically moved (in what are usually very tiny steps of only one micron each) into recording position. All of this means that for each tiny microelectrode tip, there must be considerable supporting equipment. Indeed, a complete electrophysiological recording system may be quite large, consisting of many different components as shown in Figure 2–5.

Each of the individual devices in such a system has a specific role to perform, and each device must possess certain special characteristics demanded by that role. For example, the

---

*A *micron* is a millionth of a meter.

stereotaxic micromanipulator shown in Figure 2–28 must be massive enough to damp out oscillations caused by vibrations in the surrounding environment. Furthermore it must hold the microelectrode absolutely rigidly so it does not tear the delicate cell membrane. In spite of this requirement of mass, the manipulator must also be delicate enough to advance the microelectrode by one or two micra at a time. In the small scale at which the active point of this microelectrode recording system is actually working, a successful penetration of a neuron and the ability to record signals for prolonged periods of time may depend totally on that level of precision. A micron or two too much and the tip may pass out of the neuron; a micron or two too few and the cell may not be penetrated.

Similarly the electronic apparatus must have special properties. At the very least it must be capable of amplifying the minute neuroelectric signals—typically only about 60 millivolts in amplitude—up to the multivolt levels necessary to drive recording equipment. But there are other amplifier requirements that are also of special concern in this situation. The tip of the microelectrode, being so small, has very high resistance and can distort signals with its stray capacitances. Therefore the first-stage electronic amplifier must also have a high input resistance in order to avoid inadequate amplification due to what are called voltage divider losses. It must also be able to counteract the capacitance of the electrode in order to avoid drastic reductions in the bandpass characteristics of the recorded neural signals.

Once these preamplification requirements have been met, a secondary stage of amplification is needed to raise the power of the amplified signal up to the level required either by oscilloscope displays or computer inputs. The latter consideration is relatively new. The digital computer is rapidly becoming an indispensable part of the neurophysiological recording system, particularly when the data from a single electrode must be statistically analyzed, or, even more severely, when several electrodes are simultaneously producing signals that must be correlated.

In short, the technology of microelectrode recording is complicated and demanding. It is not a casual act to use this technique. Even though the devices that accomplish the various tasks are becoming more and more standardized, it is still the case that a great deal of attention must be devoted to the technical details of this procedure before one collects any usable data. Furthermore, computer technology is a field of great complexity in its own right. One must understand the principles of analog to digital conversion, of computer programming, and enough of the hardware to apply sensibly, as opposed to wastefully or inefficiently, such a powerful tool. This brief chapter is hardly the place to pursue these matters, but the reader must appreciate that the successful neuroscientist of the future will certainly have to master all of these techniques to be productive in this exciting field.

Even though microelectrode recording of the electrical signals generated by neurons is the principal technique for the study of neuron function, several other techniques already described can also be conjoined with this procedure to produce new and powerful research possibilities. For example, drugs can be perfused around the preparation (or injected into the blood supply or even ingested by the animal) and the effects on the nervous system observed electrophysiologically. Such combined techniques are particularly valuable when dealing with the *synapses*—the interacting junctions between neurons. Synapses, as we shall see in Chapter 3, are primarily miniature chemical transmitting and receiving systems. The determination of which chemicals affect synaptic activity by means of electrophysiological techniques has been a powerful means of determining both the nature of the transmitter substances and how the synapses are effected by those transmitter substances. Future developments in this field are extremely likely to depend on ingenious combinations of some of the techniques just mentioned.

Methods for the Study of Cellular Chemistry

As useful as the microelectrode techniques are in providing measures of neural activity, the electrical signal associated with neural activity can be considered as something of an epiphenomenon indirectly reflecting the activity of complex chemical systems within the membranes of individual neurons. Although it is not entirely necessary that the underlying chemistry of the membrane be understood to appreciate the information processing carried on by neural elements, it is of considerable interest and possible therapeutic utility to have that knowledge. Chemicals are the materials of which our brains are made. To understand the nature of chemical processes in individual cells is also to begin to understand the basis of the action of drugs and hormones on behavior even if the details of that action itself remain obscure. By this somewhat cryptic comment we mean that even though chemical studies may tell us how chemicals affect neurons, they do not tell us how the overall pattern of the neural network, which corresponds to any psychological process, changes when chemicals are introduced into the nervous system. The complexity of the neural network precludes that type of analysis.

Nevertheless, a major theme of modern psychobiology is *microchemical* analysis as this relates to mental and behavioral functions. Among the first great successes of this approach was our understanding of neuronal action potentials themselves.

neurochemistry

Neurochemists substituted solutuions containing proportions of ions different from those normally occurring within or outside the neuronal membrane and determined the nature of the resulting neurophysiological effects. The jewel in this line of research was the Hodgkin–Huxley ionic theory of the spike action potential, a theory for which A. L. Hodgkin and A. F. Huxley received the Nobel prize in 1963. The details of the ionic basis of the spike action potential will be presented in Chapter 3. For the moment consider only that neurochemistry was responsible for the knowledge we now have in this field.

More recently neurochemists have made great progress in chemically analyzing the channels by means of which ions move through the cell membrane. These channels were hypothetical structures only a few years ago. Now we know a great deal about their size and shape. Techniques that allow separation of the lipid (fatty molecules) and protein components of the cell membrane, enable neurochemists to determine that the most important actions of the neuron probably depend on conformation changes in these channels which seem to be composed of protein molecules. These large protein molecules have been shown to alter their shape as the membrane potential changes. Other proteins of equal complexity have been shown to utilize the metabolic energy of the body actively to pump sodium ions out and potassium ions into the neuron. These ions play the important role of producing the ionic concentration differences responsible for the membrane resting potential. Sophisticated instrumentation, such as gel or gas chromatographs capable of sorting molecules on the basis of their molecular weights, has given us specific information about the size of these active protein molecules if not about the specific details of their chemical structure. This is not the place to discuss the biochemical research procedures only distantly related to neurochemical analysis. But the reader must not underestimate the enormous progress that has been made in this field. We will underscore this progress in the next chapter.

Another area in which neurochemistry has made great strides has been in the understanding of the synapse—the point of informational interaction between neurons. It is now quite certain that the majority of synaptic connections in the mammalian nervous system are chemically mediated. That is, "presynaptic" neurons emit chemical transmitter substances (as opposed to electrical signals) that alter the permeability of a highly specific and sensitive receptor area on the "postsynaptic" membrane. These receptors themselves are also probably large protein molecules. (Again the reader is reminded that some of these terms have not yet been adequately defined, but will be in Chapter 3.) It is now well known that a wide variety of chemicals can act as synaptic transmitters and also that an even larger group of other chemicals can interfere with the effects of these transmitters. Among other approaches, experiments using poisons such as tetrotoxin (from puffer fish) or black widow spider venom have helped to define the nature of the synaptic process. The chemical action between transmitters and their antagonists are compelling clues to the nature of the normal synaptic interactions that take place between neurons, the nature of the processes that enhance or inhibit those interactions, and the chemical structure of both the transmitter substances and the receptor site on the postsynaptic membrane.

The techniques that are used to accomplish these tasks are manifold and diverse. One of the first problems faced by the neurochemist is the segregation of the various components of the neurons. For example, it might be desired to separate the cell membranes from the cytoplasmic and nuclear components of a neuron. Procedures to sort cells into their components are well established. First, the cellular material is usually ground or pulverized by mechanical action (an ordinary kitchen blender

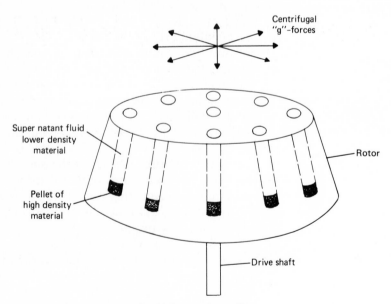

Figure 2–29 A diagram of a high speed centrifuge.

does a satisfactory job) or ultrasonic vibrations may be used. Some detergents also disrupt cell structure. Once broken up the neuronal material can be centrifuged to separate out the various components. A modern high-speed centrifuge (such as that shown in Figure 2–29) separates cellular components on the basis of their molecular weight; thus membranes and other components will be deposited at different times in different sequential orders. It is only necessary to decant the desired or undesired portions to provide a fairly pure preparation of the material to which is to be applied one or another kind of chemical analysis.

Another way in which chemical analyses or assays of neural function can be made is to culture or grow isolated groups of neurons in nutrient solutions *in vitro* (that is, in the test tube, as opposed to *in vivo*, or in the living body). Neurons can be extracted from living organisms, placed in appropriate nutrient and environmental conditions, and observed under the microscope as they proliferate. The dependence of growth on certain chemicals, including the attractive or repulsive forces exerted by particular growth stimulating substances, can be used to distinguish the substances that are embryologically significant from those that are not. Figure 2–30, for example, is a

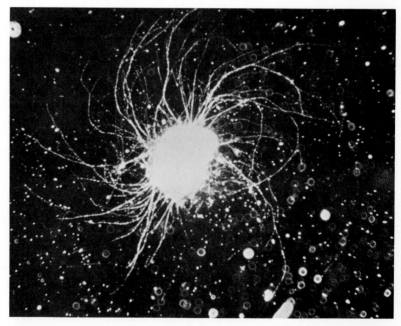

Figure 2–30 A dark field micrograph of a culture of regenerating neurites from neurons in the goldfish retina. (Courtesy of Professor Bernard Agranoff of the University of Michigan.)

micrograph of a culture of neural tissue. Of course, in some exceptional situations it is also possible to study such effects *in vivo*, but since the animal must usually be sacrificed to make such micrographs, studies of this kind are typically static and do not allow continued observation over the course of development of the cell culture. Whether the procedure is an *in vivo* or an *in vitro* one, we now appreciate that the normal development of the embryonic nervous system is strongly dependent upon chemical stimulants, triggers, and guides that regulate and organize the growth of neurons.

Methods for the Study of Behavior

So far in this chapter we have talked about the various technical tools primarily used in the neurophysiological and neuroanatomical side of psychobiology. There is, however, another side to the work that is carried on in psychobiological laboratories that is equally as important and often equally as intricate. That other technical side of psychobiology attempts to assess *mental* processes correlated with the anatomical and physiological details discussed so far. After all it is a basic premise of psychobiological research that the neural mechanisms and structures being studied are those that are relevant to mental and behavioral functions. Of course, the mental processes themselves are "private." There is no way that the psychobiologist can tell directly what is going on in a human or animal mind. Nevertheless we do have available a suggestive and highly correlated indicator of those mental processes—*behavior*—from which we can often infer the mental states. Needless to say, however, some mental processes may have no behavioral correlate.

The analogy between a behavioral assay and, say, an anatomical assay is illuminating. In the latter case, we are sometimes able to tag a particular region that is normally invisible by loading that area with a substance that can be seen under the microscope. All of the silver staining techniques, for example, deposit granules of that metal and form a replica of the original optically transparent tissue. What we see under the microscope, therefore, is a *trace* of the original cell. It may follow closely the original structure, but is not in fact the original structure. It is only an indicator and sometimes that indicator may mislead because the association between the deposition of the silver and the neural tissue may not be exact or may be confounded in some way.

In an exactly analogous way, behavioral measurements can trace, tag, or track those mental processes that are going on within an organism without directly revealing the mental processes themselves. *In this conceptual sense there is no difference between using behavior as an indicator of mind and using silver deposits as an indicator of structure.* The limitations come in when (or if) the mental states of interest are simply not revealed in behavior.*

There are, of course, special problems associated with behavioral assays just as there are those encumbering anatomical or physiological assays, and the two domains may face different problems. Nevertheless in principle the problem is the same— how do you make invisible processes visible? Furthermore, there is also a matter of complexity. It is far easier to define what we mean by a nucleus in the brain (although as we have seen even this sort of anatomical definition is not always straightforward) than it is to define exactly the mental process we seek to measure. Some would assert that mind is made up of quite separable faculties traditionally classified with names like emotion, perception, learning and motivation. However, it is not at all certain that the mind (whatever it is) can be validly analyzed into such processes. Some theoretically oriented psychologists have argued for a fundamental unity of mental functions asserting that the mental subdivisions merely reflect the particular experimental design being used by the investigator. In some cases even this pragmatic classification is unconvincing—we very often see exactly the same experiment being used to study short-term memory, perception, or motivation, where the only difference is the emphasis made by the experimenter in each case concerning how the obtained data will be analyzed. *We simply do not yet have a taxonomy of mental processes comparable to the structural analysis of the brain provided by the anatomists.* Only a very few investigators have attempted the excruciatingly difficult task of defining the behavioral components of their experiments with suitable precision. One is Philip Zeigler who has studied the eating-behavior of pigeons. Zeigler carefully "dissects" behavior just as others in other contexts dissect brain structures forming a detailed analysis of what some might have considered to be a unitary behavior, for example, a single peck by a pigeon at a piece of food. Zeigler has demonstrated by his analysis that this "simple" behavior is itself made up of a series of interrelated tasks, each performed in precise sequence.

*There are, of course, philosophical arguments to the effect that mental states have neither physical causes nor even physical correlates. Psychobiology must ignore such arguments officially or challenge them experimentally.

This type of behavioral analysis is rare, however, and psychobiologists are not generally as thorough in classifying and defining behavior (or the inferred mental states) as they are in placing their scalpels in anatomical structures. On the contrary, rather gross behavior is often measured, ranging from reflexive responses to reaction times, to tracking behavior, all the way to unquantified estimates of the degree of emotionality.

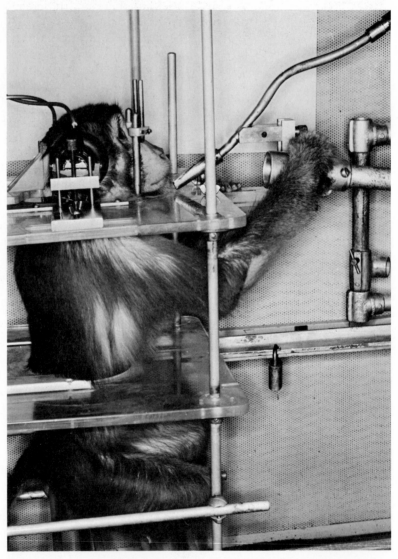

Figure 2–31 A modern Skinner Box for primates. Note the tube providing liquid reinforcement and the manual response lever. (Courtesy of Professor William Stebbins of the University of Michigan.)

Even less objective are those clinical descriptions of human behavioral changes resulting from traumatic brain injury in which such subtle personality factors as aggressiveness or mood are tagged as the critical variable.

Clearly the philosophical and linguistic difficulties involved in defining mind and its attributes are directly reflected in the coarseness of the behavioral methodology that is usually used in the psychobiological laboratory. Nevertheless, some progress has been made in quantifying and standardizing behavior. Some standardized devices have been developed that provide measures of behavior that are as quantitative and precise as anything that might come from the tip of the microelectrode. Simple activity-boxes sensitive to physical motion can determine changes in physical excitement produced by drugs or brain lesions. More sophisticated recording devices exist that do not simply integrate the total amount of activity, but track out the time-course of changes in eating, drinking, or even self-stimulation of the brain. A device often connected to such a recorder is the famous Skinner box (named after the well-known behavioral psychologist B.F. Skinner). The Skinner Box, illustrated in Figure 2–31, is designed to allow the animal to obtain reward by operating a lever or performing some other specific instrumental act. This system has made important contributions to that specialty known as the *experimental analysis of behavior.*

Other standardized devices have also been developed to measure one or another specific kind of behavior. For example, the *delayed response test apparatus* is designed to measure short-term memory. Typical use of such a device—one of which is shown in Figure 2–32—is to present an animal with a piece of food, but then to place it in a compartment covered with a particular object. The animal, usually hungry following a period of food deprivation and often with some sort of an experimental brain lesion, is then prevented from reaching for that food (and in some cases prevented from even seeing the display region) for a controlled period of time. The degree to which the animal is able to successfully select the proper compartment containing the food from among others covered with other objects after the controlled delay can be interpreted as a measure of short-term memory.

It is important to note that the particular mechanism that is used to test behavior is not as important as the fact that there is some kind of standardized behavioral test. The problem, as we have noted, is that behavior is poorly defined at best. The task imposed on an animal in a test apparatus like the one shown in Figure 2–32 may not help to define mind either. However, its value lies in the fact that whatever is tested is constant from one

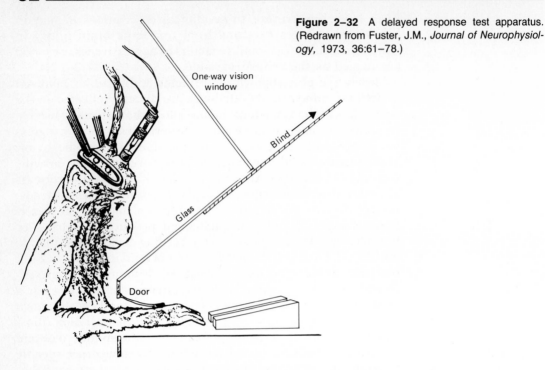

Figure 2–32 A delayed response test apparatus. (Redrawn from Fuster, J.M., *Journal of Neurophysiology*, 1973, 36:61–78.)

experiment, and perhaps more important, from one experimental condition to another.

Beyond such standardized behavior-testing devices there is an almost unlimited variety of tests and scales of psychological function in more natural "field" settings. In some laboratory test situations, the behavior of rats can be studied by simply observing them carefully. Sexual activity, either in terms of frequency or in terms of the proper sequencing of the series of preparatory steps between display and ejaculation, can be examined by observation, as can drinking, eating, or sleeping behavior. The attentive naturalist patiently observing normal behavior in the animal's natural habitat is also a necessary contributor to psychobiology.

The manifold ways in which mental activity can be measured, regardless of how poorly it is defined, is too great for us to describe in detail here. New methods for standardizing and quantifying behavior based on newly emerging technologies are constanty appearing.

Finally, we must not forget that psychobiology is no longer mainly a "rat psychology," but is increasingly concerned with human neural and mental functions and their interactions. Thus, the whole gamut of psychological scales and tests of human intellect and motor and sensory skills automatically becomes a part of the toolbox available to the psychobiological researcher.

Summary

In this chapter we have very briefly surveyed a variety of technical procedures that make it possible for psychobiologists to progress toward their goal of understanding the relationship between the neurophysiological processes carried out by the brain and the corresponding mental activities. Clearly this survey has been superficial. Many of the techniques that we have mentioned are exceedingly complex ones involving chemical, mathematical, or physical principles and procedures that are well beyond the intended level of this text. Our mention and presentation of some examples of what can be accomplished with their use is but the barest beginning of mastery of each of these skills. Psychobiologists spend a large part of their career continuously learning how to use these methods and preparing for others that will be invented in the near future.

There are, however, certain general principles of method and procedure that should be made explicit as we conclude this chapter to remind the reader that the methodological aspect of the field is not of less importance to psychobiology than its substantive or theoretical components. For example:

General Principle 1. *The methodology that is available to any science in large part determines not only the empirical progress of that field, but also the nature of the theoretical explanations that are forthcoming.*

This point is often overlooked. Nevertheless, in recent years philosophers of science such as Thomas Kuhn have emphatically drawn attention to the fact that our instrumentation guides and controls our theories. For example, the development of the intracellular microelectrode, an incredibly influential development, has made us attend much more to the dynamics of particular points in space (where the neuron is inserted) as they vary over time than to the momentary state of a broad field of neurons. How different our theories of sensory processes, in particular, would have been if we had by some happenstance invented a technology that looked at topographic patterns of activity at single moments in time rather than at the time pattern of activity of isolated points. Similarly, the fact that the microelectrode is primarily an electrical tool has constrained thinking in this field in some ways. In recent years there has been some development of "magnetrodes" that measure the magnetic, as opposed to the electrical, fields of neural activity surrounding neurons. Who knows what ideas and theories such magnetic probes might have emphasized if they had been the standard technological approach to neurophysiology?

Another example of the influence of methodology on the very substance of the science can be seen from the increasing application of radioactive and chemical tracers in neurophysiology. Where neurophysiology had primarily been a science that might well have been called "axonology" prior to 1970, recent research efforts have been directed by these new techniques to extensive study of synapses, membranes, and drug effects.

General Principle 2. *Different methodologies do not always give the same answer to a single question.*

Another important general principle concerning methodology is that the various techniques do not always agree. Cytoarchitectonic and evoked potential procedures, for example, may give entirely different estimates of the extent of the cortical regions associated with a particular sensory modality. Even more disconcerting is the fact that slight changes in a single methodology may have great effects on the outcome of an experiment. For example, the results of perimetric tests of extent of the visual field vary considerably as a function of the luminance of the test light. The conclusion we must come to, after examining such examples, is that even anatomical findings concerning the organization of neural tissue must be considered, in large part, to be uncertain *theories* rather than absolute *facts*. Students of psychobiology learn quickly enough to take an assertion like "the lateral hypothalamus is the site of a pleasure center" with a great many grains of salt, particularly when they begin to appreciate the controversy surrounding such a statement. The difficulties restricting a naive acceptance of such assertions are many; they include equivocal psychoneural associations, inadequate definitions of what we mean by a pleasure center, and the usual technical uncertainties involved in ablative surgery on very small brains. Assertions of this type, therefore, must be considered to be theoretical expressions that reflect the more or less confident point of view of some investigators, but by no means a consensus of the entire family of psychobiologists. Even more important, such assertions must be judged to be transitory and subject to continual change. Criticisms have been directed at the most widely held psychobiological dogma in recent years, and there is no reason to expect that even the most vigorously held ideas will not continue to be modified as our knowledge increases.

General Principle 3. *The history of psychobiology is intimately interrelated with that of other physical and biological sciences.*

We must also note, even though we did not discuss the history of psychobiological methodology in detail, that in the early days of this science, it was virtually indistinguishable from physics.

The elucidation of the nature of electricity, the invention of the battery, and the discovery of electrical valences were all deeply entwined with the discoveries of the electrical excitability of nervous tissue by such luminarires as Luigi Galvani (1773–1798) and Allessandro Volta (1745–1827) in the eighteenth century. The subsequent historical threads have diverged somewhat (nowadays neurophysiology is certainly more beholden to electrical engineering for the development of new instruments than the latter is to neurophysiology for the introduction of new engineering ideas). But there is at least the possibility that this flow of ideas may also reverse. The physical sciences may once again be drawing on biological science for inspiration. For example, as we learn more and more about the nervous system, particularly with regard to the details of the ways in which it processes information, insights into how one might go about developing artificial systems capable of simulating intelligent behavior become more likely. The progress of these two sciences, therefore, was originally, is now, and is likely to remain closely associated.

General Principle 4. *The specific chemistry of neurons is not a necessary condition for mental processes.*

Finally, a brief comment is in order concerning the significance of the understanding of the psychobiological processes that is forthcoming from the application of the methods discussed in the chapter. We are in the process of learning much about the chemistry of the neurons out of which our nervous systems are constructed. There have been great strides in the last few decades, both in the electrophysiology and microchemistry of neurons. Information of this kind is sure to have practical applications in psychotherapy and neurology in future decades. However, it should also be noted that perhaps the most important aspect of the nervous system is *the way in which it is organized to process information,* not *the nature of the components that are so organized.* The point being made is that even though it is true, as a matter of practical fact, that our nervous system is made up of neurons that are based on a sodium-potassium-chloride chemistry (Chapter 3), in principle there is nothing special about this particular mechanism. Theoretically, other elements (even some which operate on different functional principles than do neurons) would be able to reproduce processes of an equivalent kind if they were hooked together into networks of equivalent complexity! We should not forget this very important principle as in the next chapter, we apply the methods we have learned in this chapter to the anatomical and physiological study of the particular elements of which our nervous system is composed.

Suggested Readings

Techniques in Microscopic Anatomy
1. J. Babel, A. Bischoff, and H. Spoendlin, *Ultrastructure of the Peripheral Nervous System and Sense Organs*, Mosby, St. Louis, 1970.
2. G. Pappas and D. Purpura (eds.), *Structure and Function of Synapses*, Raven Press, New York, 1972.
3. G. Lynch, C. Gall, P. Mensah, and C. Cotman, Horseradish peroxidase histochemistry: a new method for tracing efferent projections in the central nervous system, *Brain Research*, 1974, *65:*373–380.
4. J.H. Neale, E.A. Neale, and B. Agranoff, Radioautography of the optic tectum of the goldfish after intraocular injection of [^{3}H]-proline, *Science*, 1972, *176:*407–410.
5. R. Lasek, Axonal transport and the use of intracellular markers in neuroanatomical investigations, *Federal Proceedings*, 1975, *34:*1603–1611.
6. W. Nauta and P. Gygax, Silver impregnation of degenerating axon terminals of the central nervous system: (1) technic; (2) chemical notes, *Stain Technology*, 1954, *26:*5–11.

Techniques in Macroscopic Anatomy
1. A. Brodal, *Neurological Anatomy in Relation to Clinical Medicine*, Oxford University Press, New York, 1969.
2. H.O. Peterson and S.A. Kieffer, *Introduction to Neuroradiology*, Harper & Row, New York, 1972.

Electrophysiological Techniques
1. B. Katz, *Nerve, Muscle, and Synapse*, McGraw-Hill, New York, 1966.
2. G. Ling and R. Gerard, The normal membrane potential of frog sartorius fibers, *Journal of Cellular and Comparative Physiology*, 1949, *34:*383–385.
3. E. Donchin and D. Lindsley (eds.), *Average Evoked Potentials: Methods, Results, and Evaluations.* NASA, U.S. Government Printing Office, Washington, DC 1969.
4. A. Hodgkin and A. Huxley, Action potentials recorded from inside a nerve fiber, *Nature*, 1939, *144:*710.
5. V. Mountcastle, Modality and topographic properties of single neurons of cat's somatic sensory cortex, *Journal of Neurophysiology*, 1957, *20:*508–534.

Neurochemical Techniques
1. A. Dunn and S. Bondy, *Functional Chemistry of the Brain*, Spectrum Publications, New York, 1974.
2. W. Nauta and S. Ebbesson (eds.), *Contemporary Research Methods in Neuroanatomy*, Springer-Verlag, New York, 1970.
3. R. Albers, G. Siegel, R. Katzman, and B. Agranoff, *Basic Neurochemistry*, Little, Brown, Boston, 1972.

3 Basic Anatomy and Physiological Principles of the Nervous System

Introduction

In some ways, the entire project of psychobiology or biological psychology is only a refinement of what has been taken traditionally as *functional neuroanatomy.* At the core of both branches of science are questions about what a given part or subsystem of the nervous system does to promote the well-being of the organism, what part it plays in the elaborate collection of adjustments leading to growth, survival, and propagation. Perhaps the chief difference between functional neuroanatomy and modern psychobiology is that the former, at least historically, has been primarily a *descriptive* discipline closely tied to clinical neurology, whereas the latter, at least since the late nineteenth century, has been primarily an *experimental* discipline closely tied to the balance of experimental psychology. Today, however, it is common for both the neuroanatomist and the psychobiologist to employ the same methods—those discussed in the previous chapter—often in an attempt to answer the same questions. This is one reason why specialists in neuroanatomy, neurophysiology, psychobiology, neurochemistry, and experimental neurosurgery tend nowadays to call themselves "neuroscientists"—a title that identifies their common methods and objectives rather than any particular academic department.

The fundamental facts on which all the efforts of neuroscientists finally depend are the anatomical and physiological properties of the nervous system. The purpose of this chapter is to introduce the student to enough of these facts to make the following chapters comprehensible. Thus, the present chapter does not try to be exhaustive. Neuroanatomy and neurophysiology are now vast subjects, each of which requires a separate volume to be covered completely. Indeed, as one's education in psychobiology proceeds, an ever more detailed understanding of anatomy and physiology becomes necessary. What the present chapter offers, then, is a brief introduction to the gross and microscopic anatomy of the nervous system and the general physiological principles of its functions.

The Neuron Doctrine

Until quite late in the nineteenth century and even during the early twentieth century, the prevailing scientific opinion was that the nervous system was a complex net or web of filament-like structures all connected together with a continuity of protoplasm from one part to another. In other words, it was considered to be a connected whole. The model of the vascular system was adopted and the view was that larger nervous structures broke up into smaller branches in much the same manner as arteries branch out into smaller arterioles and these into even smaller capillaries. Only with the advent of more powerful microscopes and more refined histological staining techniques was it possible to begin to unravel the fine structure—the *microstructure*—of the nervous system. Using just such techniques in a series of brilliant studies, Santiago Ramon y Cajal (Chapter 1) presented one of the earliest and certainly one of the most influential cases against the traditional view. His *Histology of the Human and Vertebrate Nervous System*, a two-volume classic published in French in 1911, is still a remarkably accurate and instructive work, and one that may be said to have established the *neuron doctrine*. According to this point of view the anatomical unit of the nervous system is the single *neuron* which exists as an independent structure and not as the merely narrowing or enlarging segment of a continuous web.

the neuron

We now know that the nervous system of all advanced species consist of many types of neurons distinguishable according to their structures and functions. Several representative examples are given in Figure 3–1. If we take the characteristics of a sensory neuron for purposes of illustration, we can identify the following four characteristics. (Note, however, that not every neuron has all of these characteristics.)

1. In the *cell body* or *soma* the metabolic work necessary to the life of the neural cell goes on. The soma is sometimes called the *perikaryon*, a word formed from the Greek for *around*

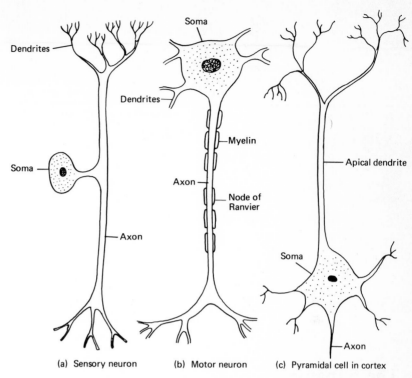

Figure 3–1   Illustrations of three "characteristic" types of neurons, (A) sensory, (B) motor, and (C) pyramidal. Myelination shown only in (B).

(peri) the *nucleus* (karyon). The soma of neural cells possesses an uncommonly large nucleus which, itself, contains one or more than one *nucleolus*. The soma is also filled with *cytoplasm* which branches out to form the axonal and dendritic branches of the neuron.

2. An *axon* is formed by the extension of cytoplasm away from the soma. Where a single axon extends from the body of the neural cell, the neuron is referred to as *unipolar*. Where there is a pair of such axonal processes, running in opposite directions away from the soma, the neuron is called a *bipolar* cell.

3. Branching *dendrites* are the receiving channels of information carried in the nervous system. The dendrites are also cytoplasmic extensions of the soma which may be numerous or few, long or short, clumped or dispersed in their branchings.

4. A sheath of *myelin* surrounds the axon and forms a cover that is interrupted along the axon's length. Note that not all axons are thus *myelinated*. Those that are display breaks in the myelin covering, typically at about every millimeter of length. At these breaks, the surface of the axon is exposed, forming an opening called the *node of Ranvier*.

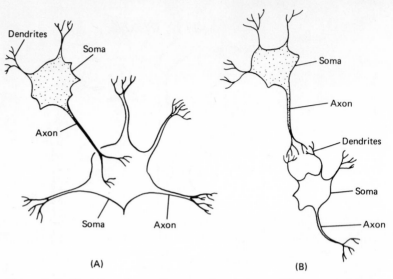

Figure 3–2 Illustation of synaptic connections between (A) the axon of one neuron and the cell body (soma) of an adjacent neuron and (B) between the axon of one neuron and the dendrites of another.

The Synapse

What the neuron doctrine asserts is that the structural units of the nervous system are discontinuous. Thus, the events occurring in one neuron cannot be transmitted to another directly, for there is nearly always some space between one and its nearest neighbor. The most common connections between neighboring neurons are those (a) between the axons of one neuron and the soma of another, a connection referred to as axosomatic, and (b) between the axons of one neuron and the dendrites of another, a connection referred to as axodendritic. Any space separating the terminal branches of an axon from the somatic or dendritic receiving area of a neighbor is called a *synaptic space* (or *cleft*). The synapse is sketched in Figure 3–2 where both an axosomatic and an axodendritic connection can be seen. The word *synapse* refers to the parts of both neurons which permit information to pass from one to the other.

Neural Pooling

Although the neuron is the basic unit of neuroanatomy, the functions of the organism require the participation of millions of neurons, with large numbers of these forming more or less *tracts, nerves, nuclei and ganglia*

distinct structures in their own right. There are two major classes of structures formed by the pooling of neurons. One results from the clustering of neural *axons* running together like the strands of a rope. When these are found within the central nervous system—that is, within the brain and spinal cord—they are called *tracts*. When they occur outside the central nervous system, they are called *nerves*. Thus, all tracts and nerves are comprised of bundles of axons (*fibers*) having shared origins and destinations.

The second major class of structures formed by the pooling of neurons are those resulting from bundles of cell bodies or somas. When such clusters are found in the central nervous system they are called *nuclei* (not to be confused with the nuclei of cells). Outside the central nervous system these pools of cell bodies are called *ganglia* (the plural of *ganglion*).

It should be remembered, however, that not every juxtaposition of several axons or several cell bodies qualifies as a tract (nerve) or nucleus (ganglion). There must be evidence not merely of anatomical pooling but also of functional pooling. A collection of axonal fibers is treated as a tract or nerve generally when all of the constituents share a common source and destination. Similarly, a pool of cell bodies is taken as a nucleus or ganglion only when, *as a pool*, the participating cell bodies either receive influences from a common source or work together in influencing a specific function. In most instances, the nerves, tracts, nuclei, and ganglia of the advanced species consist of many thousands of participating units and, for this reason, are distinctly visible either with low-power microscopes or by the unaided eye.

Planes of Observation

anatomical planes

If we are to keep our bearings as we move through the anatomy of the nervous system, it is important to have compass points. In Figure 3–3 we find these under the headings *dorsal*, *ventral*, *coronal*, *saggital*, *superior*, *inferior*, *anterior* and *posterior*. The dorsal surface is the back surface, while the ventral surface refers to the front or abdominal surface. Coronal (from the Latin *corona*, crown) refers to that plane of observation created by a window moving from the tip of the nose to the back of the head. The saggital plane (from the Latin *saggitus*, shaft or arrow) is the one that would be cut by prison bars in the person standing behind them. Superior and inferior refer to regions above and below some reference point, whereas anterior and posterior refer to forward and backward directions. There are near synonyms for some of these terms, the unfortunate consequence

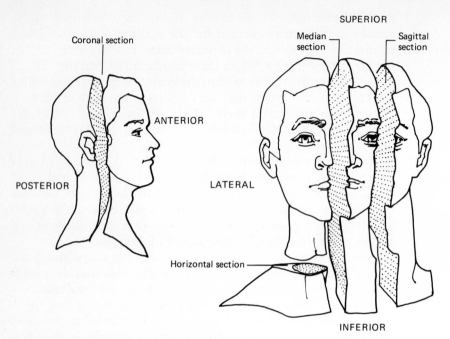

Figure 3–3 Neuroanatomical plans of regard.

of anatomy's long scientific history and its multinational celebrity. When we look at the face of a friend, we are inspecting the ventral surface, but we are also taking in the *frontal* plane. If, instead of standing face-to-face, one of us turns 90 degrees left or right, the *lateral* surface is thereby exposed. Let us now take the lateral surface of the head (Figure 3–3) and cut through in an ear-to-ear direction. In so doing, we would be cutting from the *lateral* to the *medial* regions of the head.

The Flow of Neural Information

afferent and efferent processes

In all advanced species, the most obvious functions of the nervous system are to deliver information to the brain and to conduct information from the brain to the balance of the body. Those processes involved in the delivery of information to the central nervous system are called *sensory* or *afferent* (Latin *ad* = toward; *ferro* = to bring). Information is carried away from the central nervous system by *motor* or *efferent* processes which activate the muscles and glands of the body.

The term "information" is a catch-all term, standing here for any event that enhances the organism's overall patterns of adaptation. As we shall see, however, this information can be coded in a variety of ways; for example, it can be augmented, diminished, stored, retrieved, summed, distributed, and focused. Very little of this could be achieved by a device consisting of no more than a simple conductor between two receiving stations. Thus, to speak of the flow of information toward or away from the central nervous system is to speak of a very complex network of small and large circuits, and of subsidiary transmission centers in which the information undergoes the sorts of modifications just noted. How these modifications are accomplished will be discussed later in the chapter when we turn to the principles of neurophysiology.

Gross Neuroanatomy: *The Spinal Cord*

In the adult human being, the spinal cord is about a meter in length and possesses thirty-one pairs of spinal nerves. Each pair contains a sensory (afferent) branch and a motor (efferent) branch. The human spinal cord is shown in Figure 3–4. Note

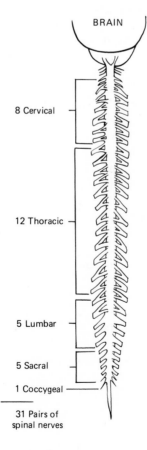

Figure 3–4 Sketch of the human spinal cord showing the cervical, thoracic, lumbar, sacral, and coccygeal pairs of spinal nerves.

BRAIN

8 Cervical

12 Thoracic

5 Lumbar

5 Sacral

1 Coccygeal

31 Pairs of spinal nerves

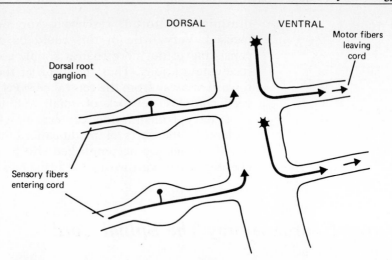

DORSAL

VENTRAL

Motor fibers leaving cord

Dorsal root ganglion

Sensory fibers entering cord

Figure 3–5 Illustration of the sensory (afferent) supply to the spinal cord and the motor (efferent) pathways leaving the spinal cord.

that the first eight pairs of spinal nerves are found at the *cervical* level of the cord and, by convention, are identified as $C_1 - C_8$. Then come twelve pairs of *thoracic* (T_1–T_{12}) spinal nerves, five pairs of *lumbar* (L_1–L_5) spinal nerves, five pairs of *sacral* (S_1–S_5) spinal nerves, and one pair of *coccygeal* spinal nerves.

All of the sensory information arising from within the body and from the body's surface enters the spinal cord on the dorsal surface. All of the motor signals originating either in the spinal cord or in the brain exit from the ventral surface of the spinal cord. The cell bodies of those efferent neurons that form the motor branch of each spinal nerve reside within the spinal cord itself. However, the cell bodies of those afferent neurons whose axons enter the spinal cord reside in a cluster just outside the cord. Each such cluster is referred to as a *dorsal root ganglion*. The arrangement is sketched in Figure 3–5. Note that it is a *ganglion* because the cell bodies are not in the central nervous system but outside it in the peripheral nervous system.

The heart, the smooth muscles, and the glands of the body are affected by a portion of the peripheral nervous system known as *autonomic nervous system* the *autonomic nervous system*. This system has two chief components which work more or less antagonistically with each other. One of these components arises within the thoracic and lumbar segments of the spinal cord and runs parallel with these segments. It is the *sympathetic branch* of the autonomic nervous system. Its neurons originate within the cord, but its cell bodies reside as a collection of *sympathetic ganglia* outside the cord. This branch and the organs influenced by it are illustrated in Figure 3–6.

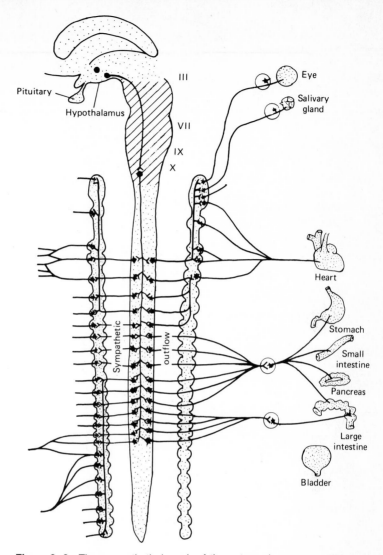

Figure 3–6 The sympathetic branch of the autonomic nervous system.

sympathetic and para-sympathetic divisions

The second component of the autonomic nervous system is the *parasympathetic branch* which arises in the cranium and in the sacral level of the spinal cord. Thus, as the sympathetic branch is said to originate at the *thoracico-lumbar* level, the parasympathetic branch is said to originate at the *cranio-sacral* level. There is still another anatomical difference between the two branches. The sympathetic ganglia lie just outside the cord, in a chain, and at a distance from the organs they serve. The parasympathetic branch, arising from four (III, VII, IX, and X) of the cranial nerves and from the second, third, and fourth

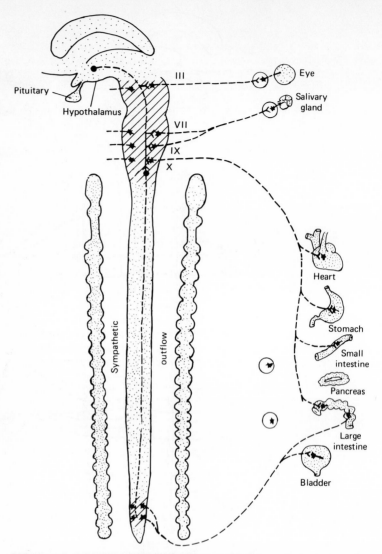

Figure 3–7 The parasympathetic branch of the autonomic nervous system.

sacral nerves, has its ganglia just outside the organs it serves. This parasympathetic arrangement is shown in Figure 3–7. Note that both branches influence the same muscles and glands. Table 3–1 summarizes these connections.

A few examples will help to explain how the sympathetic and parasympathetic branches aid in adjustment through opposition. It is sometimes said that the sympathetic branch is the stress branch because of the range of responses it triggers in the presence of stressful situations. Let us assume such a situation and note the sympathetically induced changes in just a few structures as summarized in Table 3–2.

TABLE 3–1

Parasympathetic	Organ(s)	Function
III cranial nerve	Ciliary muscles of eye	Dilation of pupil
VII cranial nerve	Submaxillary gland	Secretion
IX cranial nerve	Parotid gland	Secretion
X cranial nerve	Heart, stomach, intestines, adrenal	Tone; secretions
Sacral 2–4 (pelvic nerve)	Bladder, colon	Muscle Tone

Sympathetic	Organ(s)	Function
T1–T4	Ciliary muscles of the eye; Submaxillary gland; parotid gland; heat	Muscle Tone
T5–T10	Stomach; intestines; adrenals	Muscle Tone; secretions
L1–L3	Colon; bladder	Muscle Tone

Opposing these changes are the functions of the parasympathetic branch, which is often said to control the "vegetative" processes of the body. Digestion, for example, requires the peristaltic motions of the intestinal organs. These motions are inhibited by sympathetic influences and triggered by those of the parasympathetic branch. Accordingly, indigestion is often a consequence of stress.

Reflex Connections in the Spinal Cord

the reflex arc

The simplest neural pathway by which stimulation leads to action is the *reflex* path, and the simplest of these is what is called a two-neuron (two-element) reflex (see Figure 3–8). In two-neuron coupling, all that is necessary is that the sensory (afferent) process in the muscle be activated. The information is then delivered to the spinal cord where synaptic contact is made

TABLE 3–2

Organ	Effect	Sympathetic Ganglion
Eyes	Dilation of pupils	Superior cervical
Small intestine	Inhibition of peristalsis	Celiac
Heart	Increased heart rate, increased contractility	Superior and middle cervical
Coronary vessels	Constriction	Middle cervical

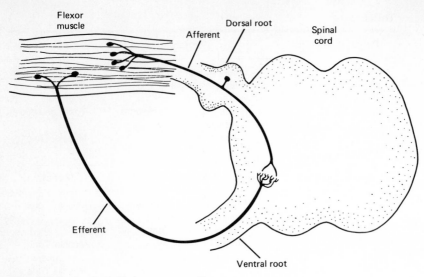

Figure 3–8 A schematic two-neuron reflex.

with a motor spinal neuron at the same level. Where only two neurons are involved, a very fast reflex occurs, usually affecting only the muscle that was stimulated (stretched).

A more complex *reflex arc* involves three neurons: (a) the sensory neuron responding to the stimulus, (b) the motor

internuncials

neuron, which leads to appropriate action, and (c) an *inter*neuron (or *internuncial* neuron) within the spinal cord, which connects the sensory and motor units.

Even with an event as simple as the knee-jerk reflex, however, a number of carefully coordinated processes must be engaged. When the knee-jerk reflex occurs, the leg kicks forward, something that could not happen unless those muscles preventing such action are inhibited. By and large, the rule of reflex actions is *for each excitation, there must be a coordinated inhibition of those muscles that otherwise oppose the action.* So even in the three-neuron example of a knee-jerk reflex, matters are somewhat complicated. In Figure 3–9 we see that the sensory neuron making contact with both a motor neuron (going to the stimulated muscle) and an *inhibitory interneuron* reducing activity in the antagonistic muscle. With this arrangement, the two-neuron reflex arc is activated, but so also is a separate arc; one that permits the knee-jerk reflex to occur by inhibiting those muscles that would otherwise oppose it.

Because of the anatomy of the spinal cord, reflexes may be segmental, intersegmental, and suprasegmental. A *segmental reflex* is one in which the motor response occurs at the same spinal level as the stimulus. An *intersegmental reflex* involves

Basic Anatomy and Physiological Principles of the Nervous System

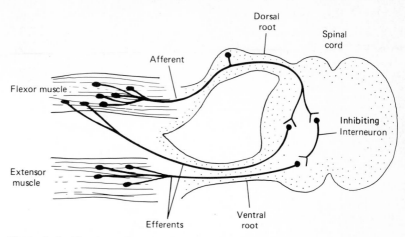

Figure 3–9 The three-element reflex are ("knee-jerk"), including an inhibitory pathway supplying the antagonistic musculature.

motor outcomes at a level different from the level of stimulation. A *suprasegmental* reflex involves the brain and the spinal cord and is completed only above the level of the cord itself. One example of an intersegmental reflex is the extension of an animal's forepaw when the hindpaw is stretched. An example of a suprasegmental reflex is the so-called righting reflex. If you push someone suddenly from the side, notice the rapid adjustments thereby engaged such that normal posture is quickly "righted." These adjustments involve the semicircular canals of the inner ear (which respond to bodily disorientation) as well as the muscles of the torso and of both arms and both legs. Such adjustments not only could not take place at one level of the spinal cord, but also could not take place solely within the spinal cord. Let us turn now to several of the principal pathways connecting the brain and the spinal cord.

Pathways Between Spine and Brain

The spinal cord contains tracts and nuclei by which it becomes functionally connected with the brain. The pathways often have compound names. It is a convention in neuroanatomy for the elements of such compounds to indicate the actual order of influence. Thus, the *corticospinal tract* originates in the cerebral cortex and passes signals down through the spinal cord. The *spinocerebellar* tract originates in the spinal cord and passes signals up to the cerebellum. The descending tracts carry the

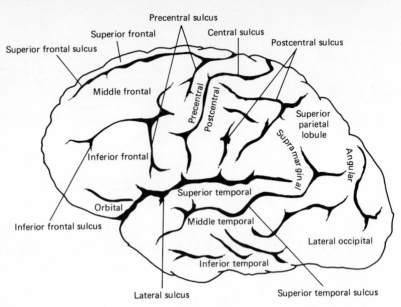

Figure 3–10 A lateral view of the human cortex indicating the longitudinal fissure and the major lobes of the cerebral cortex.

information from the brain, down through the spinal cord, and then out to the limbs and organs of the body. The ascending pathways deliver sensory information from the body to the brain. The lateral regions of the cord, shaped somewhat like the wings of a butterfly, are white in appearance owing to the large number of myelinated fibers forming the tracts, as well as shorter myelinated fibers that begin and end within the cord. The surrounding gray matter of the cord receives its appearance from the cell bodies (*nuclei*) of various neurons and interneurons.

pyramidal and extra-pyramidal pathways

The chief *motor* pathway between the brain and the spinal cord is the *corticospinal tract*, which is part of what is called the *pyramidal system*. This system originates in the region of the brain known as the *motor cortex* and has two major divisions. One of these, the corticospinal tract, contains fibers that run directly from motor cortex to spine. The other, the *corticobulbar tract*, contains fibers that run from the cortex to the *brain stem* (the "bulb," which will be noted later) where those nuclei are found whose axons control such functions as eye movement, tongue movement, and the articulatory movements associated with speech.

In addition to the pyramidal system, motor functions are served by the *extrapyramidal system*. Here again, the fibers originate in motor centers of the cerebral cortex, and they cross over early in their course to the opposite side of the brain where

TABLE 3–3

Disturbed Pathway	Clinical Signs
Right pyramidal tract in the brain (upper motor neuron disease)	Muscle weakness (*paresis*) or immobility (paralysis) on the left side of the body
Right extrapyramidal tract in brain (upper motor neuron disease)	Loss of inhibition of reflexes on left side of the body; thus, exaggerated reflex contractions as well as the *spastic* paralysis of certain muscles
Pyramidal tract at the spinal level (lower motor neuron disease)	*Flaccid* paralysis of the muscles on the same side

they make synaptic contact with cells in the brain stem. The fibers of these latter cells then pass down to the spinal cord where they have an important influence on the processes controlling the skeletal muscles.

It should be noted that the corticospinal tract of the pyramidal system has two principal branches. One is the *lateral corticospinal tract* made up of pathways that originate on one side of the cerebral cortex and end in the opposite side of the spinal cord. (The cross-over area is the medulla oblongata where the crossing fibers form what is called the *pyramids*.) About 80 percent of the corticospinal tract is devoted to this lateral corticospinal branch. The remaining fibers form the *anterior corticospinal tract*, which runs from the cortex to the spinal cord without a crossing over of the fibers. Together the pyramidal and extrapyramidal pathways provide the connecting links by which the brain can deliver signals to the muscles of the body. Several disorders associated with injury to these pathways are cited in Table 3–3.

The Brain

One of the most striking developments in all of evolutionary history is the enlargement of the brain of vertebrates in relation to the overall size of the body. And *human* evolution illustrates this more vividly than the natural history of any other species when the weight of the cerebral cortex is taken as the ground for

evolution of brain

comparison. Even confining the comparison to gross brain weight, however, the rate of change is quite remarkable. On the evolutionary account, the genus *Homo* appears some three million years ago (*Homo habilis*) and displays an average brain weight of approximately 600 grams. About 750,000 years ago there arose *Homo erectus*, with an average brain weight of approximately 1,000 grams. Then, some 250,000 years later *Homo sapiens* appears, now with an average brain weight of about 1,500 grams. We can compare these numbers with the average brain weight for *Australopithecus*, some four million years old, which is about 450 grams. Thus we discover that in somewhat less than five million years there has been a nearly 400 percent increase in brain weight. When we recall that the earliest forms of life on earth came into being four billion years ago and that hominids (of which *Homo sapiens* is a member) are only seven *million* years old, the rapidity of brain development is appreciated more fully. Over the longer period of ten million years, the brains of monkeys and apes show essentially no change at all in *cerebral* development. But in one third of this time, the cerebral development of *Homo sapiens* outdistances that attained by *Homo habilis* by a ratio of more than 2:1.

These, of course, are only gross signs of evolution and do not begin to reveal the far greater and more subtle changes that have occurred in the *functions* and the fine structure of the human brain. The brain of a bee has perhaps a million neurons; the human brain has from twelve to fifteen *billion* neurons. But more to the point, the neural organization of the human brain displays a degree of interconnectedness and synaptic richness that is orders of magnitude greater than our nearest phylogenetic relatives. Indeed, because of this very interconnectedness, it is not entirely apt to speak of the neuron as a distinct "unit", since each of its major components is involved in numerous and complex feedback circuits with a multiplicity of neighboring units. This will become clear when we examine the physiology of neural impulses and synaptic transmission later in this chapter.

In Figure 3–10 we see a sketch of the human cortex as it would appear if it was removed from the cranium and otherwise undisturbed. It is dominated by the massive cerebral mantle, which is divided into the left and the right hemispheres by the *longitudinal fissure*. Viewed laterally, the brain's gross division into lobes is more apparent, allowing the cerebrum to be roughly mapped out into *prefrontal, frontal, parietal, temporal,* and *occipital* regions. Such divisions are made possible by the presence of numerous convolutions whose "hills" called *gyri* (plural of *gyrus*) and whose "valleys" are called *sulci* (plural of *sulcus*).

If we examine the human brain in its inferior aspect, as sketched in Figure 3–11, we see the large *cerebellar hemispheres*, the *pons*, and the upper extent of the spinal cord as it enters the

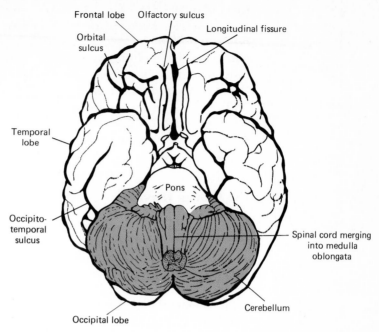

Figure 3–11 The ventral surface of the brain indicating the position of the pons and the cerebullar hemispheres.

cranium. It is at this point that the spinal cord merges into the *medulla oblongata,* which can only be seen when the cerebellar lobes are retracted. As the pons unites the two cerebellar hemispheres on the inferior surface, so the *vermis* provides a connecting link between the cerebellar hemispheres on the superior surface.

The entire brain may be broadly divided into *forebrain, midbrain,* and *hindbrain,* with further divisions abstracted from these. The *brain stem* consists of the midbrain plus the pons and

TABLE 3–4 Gross Anatomy of Brain

Major Division	Subsidiary Division	Chief Structures
Forebrain	Telencephalon	Cerebral hemispheres, Limbic system, basal ganglia
	Diencephalon	Thalamus, hypothalamus
Midbrain	Mesencephalon	Cerebral peduncles, Superior and inferior colliculi (*Corpora quadragemina*)
Hindbrain	Rhombencephalon	Pons, medulla oblongata, cerebellum

the medulla oblongata. The forebrain is subdivided into the more anterior *telencephalon* (comprised primarily of the *cerebrum*, the *limbic system*, and the *basal ganglia*) and the *diencephalon*, which includes the *thalamus* and the *hypothalamus*. The most prominent structures of the midbrain (*mesencephalon*) are the *cerebral peduncles*, which connect regions of the cerebral cortex to the brain stem and spinal cord, and the *corpora quadragemina*, the four rounded bodies that are further distinguished as two *superior* and two *inferior colliculi*. Table 3–4 summarizes the gross anatomy of the brain to this point.

The Cranial Nerves

Also found within the cranium are a dozen pairs of cranial nerves which serve the sensory functions of sight, hearing, taste, and smell as well as a number of motor functions associated with movement of the eyes, tongue, and face. Unlike the spinal nerves, howe7er, the cranial nerves are irregularly located, do not have dors1l and ventral roots, and may have either one or no ganglion. It should be noted that the twelve pairs of cranial nerves contain some that are exclusively *sensory*, some that are exclusively *motor*, and some that are *mixed*. Table 3–5 summarizes the functions and the origins and insertions of these cranial nerves. The position of the cranial nerves is illustrated in Figure 3–12. It will now be useful to take several of the more prominent structures of the brain and provide a general description of their major functions.

Medulla Oblongata

This structure is part of the brain stem and contains a number of vital *nuclei* including the *olivary nuclei* which participate in the motor functions of the cerebellum, as well as the nuclei of the X–XII cranial nerves. Through its reflex connections with both the pons and the cervical spinal cord, the medulla regulates the activity of the diaphragm and therefore breathing. As an intergral part of the entire *brain stem* system, the medulla also influences the flow of information from brain to spinal cord and *vice versa*. It is within the medulla that the brain stem *reticular* formation originates. The reticular formation is a net-like (reticulated) system of ascending and descending fibers with numerous collateral branches. It runs through the very core of the brain from the medulla oblongata to the floor of the diencephalon. Its activity is essential to the maintainance of vigilant and aroused behavior, hence the term *ascending reticu-*

reticular formation

TABLE 3–5 The Cranial Nerves in Their Anterior-Posterior Order

Number	Name	Type	Function	Origin/Insertion
I	Olfactory	Sensory	Smell	Fibers arise in nasal membrane
II	Optic	Sensory	Vision	Fibers arise in the retina
III	Oculomotor	Mixed:		
		Motor	Pupillary constriction	Fibers originate in midbrain
		Sensory	Sense of eye movement	Fibers arise in extrinsic muscles
IV	Trochlear	Mixed		
		Motor	Eye movement	Fibers originate in midbrain
		Sensory	Sense of eye movement	Fibers arise in extrinsic muscles
V	Trigeminal	Mixed		
		Motor	Chewing	Fibers originate in the pons
		Sensory	Sensation from face and head	Fibers from head and face run to the trigeminal ganglion at pons
VI	Abducens	Motor	Eye movement	Fibers originate in the pons
VII	Facial	Mixed		
		Motor	Facial movement, salivation, tears	Fibers arise at junction of pons and medulla
		Sensory	Taste (anterior part of tongue)	Fibers arise in anterior surface of the tongue
VIII	Auditory (Vestibulo-cochlear)	Sensory	Hearing and body-balance	Fibers arise in the inner ear
IX	Glosso-pharyngeal	Mixed		
		Motor	Salivation and movement of pharynx	Fibers arise in medulla oblongata
		Sensory	Taste; sensations from pharynx, tongue and ear	Fibers arise in pharynx, tongue, and outer ear
X	Vagus	Mixed		
		Motor	Movement of visceral organs and visceral secretions	Fibers originate in medulla
		Sensory	Taste; sensations from scalp and outer ear; sensations from tongue and pharynx	Fibers arise in tongue, ear, and pharynx
XI	Accessory (Spinal accessory)	Motor	Movement of head, shoulders, pharynx, larynx	Fibers originate in separate rootlets from the medulla and the cervical spinal cord
XII	Hypoglossal	Motor	Movement of tongue	Fibers originate in medulla

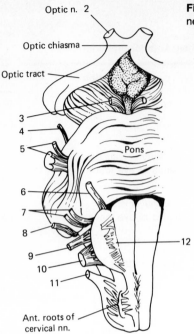

Optic n. 2

Optic chiasma

Optic tract

3
4
5
Pons

6
7
8
9
10
11

12

Ant. roots of
cervical nn.

Figure 3–12 Locations of the cranial nerves within the brain.

lar activating system (ARAS). The general nature of the projections of the ARAS is sketched in Figure 3–13.

Pons

The dorsal portion of the pons is composed chiefly of the fibers of the reticular formation. The VI–VIII cranial nerves are found at the junction of pons and medulla. Within the pons also are relay centers (nuclei) for the V–VII cranial nerves.

Cerebellum

Dense fiber bundles (*peduncles*) connect the cerebellum to the brain stem. Phylogenetically very old, the cerebellum in humans may be divided into *neocerebellum* (not found in phylogenetically lower and much older species) and *paleocerebellum* Together with the cerebral cortex and the basal ganglia, the cerebellum is essential to coordinated and refined motor activity. Moreover, through its projections to certain structures of the limbic system, it also seems to play a part in the emotional expressions of certain species. Like the cerebral cortex, the cerebellum contains layers of different types of cells: an outermost *molecular* layer, below which is a layer of *Purkinje cells*,

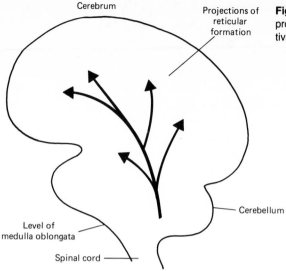

Cerebrum

Projections of
reticular
formation

Level of
medulla oblongata

Spinal cord

Cerebellum

Figure 3–13   Illustration of the diffuse pattern of projections originating in the ascending reticular activating system (ARAS).

and an innermost layer of *granule* cells, which are among the smallest of all true neurons. The *Purkinje cells* near the surface of the cerebellar cortex project downward to the deeper cortical regions where they inhibit the activity of the more deeply located neurons. There is also traffic in the reverse direction whereby granule cells and "climbing" fibers can activate the Purkinje cells. There are also so-called *mossy fibers* rising to the level of Purkinje cells and *parallel* fibers running crossways in such a way as to make synaptic contact with many thousands of Purkinje cells. Thus the opportunity for feedback, inhibition, excitation, and successive firing is immense. A sketch of the simplest sort of interaction is given in Figure 3–14, where the anatomical arrangement is illustrated in the form of a block diagram.

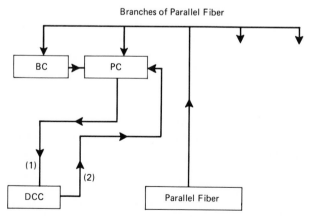

Branches of Parallel Fiber

BC

PC

(1)

(2)

DCC

Parallel Fiber

Figure 3–14   Block diagram of feedback circuit within the cerebellum. BC-basket cell which inhibits activity in the Purkinje cell (PC). The Purkinje cell is able to inhibit through (1) the activity of deep cerebellar cells (DCC). However, through synaptic connections with upward coursing *climbing fibers* (2), the deep cerebellar cells can also activate the Purkinje cell. Branches from the parallel fiber are able to activate both the basket cell and the Purkinje cell. Note, then, that inhibition of the Purkinje cell by the basket cell will *disinhibit* the deep cerebellar cell otherwise inhibited by the Purkinje cell.

The *spinocerebellar, spinoreticular,* and *spino-olivary* tracts all deliver signals to the cerebellum, either directly or by way of relays in the medulla and reticular formation. These projections carry information regarding muscle tension, tendon displacement, and limb position. Still another region of the cerebellum (the *flocculonodular lobe*) receives fibers from the semicircular canals of the inner ears which report the position of the head and which are necessary for the maintainance of postural equilibrium. Both the visual and the auditory systems provide input to the cerebellum thus permitting certain visual and acoustic effects to be integrated with special reflex mechanisms, such as eye blinking.

The chief means by which the cerebral cortex modifies the activity of the cerebellum is through the *corticopontine* pathway. Here, fibers originating over a wide area of the cerebral cortex are collected in the *internal capsule* and *cerebral peduncle* and descend to the pons. Cells in the pons thereupon send projecting fibers to the cerebellum.

In a like manner, the cerebellum is able to pass signals to the cerebral cortex via a number of intermediary steps. Recall that the Purkinje cells of the cerebellum project downward to deeper layers of cerebellar cortex. At these layers we find one of the major cerebellar nuclei, the *dendate nucleus*. The fibers arising from the cells of this nucleus constitute much of the cerebellar peduncles which, after crossing to the opposite side of the head, terminate in the thalamus. On the way, synaptic connections are also made with cells in the *red nucleus* so that the full path is sometimes called the *dentorubrothalamic* pathway: *dento* = dentate nucleus; *rubo* = red nucleus. And, from the thalamic cells receiving the fibers of this pathway other fibers ascend to the cerebral cortex via the *thalamocortical* pathways.

Thalamus

It is in the diencephalon that we find the thalamus and the hypothalamus. Their positions within the brain are indicated in Figure 3–15, where the thalmus is seen as a football-shaped structure. It is composed of a number of nuclei which may be grossly divided, according to their positions, as the *anterior,* the *medial,* and the *lateral* thalamic nuclei.

thalamic nuclei and tracts

The thalamus is the major sensory relay station between the brain and the spinal cord and within the brain itself. Through the *spinothalamic tracts* all the sensations arising on the surface of the body are passed into the brain. And through both a *diffuse* and a *specific thalamocortical* system of projections the thalamus is able to send signals to the cerebral cortex. Moreover, each area of the cortex receiving fibers from the

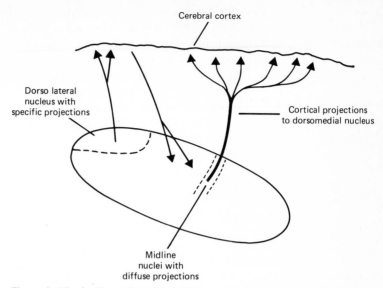

Figure 3–15 An illustration of the *diffuse* and the *specific* projections from thalamic nuclei to the cerebral cortex and an indication of feedback pathways from cortex to thalamus.

thalamus also sends fibers to the thalamus via the *corticothalamic* pathways. Again we discover that *feedback loops* are the rule in neuroanatomy.

The *ventral* region of the thalamus's lateral nucleus contains a number of subsidiary nuclei which, collectively, are referred to as the *ventrobasal complex*. Associated with this complex are nuclei that receive fibers from the optic nerve (the *lateral geniculate nucleus*) and from the auditory nerve (the *medial geniculate nucleus*) either directly or by intervening links. Fibers from the lateral geniculate nucleus (LGN) thereupon run to the visual cortex while those from the medial geniculate nucleus (MGN) pass to the auditory centers of the temporal lobe of the cerebral cortex. In the anterior region of the ventrobasal complex we discover nuclei whose cells receive inputs from the cerebellum and whose fibers run up to the motor strip of the cerebral cortex. Thus, it is through this *nucleus ventralis lateralis* that the thalamus participates in motor functions as well.

On the *dorsal* side of the thalamus's lateral nucleus is located the *pulvinar nucleus* which has elaborate feedback connections with the visual cortex. The thalamus's anterior nucleus is connected primarily with the limbic system, known to participate in the expression of emotional behaviors.

When we examine the inner core of the thalamus we discover *intralaminar nuclei* (the *centre median*) which receive inputs from the reticular formation and thus form part of a *re-*

ticulothalamocortical projection system by which large regions of the cerebral cortex may be activated. Note, then, that the thalamus is a relay for every sensory system except olfaction, that it forms part of the motor apparatus of the brain by virtue of its connections with the cerebellum, and that it is connected anatomically in both a specific and a diffuse manner with the cerebral cortex.

Hypothalamus

homeostasis

The second chief structure of the diencephalon is the hypothalamus which contains a large number of specialized nuclei regulating a wide range of appetitive and vegetative functions for example, eating, drinking, body temperature, as well as aspects of the "fight-flight" patterns of adaptive behavior. The hypothalamus is in intimate contact with structures of the limbic system,* and it contains specialized cells responsive to alterations in the chemistry of the blood. Together with the pituitary and thyroid glands, it is a central part of the body's *homeostatic* mechanisms by which states of biological and biochemical equilibrium are preserved and restored.

Limbic System

Buried in the core of each cerebral hemisphere is a collection of interconnected structures collectively referred to as the *limbic system*. The principal components, depicted in Figure 3–16, are the *cingulate gyrus*, the *amygdala*, the *septum*, the *hippocampus*, the *columns of the fornix*, the *medial forebrain bundle*, and the *mammillary body*. The fornix carries fibers originating in the hippocampus forward to the septum and the hypothalamus, picking up fibers from the former structure as well. The *septum*, primarily through fibers it lays down in the median forebrain bundle, sends influences to the brain stem and receives fibers from the olfactory pathways. The *amygdala* projects directly to the temporal lobe of the cerebral cortex and indirectly to the cortex by way of its connections with thalamic nuclei. Other projections connect the amygdala with both the hippocampus and the septum.

The anatomy alone makes clear the extraordinary degree of integration achieved by the structures of the limbic system. It is tied both to cortical and to brain stem processes, to midbrain and to diencephalic structures, to reticular formation and to its own principal components. As we shall see in later chapters, the

*So much so that it is sometimes included as part of the limbic system.

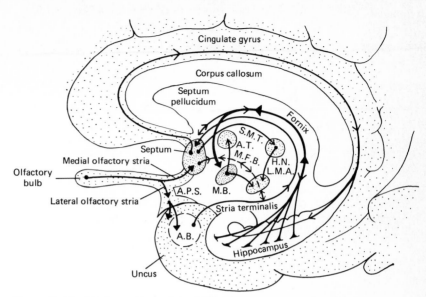

Figure 3–16 Chief structures of the limbic system. (Adapted from Peter D. MacLean, *Psychosomatic Medicine*, 1949, *11*, 388–353.)

limbic system participates directly in a wide range of psychological functions, not the least of which are memory and emotionality.

Neocortex

As noted earlier, the neocortex is the anatomical structure that clearly differentiates human neuroanatomy from anything found elsewhere in the animal kingdom. The ape's neocortex, though superficially similar, does not approximate the neuronal and synaptic richness of human neocortex.

The neocortex is of uneven thickness throughout its extent and consists of six more or less distinguishable layers of cells which, from the surface to the floor of the neocortex, are the *plexiform* layer, the *outer granular* layer, the *outer pyramidal* layer, the *inner granular* layer, the *ganglionic* layer, and the *fusiform* layer. These layers are named according to the dominant cell type found within them. By and large, however, there

cellular architecture

are only three main types of neurons: the *pyramidal* cell, the *stellate* cell, and the *fusiform* cell. Each of these major types reveals a number of variants.

Pyramidal cells are, as the name implies, pyramid-shaped and generally send out dendrites from a long branch extending from the *apex* of the pyramid—hence, their dendrites are called the *apical dendrites*. Less conspicuous dendritic branches extend from the base of the cell. The *stellate* cells are usually smaller and of a round or oval shape; the *fusiform* cells are irregular spindle-shaped neurons with relatively diffuse dendritic extensions. Of the three neurons, it is chiefly the pyramidal neuron that provides connecting links from one side of the cortex to the other, its fibers forming the major *commissures* of the neocortex. The largest of these commissures is the *corpus callosum*, which contains some 200 million fibers.

It is clear from the organization of the neurons within the neocortex that the principal anatomical goal is one of *vertical* communication. What is most common is a richly overlapping pattern of columnar processes by which the activities taking place at various levels of the neocortex may be integrated. Recent evidence, obtained radiographically through the injection of extremely small doses of radioisotopic substances, suggests further that the neocortex is anatomically organized into *modules*, each containing perhaps a few thousand integrated elements. On this view, the 10 to 12 billion neurons would be assembled into three or four million functional modules.

cortical modules

The types and arrangements of cells comprising the neocortex permit it to be partitioned into more or less distinct regions. Early in the present century K. Broadman developed a numbering system for identifying histologically distinct regions of the neocortex and his scheme, which is now conventional, was presented in Figure 2–20. The numbers of particular relevance here are 44 and 45 (the region of *Broca's speech area*), 17 and 18 (essential for communication of visual information), 21 (the auditory portions of the temporal lobe), and 4 and 3 (separated by the *central sulcus*) which respectively mark out the motor and sensory "strips" of the neocortex as shown in Figure 3–17.

Brodmann areas

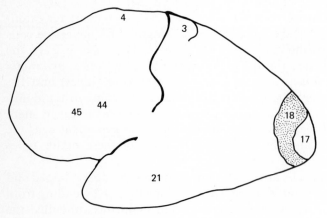

Figure 3–17 Some of the major "Brodman areas" of the cerebral cortex.

Review

Further anatomical details are supplied in later chapters in connection with specific psychological processes. What the preceding section has attempted to illustrate are the broad architectural features of the human nervous system and the chief means by which functional integration is achieved. The following comments and qualifications are offered by way of summarizing this section:

1. Although the neuron is the *structural* unit of the nervous system, the actual complexities of neuronal anatomy and neuronal connectivity make it hazardous to think of single neurons as *functional* units. In the typical instance, a given neuron is impinged upon by hundreds and even thousands of processes delivered by other neurons. And, since the target neuron may, itself, influence those very cells whose branches impinge on it, the general rule is one of *recurrent* rather than one-way influences.

2. The overall organization of the human nervous system is ideally suited to various modes of self- and mutual excitation and inhibition. The elaborate number and variety of circuits and subcircuits operate in such a way as to diminish the likelihood of extremes in the operations of the system as a whole. The incorrect picture conveyed by otherwise unavoidable block diagrams and anatomical sketches is one of a complex machine with a large number of moving parts. But the actual system is more akin to an immensely complex arrangement of hydraulic operations taking place in a closed system that includes portions of the external environment as a means of activation. The example of moving an oar through water is useful. The faster we attempt to move the oar, the greater is the counterforce presented by the water. This is an instance of (viscous) *damping* by which actions that might otherwise be jerky are smoothed out and kept within certain "tolerances." So too are the inhibitory and excitatory actions of the nervous system integrated in such a way as to permit constant corrections and modifications.

3. Precisely because the number of neural elements is so great and because the interconnections among them are so rich it is necessary to keep "errors" to a minimum. The elaborate mechanisms of *inhibition* serve this function by (chemically) opening up some circuits and closing down others.

These three points are central not only to the anatomy but to the general physiology of the nervous system to which we now turn.

The Neural Impulse

The extraordinary anatomy of the nervous system would count for very little were it not for the physiological and chemical processes that make neural transmission possible.

The precise mechanisms by which neural impulses are generated and propagated only began to be understood about a century ago, and the picture has been relatively clear for less than half that time. There is evidence of the ancients using "electric" fish for medical purposes, a practice that was not uncommon in Elizabethan times. But the suggestion that the actual movements of animals were initiated by similar electrical discharges has a history that begins only at the end of the eighteenth century with the work of Louigi Galvani. What he observed, (according to one story, for the first time in a butcher shop), was the contraction of the leg muscles of recently killed frogs when they were placed in what we now appreciate was an unplanned electrical circuit. It should be remembered that when Galvani was publishing his most important papers (during the late 1790s), the theory of electricity was in its infancy. All Galvani had in support of this thesis was the ability to activate muscles by connecting them with brass hooks to different metals. He also used lightning from the atmosphere for the same purpose, again showing that the passage of electricity through the animal reliably produced muscular contractions.

Galvani

The problem of interpretation was, however, formidable if only because electricity itself was so poorly understood. To some of Galvani's contemporaries and immediate successors, the frogs in these experiments were simply functioning as conductors. Note, for example, that if different metals are separated in a suitable conducting medium a charge will flow between them. This is no more than a kind of wet-cell battery. Thus, the frog's muscles could be viewed as no more than a conducting medium by which the circuit becomes closed. On this interpretation, there would be no justification for assuming that movement in the *living* frog is initiated by electrical events, particularly since in Galvani's time there was no evidence at all to suggest that animals possessed electrical properties. Even the great Allessandro Volta (1745–1827) concluded that Galvani's frog's were simple conductors and, fashioning a circuit along the lines suggested by Galvani's experiments, Volta proceeded to construct a "bimetallic" battery in which paper soaked in saline replaced the frog!

Only with the advent of sensitive voltmeters in the nineteenth century and with the invention of equally precise methods of generating electrical charges was it possible to test Galvani's notions. With the availability of better instruments, Carlo Matteucci reported (1841) that a current flowed between the surface of a muscle and wounded area deeper within the muscle—the so-called "current of injury"—and that the electrical events did not require muscle movement as a condition for their occurrence. This discovery was important on several counts, not the least being that it established electricity as an *intrinsic* feature of muscular tissue. Within a few years of learning of Matteucci's work, the German trained physiologist Emil Du-Bois Reymond published his influential *Theory of Electricity* (1848-1849) in which he explained such phenomena as the "current of injury" in terms of electrical *polarization* within the muscles and nerves of the body.

Polarization and the Resting Membrane Potential

The early confusion between magnetic and electrical effects is hinted at by the number of terms and principles of magnetism still applied to electricity. We still speak of the *poles* of a battery and we still describe differences of electrical *charge* as creating a condition of *polarization*.

Soon after the discoveries of Volta in the first quarter of the nineteenth century, the entire field of *electrochemistry* blossomed. Batteries were now used to separate metals, salts and gases from otherwise mixed media, and entire industries were spawned by the process of electrolysis. It was Michael Faraday (1791–1867) who imposed some order on the riot of technology by reducing the broad range of phenomena to more elementary laws—for example, that the mass of a substance liberated through electrolysis is a joint function of the strength of the current and the duration of its application. What Faraday's work showed was that electricity, like the compounds it electrolytically breaks down, must itself have an "atomic" nature. It was Faraday who substituted *electrode* for pole and who referred to the released particles of matter as *ions*. In the 1830s Faraday's work gained broad recognition and was, therefore, available to men such as Matteucci and Du Bois-Reymond who were searching for a theory to account for *electro*physiological events. The key to this theory would come from physics—from the theoretical and experimental efforts of Faraday and others— and would be fashioned out of the single fact that electricity is no more than the movement of *charged* particles governed by laws not too different from those governing the ordinary varieties of diffusion. Thus, where there is a relative abundance of such particles, there will be movement toward the region

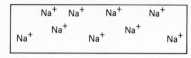

Initial State   Final State

Figure 3–18 Nine sodium ions initially deposited at one end of a cylinder are shown to distribute themselves homogeneously throughout the volume. The ions will move in such a manner as to establish an equilibrium of concentrations within the medium by the process of diffusion.

where there are relatively few. Moreover, the *potential* for this sort of movement is determined by the difference in charge between two poles. Anything done to maintain this difference leads to a state of *polarization*. Anything done to decrease this difference leads to *depolarization*. And anything done to increase the difference leads to *hyperpolarization*.

Most of the objects we have experience with on a day-to-day basis are not electrically charged. The elements combine to form compounds and thereby become electrically neutral. A single unit of hydrogen exists as an *ion* (a charged particle) in the free (unbonded) state, but hydrogen gas as it is actually found is made up of molecules (H_2), not of free ions (H^+). Similarly, oxygen *gas* has a molecular structure because each free atom of oxygen (O^{2-}) combines with another such atom to form O_2. The compound water is formed because electrical neutrality can be achieved when two free ions of hydrogen ($2H^+$) are available to a single free ion of oxygen, (O^{2-}), thus forming H_2O.

It is because of the presence of free (ionic) forms of atoms that the cells of the living body have electrical properties. And it is the membranes surrounding these cells that prevent the ions *ionic equilibrium* from establishing a perfect equilibrium of concentrations. Without a membrane to prevent diffusion, all the ions would soon establish a state of ionic equilibrium throughout any medium in which they were found. Figure 3–18 illustrates such equilibrium for sodium ions (Na^+) placed in water.

We can, however, place a barrier (in this case, a *semipermeable membrane*) in the center of the cylinder shown in Figure 3–18, thereby preventing the diffusion of sodium ions. The idealized final state of the medium would then look like that shown in Figure 3–19. As we shall see, in the actual case, Na^+ is pumped *sodium pump* across the membrane by a *sodium pump* mechanism. The membrane must allow the sodium to pass out, but must resist its return to the axoplasm. Were we to measure the *potential* across the barrier, we would find that an actual voltage had built up as a result of the ionic concentration differences across the barrier.

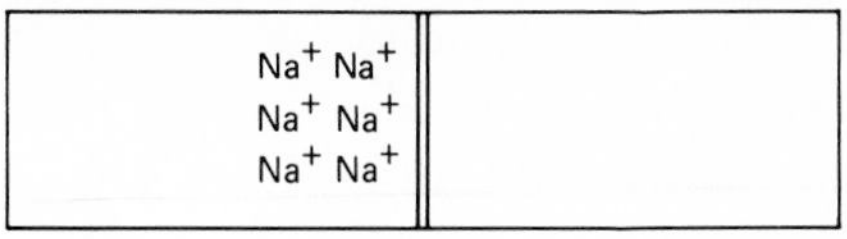

Na⁺ Na⁺	
Na⁺ Na⁺	
Na⁺ Na⁺	

Figure 3–19 With a barrier in place, the sodium ions remain close to the barrier and create a region of "charge" with a high *potential* for movement across the barrier. Note that the barrier must do work in opposing the diffusion of the ions.

membrane chemistry

When we turn to the axon of an actual neuron, we discover a state of affairs similar to but vastly more complicated than the one sketched in Figure 3–19. The membrane covering the *axoplasm* is only a few molecules thick but it is able to give shape to the mass of cytoplasmic substances comprising the axon. By and large, the medium surrounding the axon is chemically the same as the cytoplasm itself, except for the very surface of the axonal membrane. At this surface we discover significantly more sodium ions on the outer surface than are found along the inner surface; and significantly more potassium ions (K^+) on the inner than on the outer surface. There are also relatively more free chloride ions (Cl^-) and protein molecules ($Mol.^{2-}$) bearing a negative charge within the membrane than on its outer surface. A rough sketch of the arrangement is offered in Figure 3–20.

Without a membrane, the sodium ions would rush into the cytoplasmic space, the potassium would tend to move out, as would the chlorine ions and protein molecules. Indeed, it is in part because of these very differences in concentration that the ions migrate toward the membrane surfaces. But added to this process is the more active one of a *sodium pump* by which the axon is able to eliminate some sodium from the axoplasm along the membrane's inner surface. Sodium ions are pumped out through the membrane and, in the axon's resting state, these ions cannot return through the membrane at as fast a rate as the rate at which they are extruded. Furthermore, the presence of negatively charged ions works to retain potassium within the axon as does the presence of a repulsive force (Na^+) just on the other side.

It is now possible, with the use of microelectrodes and low-noise amplifiers, to measure the potential difference across the

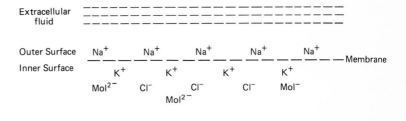

Figure 3–20 Rough sketch of the ionic distributions across the axonal membrane.

axonal membrane by placing one probe outside and another probe inside the axon. When this is done, we discover that the inside of the membrane is approximately 70 thousandths of a volt (70 millivolts) *negative* with respect to the outside. Thus we say that the *resting membrane potential* is minus 70 millivolts, and that it is in a *polarized* state. If additional positive ions are added to the membrane's surface, the resting potential becomes even greater and the membrane is said to be *hyperpolarized.* If, however, negatively charged ions are added to the outer surface the membrane becomes progressively *depolarized.*

Careful chemical analyses have uncovered the actual concentrations of the various ions found within and on the surface of mammallian axons. As it happens, the concentration difference that actually predicts the resting membrane potential is that of the potassium ion. If we take only this concentration difference, and treat the axon as if it were a simple battery, we would predict a minus 70 millivolt value across the membrane. This value is an expression (electrically) of the physical *work* done by the membrane in maintaining the concentration differences of the ions on each side of it. Because of this, the term resting membrane potential is something of a misnomer. The membrane is certainly not resting, but rather *working* to oppose the movement of ions down their concentration gradients—that is, ions seeking to establish equilibria.

The Neural Impulse

The chief consequence of stimulating the neuron is to alter the *permeability* of the axonal membrane. The membrane that once resisted the passage of sodium and potassium ions across it now enters a state of relative permeability and permits the sudden flow of ions. Sodium begins to rush in and then potassium begins to move out. As the Na^+ ions enter the axon through the membrane, resulting value of −70 millivolts changes, becoming more and more positive. At the peak of the process, the inner surface of the membrane is actually *positive* with respect to the outside by a value of some 50 millivolts. A graphic depiction of these changes, showing both the ionic and the electrical changes, is given in Figure 3–21. Note that the flow of sodium into the membrane is quite rapid relative to the flow of potassium out of the membrane. Note, too, that it takes nearly 4 milliseconds for potassium to return to the resting concentration, whereas sodium returns to the initial level in about half the time. The waveform (A) in this figure designates the *action potential* which travels down the length of the axon as the neural impulse.

the action potential

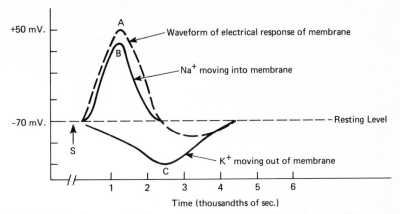

Figure 3–21 Course of ionic movements in and out of membrane and the resulting changes in the electrical potential across the membrane. Stimulus is applied at (S).

The action potential is the result of the movement of ions which, in the unstimulated state, the membrane tends to keep apart. If we think of the membrane as a very thin sheet separating two aqueous solutions, we can predict at least roughly the consequences of completely removing the sheet. In terms of the most relevant ions, the external solution contains only about 4 percent as much K^+ found in an equal volume of the internal solution whereas it contains ten times as much Na^+ as an equal volume of the internal solution. The *electrical* potential of 70 millivolts is just the amount of labor the membrane expends in maintaining this difference in concentrations.

With the advent of stimulation the membrane's permeability to both ions rapidly increases—first to Na^+ and then a little later to K^+—and so both ions begin to run down their concentration gradients toward an equilibrium state. Research has made it possible to measure the membrane's *conductance* for various ions and Figure 3–22 indicates the time course of the conductances for K^+ and for Na^+.

It has also become clear that the two ions move through different "gates" in the axonal membrane. Toxic agents applied to the outer surface of the membrane will prevent the movement of Na^+ inward, but will not prevent the migration of K^+ to the outside. Similarly, toxins infused into the axoplasm will prevent the outward movement of K^+ but will not significantly influence the inward movement of Na^+.

Concentration differences on each side of the membrane surface are the chemical source of neuroelectric events along the axon. The resting membrane potential, as has been noted, is

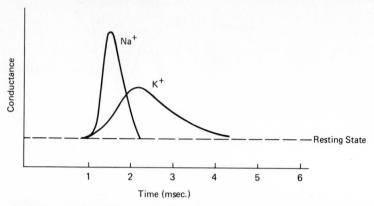

Figure 3–22 Conductance for Na^+ and K^+ ions during the initiation of the neural impulse. Note that the sodium conductance is greater and occurs more rapidly. The rise in K conductance coincides with the decline of the magnitude of the impulse back toward the resting level.

the voltage clamp

chiefly the result of potassium differences, whereas the amplitude of the action potential is best predicted by the concentration differences for sodium. And, finally, the return of the membrane potential toward the resting value is best explained in terms of the migration of K^+ to the outside, its slow return to the inside, and the reactivation of the "pump" that actively extrudes Na^+ from the inside surface of the membrane. Much of this was learned through the extraordinary studies of Hodgkin, Huxley, and Katz who used radioactive tracers and a *voltage clamp technique* to examine the movement of various ions across axonal membranes. The *giant axon* of the squid is ideal for these purposes because of its size and its ability to survive in a saline solution once it has been removed from the animal.

The *voltage clamp technique* requires that the axon be incorporated into an electrical circuit such that the voltage drop across the membrane can be set by the experimenter. That is, the membrane voltage can be clamped while the movement of ions is electrically tracked. Such a feedback circuit informs the experimenter of how much voltage must be applied to the axon in order to keep the voltage fixed during the migration of ions back and forth across the membrane. It thus establishes the electrical analog of the chemical events. What we discover from such research is the *explosive* and self-generating nature of the neural impulse. The application of any stimulus that momentarily alters the permeability of the axonal membrane results in what is initially a purely local flow of Na^+ and K^+ in opposite directions. However, once these changes alter the resting potential by about 20 millivolts, the entire equilibrium is disrupted in the immediately adjacent region of the membrane and thus the depolarization spreads. Actually, the spread is in *both* directions—down the axon (*dromic*) and up the axon (*antidromic*), the latter being in the "wrong" direction. How this is all corrected will be discussed shortly.

all-or-none law

What is important to recognize here, however, is that the collapse of the membrane leads to ionic movements whose physical (electrical) properties are determined by the preexisting concentration differences. Thus, once the process is initiated, the resulting amount of potential change is completely determined. It is on this basis that neural conduction of impulses is said to conform to the *all-or-none law*. With only partial depolarization there is the spread of an effect which is insufficient to trigger the changes in permeability at adjacent locations. As a result the alterations are entirely local and no traveling impulse arises. Only when a critical amount of Na^+ has entered the axon is the threshold reached. With the partial collapse of the membrane, even more Na^+ can enter and once the 20–25 millivolt change has occurred the resulting potential moves with constant amplitude and velocity along the entire axonal extent.

As can be seen in the preceding figures, the events culminating in a neural impulse take time. Gates must be opened and closed, and pumps must be started and stopped. In these respects different axons have somewhat different properties. In the limiting case, however, the interval from the initiation of ionic movement to the restoration of the resting level is at least 1 millisecond and is usually on the order of several milliseconds. Once K^+ ions have begun to return to the axoplasm and sodium is again being pumped out, the axon cannot initiate a new action potential no matter how intensely it is stimulated. The interval covering this period of nonstimulability is called the

absolute and relative refractory periods

absolute refractory period, generally on the order of a millisecond to several milliseconds long. Just beyond this interval an action potential can only be initiated by stimulation stronger than is necessary when the axon is in the resting state. This is the *relative refractory period*.

saltatory conduction

Axons vary in a number of characteristics. They may be long or short, thick or thin, myelinated or unmyelinated. The velocity with which an impulse moves down the length of an axon is proportional to the thickness of the axon; the thicker the axon the faster the velocity of propagation. Myelinated fibers display greater conduction velocities than is found in unmyelinated fibers for, in the former, the impulses skip from node to node. Such conduction is called *saltatory* (from the Latin *saltare*, to skip). In the unmyelinated axon the spread of activity is like that of a flame moving along a wick. In myelinated axons it is like a ball bouncing, where the bounces are all equal in height and in

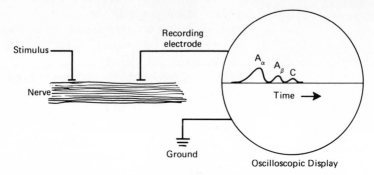

Figure 3–23 Recordings from two groups of A fibers (A_α and A_β) and one group of C fibers illustrating the different conduction velocities of the fibers in the nerve. Since the action potentials in all the fibers are of the same amplitude (+50mV), the amplitudes of the different components shown here reflect the relative abundance of the three types of fibers.

distance—the distance between adjacent *nodes of Ranvier*. In the thicker axons, these nodes occur at about 1 millimeter intervals and the velocity of conduction is about 80–100 meters per second. In the thinnest unmyelinated axons, the velocity may be only a fraction of a meter per second. It is customary to refer to the largest myelinated axons as *A* fibers, to the less thick myelinated autonomic axons as *B* fibers, and to the thinnest and unmyelinated axons as *C* fibers.

Nerves and tracts are composed of such axonal fibers. When an entire nerve is stimulated it is possible to record a *compound potential* of the different contributions made by the different classes of fibers of which the nerve is comprised. If the nerve contains two classes of *A* fibers and a few *C* fibers, a record like the one illustrated in Figure 3–23 is obtained. There are three distinct electrical events shown. The earliest is provided by the rapidly conducting *A* fibers and the latest by the slowly conducting *C* fibers.

Synaptic Transmission

Although it is true that the spread of electricity in the axon is multidirectional—in that a stimulus applied at indifferent points along the axon will produce recordable electrical changes both dromically and antidromically—the actual flow of information in the intact nervous system is primarily from dendrites and cell bodies *to* axons, and from the axon of one neuron to the dendrites and cell bodies of adjacent neurons. What guarantees this is the unique nature of the synaptic physiology and biochemistry.

We should note here the different types of synapses. Some

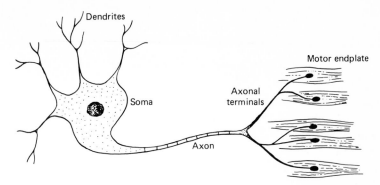

Figure 3–24 Schematic illustration of a motor neuron with its axonal terminals converging on motor endplates.

synapses, found chiefly among invertebrates, conduct by means of electricity. Others, which are common in the vertebrate nervous system, conduct by chemical means. We will focus on the latter type, using the neuromuscular junction illustratively.

Figure 3–24 illustrates schematically the terminal branches of an axon separated from the receiving terminals of a muscle fiber. Here we have the typical *neuromuscular* junction where each muscle fiber receives controlling signals from a single axonal terminal. The region of the muscle fiber on which the axon terminals converge is called the motor *endplate* and electrical activity here is referred to a *endplate potentials* (EPP). A typical motoneuron will have more than one hundred such axonal terminals, each one functionally connected to a specific muscle fiber. If the axon itself is stimulated, muscle contractions will occur as a result of the activation of all the fibers driven by the axonal terminals of the stimulated axon.

Through electronmicroscopy it has become possible to examine the fine structure of the axonal terminals and the receiving areas of the motor endplates. What has been discovered is that a narrow (synaptic) gap separates these structures into the *presynaptic* axonal terminals and the *postsynaptic* endplates. On the presynaptic side, there is a membrane to which is attached a number of vesicles containing chemical transmitter substances. The arrangement is sketched in Figure *chemical transmitters* 3–25. The primary consequence of the electrical impulse carried by the axon is to trigger the secretion of chemical *transmitter substances* contained in the presynaptic vesicles. At the neuromuscular junction the transmitter is known to be *acetylcholine* (ACh) whose arrival at the motor endplate results in the formation of electrical endplate potentials (EPP). Toxic agents that prevent the formation of ACh will result in the failure of axonal activity to induce contractions in muscle fibers.

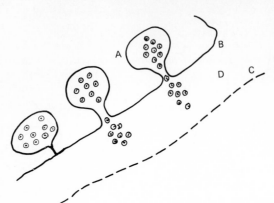

Figure 3–25 (A) is the pre-synaptic vesicle found at the tip of the axonal terminal and imbedded in presynaptic membrane (B). At the time of activation this vesicle fuses with the membrane and its contents are secreted into the neuromuscular synaptic space (D) and migrate across toward the postsynaptic membrane (C) of the motor endplate.

A variety of other transmitters can be found in the nervous system including dopamine, glycine, gamma-aminobutyric acid (GABA), epinephrine, and norepinephrine.

On the postsynaptic side it is clear now that only particular locations or channels are available to the secreted substances. The application of microscopic quantities of ACh to various regions of a muscle fiber is ineffective unless it is very close to those endplates that appear to have specific ACh "receptors." But the postsynaptic membrane also contains a substance of its own—acetylcholine *esterase* (AChE)—which has the effect of neutralizing the ACh secreted by the presynaptic terminals. In this way the postsynaptic events can block further activation by the presynaptically released ACh.

A somewhat simplified way of thinking of the presynaptic and postsynaptic events is to take them as doorways facing each other in a long corridor. On one side we can number the doors 1A, 2A, 3A, and so on, and on the postsynaptic side of the corridor we can number them 1B, 2B, 3B, and so on. The doors on the B side can be opened either electrically (by depolarization) or chemically by the material coming from the facing doors on the A side. Once the doors on the B side have been opened for a time, pumps on the B side begin to inject barriers into the corridor such that material from the A doors ceases to affect the B side of the corridor. In the actual physiology of neuromuscular junction, different materials are required on both sides. The presynaptic vesicles, for example, require calcium ions (Ca^{2+}) if the vesicles are to release ACh. The calcium needed for this is released through depolarization. We see therefore that the spread of the impulse into the presynaptic terminals causes a wave of depolarization resulting in the release of Ca^{2+} which then causes the release of ACh from the vesicle. On the postsynaptic side this ACh opens still other doors or gates which then permit the passage of Na^+ and K^+ ions

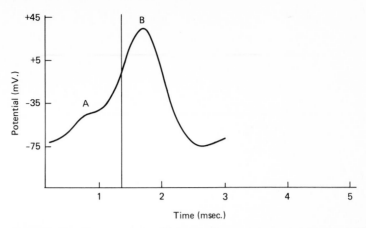

Figure 3–26 The component (A) shows the graded endplate potential (EPP) building to a value of approximately -4 mV, whereupon an action potential (B) is recorded in the muscle fiber. There is no sign of (B) when (A) fails to reach a threshold value. The vertical line separates the events into a period during which there is no evidence of muscular contraction from the first signs of contraction.

toward their equilibrium concentrations. The EPP is the electrical consequence of this ionic movement and the effective stimulus for contraction by the muscle fibers. Once the EPP reaches a critical or threshold value, a muscle action potential is initiated.

graded potentials

The EPP itself is not an *all-or-none,* nondiminishing potential. Rather, it is one version of what is called a *graded potential,* one that expresses the degree of depolarization that has taken place in the stimulated unit. It is only when this graded potential has reached a certain level that an all-or-none action potential is triggered. That there are two such components can be seen in Figure 3–26 which illustrates the EPP resulting from depolarization caused by a transmitter and the impulse that results once the EPP goes from the resting level of minus 70 millivolts to the depolarized level of minus 50 millivolts. A poison such as curare will eliminate the EPP component, showing that the overall waveform is made up of two different processes.

Synaptic Excitation and Inhibition

Not every postsynaptic event results in excitation. If we take a simple reflex for illustrative purposes—say the knee-jerk (or patellar) reflex—we discover that some muscles must contract and others must become extended if the reflex is to occur. It is clear, therefore, that even relatively simple movements require the combined action of *excitatory* and *inhibitory* mechanisms.

Excitation typically involves the depolarization of membranes and the initiation of action potentials. Inhibition is any process that opposes this, the most obvious being that which generally leads to states of *hyperpolarization* or that which actively blocks the action of excitatory influences.

In a monosynaptic path, such as the one involved in the knee jerk, sensory receptors in the tendons of the knee are stimulated by the application of a blow to the tendon. The fibers thus activated carry impulses to the spinal cord, entering on the dorsal surface and making synaptic connection with the spinal motoneuron whose impulses will lead to the knee jerk. For this to occur it is necessary for the sensory fibers, through their axonal terminals, to initiate impulses in the motor neurons. This, as we have seen, is accomplished by synaptic transmitters that depolarize the postsynaptic neurons. Here we have an instance of what is called an *excitatory postsynaptic potential* (EPSP) caused by depolarization and in this case leading to the contraction of the extensor muscles of the thigh. However, at the same time as these events take place, we will discover that other sensory neurons sending fibers to the spinal cord are making

EPSP

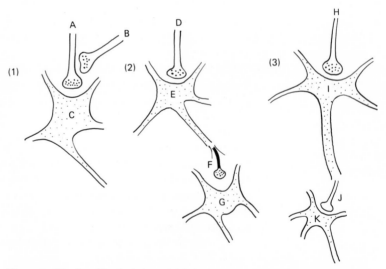

Figure 3–27 Graphic depiction of (1) the inhibition of synaptic inhibitors, (2) the excitation of inhibitors, and (3) the inhibition of exciters. In (1) is illustrated the mechanism of *presynaptic* inhibition where the inhibiting axonal terminal (B) has the effect of preventing (A) from releasing a postsynaptic inhibitor. Thus there is *inhibition of inhibition* or a form of disinhibition. In (2) the axonal terminal (D) results in the EPSP in E whose own axonal terminal (F) results in an IPSP in (G). Thus we have the *excitation of an inhibitor*. And in (3) the axonal terminal (H) results in an IPSP in (I) whose axonal terminal (J) normally produces an EPSP in K. The overall effect here is the *inhibition of excitation*.

IPSP

synaptic connections with motor cells whose fibers normally cause contraction of the flexor muscles that pull the leg toward the body. For full extension to take place, the flexors must be inhibited, which they are. This is achieved by *hyperpolarizing* the postsynaptic (motor) neuron and it is an example of an *inhibitory postsynaptic potential* (IPSP). The inhibitory transmitters in the central nervous system include two different amino acids, glycine and gamma-aminobutyric acid (GABA). They achieve their effects essentially by closing the "gates" that must be opened if excitation is to occur. That is, just as in the case of excitation, inhibition is also an ionic process.

All inhibition is not confined to the postsynaptic membrane, however. The complexities of the microscopic anatomy of the central nervous system permit any number of possibilities. A few of these are illustrated in Figure 3–27 in which we view the inhibition of inhibitors, the excitation of inhibitors and the inhibition of exciters.

*cholinergic and anti-
cholinergic mechanisms*

The achievement of these effects is apparently the task of specific neurochemical agents, the number and exact nature of which modern science has only begun to determine. We have already noted the action of acetylcholine whose chemical structure is given in Figure 3–28(A). Synapses activated by this substance are called *cholinergic* and substances that inhibit the formation of ACh (such as AChE) are called *anticholinergic*. There are other synapses which are activated by *epinephrine* (adrenaline) and *norepinephrine* (noradrenaline) whose actions are called *adrenergic*. These cholinergic and adrenergic transmitters are active in the autonomic nervous system and their chemical structures are given in Figure 3–28(B),(C). In the eye, for example, cholinergic synapses cause constriction of the pupil whereas adrenergic synapses cause dilation. Within the gastrointestinal tract the cholinergic influence is one of causing peristalsis which is inhibited by adrenergic synapses. Similarly, the cholinergics increase heart rate while the adrenergics decrease it. It is known that norepinephrine is synthesized by cells in the brain stem's reticular formation and that the fibers from these cells run downward to the spinal cord, outward to the cerebellum, and forward into the forebrain. Dopamine [Figure 3–28(D)] and serotonin [Figure 3–28(E)] are also synthesized by cells in the brain. Dopamine synthesizing cells occur in the hypothalamus and in certain structures of the limbic system and serotonin is known to be synthesized by cells in the brain stem. These agents like other transmitters regulate the "gates" controlling the entry and the exiting of ions. No doubt other transmitter substances are to be found but these too will have their effects at the ionic level of neural physiology. The

(A) Acetylcholine

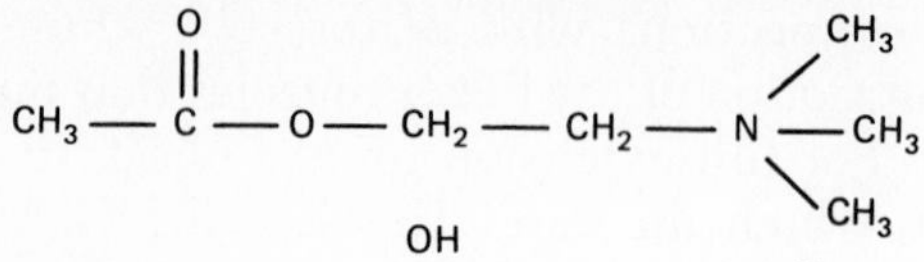

(B) Epinephrine

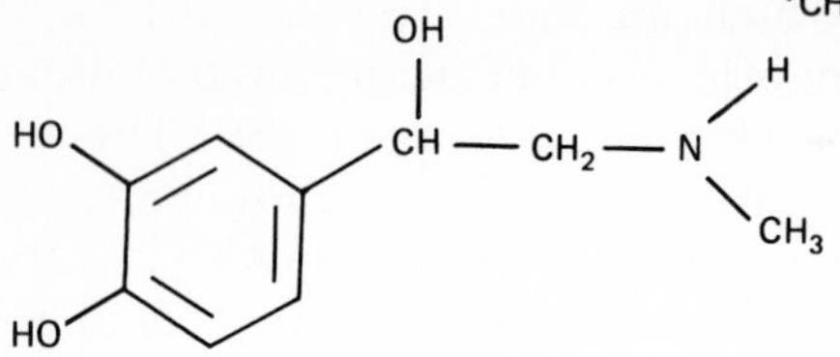

(C) Norepinephrine

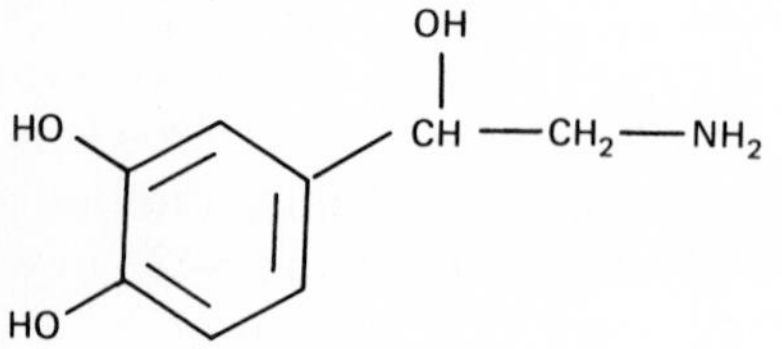

(D) Dopamine

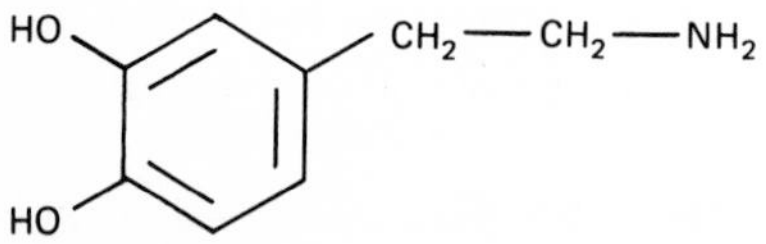

(E) Serotonin

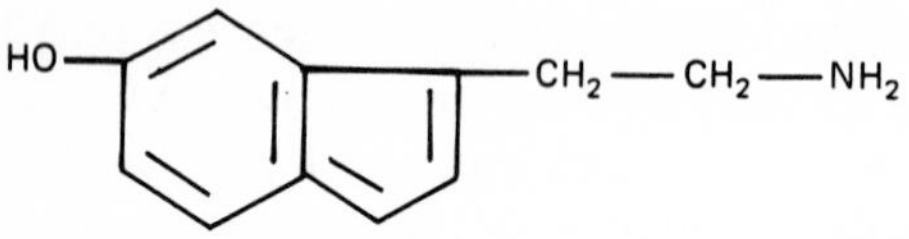

Figure 3–28 Synaptic transmitters including cholinergic (A) and andrenergic (B,C) types. Norepinephrine and dopamine are sometimes called *monoamines* because of the presence of a single amine (NH_2) group. Serotonin is an indoleamine since it is built on the indole structure (a benzene radical to which a cyclopentene has been affixed). The basic benzene ring with bonded oxygen is called the catechol structure and thus (B), (C), and (D) are also referred to as catecholamines.

specific psychological correlates of the substances briefly described here will be noted in later chapters. These, as we shall see, run the gamut from relatively simple sensory effects to profound changes in the emotional and motivational life of the organism.

In light of these properties and in light of the fact that neurons in the brain are generally encrusted with synaptic terminals, the possible excitatory and inhibitory combinations are, for all practical purposes, infinite.

Here, then, is the "hardware" of the nervous system and the main principles governing the initiation and the transmission of signals. How this all relates to psychological processes will be taken up in the following chapters. Before turning to this, it may be useful to summarize the highlights of this chapter.

Summary

1. The nervous system is characterized by relatively independent lines of communication from the periphery of the body to the central nervous system and from the central nervous system to the periphery, but by highly interconnected and interdependent lines within the central nervous system.
2. The anatomical organization of the spinal cord is one of functionally overlapping segments with each segment controlling the musculature of and receiving the signals from the same location. The sensations arising from the body surface and the movements of the trunk and limbs are processed by the thirty-one pairs of spinal nerves whose contact with the brain is made possible by vertically ascending and descending pathways.
3. Sensory and motor functions of the head—including sight, smell, hearing, and taste—are accomplished by twelve pairs of cranial nerves, some of which are exclusively sensory, some of which are exclusively motor, and some of which are mixed.
4. Organization within the brain is dominated by feedback connections within and among the three main divisions of the brain: forebrain, midbrain, and hindbrain. Gross effects of an activating or depressing nature are made possible by the elaborate connections between the reticular formation, which runs through the core of brain stem and midbrain, and more specific regions associated with sensation and movement.
5. The cerebral hemispheres, which dominate the central neuroanatomy of the most advanced species, display a vertical organization ideally suited to communication between the depths and the surface and the cerebral cortex. The multibillions of cerebral cells appear to be functionally organized into several million "modules" or columns in which exquisite patterns of excitation and inhibition result.
6. Communication within the nervous system is electrical and is made possible by mechanisms of synaptic transmission. Owing to different kinds of transmitters, communication has both excitatory and inhibitory consequences. The rule rather than the exception in the brain is that each neuron is influenced functionally by hundreds to thousands of neighboring neurons which have both inhibitory and excitatory effects. The output of any one neuron thus expresses the average effect produced by influential neighbors.

7. The characteristically impulsive nature of neural transmission is the result of *graded* changes occurring within the neural anatomy. These are of an ionic nature leading to a degree of depolarization that culminates in the *all-or-none* response of the axon as a whole.

8. The ionic and electrical properties of neural units are ultimately controlled by specific synaptic "gates" and receptor sites which are uniquely accessible to excitatory and inhibitory molecular substances (for example, ACh, AChE, glysine, and GABA). Thus, the functions of the nervous system are to be understood as the joint consequence of anatomical connections and specific biochemical processes.

Suggested Readings

Gross Neuroanatomy
1. M. L. Barr, *The Human Nervous System*, Harper & Row, New York, 1974.
2. M. Roberts and J. Hanaway, *Atlas of the Human Brain in Section*, Lea, and Febiger, Philadelphia, 1970.

Neuronal Anatomy and Physiology
1. H. Hyden (ed.), *The Neuron*, Elsevier, Amsterdam, 1967.
2. H. Kuhlenbeck, *The Central Nervous System of Vertebrates*, Vol, 3, Part I, *Structural Elements: Biology of Nervous Tissue*, Academic Press, New York, 1970.
3. E.R. Kandel, *Cellular Basis of Behavior*, Freeman, San Francisco, 1976.
4. J. Szentágothai and M.A. Arbib, *Conceptual Models of Neural Organization*, MIT Press, Cambridge, 1975.
5. K.R. Porter, and M.A. Bonneville, *Fine Structure of Cells & Tissues*, Lea & Febiger, Philadelphia, 1968.
6. R.F. Schmidt, *Fundamentals of Neurophysiology*, Springer-Verlag, New York, 1975.

The Synapse and Reflex Mechanisms
1. J. Eccles, *The Physiology of Synapses*, Springer-Verlag, Berlin, 1964.
2. G. Shepherd, *The Synaptic Organization of the Brain*, Oxford University Press, New York, 1974.
3. J. Axelrod, Neurotransmitters, *Scientific American*, 1974, 230:58–71.

The Neural Impulse
1. A. Hodgkin, *The Conduction of the Nervous Impulse*, Charles C. Thomas, Springfield, IL, 1967.
2. B. Katz, *Nerve, Muscle, and Synapse.* McGraw Hill, New York, 1966.
3. W.R. Utall, *Cellular Neurophysiology and Integration: An Interpretive Introduction.* Erlbaum, Hillsdale, N.J., 1975

Autonomic and Endocrine Functions

1. O. Appenzeller, *The Autonomic Nervous System*, Elsevier, Amsterdam, 1970.
2. C. Turner and J. Bagnara, *General Endocrinology*, Saunders, Philadelphia, 1971.

4

Sensory, Perceptual, and Elementary Cognitive Processes

Introduction

In the past two chapters we have considered a substantial amount of technical detail concerning the neuroanatomy and physiology of the nervous system and the techniques used to study these topics. In this chapter we begin our discussion of the psychobiological issues for which these materials have been preparatory. To appreciate the meaning of what we discuss here, the reader should recall from Chapter 1 that psychobiology is not the same science as neurophysiology or neuroanatomy; it has its own special problems and goals, and while it depends heavily on these other fields of neuroscience, it is not identical to them. Psychobiology's separate and distinctive goal is to identify the relationships between the properties of the nervous system and psychological functions. This chapter is the first in this book to emphasize this unique role.

Sensory processes have proven to be the easiest psychological functions to analyze from a psychobiological perspective. The two major reasons for the extraordinary amount of progress in this area are:

1. Sensory processes are anchored to a specific and concrete reference system, the characteristics of the physical stimulus.
2. The afferent pathways (those going toward the central nervous system) that play such an important role in sensation are conceptually simpler than the neural mechanisms underlying other more central and more complicated psychological functions: Information flows mainly in one direction.

Research on sensory systems thus enjoys an advantage that other areas of psychobiological research do not—there exists an

133

independent reference or anchor against which all results, both psychological and neurophysiological can be compared. That anchor, of course, is the physical stimulus. Every sensory experiment is initiated by some kind of a manipulation of physical events. There is an elaborate background of precise measurement and standardization established in the physical sciences that can be used to precisely quantify this independent variable—the stimulus—in any sensory experiment. We can be precise (to a degree that usually exceeds the needs of sensory scientists) concerning the nature of a visual, somatosensory, or auditory stimulus against which the behavioral response is compared. It is far more difficult to be precise about the antecedent conditions triggering such a cognitive process as creativity. How, indeed, could we precisely specify the exact stimulus conditions that lead to the mental responses that, in turn, lead to the solution of a mathematical problem. On the other hand, visual responses are anchored to the outputs of physical machines of which *all* relevant dimensions are known. Even though we can be absolutely precise about the dominant wavelength, the purity, and the luminance of a stimulus presented to the eye, it is not always possible to be sure that one has identified the salient dimensions of the stimulus in a cognitive task.

The second advantage enjoyed by sensory psychobiologists is that in most cases the peripheral mechanisms underlying sensory processes are relatively simple. The neurophysiological mechanisms are easy to conceptualize since they usually consist of regular, repetitive networks. Furthermore, the relationship between the stimulus and response is logically straightforward. One reason for this conceptual and logical simplicity is that sensory processes are influenced mainly by a flow of information in a single direction. Indeed, sensory processes initially are defined as the intake of information along the afferent or ascending pathways of the nervous system. This unidirectionality organizes and simplifies thinking about sensory processes in a way that could never be matched for those complex central mechanisms involved in intelligence, problem solving, or even other such high-level processes as retrieval from memory. Although there are now known to be some centrifugal (that is, from the central nervous system out to the sensory receptors) influences on sensation, for the most part the flow of information is from the outside to the inside.

Finally, the kinds of neural interactions that occur in the sensory pathways, while not always trivial, are also conceptually simpler than those that occur more centrally. Peripheral sensory processes, at least, seem to be executed by neural mechanisms that are more or less spatially similar or congruent to the stimulus. Central cognitive mechanisms are almost certainly executed by what we call symbolic mechanisms that are probably spatially unrelated to the stimulus.

This leads us to one of the vexing conceptual problems that faces sensory psychobiology today. "What is the significance of the many important discoveries that are currently being made in neurophysiological laboratories?" This is not a trivial or frivolous question, and the answer to it is not obvious. It is important for the reader to appreciate that what we know about the neurophysiology of the sensory pathways has more to do with how information is encoded and communicated along those pathways than how that encoded information becomes the stuff of conscious experience. Of the latter relationship—the transmutation of brain activity to experience—we have virtually no understanding. What we are learning to appreciate is the nature of the constraints placed on the flow of afferent information by the anatomy and physiology of the peripheral pathways. We know, too, that these constraints leave traces that can be detected by psychological experiments. But, the reader is cautioned against accepting the notion of a "line detector," for example, in the retina, thalamus, or even in the visual cortex of a mammal as *the* physiological explanation of how we see linear patterns. Neurophysiological findings tell us something important but not what sensation or perception *is*.

Now that the idea of sensory processes has been introduced in general, we next consider another important idea. In many textbooks it is common for the various sensory modalities to be presented separately, with an ensemble of facts associated with each of them. For example, chapters titled "Vision" or "Hearing" (and all too often, "The Other (or lower) Senses") usually independently discuss the various physical, physiological, and psychological facts known about each of these modalities. We are now approaching a stage in the study of sensory processes at which it is possible to consider what are the general principles common to all of the senses and to develop a coherent organizational theme. We have organized this chapter in an unusual way in order to emphasize factual and conceptual similarities among the senses rather than the distinctions among them. In the following sections we will consider these general aspects in turn:

- The stimulus
- Pretransductive modification of stimulus
- Receptor anatomy
- Transduction
- Sensory coding
- Pain

The Stimulus

receptor selectivity

the adequate stimulus

The basic function served by the sense organs is the conversion of patterns of physical energy in the external environment into patterns of electrochemical activities within neurons. To begin our discussion of this process of stimulation, we shall first consider the nature of these physical energies—called *stimuli* when studied in the sensory context. Perhaps the main point to be made in this section is that sensory receptors are extremely selective in terms of the energies to which each can respond. Each receptor also is sensitive to only a relatively small range of all the possible stimuli to which it could conceivably respond. The eye, for example, is not a general purpose detector of electromagnetic energy, but it is highly sensitive to only the small window of the electromagnetic spectrum shown in Figure 4–1. This narrow range of wavelengths is the visual spectrum. Similarly, the human ear is selectively sensitive to only a relatively small portion of the full range of possible acoustic oscillations; only sounds between 20 and 20,000 Hz (cycles per second), depending on the listener's age, can be detected by the human ear. Within the olfactory and gustatory sensory systems, chemical sensitivities to only a relatively few chemical molecular types are exhibited. It is this extreme selectivity of the receptors that determines whether photons of light will activate the neurons of the optic nerve, that acoustical stimuli will activate the auditory nerve, and that vaporized chemicals will activate the olfactory nerve. This highly selective response of the various modalities has nothing at all to do with the nature of the neurons in those nerves; those neurons are all virtually identical. Rather, it is determined by the respective sensitivities of the sensory receptors.

This leads us to several important concepts concerning the nature of stimuli. First, there is for each sensory modality a best or *adequate stimulus* that can activate its sensory receptor with minimum physical energy. For the eye, the adequate stimulus is

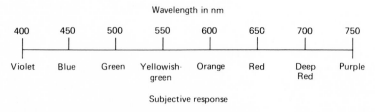

Figure 4–1 The visible spectrum. Wavelength is given in nanometers (nm) or billionths of a meter.

electromagnetic radiation with wavelengths varying approximately from 400 nm to about 760 nm. (Depending on whether one is considering rod or cone vision, the optimum wavelengths are about 510 nm and 555 nm, respectively.) For the ear, pneumatic pressure fluctuations of about 3000 Hz are heard at the lowest energy levels. Electromagnetic radiation could be focused on the acoustic receptor, but because the receptors are so insensitive to that kind of energy it is likely that the tissue would actually be cooked before any activity was elicited by light delivered to the acoustic nerve.

specific nerve energies

The idea of an adequate or best stimulus for each sensory modality is intimately related to a very important law of sensory processing. *The law of specific energies of nerves*, originally proposed by Johannes Müller (1801–1858), states that the response produced by activity in a nerve depends only on that nerve and not on the stimulus, whatever it was, that originally activated the nerve. This law is meaningful because the fact is that even though the adequate stimulus can most easily evoke a sensation in a particular modality, in some instances it is possible to produce a sensory experience with a nonadequate stimulus. For example, one can press on the eyeballs to initiate activity in the optic nerve. The fact that light is perceived (a *phosphene*) when one uses this mechanical stimulus is both indicative of the fact that nonadequate stimuli can, in some cases, produce activity and also that no matter how the activity is generated in the nerve, the perceived response is characteristic of that nerve and not of the nonadequate stimulus. It is totally independent of how the nerve was initially activated. In other words, all information about the nature of the original stimulus is lost. Thus one can stimulate the eye with light, electrical shock, chemical infusions, or even mechanical pressures, and yet one will always *see* something, never feel, smell, or hear as a result of optic nerve activation.

Müller's law of specific energies of nerves has been a part of our thinking for many years and is generally accepted as a valid law describing the activity of nerves made up of many neurons. However, new understanding has led us to modify its significance in the context of individual neurons. It is now appreciated that within a nerve or tract, the activity of a single neuron does not uniquely define a particular perceptual experience. All neurons are broadly tuned to a wide range of the adequate stimulus. Therefore, whether the activity of a particular neuron in the optic nerve is indicative of the effects of a long, medium, or short wavelength stimulus and will ultimately be perceptually decoded as a red or some other color depends on activity in neighboring neurons. In other words, the meaning of a neural response at the level of the individual neuron is not dependent solely on which neuron is firing, but is conditional on the activity of other neurons. Thus, Müller's law fails in the microcosm of individual neurons. The law of specific energies of nerves is not specific, but rather is dependent on other factors. We shall return to this topic later when we discuss sensory coding.

There are many special problems to consider in cutaneous or skin stimulation. We are not really sure exactly what the adequate stimuli are for the various skin senses. It is known with certainty that we respond to *pressure gradients* (a constant pressure uniformly distributed across the skin is not felt), to thermal stimuli, and to noxious or pain-producing stimuli. However, it is not yet known what the critical stimulus is in these cases. Is pain simply a response to too much of an otherwise inoffensive stimulus that would normally produce a sense of touch or warmth? Does thermal energy activate sensory receptors through the medium of induced mechanical changes perhaps associated with the expansion or contraction of blood vessels; or does temperature affect some specialized neurons directly? These are among the many questions involving cutaneous stimuli that have not yet been satisfactorily answered.

Questions like these represent the basis of the differences among some of the contending theories of cutaneous sensitivity. Some theories, for example, assert that there are special receptors for each of the cutaneous modalities—touch, warmth, cold, and pain. Specific receptor explanations of this kind are countered by what is known as *pattern theories*. Pattern theories assert that there really is only a single mechanically sensitive system in the skin, but the pattern of physical energies that impinges on the skin determines a pattern of neural activity that differentially encodes the various cutaneous experiences. No resolution of this controversy has yet been achieved.

To conclude these comments on the physical stimulus, we present Table 4–1. This table summarizes many different kinds

TABLE 4–1 The Nature of the Adequate Stimuli for the Various Senses

Sensory Modality	Adequate Stimulus
Mechanical	
Acoustic	Pneumatic force
Vestibular	Acceleration
Mechanical cutaneous	Mechanical force or gradient of force
Proprioceptive	Position and velocity
Photic	Electromagnetic waves (photons)
Chemical	Specific atoms, ions, or molecules
Electrical	Electricity
Thermal	Temperature or temperature change

of information concerning the adequate stimuli for the various senses—information that will not be spelled out in detail in the text of this chapter. Each of the adequate stimuli is then considered in terms of its sources (that is, the devices capable of generating that kind of physical energy), and the metrics that are used to measure its quality and quantity. Finally, we consider the *universal stimulus*, electricity, which by virtue of the electrochemical basis of neural functions is able to excite all sensory systems at relatively modest (though not as low as the adequate stimulus) energy levels.

Pretransductive Modifications of Stimulus Energy

Since we have considered the nature of physical stimuli, the next step is to realize that the tissues and organs containing sensory receptor cells are not perfect transmitters; they do not convey the information falling on them without distortion. There are dramatic and perceptually influential transformations of the physical stimulus energy that strongly affect sensation and perception before stimuli are converted from the physical energies of the external world to the electrochemical energies of the nervous system. Often these preneural transformations can be enormously influential in determining the final nature of the sensory experience. Indeed in some instances some psychological phenomena reflect the exclusive infuence of these preneural modulations of the physical stimulus. For example, the eye acts in several ways to modulate the amount of light that actually reaches the retinal photoreceptors. There is a substantial reduction in the amount of incident light as a function of the size of the pupil. Various materials and debris within the eye can interfere with the passage of some portion of the stimulus or even absorb certain selected wavelengths. There are also materials within the eye that selectively absorb light that is polarized at particular angles. The end result of all of these obstructions and absorptions is that we often see things that are not in the external stimulus environment. We see *Haidinger's brushes*—a colorful blue and yellow hourglass percept that occurs because of the selective absorption of polarized light by oriented molecules in the macula lutea (the ring of pigmented material that surrounds the fovea). We see shadows of debris lying on the cornea or even behind the lens in the vitreous humor where these materials may block the pathway of some incident light rays. All such psychological phenomena can be directly attributed to preneural processing by the optical (as opposed to neural) processes in the eye.

pre-neural influences

*phasic and tonic
responses*

In the skin there are also *preneural* modifications that tend to modulate what we feel. One of the receptor structures in the skin, the Pacinian corpuscle, consists of a neuronal ending surrounded by a multilayered encapsulation. The actual transducer in this case is the neuronal ending; of that there is little current doubt. However, the capsule does modify the actual stimulus in a physiologically and psychologically significant way. Because of the elasticity of the capsule, it tends to allow only pressure transients (that is, changes in pressure) to impact on the neuronal ending. Continuously applied signals do not pass—only transients do—as shown in Figure 4–2. The result of this selective passage of only the transients (which is equal to differentiation in the mathematical sense) is that cutaneous neurons tend to fire only when stimuli begin and when they end. Typically, therefore, Pacinian corpuscles produce responses in the enclosed neurons that are *phasic* (occurring only at stimulus onset and offset) and not *tonic* (occurring as long as the stimulus is present). This is a profoundly important feature of the neural coding of these cutaneous receptors, and is probably an important factor in determining that we are not continuously aware of our clothing and all of the other stimuli that are constantly impinging upon our bodies. The sensitivity to transients, however, is not the result of a neural process, but rather of a modification of the stimulus by a nonneural appendage to the actual receptor structure.

In another context, that of the chemical senses, it is quite clear that the dissolution of chemical molecules in body fluids is an important preneural modification of adequate olfactory and

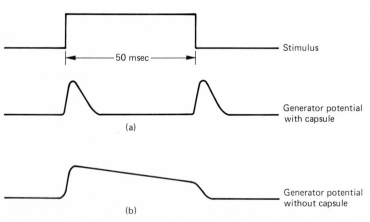

Figure 4–2 The effect of a cutaneous receptor capsule. Only the transient portion of an applied stimulus is passed. (Adapted from Loewenstein, W.R. and Mendelson, M. *J. Neurophysiol.*, 1965, *177*, 377–397).

gustatory stimuli. Unless molecules dissolve in some solution, they remain ineffective nonstimuli—only ions are effective as taste or smell stimuli. Preneural dissolution of these chemicals, therefore, is a key step in the process that leads to our ultimate awareness of the whole gamut of chemical stimuli that enrich our lives or protect us from harm.

By far the most dramatic preneural modification of stimuli, however, occurs in the ear. The cochlea of the inner ear, the true auditory receptor, is a fluid-filled tube whose hydromechanical properties are especially significant in the preneural modification of acoustic energy. The physical stimulus for hearing, of course, is the sequence of waves of rarefaction and compression that occur in the external environment surrounding the head. Generally this external environment is air but we also hear fairly well when immersed in water. Snorkelers and scuba divers are often entertained with a clatter of clicks and ticks, whistles and wheezes, and pips and pops when exploring an ocean habitat. Whatever the external medium filling the outer ear, the middle ear is normally filled with air from the throat through the Eustachian tubes, (see Figure 4–9), and the cochlea is normally filled with a mild saline solution. The action of the oscillations of pressure in the external medium on tympanic membranes is to produce a mechanical action in the three tiny bones, the *malleus, incus,* and *stapes,* of the middle ear, which in turn produces a plunger-like action on the oval window. The three bones, the *ossicles,* themselves exert one kind of preneural action; they tend to amplify the power of the acoustic energy with a lever-like action. However, the physics of the cochlea produces a much more potent preneural modification.

The plunger-like action of the oval window (a temporal variation) produces a series of traveling waves that move through the cochlea. Since the cochlea varies in size and its walls have varying elastic properties, and since the incoming wave from the oval window will encounter a reflected wave of activity from the far end of the cochlea, there is a tendency for the amplitude of each traveling wave to vary from one point to another in its course along the cochlea. Figure 4–3 shows how this may occur for a traveling wave of intermediate wavelengths. This figure shows the envelope of the wave—that is, a plot of the obtained amplitude of the travelling wave—at the various positions along the cochlea. The important thing is that this envelope has a maximum that occurs at a particular place on the cochlea. That is, there is one place on the cochlea at which the traveling wave is larger than at any other place.

spatial coding

This *point of maximum amplitude on the cochlea (a spatial measure) varies as a function of the frequency (a temporal measure) of the original acoustic stimulus.* This is shown in

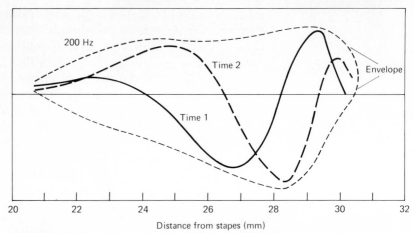

Figure 4–3 The variation in the amplitude of a travelling wave as it passes down the cochlea. (Redrawn from Bekesy, G., *Journal of the Acoustical Society of America*, 1949, 21:245–254.)

Figure 4–4. There is now a distinctive place (a spatial code) on the cochlea that responds maximally as a function of the frequency (a temporal code). In other words, the temporal representation of the frequency of the original stimulus has been converted or transformed by the hydromechanical properties of the cochlea into a spatial representation of that frequency.

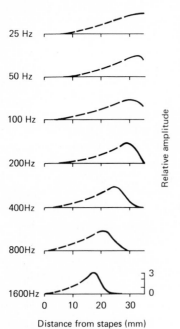

Figure 4–4 The variation in the point at which the travelling wave reaches its maximum amplitude as a function of the frequency of the applied auditory signal. (Redrawn from v. Bekesy, G., *Journal of the Acoustical Society of America*, 1949, 21:245–254.)

Some frequencies (the lower ones) produce the maximum traveling wave amplitude near the *heliocotrema,* the tiny hole at the end of the cochlea. Some frequencies (the higher ones) produce the maximum amplitude of the traveling wave near the oval window. Information once encoded along a time dimension is now encoded by variations along a spatial dimension—frequency has been converted into place, totally on the basis of a preneural hydromechanical process.

We now know that the auditory nervous system is exquisitely sensitive in its ability to distinguish among differences in spatial patterns of this kind. It is probably not the absolute value of the peak that is the key clue to acoustic frequency, but rather the amplitude at a given point along the cochlea *relative* to other amplitudes elsewhere that is critical. Indeed, it seems that the neural apparatus is better able to make this kind of spatial discrimination than it is to make temporal discriminations per se. We know this to be the case since the stimulus frequency can only be discriminated poorly if a repetitive train of electrical stimuli is applied to a single point on the cochlea. Obviously the preneural mechanics of the cochlea, like the preneural optics of the eye, can and do play a very important role in determining what our perceptual experiences will be.

In concluding this section we must also point out that there are other preneural modifications of stimuli that occur in the *external* environment as well as in the body that are also significant in determining our perceptual responses. Light can be reflected, refracted, and absorbed by a wide variety of enviromental mechanisms. Over the desert the light may be spuriously refracted by giant atmospheric "lenses" produced by the effects of temperature on the air's index of refraction. Natural and man-made colored filters such as those produced by dust, smog, and so on selectively remove various wavelengths of light from a visual stimulus. Rainbows are produced by the refraction of light by water droplets. Many of these preneural (indeed, preocular) alterations of the stimulus also produce fascinating perceptual phenomena. However, it is very important to keep in mind the essential fact that even though these external modifications of the stimuli do produce perceptual experiences they do not do so because of the nature of the nervous system. Desert mirages produce perceptual experiences that are distorted from reality, but these distortions can also be photographed. The mirage, therefore, is a more or less appropriate response of the visual system to the stimulus that actually falls on the retina. Perception in this case is *veridical*—correct—even though bizarre and in disagreement with independent measures of the objective reality of the visual scene—the distal stimulus. Mirages thus tell us nothing about the nervous system. *Illusions,* on the other hand, are discrepancies between the stimulus that actually falls on the retina—the *proximal* stimulus—and the perceptual experience. Illusions are caused by the transformations imposed by the sensory nervous system and tell us about the nature of that system.

The Anatomy of the Receptors

In the previous section it was necessary to refer to many aspects of the structure of the receptor organs. It is now time to begin a more complete excursion into the anatomy of the sensory mechanisms. Again, the reader is reminded that in this section we cluster together anatomical information on the basis of function rather than modality. We do this to emphasize the general similarities of the various receptors even though we may be forced to talk about the anatomy of any single receptor system in several different places.

In order to provide some coherence to what otherwise would be merely an ensemble of anatomical curiosities, let us first point out certain similarities in receptor anatomy.

1. Receptors can be categorized on the basis of the distance from which their stimuli come. For example, some receptors have specifically evolved to respond to events occurring at great distances. The eyes, for example, respond to lightwaves reflected from distant objects; the ears respond to sound transmitted from distant sources. Smell, of course, also acts similarly. Gustation, the vestibular senses, and the skin and joint senses, however, are sensitive to stimuli that are generated right at the receptor. All receptors of stimuli from distant sources are located on the head—an anatomical process called *encephalization.* Receptors sensitive to the immediate surroundings are found both on the head and on the rest of the body.
2. As noted earlier, all receptor mechanisms have some kind of nonneural apparatus that does tend to modify the stimulus prior to transduction. The external pinna of the ear, the optical machinery of the eye, the encapsulations of the cutaneous neurons, and the fluid media of the olfactory and gustatory organs are examples of preneural apparatus.
3. All receptors have some kind of an especially sensitive region, either a specialized neuron or a specialized portion of a neuron, capable of converting (transducing) the physical energy into electrochemical energies.
4. Receptor neurons tend to be of two different classes. One class includes a short neuron synapsing almost immediately with another neuron. Receptor neurons of this first class have

no axons of their own and cannot produce spike action potentials; these cells respond only with graded action potentials. Receptor neurons of the second class do possess long fibers and they can propagate spike action potentials over their own axons.

5. Regardless of the particular details of receptor anatomy, all function in much the same way to transduce the stimulus information—some portion of the membrane is induced to change its permeability to sodium and potassium ions by the stimulus. We shall discuss this process later.

With these general points of similarity in mind, we can now consider receptor anatomy in detail. In doing so we shall follow a sequence based on increasing magnification.

First, let us consider the visual receptor mechanism. Figure 4–5 is a diagram of the human eye. With the exception of its

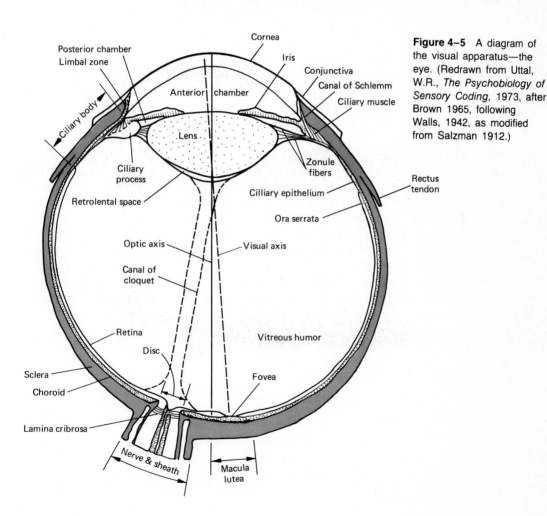

Figure 4–5 A diagram of the visual apparatus—the eye. (Redrawn from Uttal, W.R., *The Psychobiology of Sensory Coding*, 1973, after Brown 1965, following Walls, 1942, as modified from Salzman 1912.)

very thin layer of neurons which is called the *retina*, the eye functions as an optical instrument not a neural instrument. The eye has evolved to project a well-focused image of an external scene on the array of photosensitive receptors. In the front of the eye there is a transparent region, the *cornea*, responsible for most of the sixty diopters of optical power exhibited by the whole eye. (The number of *diopters* of power of a lens is the reciprocal of the focal length of that lens measured in meters.) In fact, it is the interface between the air and the cornea that accounts for most of the eye's optical power. This is the reason that we do not see as well underwater as in air. The index of refraction of water and the cornea are much closer than are those of air and the cornea. Since the difference in indices of refraction is the critical determinant of optical power, the optical power of the water/cornea interface is much less than that of an air/cornea interface.

Behind the transparent cornea, an anterior chamber is filled with the *aqueous humor*—a liquid of very modest viscosity. Separating the aqueous humor from the larger chamber of the orb of the eye itself is a circular ring of heavily pigmented muscles—*the iris*—capable of either being dilated (under sympathetic nervous control from the autonomic nervous system) or being constricted (under parasympathetic control). The iris acts as a gain controlling device and regulates the amount of light passing into the eye in much the same way as does the diaphragm behind a camera lens. And, to strengthen the analogy, an optical lens exists behind the iris of the eye. This lens, usually quite transparent, can sometimes be afflicted with opacities (*cataract*) that can reduce the quality of an image to the point of blindness. The transparent *vitreous humor* fills the larger cavity of the eye, but is of little optical significance.

The cross section of the eye presented in Figure 4–5 indicates the point of entry into the eye of the blood vessels necessary to provide the eye with nutrients and carry off metabolic waste products. This is also the exit point from the eye of the optic nerve conveying the visual information (transduced by the receptors) from the eye to the brain. The point at which the blood vessels enter and the optic nerve exits is devoid of visual receptors; thus, there is a *blind spot* or *lacuna* in the visual field in this region. One other anatomical singularity to which attention should be drawn is the small pit slightly temporal on the retina. This is the *fovea*, the region of greatest visual acuity.

The main function of the eye is to focus images on the retina, the thin sheet of neurons that lies along the inside of the eyeball. Figure 4–6 shows a magnified cross section of the retina. A surprising fact concerning this structure is that it is functionally inverted. That is, light passing into the eye must pass through

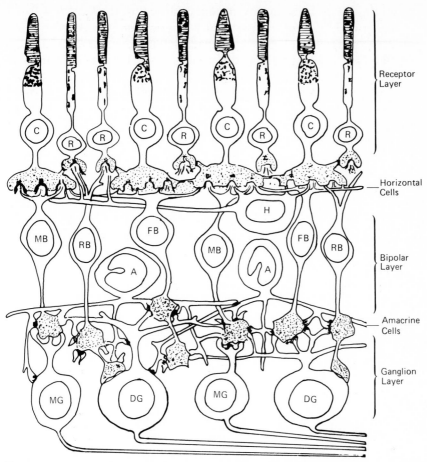

Figure 4–6 A magnified cross section of the human retina. (Redrawn from Dowling, J.E. and Boycott, B.B., *Proceedings of the Royal Society of London*, 1966, Ser. B, 166:80–111.)

third-order (*ganglion cells*) and second-order (*bipolar cells*) neurons, as well as the long fibers of the optic nerve, before it reaches the receptors. The photosensitive cells actually point away from the pupillary opening. Fortunately, all of this neural tissue is relatively transparent. As much as 90 percent of the light that enters the eye, however, may be lost before being absorbed by the receptors.

Figure 4–6 also shows that the retina is made up of three layers of neurons. The first is the receptor of which there are four different kinds in the human eye—one kind of rod and three kinds of cones. The factor distinguishing these four different kinds of receptor cells from each other is the kind of photochemicals resident in each. It has in the past been fashionable to refer

rods and cones

to the retina as a duplex system referring to the fact that there are two different anatomically shaped photoreceptors—one cone shaped and one cylindrically or rod shaped. In fact, however, the functional differences among the three kinds of cones are conceptually as great as the difference between the rods and cones. The really important differences among these receptors are their absorption spectra; that is, the specific wavelengths of light that are selectively absorbed by the four photochemicals. Of this we will have more to say soon. For the moment we note only that the retina might properly be referred to as being quadriplex rather than duplex.

The second neural layer in the retina (shown in Figure 4–6) consists of short *bipolar* neurons connecting the receptors to the third layer—the *ganglion* cells—whose long axons make up the fibers of the optic nerve. At the interface between each of these layers there are laterally connecting cells; the lateral connectives in the outer plexiform layer (between the receptors and the bipolars) are called *horizontal* cells. This region consists of a

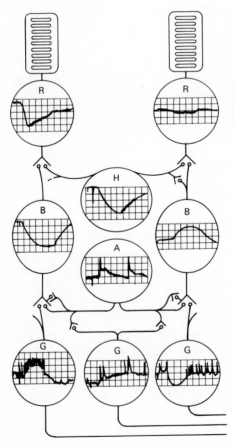

Figure 4–7 The kinds of responses that can be obtained from the various neurons in the retina. Only amacrine and ganglion cells produce spike action potentials. The other cell types produce only graded potentials. (Redrawn from Dowling, J.E., *Investigative Ophthalmology*, 1970, 9:655–680.

very complex network of synaptic interconnections between the receptors and the bipolars and the laterally interconnecting horizontal cells. The inner plexiform layer between the bipolars and the ganglion cells consists of an equally complex network of interconnection between these cells and the laterally communicating *amacrine* cells. Running parallel, but in the opposite direction to the sensory chain just described, are also some *centrifugal* (from the center outward) fibers that convey regulatory information from the central nervous system to the receptors.

The neurons in the retinal plexus are quite different, it should also be noted, in terms of the electrophysiological responses of which each is capable. The receptors, bipolars, and horizontal cells can only respond with graded potentials and are incapable of producing a propagating spike action potential. The ganglion and amacrine cells, on the other hand, do produce spike action potentials. Figure 4–7 sums up this varying kind of responsiveness for each of the types of cells.

If we increase the magnification even further, we can look at the anatomical details of a typical rod and a typical cone. Enlarged views of these two cell types are shown in Figure 4–8. The cylindrical rod and the somewhat more conical cone both display other anatomical features that are quite significant in understanding their function. Note that the outer-segment of each cell type is actually made up of a series of discs enclosed within the outer membrane of the receptor cell. These discs are thought to contain the actual photosensitive material. In the rods these discs are continuously created at the base of the outer

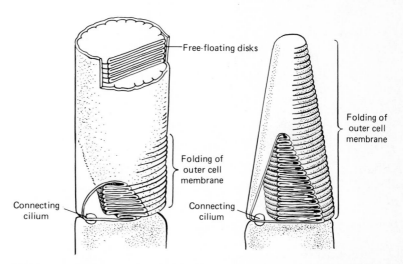

Figure 4–8 Enlarged view of a typical rod and cone. (Redrawn through the courtesy of Dr. R.W. Young.)

segment and migrate to the tip where they are cast off into the extracellular space. The discs in the cone, however, are permanently attached to the cell membrane and seem to remain in one place over the entire life of the cell. It is thought that the typical conical shape of the cone results from the fact that the smaller outer discs were formed early in the embryological development of the organism, while the larger discs formed during the later stages.

Note also that the receptors consist of both an outer segment containing the discs and a cell body containing the nucleus and other intracellular organelles involved in cellular metabolism. We know now that the cell body and the outer segment are connected by a very fine tube through which must flow all of the nutrients necessary for the metabolism of the photoreceptor.

At the foot of even an individual receptor cell there exist very complicated synaptic interconnections with large numbers of other neurons. The neuroanatomist Sjöstrand for example, has shown that a typical cone in a rabbit may be connected to as many as thirty other receptors, bipolars, and horizontal cells in an extremely complicated manner. Clearly a high degree of neural interconnection is possible even here at this first synaptic junction.

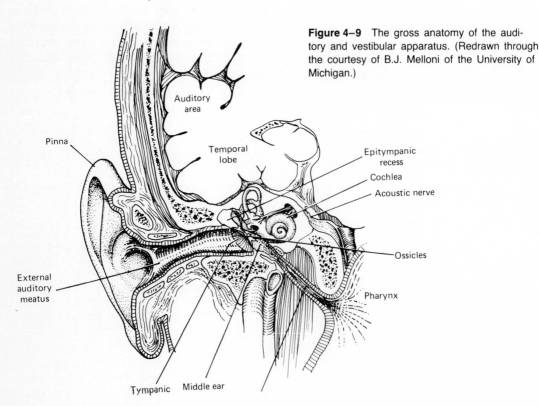

Figure 4–9 The gross anatomy of the auditory and vestibular apparatus. (Redrawn through the courtesy of B.J. Melloni of the University of Michigan.)

the auditory system   The anatomy of the auditory and vestibular systems is also well known. Figure 4–9 presents the gross anatomy of the external, middle, and inner ear. The external pinna acts like a miniature megaphone mechanically collecting acoustic signals and channeling them through the external auditory meatus. These concentrated sound waves then impinge on the tympanic membrane, a tissue connected by the three ossicles to the oval window, one of two membrane-covered openings of the middle ear. (The other is the round window.)

The bulbous region of the inner ear shown in this diagram is referred to as the *vestibule,* and it is for this reason that the organs of balance—*the semicircular canals* and the *saccule* and *utricule* which branch off at this point—are referred to as the vestibular system. The other larger chamber emerging from the vestibule is the snail-shaped cochlea, the actual organ of auditory transduction.

If one enlarges a cross section of the cochlea sufficiently, as has been done in Figure 4–10, it can be seen that the cochlea is

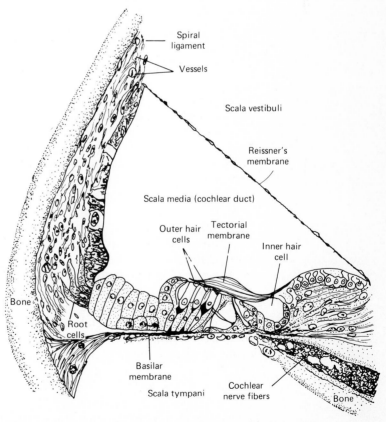

Figure 4–10 A magnified cross section of the cochlea. (Redrawn through the courtesy of Professor Joseph Hawkin of the University of Michigan.)

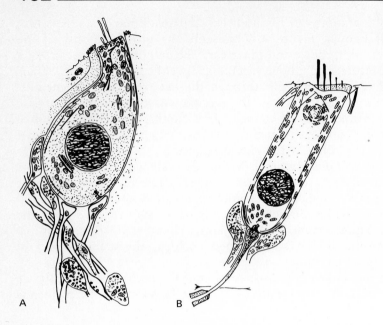

Figure 4–11 Enlarged views of a typical (*A.*) inner and (*B.*) outer hair cell from the cochlea. (Redrawn from Engstrom, H., Ades, H., and Hawkin, J., in Neff, W.D., eds., *Contributions to Sensory Physiology*, N.Y., Academic Press. 1965.)

A

B

hair cells

divided into three cavities with two membranes running along its total length. Meissner's membrane is a very thin tissue, actually only one flattened cell in thickness. The basilar membrane upon which rest the inner and outer hair cells—the actual sensory cells—is a somewhat more elaborate structure consisting of several different cell types. All three of the cochlea chambers are filled with lymphatic fluids. However, these fluids vary in their ionic constitutents and as a result there are substantial and important voltage differences among the three chambers. We shall reconsider the importance of this fact when we discuss transduction.

At the highest level of magnification at which we examine auditory anatomy, the details of the short stubby auditory receptors become clear. Figure 4–11 illustrates that the one row of inner hair cells has a typical flask-shaped body with nothing that corresponds to any dendritic aborization. The three rows of outer hair cells are more cylindrically shaped and also devoid of any dendritic protrusions. At the base of both of these cell types are very elaborate neural networks comparable to those existing at the base of photoreceptors. Some second order neurons obviously must pick up signals from the base of the auditory hair cells when they are activated. These are the neurons of the cochlear or acoustic nerve; their function is to convey sensory information to the central nervous system. However, there also appear to be other junctions conveying

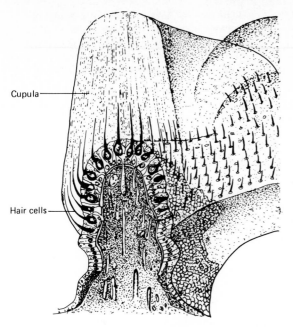

Cupula

Hair cells

Figure 4–12 A magnified view of the receptor region of the semicircular canals. (Redrawn from Flock, A., in Loewenstein, W.R. (Ed.) *Handbook of Sensory Physiology*, 1971, New York, Springer-Verlag, 1:396–441.)

information *from* the central nervous system; these fibers are indicated anatomically by the presence of synaptic vesicles in the cochlear nerve neurons rather than in the body of the hair cell. The receptor in this case must be acting as the postsynaptic cell, and information must be passing from more central portions of the nervous system to the receptors, another example of vestibular conduction.

The vestibular sensors are also presented at high magnification in Figures 4–12 and 4–13.

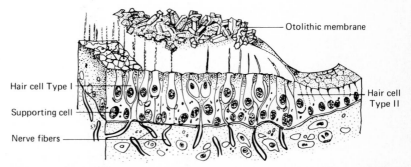

Otolithic membrane

Hair cell Type I

Supporting cell

Nerve fibers

Hair cell Type II

Figure 4–13 A magnified view of the receptor region of the utricle or saccule. (Redrawn from Iuarto, S., in Iuarto, S. et. al., eds., *Submicroscopic Structure of the Inner Ear*, Oxford, Pergamon 1967.)

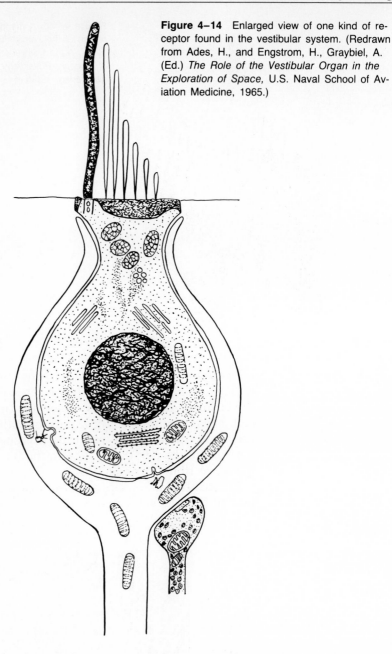

Figure 4–14 Enlarged view of one kind of receptor found in the vestibular system. (Redrawn from Ades, H., and Engstrom, H., Graybiel, A. (Ed.) *The Role of the Vestibular Organ in the Exploration of Space,* U.S. Naval School of Aviation Medicine, 1965.)

vestibular receptors

The utricle and the saccule are lined with a specialized type of hair cell (see Figure 4–14) quite similar to the auditory receptors, but of somewhat different construction. The three semicircular canals contain another type of hair cell (see Figure 4–15.) However, the most novel aspect of the sensitive surfaces in the vestibular system is the presence of gelatinous material

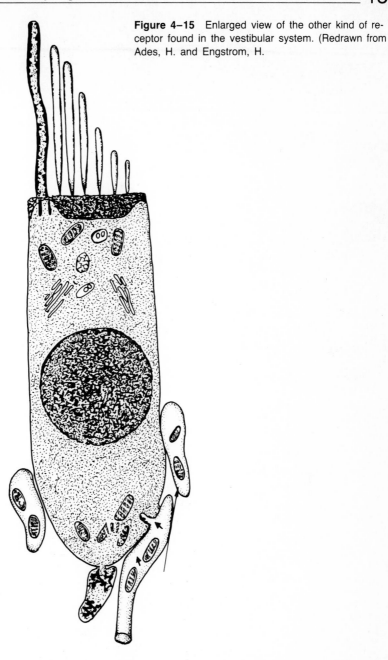

Figure 4–15 Enlarged view of the other kind of receptor found in the vestibular system. (Redrawn from Ades, H. and Engstrom, H.

that plays an important role in the sensory process. For example, in the semicircular canals there exists a *cupula* of stiff jelly that transmits dynamic accelerative information to the hair cells, as shown in Figure 4–12. These receptors thus respond to changes in the motion of the body. The utricle and saccule, on the other hand, are activated by static accelerative

A

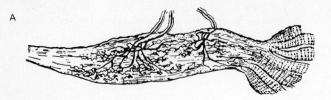

Figure 4–16 Several different types of somatosensory receptors. (A.) Golgi tendon organ. (B.) A Muscle Spindle ending. (C.) A Pacinian corpuscle.

B

C

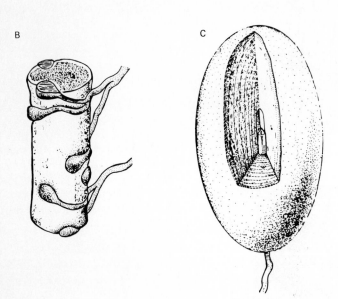

forces, that is, gravity. Here the jelly is arranged into a flat sheet covered with a stony or *otolithic* membrane consisting of tiny crystals of calcium carbonate as shown in Figure 4–13. It is the action of gravity on these relatively dense crystals transmitted through the gelatinous membrane that activates the utricular and saccular hair cells.

The *somatosensory* receptors of the skin, muscles, and tendons are also highly developed for their specific tasks. Figure 4–16 shows several of the many types of receptors that exist in the body. For many years it had been thought that the type of encapsulation surrounding these endings was responsible for sensitivity. It now seems more likely that the various kinds of encapsulations are nothing more than tiny *neuromas* or *neurotumors* that play only a minor preneural role in sensory processing. A currently more popular view is that the nerve ending itself is the actual receptor organ and where it is located is more important than its shape. The gross anatomy of the olfactory and gustatory receptors—the nose and tongue—are

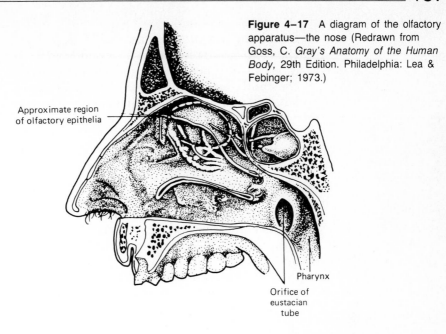

Figure 4–17 A diagram of the olfactory apparatus—the nose (Redrawn from Goss, C. *Gray's Anatomy of the Human Body*, 29th Edition. Philadelphia: Lea & Febinger; 1973.)

Approximate region of olfactory epithelia

Pharynx

Orifice of eustacian tube

shown in Figures 4–17 and 4–18 respectively. The actual olfactory receptor cells are embedded deep within the nasal passages on a patch of yellow pigmented cells. Olfactory receptors, like the somatosensory ones, possess their own elongated axon. The gustatory receptor cells on the taste buds of

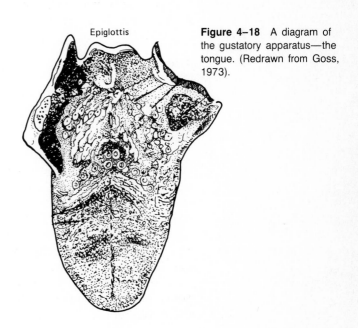

Epiglottis

Figure 4–18 A diagram of the gustatory apparatus—the tongue. (Redrawn from Goss, 1973).

the tongue have undergone a different evolutionary adaptation. Of all the receptors of the body, they are most exposed to chemical insults by their savory and tasty environment. Many different chemicals of more or less modest corrosive powers constantly bathe the tongue's receptors. As a result, these cells have a relatively short life expectancy and therefore have evolved a unique reproduction mechanism among sensory receptors. Gustatory receptor cells are continuously created from the epithelial cells of the epidermis of the taste bud. As the older cells disintegrate and new cells migrate into their place, the synaptic connection is passed from the old to the new.

All in all, these extraordinary receptor structures represent our only means of contact with the external world. It is only through the sensory mechanism that information can be acquired from the environment. No matter how powerful our brains might be, they would be perceptually useless without these delicately tuned sense organs.

Once information has been transduced by the receptor cells, it must be sent to the central nervous system for interpretation and action. This is the function of the afferent pathways. Each receptor cell is connected in sequence to several other neurons. These neurons form a chain from the individual receptor to the brain. The exact number of neurons varies in this chain. In the visual system there are chains of three or four neurons; in the auditory system, five or six; in the somatosensory three is the usual number for the main pathways. At least four neurons are involved in the chain making up the vestibular pathway, and probably five in the gustatory system. Figure 4–19 summarizes the steps in the various afferent pathways.

Transduction

So far we have discussed the wide variety of physical energies to which the sensory systems respond and the many shapes and forms of the evolved receptor organs. In the previous chapter we considered the basic fact of psychobiology that responses of all neurons are very much alike; they are electrochemical potentials produced by shifts in membrane permeability. The question to which this section is addressed is "How are physical stimulus energies converted into these electrochemical signals?" The answer is briefly summed up in the single word *transduction*. Of course, this word has too much meaning; it includes a very large number of processes, each of which is specialized for the particular physical energy to which the receptor is most sensitive. But there are several properties of transductive mechanisms that are common. Before we discuss their differences, let us consider these similarities.

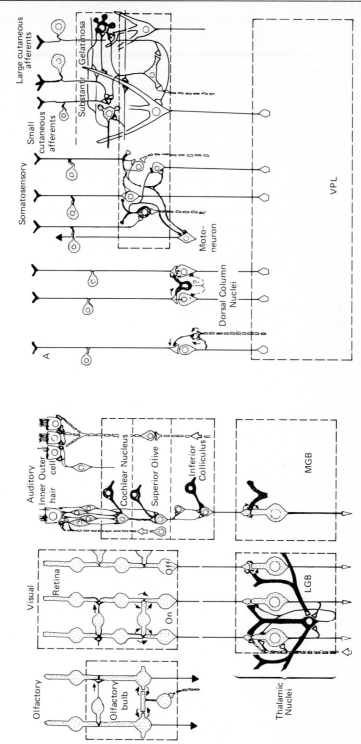

Figure 4-19 A summary of the neural steps from the receptors to the major sensory nuclei for the various sensory pathways. (Redrawn from Szenthagothai, J. and Arbib, M.A., *Conceptual Models of Neural Organization*, Cambridge, Mass. MIT Press, 1975.) LGB = Lateral geniculate body; MGB = Medial geniculate body; VPL = Ventral-posterolateral nucleus.

primary sensory action

In Chapter 3, we saw how a resting potential was established by the metabolic pumps and the passive forces that acted to distribute ions across a semipermeable membrane. After a stage of equilibrium is reached, the typical neuron exhibits a resting potential across the membrane such that the inside of the neuron is about 70 millivolts more negative than the outside fluid. Let us assume for the moment that some agent is able to alter the permeability of the membrane. When that occurs, the ionic equilibrium would be altered as a new balance is established by the several forces (the active pumps and passive forces) involved. This idea of an induced permeability change is the key to understanding the transductive mechanisms in all of the sensory modalities. Each of the receptors has evolved some physical action that allows a particular energy (the adequate stimulus) to alter the membrane permeability of a specialized receptor. This physical action is the last action of the stimulus prior to transduction; another term for this last action of the physical stimulus is *primary sensory action* because it is also the trigger that releases the electrochemical action of the neuron. Although the primary sensory action differs from one receptor to another, the outcome in each case is an induced variation in membrane permeability.

receptor and generator potentials

The result of this altered membrane permeability is a graded neural signal that is referred to either as a *receptor potential* or a *generator potential*. As we saw earlier in this chapter, some receptor cells have long axons while others are short processes that synapse almost immediately with another neuron. If the receptor cell has its own axon, the graded change in the receptor potential (resulting from the change in the membrane permeability) is itself the immediate cause of a spike action potential in that same neuron. In this case, the response is referred to as a generator potential. If, however, the receptor cell has no axon, then the information in the graded potential (triggered by the primary sensory action) must be communicated to a neuron that does have an elongated axon for transmission to some more central portion of the nervous system. Within the receptor cell itself, however, there is no direct generation of a propagated spike action potential. In this case we refer to the stimulus induced graded potential shift as a receptor potential. Figure 4–20 diagrams this distinction between the two terms.

The key to the transduction process in all sensory receptors is that the membrane potential of the receptor must be changed to produce the receptor or generator potential. Membranes have evolved a number of different primary sensory actions. In fact, however, if we consider the process in terms of the membrane itself, there are only three kinds of *sensitivities*—to electrical stimuli, to mechanical deformations and to certain chemicals.

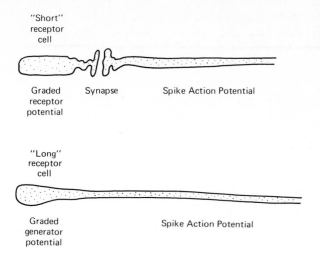

"Short" receptor cell

Graded receptor potential   Synapse   Spike Action Potential

"Long" receptor cell

Graded generator potential   Spike Action Potential

Figure 4–20 A diagram depicting the difference between a receptor and a generator potential.

Even at this level, modern developments in membrane biochemistry suggest that there is an even more fundamental common mechanism relating transduction in all known receptors.

membrane structure

The current model of neuronal cell membrane structure is shown in Figure 4–21. A bilayer of lipid molecules forms the main portion of the cell or plasma membrane of all neurons, as well as all other cells of the body. Scattered over this lipid bilayer are relatively large protein molecules. Some of these

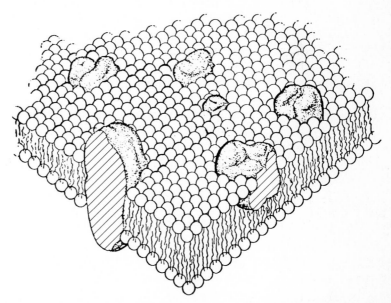

Figure 4–21 A current model of the neuronal cell membrane. (Redrawn from Singer, S.J. and Nicholson, G.L. *Science,* 1972, *175,* 720–731.)

protein channels

molecules, as we have seen, are the pumps that push sodium out and potassium ions into the neuron and thus establish the resting potential. Other protein molecules, however, are specialized for other functions. In particular, a large number of these protein molecules act as channels allowing the passive flow of ions when the configuration or chemical constitution of these molecules is varied. Some protein channels are activated by electrical activity in the membrane itself. Such channels are probably responsible for the sequential propagation of a spike action potential along the neuron—the electrical activity in one place activates the channel in the next. Some are activated when they combine with certain substances secreted by other neurons. These channels are best represented by the post-synaptic receptor sites that allow synaptic transmission. Other protein channels, however, are activated by either chemical or mechanical stimuli applied from the external environment. These are the sensory receptors of interest to us in the current context. Figure 4–22 sums up this family of membrane protein channels.

All of these protein channels, regardless of how they are activated, perform the same function—they all act to allow ions to be redistributed across the plasma membrane. In doing so they produce a *neuroelectric response*. Whether it is a synaptic response, an action potential within a nerve, or a response to a stimulus, the effect is the same—the conduction of information from one point to another within the nervous system often accompanied by a change in the physical form of the energy by which the information is carried (transduction) or in the kind of electrical signal representing it (coding).

We now can consider several important questions. First "What is the physical basis of transduction—the conversion of physical to neural energy?" This question is best answered in molecular terms. Transduction results from the alteration in the state of some protein molecule in the receptor membrane in a way that changes the membrane's permeability to sodium and potassium ions. Transduction considered at this level is nothing other than what we have just been talking about—an induced

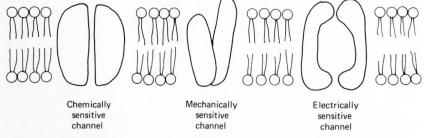

Chemically   Mechanically   Electrically
sensitive   sensitive   sensitive
channel   channel   channel

Figure 4–22 Schematics of the kind of channels that may exist on the membrane.

change in the conformation (and thus permeability) of one of a set of specialized protein molecules.

The next question might be "What are the adequate stimuli at this level of analysis?" As we said, when you get down to the brass tacks of this microscopic level, the only effective stimuli are chemical and mechanical energies (ignoring for a moment the ubiquitous effects of electricity). Clearly olfactory and gustatory events are initiated by the direct chemical action of the appropriate substances on the receptors, but surprisingly, so also is the visual process. As we shall shortly describe, the visual receptor membrane potential is activated by the *chemical* breakdown products of photosensitive substances; light itself does not act directly on the membrane. On the other hand, touch, hearing, and vestibular sensitivities as well (probably) as all of the somatosensory processes seem to result from a direct mechanical effect on the membrane. But here again some protein molecule especially sensitive to mechanical distortion presumably must be involved in the transduction process.

The main point for the student to appreciate here is that the common response in the transductive process is the alteration of the membrane potential, that is, the signal that the neurophysiologist observes in the form of a generator or receptor potential. The primary sensory action, the last task of the stimulus, does vary from sensory modality to sensory modality, but its effect is always to change membrane permeability. In the following paragraphs we consider the details of transduction for the various senses.

visual receptor chemistry

In vision, the chemistry of the photosensitive chemicals is well known. Four types of photochemicals have been identified. These are *rhodospin* in rods, and *erythrolabe, chlorolabe,* and *cyanolabe* in the three types of cones, respectively. These four substances have distinctive sensitivites to light, as shown in Figure 4–23. However, they are similar to each other in their

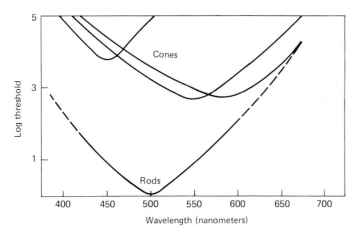

Figure 4–23 The spectral sensitivites of the four receptor chemicals in the photoreceptors.

respective chemical structure. Each photochemical consists of a combination of two organic parts; one part is a relatively small molecule called *retinal* and the other is a relatively large molecule called *opsin*. The different spectral sensitivities of the four receptors—three cones and one rod—are determined by differences in four different kinds of opsins; a single retinal is common to all four substances.

To understand the transductive process in vision one must understand a little bit about the stereochemistry of organic molecules. (*Stereochemistry* is the area of chemical science that deals with the three-dimensional shape of molecular structures.) It is a fact that even substances with identical chemical formulas (for example, the formula for human retinal is $C_{19} H_{27} CHO$) may display substantially different chemical properties if the three-dimensional shape of the structure varies. Retinal, for example, can exist in a number of stereogeometric configurations. Two that are important to us in the present discussion are the forms called all-*trans* retinal and 11-*cis*-retinal; these are the chemical names associated with the two shapes shown in Figure 4–24. Note that the constituent elements in each are identical one to the other. The only difference is that there is a kink in the tail of 11-*cis*-retinal that is not present in all-*trans* retinal. The kink is caused by different bonding energies being exerted at that eleventh carbon atom including those of the hexagonal ring.

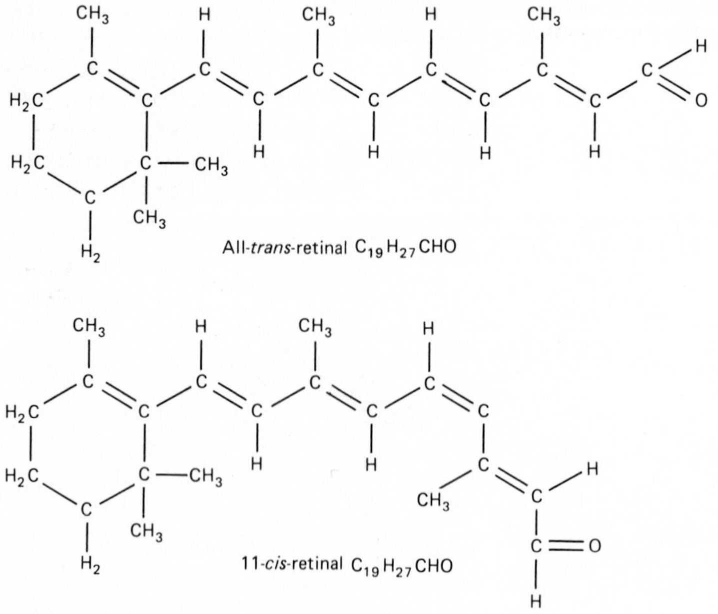

All-*trans*-retinal $C_{19} H_{27} CHO$

11-*cis*-retinal $C_{19} H_{27} CHO$

Figure 4–24 Two of the isomeric forms of retinal₁.

The important chemical fact concerning these two stereo-isomers is that, like many other stereoisomers, they differ in their chemistry in a very important way. This key difference is that 11-*cis*-retinal forms an exceedingly stable substance—rhodopsin—when combined with rod opsin. However, all-*trans* retinal does not produce a stable combination; when combined with rod opsin, it is so unstable that at normal body temperatures, the available thermal energy is sufficient to break the two parts of rhodopsin apart spontaneously!

stereoisomerization   The central principle of the primary sensory action of light in the visual process is that *all that light does is change 11-cis-retinal into all-trans retinal*—a process referred to as *stereoisomerization*. This is all that light does—nothing more; the rest of the process is driven by thermal energies and occurs spontaneously. In other words, the primary sensory action in vision is the interaction between a single photon of light and a particular kind of molecule. Even more particularly, it is the absorbtion of that photon of light by the particular kinked bond in 11-*cis*-retinal. The shape of this substance thus is changed by this final physical (primary sensory) action and the process that leads to the receptor potential then occurs spontaneously.

The next question one must ask is, "How does the stereo-isomerization of 11-*cis*-retinal lead to the receptor potential?" Some parts of the answer to this question are beginning to be understood but other parts still remain obscure. After the moment of stereoisomerization of 11-*cis*-retinal into all-*trans* retinal, as we have seen, there is a vastly increased tendency for the rhodopsin molecule to begin to break up. When it does, it does not separate all at once. Rather the altered rhodopsin decomposes into a series of intermediary chemicals known as *breakdown products*. The chemistry of these breakdown products is well known. There may be as many as a dozen stages in the process occurring before the stereoisomerized all-*trans* retinal and the opsin are fully separated. Here is where the uncertainty begins: We are not sure, but it appears that either one or more of the breakdown products or free opsin is the specific chemical that acts on the protein molecules (channels) in the membrane of the discs or the receptor cell membrane itself. This would alter the permeability of the membrane, allow a redistribtion of the sodium and potassium ions, and thus produce the receptor potential.

In the vertebrate photoreceptor, curiously, the effect of these breakdown products is to decrease the permeability of the protein channels, and thus to increase the membrane potential. There is no reason to think, however, that a change in this direction—a hyperpolarization—is less able to carry information than a decrease in the membrane potential—a *depolariza-*

tion. It is simply a different convention, equally capable of being decoded by the nervous tissue involved. Indeed, in invertebrates that is exactly what happens.

This, briefly, is the story of the transductive mechanism for what we now understand is the chemically mediated visual system. Other chemical senses presumably act more directly, since the adequate stimulus is a chemical itself and there are no known substances or processes (such as photoisomerization) interposed between the presentation of a chemical and the olfactory or gustatory receptors and their neural responses. Presumably different molecules exist on the membranes of their respective receptor cells that are especially sensitive to some feature of chemicals that can be smelled or tasted.

The most widely accepted theory of olfactory transduction is, like vision, based on the stereogeometry of the involved chemicals. J.E. Amoore has proposed a lock-and-key model that he believes accounts well for the characteristics of olfactory transduction. According to his theory there are seven different basic smells. Five of these smells are associated with a particular molecular shape. Figure 4–25 shows the five particular shapes that he has suggested as representative of these five sensitivities, as well as the two small positively or negatively charged particles that do not fit his stereogeometric hypothesis. According to Amoore, these five key shapes match the five equivalent membrane site shapes shown in Figure 4–26. When a particular chemically odorous "key" fits into the particular "lock," a

olfactory transduction: the "lock and key" theory

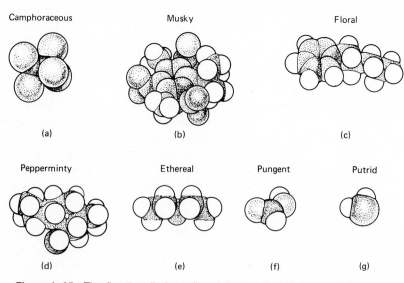

Figure 4–25 The five "smell shapes" and the two "smell charges." (Redrawn from Amoore. J., *Proceedings of Scientific Section of Toilet Goods Association,* 1962, 37:13–23.)

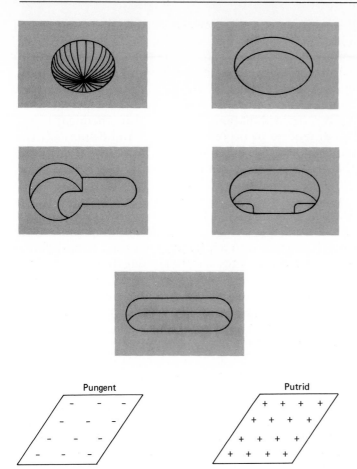

Figure 4–26 The five "smell receptor-site shapes" and the two "smell receptor-site charges." (Redrawn from Amoore, J., 1962.)

Pungent   Putrid

generator potential is produced. It seems likely that the lock in this case is a specialized protein molecule of the membrane similar to the ones already discussed.

It is likely that Amoore's theory must be something of an allegory and that the shapes of the lock and the keys probably are not the essential aspect of the process. It is the chemistry of the olfactory stimuli as well as the protein channel molecules and how they interact that is critical. But the shapes and the chemical activities of the involved molecules are closely related. Geometrical "keys" need not fit physically into geometrical "locks" as much as chemical "keys" may fit into chemical "locks."

Clearly there is much uncertainty concerning exactly what is happening at the point of olfactory transduction, but equally clearly whatever is happening is a chemical process of some sort. The unifying concept that ties this sense to vision and all of the other modalities is the idea of a chemically sensitive molecule acting to vary the permeability of the receptor cell membrane.

The story that can be told concerning taste is similar, though it must necessarily differ in detail because the adequate stimuli and receptor anatomy differ. There are several theories of taste that attempt to explain why there appears to be four basic tastes. Again, the explanations are framed in chemical terms. *Bitter* stimuli tend to incorporate nitrogen and display heavier molecular weights than other flavorful stimuli; *sweet* stimuli tend to be proton-acceptor substances or the salts of a heavy metal like lead; *salty* stimuli ionize very well in water; *sour* stimuli tend to be acids. However, in each case there is no exact relationship between chemical structure and perceptual experience, and exceptions to each of these generalities abound. What does seem to be certain is that different taste buds have different distributions of receptor sites selectively sensitive to these four classes of stimuli. A general idea of receptor distribution is presented in Figure 4–27. These receptor sites once again appear to be rather large protein molecules with weights near 150,000 Daltons. What is not certain, but plausible and theoretically comforting, is that the same model of a chemically sensitive protein acting as an ionic channel operates here as it does in the other chemically sensitive transduction mechanisms.

We now may turn to the mechanical transducers. Whether one is dealing with hearing, balance, or any of the body and skin senses, the primary sensory action is the mechanical distortion of some specialized portion of the receptor neuron. On the other hand, it is clear that not all portions of each receptor cell are sensitive to such deformations. There are many portions of the

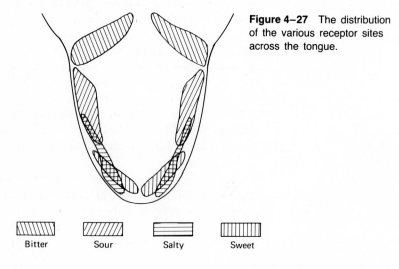

Figure 4–27 The distribution of the various receptor sites across the tongue.

Bitter   Sour   Salty   Sweet

the pacinian corpuscle

plasma membrane of a hair cell or a cutaneous axon that can be distorted until they are torn asunder without producing even a minimal generator or receptor potential. Only certain portions of a receptor neuron respond to the stimulus. To make this clear, let us consider the transductive process of the somatosensory receptor known as the pacinian corpuscle (illustrated in Figure 4–16C) in detail. Werner Loewenstein has been the major contributor to what we know about the specialized regions of the Pacinian corpuscle. Figure 4–28 depicts the several critical regions of this neuron. First, a specially sensitive region (Region I) exists at the tip of the neuron that is devoid of the myelin sheath. Instead of myelin, this tip is enclosed within an onion-like encapsulation. This encapsulation is not neural tissue, but as we have noted earlier it is not entirely inert; it does serve to accentuate the stimulus at its onset and at its offset to differentiate it. With regard to the neural membrane itself, Loewenstein discovered that only this limited region near the tip was capable of producing *generator potentials* when mechanically distorted. Beyond this small region of the tip no amount of mechanical bending was effective in producing a generator potential. On the other hand, only those portions of the membrane beyond the first node of Ranvier (Region III) were capable of propagating spike action potentials. Two distinct regions with quite different properties therefore exist within a few microns of each other on the same membrane—one (Region I) can produce generator potentials, but not spikes, and one (Region III) can produce spikes but not generator potentials. Separating them exactly at the first node of Ranvier, Lowenstein discovered that there was a narrow ring of membrane (Region II) that had its own very special properties. It was here, and only here, that the generator potential was capable of actually generating spike action potentials. If this region were inactivated (by a pressure block) no spikes were produced even when the generator potential was of substantial amplitude.

How can this all be explained? To be honest, we do not know exactly what the membrane properties are that distinguish these three regions. The speculative answer that best fits current

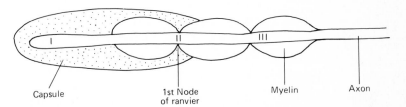

Figure 4–28 The critical transducing regions of a peripheral somatosensory neuron.

ideas of membrane characteristics is that the membrane differs in this region in terms of the kind of protein molecules present. The tip of the neuron, which is capable of producing a generator potential but not a spike, probably has scattered on its surface protein channels which are exquisitely sensitive to mechanical deformation. On the other hand, the protein molecules that are scattered about on the portion of the membrane near the first node of Ranvier are probably very insensitive to mechanical stimulation but are likely to be tuned to respond to the slight electrical signals produced in the form of generator potentials. Along the other regions of the axon beyond that first node of Ranvier, the proteins present have the joint properties of virtually total inertness to mechanical stimulation and a relatively high threshold to electrical fields. This high threshold, however, is regularly exceeded by the relatively high level voltage swings produced by a spike action potential in the preceding portion of the neuron.

the hair cells

In the inner ear the situation is somewhat different but in many ways the vestibular and acoustic hair cells share properties common to all the other mechanically sensitive receptors. We are fairly certain that these acoustically sensitive cells also have membranes that are not identical in sensitivity over all of the cell. The movement of the cilia or hairs of these cells (shown in Figure 4–11) leads to a distortion of the cuticular base plate from which the hairs emerge. The current consensus is that it is this base plate that is the critical region, and that its deformation is the key cause of the production of the receptor potential. Other portions of the hair cells do not seem to be sensitive to mechanical deformation in anywhere near the same degree. Presumably, therefore, it is here that the necessary special protein molecules, particularly sensitive to deformation, reside.

The transduction process in the auditory system is made even more effective by a curious fact of the body's chemistry. In Figure 4–10 we saw that the cavities of the cochlea are filled with solutions with different ionic concentrations. While the scala vestibuli and the scala tympani have virtually the same voltage level as blood, the scala media consists of fluids whose ionic concentrations produce a voltage level 80 millivolts more positive than blood.

Now consider the following fact: It is into the fluids of the scala media that the hairs of the hair cells protrude! Given that the inside of the hair cell is about 60 millivolts more negative than the blood, and the scala media is about 80 millivolts more positive, a total voltage difference of over 140 millivolts exists across the same cellular base plate that we have already identified as the key element in acoustic transduction. The passive voltage and ionic concentration forces tending to move sodium and potassium through the membrane of the auditory receptor cell are more than twice the normal level at this point. Indeed, very tiny changes in membrane permeability would, under the influence of these forces, produce an enormous rush of sodium ions and potassium ions out of the cell. The word "enormous" may strike the reader as being a little highblown in the context, but its use here is most appropriate. The 140 millivolt difference between the inside of the hair cell and the fluid of the scala media is the largest electropotential existing inside the human body. The system thus acts as a very powerful amplifier. The tiny energies of the stimulus act to "gate" or control the relatively large 140 millivolt power. A small stimulus can thus produce a very large response, and indeed this is exactly the case in auditory transduction. The receptor potential is so large that at first it was not accepted as the result of the membrane, but was thought to be a "microphonic" effect produced by nonnervous properties of the cochlea.

the cochlear "microphonic"

In summary, we have seen how transduction is probably mediated by chemically and mechanically sensitive protein molecules penetrating the membrane of highly evolved and specialized receptor cells. These receptors are neurons, it must be remembered, and they are the first step in communicating information from the external world to the central nervous system. The medium in which the information was carried in the external world—some form of physical energy—has, by virtue of the act of transduction, been converted into the new medium of electrochemical signals of the nervous system. It is as if the message had been translated into a new language. The words of this new language are to be found in the various ways in which individual neurons can respond. This is the topic of the next section.

Sensory Coding

Once information has been translated from the external "language" of the physical stimulus to the internal "language" of neurons, it must be conveyed from the receptor to the central nervous system in the form of neural activity of one kind or another. The two questions we now face are "What is the language (or languages) used by the nervous system?" and "What are the messages that are to be carried?" If we focus on the problem and look at something less grandiose than *"the overall spatiotemporal pattern of nervous activity"* and *"the complex real world scene,"* some general features of sensory coding quickly become apparent. To begin, let us note that physical stimuli, while they may be carrying highly complex messages, are actually constrained by their own physics. Though elaborate significance and meaning may be conveyed by either the simplest or the most complex physical stimulus, in fact that stimulus may vary only along relatively simple dimensions. Physical stimuli *vary in intensity, in quality,* and *in their spatial* and *temporal distributions.* These variables are the words of the external medium, but they are not the message, to distort the aphorism of the late Marshall MacLuhan. The message is quite different from the physics of the stimulus. It may, indeed, be much more complex, bearing as it does only a symbolic relationship to the physics of the stimulus.

After transduction, the formation or meaning of the message is represented or encoded in an entirely different language. It may have been translated into frequency of spike action potentials, the amplitude of a graded signal pattern, or even a topographic pattern of neural activity. Even so, these new signals still represent the same message. The analogy between this transformation or recoding, and spoken language is instructive. "Gutten morgen" in German *means* the same thing as "Ohio gozimasu" in Japanese, even though the two languages are totally noncognate and there is no similarity between the physical signals. In the same way a pattern of light and a burst of neural activity—two different "languages"—may also both represent the same idea of "Good morning."

The point we make is that it is possible to distinguish between the message "Good morning" carried by the code on the one hand, and the physical medium or code itself on the other. The message may remain constant regardless of the physics of the stimulus, the biochemistry of neurons, or atmospheric pressure. Our task here is to examine how the nervous system represents the dimensions of the physical stimulus, not to consider the nature of the messages. This is the goal of that subspecialty within psychobiology called *sensory coding theory.*

To begin this discussion properly it is necessary to consider two aspects of the problem. First, we have to establish the relevant dimensions of variation in the physical stimulus, and second, we have to consider the relevant dimensions of variation in the neural response. The task of the sensory coding theorist is then to define the relationships between the two. To make this idea more concrete, consider the following example. A neurophysiologist finds that increasing the intensity of an external light causes a neuron in the peripheral nervous system to fire spike action potentials more frequently than it did prior to that increase. The meaning of this message may be that dawn has arisen in the external environment. In the language of the external environment, dawn was represented by luminance. In the internal language, the same message was represented by an increase in the number of spike action potentials. But consider the situation from a little more abstract point of view. The message has remained constant throughout this entire process of transduction and coding regardless of the language in which it was encoded. Increased luminance has exactly the same meaning as increased firing rate. The codes are different but the meaning is the same. If this is taken for granted, from this point on we can ignore meaning and concentrate only on the translation of the codes as we go from point to point in the nervous system.

neural codes

To systemize this discussion (it would be a terrible task to try to work out the code for every meaningful message) we must consider what are the generalizable characteristics of physical stimuli and what are the generalizable characteristics of the neural language. Physical stimuli, as we have asserted, vary in amplitude, quality, temporal pattern, and spatial pattern. These terms may be referred to collectively as the *common sensory dimensions*, the dimensions defined in a way that is independent of which physical stimulus we are studying or what the message is. Electromagnetic, acoustic, and even chemical stimuli all vary along each of these dimensions.

How, then, do we identify the equivalent coding dimensions in the neurophysiological language? We do so by performing the classic sensory-electrophysiological type of experiment. In this prototypical class of experiments an electrode is implanted either near or in a neuron. When the preparation is stable (following the sometimes traumatic surgery such an implantation requires) some dimension of the stimulus is varied in a systematic way. Variations of the recorded neural response are then observed. We have already mentioned repeatedly one such neural response dimension—the frequency of firing of a single neuron. But there are many other possible dimensions of neural encoding. Some of these response dimensions often are quite simple—for example, the size of the response, its location in the nervous system, and the amount of transmitter substance that is released at a certain synaptic junction. However, some response dimensions can be much more complex. For example, the spatial or topographic pattern of activity produced on a particular portion of the cerebral cortex may itself represent some aspect of the stimulus. Indeed, the frequency of an acoustic stimulus is represented by just such a pattern of activity on the surface of a dog's temporal cortex. The irregularity or variance on the intervals between successive spike action potentials in some neurons (quite a different dimension from the mean frequency) is also a possible code. It is even possible in some neurophysiologically relativistic world that the *relative* amount of activity in two different places may signify some aspect of the stimulus. Thus both absolute and relative aspects of the neural response of both single neurons and groups of neurons are, in principle, able to encode stimulus dimensions in widely diverse ways. In fact, a basic law of sensory coding is that virtually any neural response dimension can represent or encode virtually any stimulus dimension.

After one has defined the stimulus and neural response dimensions, a question like "What are the actual correlations between the stimulus dimensions and the neural dimensions" might be asked. We may conceive of something like a matrix, similar to the one shown in Figure 4–29 between the common stimulus dimensions and the possible neural codes. Our task would be to correlate the former with the latter. This is the program of an extensive research agenda, it goes without saying, and the filling in of this table (with statements such as "Stimulus quantity is encoded by an increase in spike action potential frequency") has only begun. There are, however, a number of things we do know about sensory coding that may help us to appreciate the general nature of the correlations most likely to emerge.

First, it seems likely that there are many coding features that are common to the senses. As we have seen, not all of the transduction mechanisms are identical, but in large part it seems probable that common stimulus dimensions are encoded by similar neural response patterns independent of the specific modality being studied. Increased stimulus intensity, for example, seems to be associated with an increase in spike action

			Neural Response Dimensions (The Candidate Codes)								
							Temporal Parameters				
			Place	Topographic Pattern	Number of Activated Units	Neural Event Amplitude	Frequency	Frequency Microfluctuations	Frequency Macrofluctuations	Derived Statistical Measures	Temporal Comparison Between Two Places
Common Sensory Dimensions		Quality									
		Quantity									
	Temporal Parameters	Relative Temporal Order									
		Temporal Acuity									
		Duration									
	Spatial Parameters	Spatial Localization									
		Spatial Interaction and Patterns									

Figure 4–29 A sensory coding matrix. (From Uttal, W.R., *The Psychobiology of Sensory Coding:* New York, Harper & Row, 1973).

potential firing rate in vision, hearing, and somatic sensations.

Second, we are fairly confident that there is no single best code. As we also noted previously, any neural code can represent any stimulus dimension. But it is also probably the case that coding is redundant and stimulus intensity is not only encoded by stimulus frequency, but also by such dimensions as the number of responding neurons.

Third, coding cannot be considered to be understood even when and if a single table like the one shown in Figure 4–29 is completed. There is no single code, but rather a chain of different codes in sequence as the signal moves from the receptor to more central portions of the nervous system. Thus while one neural code for stimulus intensity may be the amplitude of the receptor potential, the same information of necessity is recoded at the first synapse into a correlated amount of chemical transmitter substance; at the next neuron first as a graded postsynaptic potential, and then as the frequency of spike action potential firing. Perhaps at some higher level the same stimulus dimension of intensity will be encoded as the difference between two different firing rates of two nearby neurons. Thus a large number of tables like the one shown in Figure 4–29 must be prepared to describe fully the sensory coding system. A comparable table must be developed at each of the *levels* of neural processing. This includes the highest centers of the brain where some coded pattern becomes the equivalent of a psychological state.

The fourth general point about sensory coding reveals that there is no need for a coded signal to be decoded by a central processing unit in order for the signal to become a psychological experience. All that is required is that after a number of codings and recodings, and after the integration of the immediate sensory signal with stored information, a certain state of a very complex network comes into being. That network state *is,*

mind/brain-state equivalence

according to the monistic philosophies of the brain/mind problem, the equivalent of a psychological state. As we pointed out in the first chapter, however, this is a speculative belief that is probably not amenable to direct confirmation in the laboratory. Indeed, reasonable persons may argue this point from many different points of view and still find themselves in agreement with this *hypothesis of intrinsic nonconfirmability;* that is, that the speculation may not be experimentally verifiable. Whether one believes this hypothesis because of practical considerations—there are simply too many neurons involved to ever expect that we will be able to analyze them—or because of some more subtle principle, the nonconfirmability of mind/brain state equivalence is held by many psychobiologists today.

We do know a great deal about the particular codes that are

used in communicating the various dimensions of the stimulus for at least a few of the afferent levels and are beginning to appreciate the similarity that exists among the various modalities. In the following sections of this chapter we shall consider, in turn, what is known about quality coding, quantity coding, and spatiotemporal coding in the afferent sensory systems.

Quality Coding

Even though the kind of physical stimulus differs greatly among the several sensory modalities (for example, vision, hearing, taste, touch, and so on) there are a number of common sources of how the quality of any individual stimulus is encoded. To understand this coding concept, it is necessary to define what we mean by *quality*. Obviously each of the human senses is particularly responsive to a particular *kind* of physical stimulus. The eye is sensitive to electromagnetic radiation varying between 400 and 750 nm,* the ear is sensitive to pneumatic pressure fluctuations varying between 20 and 20,000 Hz, and the tongue and nose are sensitive to different kinds of chemicals.

However, within each of these sensory modalities there are also differences in kind that transcend the other differences in amount, temporal pattern, and spatial pattern. Light and pneumatic pressure waves are different in quality in a massive way (one is electromagnetic and one is pneumatic) but in a more delicate manner so also do 450 nm and 700 nm electromagnetic radiations differ in kind. This definition of quality of the physical stimulus is often (but not always) associated with subjective differences, such as psychological qualities like red, yellow, high pitch, and salty. As we progress through the following discussion it is vitally important that both physical quality and perceptual quality are kept distinct. No physical stimulus *is* red; its quality is defined only in terms of its wavelength. To say that a "red" light is emitted by a monochromater is meaningless. To say that a "650 nm" light is emitted by a monochromater is meaningful.

receptor tuning

If we stay within the context of the problem of explaining how the quality of the stimulus (as defined in these physical terms) is encoded by the activity in the nervous system, however, we can see that certain general rules are followed by the nervous system. One general rule of quality coding is that the receptors are typically broadly tuned. That is, there is no receptor that is so precisely tuned that it will respond to only a single chemical, or a single wavelength of sound or light energy. All receptors respond to broad ranges of whatever stimulus dimension is

*Recall that a nanometer (nm) is a billionth of a meter.

associated with its quality. The four photoreceptor substances in the retina have considerably overlapping sensitivity curves. The type of cone whose peak sensitivity is furthest into the long wavelengths is actually sensitive (to a variable degree) to wavelengths from about 450 to 650 nm. The other two cone absorption curves are equally broad. Furthermore, the rod photopigment absorption curve is sensitive from at least 400 nm to more than 750 nm. All of these four absorption curves are plotted in Figure 4–23. Obviously the high degree of precision exhibited by our ability to discriminate between wavelengths only a few nanometers apart is not due to the tuning of the receptors.

A similar argument can be made for acoustic nerve neurons and higher order neurons of the auditory system. The auditory tuning curves shown in Figure 4–4 also display very broad ranges of sensitivity. Curves such as these indicate that the basilar membrane is activated broadly by a given frequency of stimulation. In the chemical senses, the dimension of variation of quality—different chemical structures—is not so precisely measured, but clearly sensitivity on the part of each neuron to a wide range of chemicals is also the rule.

The impact of broad tuning is most clearly evident in the visual sense. The photopic and scotopic curves are psychological functions that indicate the threshold to light in both light and dark adapted conditions, respectively. These curves are plotted in Figure 4–30. The breadth of these psychophysical functions attests to the breadth of the receptor tuning curve.

relational coding

Another general principle of the encoding of quality emerges from the fact that, in spite of these broadly tuned curves, our ability to discriminate among different stimulus qualities is very precise. How can this be? The answer to this query is that it is not the *absolute* amount of neural activity in any of the visual or acoustic channels that is significant in determining perceived quality, but rather it is the *relative* amount of activity among the various systems of neurons. Thus, the experience of "red" is not produced by the absolute amount of activation of any single broadly tuned wavelength sensitive system, but rather by some kind of comparison of the amounts of activity in the three different cone systems. The response of the individual system is indeterminable. The reason for this indeterminacy, of course, is that the response of the long wavelength system could be caused either by very intense "white" light with distributed energies or by a red appearing light in which all of the stimulus energy was concentrated in the region of that system's greatest sensitivity. The only way to tell the difference between the two stimulus conditions is to have information concerning what the other two channels—the medium and short wavelength sensi-

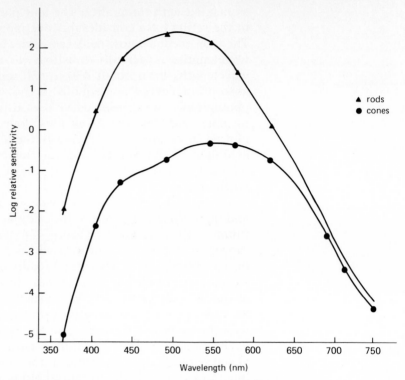

Figure 4–30 The photopic and scotopic visual sensitivity curves.

tive system—are doing concurrently. Figure 4–31 shows a coding scheme for visual stimulus quality based on such a relational scheme.

The same argument holds for the auditory system. Individual neurons are so broadly tuned that it is not possible to tell what kind of stimulus each is responding to without knowing what others are doing. The only difference in this case is that the auditory system does not have three sets of nearly identical cone receptors, but a much larger family of broadly tuned acoustic energy detectors whose spectral sensitivities are scattered across the auditory spectrum. In either case, however, the nervous system is incapable of determining what the quality of a stimulus is from a single receptor—that kind of information can only be encoded by a comparison process. We should also note in reference to the auditory system that auditory nerve fibers, each of which is connected to broad regions of the cochlea, are actually responding to the levels of activity at various places. Recall that there has been a preneural distribution of the temporal patterns of acoustic energy across the spatial extent of the cochlea.

Response In

	R	G	B
Saturated Red	+++	+	
Unsaturated Pink	++	++	+
Saturated Green	+	+++	+
Unsaturated Green	++	++	++
Saturated Blue		+	+++
Unsaturated Blue	+	++	++

Figure 4–31 A plausible coding scheme for visual quality based upon relations among the responses of the three types of color responses. Increasing numbers of plus signs indicate increasing response activity.

Abundant evidence also exists in the chemical senses for the same kind of relational coding of quality. Figure 4–32, for example, shows the pattern of responses of nine chorda tympani (gustatory) nerve cells in the rat when five different chemicals are used as stimuli. Clearly there are differences in the pattern of response; nevertheless there are many cells that respond to several chemicals. No one cell, therefore, can adequately repre-

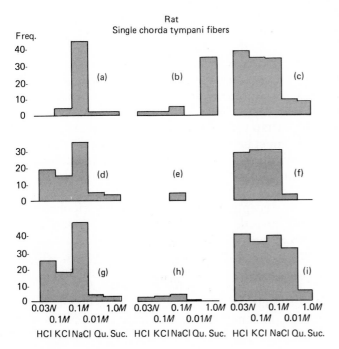

Figure 4–32 The pattern of responses of nine chorda tympani cells in the rats tongues to five different chemical stimuli. (Redrawn from Pfaffmann, C., *Journal of Neurophysiology*, 1955, 18:429–440.) The baseline gives the molar concentration of the chemical stimuli: Hydrochloric acid (HCl), potassium chloride (KCl), sodium chloride (NaCl), quinine (Qu.) and Sucrose (Su.).

sent information about the quality of the tasty material. Comparisons among the various receptors are required to determine the nature of the stimulus.

The coding of the quality of visible color involves analogous principles. Note in this connection that the trichromatic (three system) coding system of the cones, however, is not the only coding language used by the visual pathways to represent color. Even at the second neuron—the bipolar cell—there is a considerable change in the coding scheme. At the bipolar level, the language is still *trivariant* (that is, it still depends on the relations among three types of neurons); however, the code is no longer the same as that used in the receptors. Rather than having three types of cones, which are dormant in the absence of a stimulus and activated to some variable degree by a stimulus, the bipolar system is made up of two or more opponent-type neurons and one or more neurons that act as an overall luminance encoder. An *opponent neuron* is one in which there is a substantial amount of spontaneous activity and the typical pattern of response of such a cell is to increase the level of spontaneous activity when certain kinds of stimuli occur and decrease it when other kinds occur. The net result is a balanced response, sometimes increasing and sometimes decreasing, depending upon the *quality* of the incoming stimulus. A wide variety of neurons use opponent codes; not only bipolars but also many neurons of the lateral geniculate nucleus of the thalamus and even the visual cortex. For example, Figure 4–33 shows a sampling of the different kinds of opponent cell responses that occur in the lateral geniculate body.

opponent-process cells

It is important to remember that no single opponent cell can any more uniquely define a stimulus wavelength than can a single trichromatic type cone. Therefore, it is equally as necessary to possess a comparative or *relational* system for wavelength encoding here as it is in the receptors. Quality within a modality, whatever the level of the nervous system and whatever the code, must be represented by the relative amounts of activity in many different neurons. This is the most general law of quality coding and is true, as far as we can tell, for all of the senses.

The trichromatic receptors and the opponent bipolar and higher level cells just described each represent the same message—the wavelength of the incident stimulus. Each does so, however, with a different coding scheme—that is, with a different neural language. This is another example of the multiplicity of languages used by different levels of the sensory nervous system. Though different, each of these languages is bound by the common constraint of requiring a comparison of

Figure 4–33 Several alternative kinds of opponent type responses in visual cells of the lateral geniculate body. (Redrawn from Devalois, R.L., Abramov, I., and Jacobs, G.H., *Journal of the Optical Society of America,* 1966, *56,* 966–977).

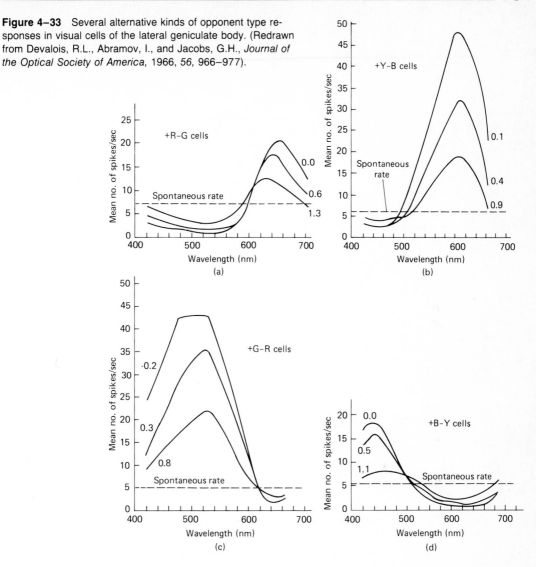

the outputs of multiple channels to represent information regarding quality.

Whatever the code is at any level, it does tend to modify the afferent signal in ways that can be detected in human psychophysical experiments. Each code at each level introduces into color perception some trace of its own properties and characteristics. For example, the fact that we have three cones is detectable in the trivariant nature of all subsequent codes and by the fact that any color may be matched by a mixture of any other three wavelengths (under certain restrictions that are not developed here). The point is, in the current context, that it

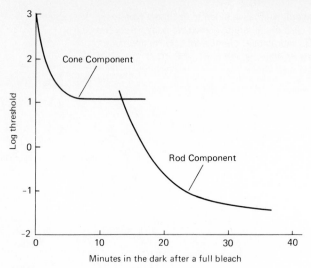

Figure 4–34 The dark adaptation curve.

takes three lights not two or four, in the normal eye to match any other color. This aspect of our psychological response is largely explained in terms of the chemistry of the three-cone photosensitive substances and the resulting trichromacy of the visual system.

Similarly, after the same information is represented in the opponent codes used by higher levels of the visual system, a trace of that opponent coding scheme can also be found if other types of psychological visual experiments are carried out. The existence of complementary colors and the fact that the subjective reddishness of a light can be counterbalanced by mixing it with an appropriate proportion of a light that appears green (and vice versa) are also examples of the persistent influence of the coding scheme.

It is also possible to obtain psychophysical functions reflecting the fact that there are four kinds of photoreceptors in the retina—three cones and one rod. The dark adaptation curve, if measured in a region of the retina in which both cones and rods are present, exhibits a two-limbed form. This is entirely accounted for by the fact that cones adapt to the dark more quickly than do rods, but not to as sensitive a level as that achieved by the rods. This is illustrated in Figure 4–34.

Quantity Coding

psychophysical laws

The encoding of the magnitude of a stimulus is characterized in most sensory systems by neural response functions that are *compressed*. That is, the function relating stimulus amplitude

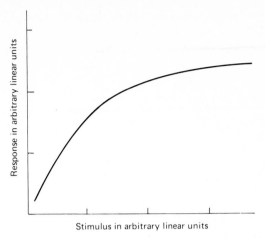

Figure 4–35 A typical compressed response curve showing the diminishing change in response amplitude as stimulus strength increases.

Response in arbitrary linear units

Stimulus in arbitrary linear units

and neural response frequency or amplitude (among many other possible coding dimensions) is, negatively accelerated. Thus it takes a far larger change in the stimulus to produce a given change in the neural coding dimension when the stimulus is strong than when it is weak. A typical compressed function is plotted in Figure 4–35. This compressed coding function is the neural analog of the psychophysical *Weber's law*, asserting that the just noticeable difference along any stimulus dimension is proportional to the absolute value of the stimulus.

$$\Delta I/I = C \qquad \text{(Equation 4–1)}$$

It is likely that the physiological fact of compression in the neural dimension is the cause of psychological fact expressed by Weber's law. Another important relation—the Weber–Fechner law—speaks not to the size of the just noticeable difference but rather describes the suprathreshold amplitude of the psychological experience. The Weber-Fechner law is formulated in the following manner

$$\psi = K \log_{10}I \qquad \text{(Equation 4–2)}$$

where ψ is the magnitude of the psychological experience, K is a constant of proportionality, I is the intensity of the stimulus producing that experience, and I_0 is the threshold stimulus amplitude.

Though there has been considerable debate over the exactness of this representation of psychophysical magnitude, and many discrepancies between it and empirical data are known to exist, there is no question that compression of the neural response occurs ubiquitously in the sensory system. That it does so is a highly adaptive and useful outcome. Response compression allows us to expand the intensity range over which our sense organs can function while at the same time maintaining high sensitivity at low stimulus levels. When one considers that the threshold of hearing, as one example, may be a trillion times less than the loudest sound we can tolerate, the advantages of compression become immediately obvious. It allows us to be sensitive to very tiny changes, when stimuli are small, while at the same time to tolerate (without response saturation) very high level stimuli. (Saturation is a condition in which a medium level stimulus produces a maximal response thus precluding further discrimination.)

One alternative formulation of response compression is Stevens' power law. While the Weber–Fechner relation allows us to represent only compressed functions, the power law

$$\psi = K (I - I_0)^n \qquad \text{(Equation 4–3)}$$

allows a much wider range of response types. In this expression all of the symbols mean the same thing they did in Equation 4–2 but we have one added factor—n—the exponential power to which the difference is raised. The advantage of the Stevens' power law is that n can vary over a wide range of values. If this exponent is less than 1, the function represented is compressed as it was with the logarithmic Weber–Fechner function. If n is equal to 1, on the other hand, the function is linear. Finally, if the exponent is greater than 1, the function exhibits an expansion rather than a compression of the range. Expansion has just the opposite effect of compression. It tends to constrain the range over which the sensory system may work. Medium level stimuli produce responses that are inordinately large and the mechanism quickly saturates: further increase in the stimulus has no effect or may produce one of the results of overstimulation—pain.

The empirical facts of the matter are that some psychological relations between stimulus intensity and subjective magnitudes are not compressed, but are quite expanded. Indeed, to offer one unpleasant example, electrical stimuli applied to the teeth, the exponent of the power function relating stimulus intensity and subjective magnitude can be as high as 7.0. This essentially means that every small increase in the stimulus above the threshold level produces an inordinately large difference in sensation. If the threshold is one milliampere, for example, adding an additional milliampere to the stimulus may increase the psychological experience a hundredfold. This is known as the "ouch" response! Table 4–2 lists some of the exponents that have been found for various sensory dimensions.

TABLE 4–2 The Power Function Exponents That Have Been Obtained for Various Sensory Modalities

Exponent	Paradigm
0.33	Brightness of 5° target in dark (continuous)
0.5	Brightness of brief flash
0.6	Smell of heptane
0.6	Vibration of 250 Hz on finger
0.67	Loudness of 3000-Hz tone
0.7	Visual area
0.8	Factual hardness
0.95	Vibrations of 60 Hz on finger
1.0	Temperature
1.0	Visual length
1.1	Duration of white noise stimulus
1.1	Pressure on palm
1.1	Vocal sound pressure
1.3	Thickness of blocks
1.3	Taste of sucrose
1.4	Taste of salt
1.45	Lifted weights
1.5	Temperature (warmth on arm)
1.5	Tactual roughness
1.7	Handgrip
2.0	Electric stimulus in hearing
3.5	Electric stimulus to skin
7.0	Electric stimulus applied to teeth

Source: Adapted from S. S. Stevens, in Lowenstein (ed.), *Principles of Receptor Physiology*, Springer-Verlag, 1971.

stimulus compression

In spite of this wide range of psychological expanded functions, it is, however, also a fact that the relationship between the neural response and the stimulus intensity is almost always compressed (that is, their exponents are usually less than 1.0 over most of their range). A variety of experiments has shown that the coded neural response dimensions, whatever it is that is encoding quantity, is, typically, compressed in the way shown in Figure 4–35. Somatosensory neurons display compression equal to an exponent of 0.52 in the Steven's power law formula; kinesthetic neurons display a compression exponent equal to 0.42; vertebrate visual receptors potentials have exponents of about 0.6; invertebrate visual receptors about 0.3; the olfactory receptor potentials about 0.4; and the integrated responses from the gustatory nerves of the tongue typically about 0.6. All of these neural functions, and presumably many others that might be examined, are, therefore, highly compressed.

Now to conclude this discussion, note that in all of the cases discussed so far we have examined the relationship between the stimulus and some aspect of the neural response. In doing so we have briefly mentioned some of the neural codes that may be used to represent intensity—for example, the amplitude of the generator potential, the integrated response of an entire population of neurons, the frequency of the spike action potential firing, and so on. But this list is incomplete; there are obviously other candidate codes that also vary concomitantly with variations in the stimulus intensity including, for example, the spread of the response or the regularity of the intervals between sequential spike action potentials. And certainly there must be others even more subtle that will someday be shown by neurophysiological research to covary with stimulus intensity. Whatever these new dimensions turn out to be, we can be sure that they will be compressed; virtually all codes for intensity that have been examined so far are, and there is little reason to expect any surprises in this regard given its high adaptive utility.

One final question concerning response compression should be considered before we move on to other common stimulus dimensions. That is, "Where in the nervous system does compression occur?" We have already had a clue to the answer. Recall that electrical stimulation produced unusually high exponents when it was used as a stimulus. We know that

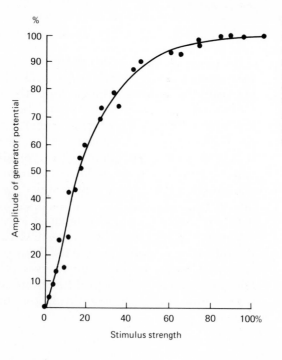

Figure 4–36 A typical response curve for a somatosensory receptor as the stimulus strength is increased. (Redrawn from Loewenstein, W.R., *Annals of the New York Academy of Science*, 1961, 94:547–591.)

electrical stimuli have the property of activating neurons directly and bypassing the usual transduction mechanisms located in the receptors. In general, neurophysiologists find that when electricity is used to excite neurons, there is a tendency to find higher exponents for the power law representation of the induced neural responses. Many experiments have shown the response of somatosensory neurons to electrical stimuli. The range is very narrow; the slope (exponent) is high; only a few milliamperes are necessary to go from the very smallest response to the maximum possible. The conclusion to be drawn from such findings (and others not discussed in detail here) is that the mechanism responsible for response compression is the transduction process itself; *compression,* in other words, is a function of the receptor. No further mechanism beyond the receptor needs to be invoked to explain virtually all compression of the stimulus range. Of course, there are other higher-level influences on subjective magnitudes—the ultimate psychological response—but the trace of the *receptor-induced compression* throughout the entire afferent pathway is persistent.

Spatio-temporal Coding

It is in the area of spatio-temporal coding that the greatest and most exciting advances have been made in recent years in sensory psychobiology. The major discovery occurred in 1959 when it was shown that the most effective stimuli to activate many sensory neurons are those that possess a specific patterning in time and space. Prior to that time it had been implicitly accepted by sensory coding theorists that the response of a neuron was dependent simply upon the intensity of the stimulus which impinged on it. In 1959 two experiments were carried out, one by a group at MIT (Lettvin, Maturana, McCollough, and Pitts) and one at Harvard by Hubel and Wiesel, in which it was shown that in fact the total amount of light falling on visual receptors was *not* the most significant variable in determining the neural response. Rather the *pattern* of that light in time and space was most important; the stimulus had to be shaped in a certain way and had to move, enlarge, or shift in a certain direction before a neuron would respond to its presence. Otherwise, even if it were very strong, it might be totally ineffective in eliciting a neural response.

To make this point clearer let's consider some of the early studies by David Hubel and Thorsten Wiesel. They inserted a tungsten microelectrode into the visual cortex of a cat. Thorstein Wiesel discovered almost immediately that most of these cortical neurons were insensitive to large diffuse light stimuli even when the intensity of that light was fairly high. Many neurons in the visual cortex were also insensitive to simple darkening and brightening of the whole field. Since these cells were in what was known to be visual cortex and presumably had something to do with vision, Hubel and Wiesel ingeniously decided to try a large number of variously shaped stimuli to determine if any of the cortical neurons responded to anything at all. This time the results were quite surprising. If a slit- or line-shaped stimulus was presented in the visual field of the cat, certain neurons in the brain responded strongly to these patterns. However, the line had to be aligned in a specific direction, as shown in Figure 4–37 to be effective. If the slit were not aligned in the critical direction, then the magnitude of the response of that particular neuron (measured in the number of evoked spike action potentials) diminished sharply. An orientation change of as little as 10–20 degrees was sufficient in some cases to inactivate the neuron totally. The rotated line stimulus then might maximally activate some other neuron, of course, but as far as the first one was concerned, it "saw" nothing. The simple and dramatic fact discovered by Hubel and Wiesel is that even though the amount of light falling on the retina may be exactly the same for all orientations of a line, each particular neuron can respond only to a very particular orientation of that line. Essentially, this finding says that shape is being represented in the afferent signal by a place code; the various shapes of the stimulus are being encoded by neurons located in different places.

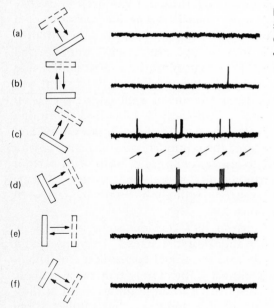

Figure 4–37 A demonstration of the selective sensitivity of a simple cortical cell to line orientation and direction. (Redrawn from Hubel, D.N., and Wiesel, T., *Journal of Physiology*, 1959, 148:574–591.)

Before we discuss some of the further outcomes of Hubel and Wiesel's research, it is very important to point out that what we are talking about here is the *transmission code.* We are not talking about perception or pattern recognition, but only about the way in which information about shape is conveyed to the central nervous system where, most probably, much more complex systems of neurons mediate more complicated psychological processes. It has been a fad for some years in sensory coding research to assume that because we have identified a neuron that is capable of encoding some aspect of shape, we have also learned something about pattern or shape recognition. That is definitely not the case. Hubel and Wiesel's discoveries (as David Hubel himself has so strongly asserted) do nothing more than tell us information is transmitted to the central nervous system; they do not tell us how we perceive, recognize, interpret that information, or imply that that afferent flow of information is equivalent in some way to the percept.

With this caveat in mind, we can return to the discussion of the nature of the transmission codes for space and time. Hubel and Wiesel found that there were several different kinds of visual cortical cells, each of which displayed a specific kind of pattern sensitivity. Neurons that are sensitive to oriented lines or shapes came in several different types. *Simple cells* were sensitive to a particular line orientation, but the line has to occur in a specific portion of the receptive field of the neuron. (The *receptive field* of a neuron is defined as the extent of the external world in which a stimulus may be placed and effectively evoke a response in that neuron.) *Complex cells* also respond to oriented lines, but the line can be placed anywhere in the receptive field of this type of neuron and still evoke a response. The response of a complex cell was enhanced if the line moved in a direction perpendicular to its orientation. Hubel and Wiesel also discovered certain neurons they classified as *hypercomplex cells* that seemed to be especially sensitive to edges, corners, or angles, stimulus features that terminate within the cell's receptive field.

simple and complex cells

It must also be appreciated that these cell types differ from species to species and from level to level even within the same animal. The critical spatiotemporal factors that best affect the response of the retinal ganglion cells of a cat, for example, are quite different from those that affect the neurons of this same animal's visual cortex. In the cat's retina (as well as in the lateral geniculate body of the thalamus) stationary round spots of light falling in the very center of the receptive field are much more effective than lines or even slightly larger spots. The reason for this is that the receptive field of this portion of the cat's visual system is bipartite. The inner part is usually excitatory; a response placed in that part of a neuron's receptive field activates the neuron. However, this central region is surrounded by a ring-shaped portion of the receptive field that may be inhibitory; here stimuli reduce the response of that cell. This arrangement is shown in Figure 4–38, (along with a possible opposite arrangement, an inhibitory center and an excitatory surround). In the cat, movement does not add appreciably to the response in this type of cell. On the other hand, there are ganglion cells in the rabbit retina discovered by Barlow, Hill, and Levick that are exquisitely sensitive to the direction of movement of a spot of light.

We can speculate that beyond the primary visual cortex in which Hubel and Wiesel worked, the spatiotemporal sensitivities of individual neurons are far more complex than even the hypercomplex cells just described. Scattered reports of cells uniquely sensitive to such curious spatial patterns as the shape of the paw of the experimental animal itself have filtered into the general literature of sensory psychobiology. It seems far more likely that the specific spatiotemporal sensitivities of visual neurons grow ever more fuzzy as one pushes further into the nervous system. More and more symbolic aspects of the stimulus are encoded as the immediate stimulus interacts with other previously stored neuronal information.

It should also not be assumed that visual neurons are sensitive only to spatiotemporal patterns. As we have already discussed, there are other dimensions of the visual response that the organism also must be able to encode.

Hubel and Wiesel have emphasized another basic principle of neural representation. In their studies they noted that many of

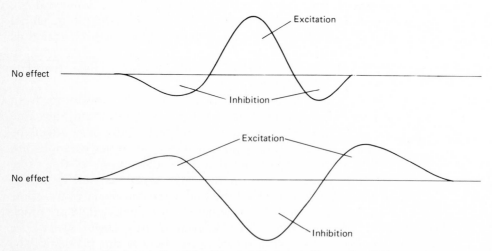

Figure 4–38 The "Mexican hat" and the "inverted Mexican hat" receptive field arrangement.

the neurons that are activated by both eyes were also selectively sensitive to the eye from which the stimulus was coming. Neurons of this type are said to be exhibiting *ocular dominance*. This process is quite likely to have something to do with the transmission of the signals necessary to produce stereoscopic vision. Thus, many different types of neurons encoding many different dimensions of the stimulus must simultaneously be working to signal the nature of our environment.

All of these observations notwithstanding, the important general principle is that our nervous system encodes many different dimensions of the stimulus with many different codes. But these codes *are not* perceptions, they are merely representations of the stimulus world that initially led to the activity in these neurons. We simply do not yet know, and perhaps may never know (if the system turns out to be too complicated for analysis) how these neural codes are transmuted into the stuff of conscious awareness.

In this section we have emphasized vision for a simple reason—much more is known of visual coding than of any of the other senses. However, it seems likely that many of the principles that have been discussed here must also hold for all modalities. Evidence is already accumulating concerning temporal pattern (and because of the action of the cochlea, this certainly must mean spatiotemporal pattern) detectors in the auditory system. Our olfactory and gustatory receptors are not as efficient in handling spatial patterns, but certainly what is now known about the skin suggests that many of the same principles of coding that hold for vision also hold there.

Pain

Having now discussed the usual sensory channels, we are faced with a problem of quite a different nature. When dealing with vision, hearing, or even smell it is possible to specify the nature of the stimuli that led to the particular coded responses. For many reasons the study of pain is much more difficult to conceptualize. One reason is that it is not entirely clear what particular antecedent stimulus conditions are required for pain. Any stimulus may evoke painful consequences if intense enough, and sometimes quite moderate stimuli will produce intense pain. Another reason is that pain is more heavily modulated by the psychological state of the person than are the other sensory mechanisms. We have all heard stories of instances in which pain seems to have been completely overcome under the stress of the moment. Another impediment to understanding pain is that its definition is still elusive. Perhaps the best way to define pain is to say it is a complex of experiences produced by stimuli that, at least, have the potential of causing tissue damage. Inflammatory conditions, trauma, and certain chemicals all lead to the withdrawal responses that lead us to infer that others are experiencing the unpleasant sensation we feel when we behave similarly.

It is interesting that not all parts of the body are capable of generating pain. The brain can be cut and slashed without any pain and muscle tissue is also relatively insensitive to the insertion of needles or the cut of a scalpel. The tissues that do respond strongly when stimulated with noxious stimuli are those that lie at the interface between some part of the body and some part of the external or internal environment. The skin, the capsules of the internal organs, blood vessels, and the pericardium are sites at which even moderate stimulation can lead to excruciating pain.

For sound ethical reasons we have very little data concerning the neural coding of pain stimuli in either animals or human beings. The arguments against inflicting pain on animals purely for the sake of studying pain are formidable. For these reasons we have very little in the way of empirically based theories of pain.

Some rather speculative theories exist, however. For example, it has been suggested that pain is represented by what is essentially a very high frequency of virtually random bursts of action potentials in the same fibers that encode touch or heat with regular bursts of activity. The proposed code here is that of *temporal pattern*. Others have proposed that pain is represented

pattern and place theories by what is essentially a *place code*. The theory is based on the proposition that the smaller fibers in the afferent somatosensory nerve carry pain, whereas the larger fibers carry touch and pressure sensations. It has been long known that a remedy for reducing pain is to rub the skin or massage the body. The *place code* theory developed by Melzack and Wall suggest, therefore, that the large fibers conveying touch and pressure signals act to inhibit pain signals carried by smaller fibers. Presumably a nucleus in the spinal cord (the *substantia gelatinosa*) is the source of these inhibitory signals. Both large fiber signals and small fiber signals enter the substantia gelatinosa, but the small pain conducting neurons are connected within it in an inhibitory fashion, while the large pressure signals excite this nucleus. The only output from the substantia gelatinosa, according to this theory, is an inhibitory signal that inhibits other small fiber pain signals. Figure 4–39 diagrams this theory of pain.

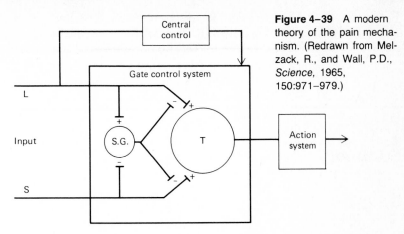

Figure 4–39 A modern theory of the pain mechanism. (Redrawn from Melzack, R., and Wall, P.D., *Science*, 1965, 150:971–979.)

Clearly this theory is incomplete, and there has been substantial criticism of it on both physiological and conceptual grounds. However, no more plausible alternative has been proposed. Whatever the physiological facts, this theory does incorporate much of the known physiology and phenomenology concerning the interaction of touch and pain. Melzack and Wall also refer in their theory to some central feedback signals that, to at least a partial degree, modulate the pain experience. This is also in accord with the obvious fact that pain is closely associated with the psychological state of the situation in which a person may be.

chemical theories

Neurophysiological place or temporal pattern theories of pain, however, are not the only approaches to the problem. Others have suggested that pain is the specific response to particular substances which are released when tissue is damaged. Many different chemicals have been proposed to fill this role including histamines, intracellular potassium, and *kinin* (a polypeptide that is particularly effective in dilating blood vessels). However, these chemical theories only beg the question for even if chemicals were required in the area of tissue damage, one would have to account for the transmission of information specifically signaling their presence to the brain. That would leave us exactly where we were when we explored the applicability of the spatiotemporal pattern theories to the solution of the difficult problem posed by pain.

Pain is exceedingly important in maintaining the physiological integrity of the body. Unfortunately, pain can sometimes be inadvertently evoked when the danger of tissue damage is not actually present. The stumps of amputated limbs can be painful, in fact the pain can be referred to the nonexistent limb. *Phantom*

phantom limb

limb pain does not confirm or deny any particular theory of

pain; mainly it tells us that pain is no more (and no less!) mysterious than any other sensation. It is produced by stimuli, it is conveyed by neural signals; it is perceived. Unfortunately, we do not yet know what the code is that allows the brain to distinguish between a painful stimulus and an innocuous one.

Summary

In this chapter we briefly surveyed a wide range of topics and problems concerning the psychobiology of sensory processes. To say that we have only touched the surface of this field would be a gross understatement. One has only to look at the thirty or so volumes of the *Handbook of Sensory Physiology* to appreciate the enormous amount of empirical knowledge that is available in this field. The examples we presented in this chapter are only a small portion of this enormous data base. To sum up this chapter we may note that it is clear that there are certain principles that can be discerned in the data at the present time.

First, it must be appreciated that the simplicity and stimulus anchor of the sensory mechanisms are both an advantage and a disadvantage. Simplicity makes it possible to understand these peripheral mechanisms, but keeps us from generalizing findings obtained here to more complicated psychoneural mechanisms deeper in the nervous system. The reader must appreciate that we have been considering only the *neural* mechanisms of transmission of information from the periphery to the central nervous system. Nothing we have said in this chapter pertains to the problem of imagery, visual thinking, pattern perception, or any of the other higher level processes that involve the central interpretation of that information.

What we have learned is something about the transmission codes and the way in which they function. Codes are generated initially by *transduction mechanisms* that seem to universally involve the alteration of neuronal membrane permeability by means of protein channels—large molecules that penetrate the membrane. For each of the senses there is a primary sensory action—the final physical action of the stimulus. For any of the senses, the primary sensory action acts directly on these protein molecules to alter membrane permeability and thus initiate the neural signal.

From the point of transduction onward, information is represented in electrochemical energies. Certain dimensions of the stimulus are represented by certain neural codes, but there is no need for any particular dimension to be used rather than any other. Any code can represent any stimulus dimension. However, there are certain general principles that do seem operative throughout all sensations. Quality is universally encoded by comparative or relational codes. Several broadly tuned receptor systems act simultaneously to represent quality in any modality; all of the receptors are broadly tuned and respond to broad ranges of the stimulus quality dimension, whatever it is.

Stimulus intensity, on the other hand, seems to be nearly universally compressed when processed through the normal receptors—the function relating intensity and neural response is virtually always negatively accelerated. This acts to expand the intensity range over which the sense can work. This compression seems to be a result of receptor function more than any other part of the nervous system.

We also see the close linkage between space and time in sensory codes. Certain neurons in certain places respond best to particular spatiotemporal patterns. In many kinds of neurons, neither a particular shape nor a particular temporal pattern is, by itself, capable of eliciting responses.

Pain remains an elusive phenomenon and we have little solid information about the codes used to transmit information about potentially tissue damaging stimuli to the central nervous system. Obviously there is still much to be learned about the neural coding of noxious environmental stimuli.

In conclusion, we are just barely beginning to understand the peripheral mechanisms of sensation. Perhaps at some time in the future we will also begin to understand the much more difficult issue of how neural codes are transformed into psychological experience.

Suggested Readings

Sensory Psychobiology—General
1. W.R. Uttal, *The Psychobiology of Sensory Coding*, Harper & Row, New York, 1973.
2. J.L. Brown, *Sensory Systems*, Reprinted from the 9th edition of Best & Taylor's *Physiological Basis of Medical Practice*, Williams & Wilkins, Baltimore, 1973.
3. W.R. Uttal (ed.), *Sensory Coding: Selected Readings*, Little Brown, Boston, 1972.
4. F.A. Geldad, *The Human Senses* (2d ed.) Wiley, New York, 1972.

Visual Mechanisms and Functions
1. H. Davson (ed.). *The Eye*, vol. 2 (*The Visual Process*), Academic Press, New York, 1962.
2. C.H. Graham, *Vision and Visual Perception*, Wiley, New York, 1965.

3. W.R. Uttal, *A Taxonomy of Visual Processes*, Erlbaum, Hillsdale, NJ, 1981.

Auditory Mechanisms and Functions
1. W. Gulick, *Hearing: Physiology and Psychophysics*, Oxford University Press, New York, 1971.
2. G. von Bekesy, *Experiments in Hearing*, McGraw-Hill, New York, 1960.

Olfactory & Gustatory Mechanisms and Functions
1. C. Pfaffmann (ed.), *Olfaction and Taste*, Proceedings of the Third International Symposium, Rockefeller University Press, New York, 1969.

Pain Mechanisms and Cutaneous Sensitivity
1. R. Melzack and P. Wall, Pain mechanisms: A new theory, *Science*, 1965, *150:* 971–979.
2. B. Libet, W. Alberts, E. Wright, and B. Feinstein, Responses of human somatosensory cortex to stimuli below threshold for conscious experience, *Science*, 1967, *158:* 1597–1600.
3. A. de Reuck and J. Knight (eds.), *Touch, Heat, and Pain*, Little Brown, Boston, 1966.

5   Mechanisms of Behavioral Adjustment

Introduction

Now at about the half-way point in this text, this is a useful place to pause, and take a brief look back and a brief look ahead. Preceding chapters have concentrated on the overall perspective guiding modern psychobiology (Chapter 1), the principal research methods and instruments available to today's investigators (Chapter 2), the anatomy and physiology forming the boundaries of contemporary research (Chapter 3), and the organization of sensory systems and the principles of information-processing characteristic of all the advanced species (Chapter 4). Although the material presented in Chapters 2, 3, and 4 summarizes what is fundamental to psychobiology, it is far more "biological" than "psychological". It provides, however, the necessary foundation on which we may now begin to build the distinctly *psychological* side of psychobiology.

The current chapter examines those physiological processes and mechanisms most directly involved in the patterns of behavior by which animals become adapted to the demands of the external environment. After a brief exploration of *unlearned behavior* (instincts, reflexes, and tropisms), the chapter moves on to that domain of *acquired* and *motivated* behavior in which we find the psychologically most significant modes of adaptation. This review provides the context for Chapter 6 on learning and memory, which attempts to unravel the complex physiological and chemical events that must occur if experience, training, and conditioning are to have lasting effects.

Together Chapters 5 and 6 introduce both a *behavioral psychobiology* and a *psychobiology of memory*. These terms refer

197

to research and theory designed to establish the biological foundations of conditioned responses and related forms of associative learning and memory. *Cognitive* psychobiology goes beyond this and attempts to establish the biological foundations of more complex functions, such as those that involve thought and language. As we shall see, however, (Chapter 8) the facts emerging from behavioral psychobiology are not sufficient to account for the genuinely cognitive, linguistic, and symbolic processes typical of human mental life. Nor are they sufficient to explain those emotional and social factors that stand at the very foundation of what is called *personality* (Chapter 7).

These latter properties of human psychology call for special methods of investigation and for rather unique theoretical analyses. Accordingly, separate chapters have been reserved for *emotion, personality, and psychopathology* (Chapter 7) and for *consciousness, language, and thought* (Chapter 8). As will become clear, these topics do not exist in total isolation from the balance of psychobiology. Thought, for example, is thought *about something* and, if only to this extent, the psychobiology of learning and memory must be included in any general account of cognition. The same is the case with personality, consciousness, language, emotion and related psychological processes and states. These terms, after all, are only words we use to refer to the feelings, actions, and deliberations of ourselves and others. The events and states to which these words refer are all occurring within the same person and all involve the same nervous system which, itself, is governed by the same principles no matter how varied the psychological states may be. Therefore, although the division of such topics is necessary for purposes of study and discussion, we must not jump to the conclusion that the same division takes place within the nervous system. The emotional patient is also a patient with memories, motives, thoughts, and the like. The person engaged in linguistic communication—conversation, for example—is not only totally "cognitive" but also, at the same time, is emotional, motivated and conscious. The reader must be mindful, then, that the topical divisions are tools of convenience and not the mirror of reality.

This chapter's title intimates a somewhat neutral position on a range of issues that still create difficulties for psychologists and biologists. From the perspective of psychobiology the ultimate fate of behavioristic or cognitive or (even) humanistic theories is not of central concern. As we noted in the first chapter, the psychobiologist takes for granted that the achievements and experiences of any organism are made possible by the nervous system and can be explained in terms of its functions. Thus, whether a given sample of behavior is interpreted as being *learned* as opposed to *instinctive*, or as the outcome of some form of mental operation as opposed to a purely associative one is not something that must be settled by psychobiology. Instead, the psychobiologist seeks to determine those necessary and sufficient conditions of the nervous system for the behavior in question to be produced or for the experiences in question to be reported. What is clear, however, is that animals do make *adjustments* in their behavior and that these adjustments often have consequences of significance to the animal, to its species, or to both. Some of these adjustments are reliably engaged by specific stimuli impinging on specific receptors. Other adjustments are not as reliably tied to a specific stimulus, nor are they dependent on the specific receptors stimulated. Still other adjustments seem to depend not on the physical but on the symbolic properties of stimuli, and the adjustments themselves require what, at the level of human discourse, we would call problem-solving. The aim of this chapter is to examine the relationships among adjustments like these and the associated events in the nervous system. But before turning to the facts and their implications, it will be useful to raise some general warnings regarding interpretation and currently fashionable hypotheses.

Heredity, "Sociobiology," and the Taxonomy of Adjustment

The digger wasp engages in an elaborate series of activities essential to the survival of its offspring. Not only is a nest built but it is furnished with dead insects, killed by the mother wasp, and located in such a manner as to prevent poaching. The mother robin also builds a nest, returns daily with worms for the young and, at the appropriate time, evicts the young from the nest. Human parents return home with food and clothing for their offspring.

Since remote antiquity people have reported on the number of actions performed by nonhumans which serve functions quite similar to those served by the intentional actions of human beings. Long before Charles Darwin wrote his influential books there was already general agreement among scientists that the entire so-called animal economy was governed by general principles leading to the survival of species. Indeed, the idea of *progress through competition* was quite popular in the eighteenth century when *laizzez-faire* theories of the market were avidly endorsed. Evolutionary theory was not necessary to alert us all to what is finally no more than a truism: Scarce resources lead to competition and only the successful competitor survives.

But neither this truism nor the monumental contribution of Darwin permits us to arrive at a sound and an unarguable position on what can be said of the digger wasp, the robin, and the human parents. If we begin from the psychobiologist's perspective, we must conclude that the activities in question are of a radically different sort because of the profound differences among insect, avian, and human nervous systems. Thus, from the mere fact that the behaviors in question all lead to the survival of offspring we could not conclude either that they are served by the same mechanisms (for they are not) or organized around the same considerations. It is in just this respect that we discover, perhaps surprisingly, a certain incompatibility between psychobiology and sociobiology. All too common in the sociobiological literature is the implication that similar effects entail similar causal agencies. Note that a door can be kept closed by a magnet, by a person on the other side, by a lock, or by an iron bar. The physical principles bringing about the same result can be and in this case are quite different. The monkey emits bursts of vocalization which *to us* may seem like a kind of laughter just as it can control its facial muscles in a manner that appears similar to a smile, a frown, or a look of amazement. But the monkey is a member of a species different from our own; its genetic endowment comes from a different gene pool; its brain is different. Thus it is perilous to treat similar behaviors as proceeding from similar processes or as governed by similar principles or as having similar functions—let alone as arising from similar motives or feelings. A hand can be raised by a pin prick or in order to ask a question. On the purely *efferent* side these two events may be indistinguishable. From this fact we are forced to conclude that even identical motor events can be brought about by radically different antecedents.

anthropomorphism

Students of comparative psychology are taught early to avoid the temptation of *anthropomorphism*, the "ism" which imputes human motives and emotions to any animal whose behavior somehow "looks" like ours in situations in which *we* would be motivated or emotional. But there is also a kind of *reverse anthropomorphism* by which we impute to human beings only the motives or emotions of nonhumans. On this view, we are to understand warfare as a "territorial imperative"—such as that displayed by fighting fish—and acts of human kindness as the altruism displayed by birds who emit warning calls even at their own peril. The conceptual problems connected with interpretations of this sort are deep and numerous and go beyond the objectives of this chapter and this book. They are rooted in the very meaning of the words we use to establish the alleged comparability between human and nonhuman processes. Words like "fighting", "warning", and "altruism" have meaning only when tied to motives and intentions of a particular type. That natural selection would favor a species of bird whose members make characteristic sounds in the presence of a predator—even though the vocalizing member is thereupon caught by the predator—is a plausible deduction from the central premise of the theory of evolution. But neither logic nor science will permit us to move from an instance of this sort to one in which a parent says to a child, "I warn you, if you do not attend to your studies now you will have great difficulty later on."

This brings us to the matter of heredity and the range of characteristics that can be passed from one generation to the next. When Darwin wrote, Mendel's genetic theory was unavailable and so it is not surprising that early forms of evolutionary biology were utterly naive on the question of hereditary transmission. Darwin himself, as with most of his contemporaries, tended to adopt the theory developed by Lamarck according to which the thoroughly ingrained but acquired *habits* of the parent stock were passed on to the offspring.

Mendelian inheritance

We now know that the hereditary mechanisms are governed by the molecular biology of individual and independent *genes* and that these genes are responsible for the production of specific proteins. The genetic equipment of the individual organism is its *genotype* which is derived from the parental genotypes. According to Mendel's First Law (the *Law of Independent Segregation*), the genes passed on by the parental strain are passed on independently. The physical characteristics controlled by these genes are called the *phenotype* and, although a given phenotype may disappear in one generation, it can be recovered in the next. In Figure 5–1 we have the crossing of a *pure yellow* and a *pure green* plant yielding four yellow offspring—all yellow because the *y* gene is dominant in the hybrid (yg) strain. Now the offspring are crossed and the next generation displays the (never really lost) green type.

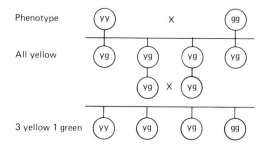

Phenotype				
	(yy) X (gg)			PARENTS
All yellow	(yg) (yg) (yg) (yg)			FIRST FILIAL
	(yg) X (yg)			
3 yellow 1 green	(yy) (yg) (yg) (gg)			SECOND FILIAL

Figure 5–1 A cross of pure yellow with pure green and the resulting first and second filial generations.

At the level of such phenotypes as color, shape, and size the processes of genetic transmission and the manner in which the genes actually regulate the phenotype can be specified. Color, after all, is determined by the kind and amount of a given pigment which itself is manufactured in the cells. But even at this relatively simple level the story becomes quickly complicated by the fact that such pigments can only be made if the necessary ingredients are present. (Without sunlight and nourishment green plants *turn* yellow!) Note, then, the caution that must be exercised in asserting that even the color of a plant is "hereditary." Assertions of this sort must always include the implicit "all other things being equal" qualification. The interaction of genes occurs *on* something and *with* something. The work itself is confined to the regulation of the metabolic physiology of cells. It makes sense, therefore, to say that we inherit our parents' *genes* but not that we inherit our parents' *traits*. Traits or phenotypes are invariably the result of an interaction between genetic and environmental resources.

heritability

The technical term employed as a measure of the degree to which a given phenotype is regulated by genetic factors is *heritability (h^2)*. Heritability can take on values from 0.0 to 1.0 and it is a measure of the fraction of the *total variance* displayed by a population of phenotypes attributable to additive genetic factors. The key term here is *variance* in that it shows that h^2 is a population measure, not a measure of the individual. Technically and quite literally, it makes no sense to ask whether John's blue eyes are "inherited." What we can say is that John's genetic structure established a *reaction range* over which John's physiological processes can function. The color of his eyes will express not only the genetically established reaction range but also his exposure to nutrients, to disease, and to various impediments to normal maturation. Eye color is, in fact, a good case in point. The value of h^2 for eye color in one variety of fruit fly is 1.0. What this means is that all of the *variance* displayed by the eye colors of the fruit flies is attributable to genetic variation. Nevertheless, the *average* eye color displayed by a population of fruit flies with an h^2 value of 1.0 will depend upon the altitude at which the flies develop. It is essential, therefore, to recognize that even when a phenotype displays high *heritability*, the question remains open as to the extent to which the environment might affect its *average* value. If the children of all parents over six feet tall were isolated and exposed to conditions of malnutrition, the *average* height attained by this sample would be less than that attained by properly nourished children of parents of average height; and this notwithstanding the fact that height displays a value of h^2 greater than 0.90.

When all this is taken into consideration we begin to appreciate the arbitrariness of designating certain behavioral adjustments as *learned* and others as *instinctive*. An elephant cannot be taught to fly and a bird needn't be taught. It is quite clear that, all other things being equal, each species enters the world equipped with mechanisms of adaptation and that little more than a nurturing environment is needed for these mechanisms to attain their mature functional status. It is equally clear, however, that no one plays the piano at birth and that no one who has been kept away from music since birth will sit down and play a Bach Fugue on his or her first access to a keyboard. To speak, therefore, of *learned* or of *instinctive* behavior is to speak of patterns of adjustment that are *relatively* dependent on or *relatively* independent of systematic training. With these cautions in mind we can move on to the traditional classification or taxonomy of behavioral adjustments.

Tropisms

The term *tropism* refers to whole-body or nearly whole-body responses to a specific class of stimuli. Thus, in *phototropistic* behavior, such as that displayed by unicellular organisms, the presence of light leads to movement of the entire organism toward (positive phototropism) or away from (negative phototropism) the stimulus. Tropistic behavior is said to be *nonhabituating* in that the response is not weakened by repeated elicitations. It is also said to be *irreversible* in that the organism cannot be trained to respond differently. In many instances the effective stimulus is not the mere presence or absence of a given form of energy but a change in the level of intensity. The unicellular Stentor, for example, is negatively phototropistic in its behavior and will move directly to the darkened half of its small aquarium. If, however, the gradations from light to dark are made continuous, the tropistic response is not emitted and the Stentor displays no preference for one location over another.

Reflexes

The term *reflex* generally refers to reactions by parts of the body (in contrast with the whole body) to specific stimuli. Table 5–1 provides just a small but suggestive number of reflexes to illustrate the range of processes reflexively controlled. The physical properties of a given reflex are highly stereotypical, and display variability only during the course of maturation or in the presence of neurological disturbances and diseases.

TABLE 5–1

Reflex Name	Eliciting Stimulus	Behavioral Adjustment
Labyrinthine-righting reflex	Animal (blindfolded) lifted in the air	Head turns to normal horizontal position
Pupillary light reflex	Light delivered to *either* eye	Equal constriction of *both* pupils
Biceps jerk reflex	Biceps muscle struck with a sudden blow	Flexion of the elbow
Corneal reflex	Light touching of corneal surface	Blinking of *both* eyes
Crossed extensor reflex	Painful stimulus applied to limb	Extension of limb on opposite side

Instincts

Instinctive behavioral adjustments differ from reflexes in that they involve complex and coordinated steps sometimes extending over long periods of time and emitted in an order that changes as the relevant features of the environment change. Whereas the order in which the neural and motor phases of even the most complex reflexes is fixed, instinctive chains of behavior display novel sequences. For example, when the spider's web is destroyed in a particular region, the spider does not create a duplicate of the entire web, but proceeds to the damaged area and repairs it, often with a weave different from that used to spin the remainder of the web. Similarly, nest building birds construct nests out of available resources and will make different nests even with the same materials. The traditional justification for classifying such complex patterns of behavior as *instinctive* (as opposed to *learned* and *intentional*) is that they are emitted by animals reared in isolation and thus unable to learn the behavior from adult members of the species. Moreover, the most carefully studied instinctive behaviors suggest that they are under the control of relatively specific environmental or internal events. The mating responses of the male stickleback fish, for example, can be triggered by any oval-shaped object half of whose surface is painted red. These visual cues are said to activate an *innate releasing mechanism*, which thereupon causes the complex mating response to unfold. Other instinctual patterns of behavior can be utterly disrupted by masking relevant odors, by altering the frequency of relevant sounds, by artificially lengthening or shortening day and night, or by changing the temperature of the surrounding environment. Such effects tend to support the thesis that instinctive behavior is not a sign of goal seeking or truly intentional and planned

innate releasing mechanisms

adjustments, but the unfolding of innately programmed chains triggered by a specific class of stimuli.

Learned Behavior

Any number of characteristics have been set forth to distinguish this type of adjustment from tropisms, reflexes, and instincts. *Learned behavior* is said to involve a *progressive modification of activity* rather than its sudden onset. It is said also to benefit from practice, to be reversible, and to involve truly novel solutions to a given problem. Unlike the other types of behavioral adjustment, learned behavior can be eliminated either by establishing alternatives or by punishing the animal for performing the behavior. Historically the learning process has been described as *associative* and of a *trial-and-error* nature in which past experience is essential. To this extent, then, learning entails memory, since previous experience can benefit only the animal capable of storing and retrieving it (Chapter 6).

Cognition

Modern psychology has yet to make clear and concise distinctions between the sorts of adjustments normally taken to be evidence of *learned behavior* and those that appear to require something more than trial-and-error forms of problem solving. Debates on the subject are interesting and spirited but fall beyond the aims of the present text. At the level of common sense and daily observation, however, it is abundantly clear that human beings organize their behavior around considerations of a *symbolic* nature and that they are not entirely governed by the purely physical attributes of impinging stimuli. The mathematician who knows that in Riemannian geometry parallel lines intersect and triangles contain more than 180° does not go about solving problems in this system of geometry by looking at the size of the numbers or the color of the printed page. And the judge in an equity court, called upon to determine what is *fair* in a given case, must work through a complex argument whose terms are entirely nonperceptual; for example, terms like law, justice, intent, fraud, and so on. To put the matter simply, we can say that a substantial fraction of the behavioral adjustments made by human beings must be understood as the result of cognitive or conceptual processes which are not tied in any direct way to the so-called physics of the situation. The most developed forms of such processes are those we call *language and thought* and these will be examined in Chapter 8. Here we will confine our study of cognition to those behavioral adjustments common among the advanced species and suggestive of processes that go beyond associative trial-and-error learning.

In the taxonomy we have adopted, tropisms and reflexes are surely the least psychological modes of behavioral adjustment, whereas *learned* behavior and *cognition* clearly imply psychological processes. At the level of common sense, learned behavior or, more simply, *learning* is taken to be a form of problem solving leading to a goal and influenced by practice, by reward, and by punishment. Cognition, too, even though it involves complex mental processes, is a kind of problem solving in which practice, reward, and punishment are at least somewhat involved. In both cases, therefore, the psychobiology of learning and cognition must examine the conditions of *motivation* for these appear to be both the starting point and in many cases the goal of learned behaviors.

Motivation

From the very root of the word (*motus*, movement) we discover that *motivation* refers to the conditions that lead an organism to move or respond or change its responses. In psychology the term is generally confined to patterns of behavior that are *goal oriented*. Thus, the rat deprived of food is said to be "motivated" by hunger to run down a runway and turn left toward the compartment containing food. By introducing the notion of *goals* the psychologist attempts to distinguish between motivated and reflexive behavior, but the distinction is not entirely convincing. Why not say, for example, that limb flexion in response to a pin prick is a *motivated* response which has the removal of pain as its goal? What makes motivated behavior different from reflexive behavior is not the presence of an actual (or alleged) goal but the fact that the behavior itself is not stereotypical. The hungry animal will display an immense range of behaviors in an attempt to secure food, whereas the reflexively behaving animal will display only the narrowest range of responses. Indeed, the same reflex can be elicited by a wide range of stimuli whereas a wide range of (motivated) behaviors may be emitted by an animal under a single motivational state.

Conditioning

Differences between motivated and reflexive behavior can be illustrated by comparing the two traditional forms of conditioning; the *classical* form studied by Pavlov and the *instrumental* or *operant* form common in contemporary behavioral research.

stimulus substitution

Figure 5–2 depicts the sequences characteristic of each form of conditioning. What is obvious in the case of classical conditioning is that nothing the animal does will prevent the salivary reflex from occurring once the powdered food is placed in its mouth. The bell's apparent power to control this reflex—an example of *stimulus substitution*—is established by the frequent pairing of the bell (conditioned stimulus) with the food (unconditioned stimulus). The latter is *unconditionally* effective in eliciting salivation. What classical conditioning establishes is some sort of (associative) connection between two *stimuli*, one of which unconditionally controls the salivary reflex. What operant conditioning establishes is a connection between a *response* and some stimulus produced by it.

Another common distinction drawn between the two modes of conditioning is that classical conditioning operates primarily on cardiac and smooth muscles and glands whereas operant conditioning chiefly involves the striate muscles—those that actually move the animal. However, such responses as limb flexion can be classically conditioned and heart rate can be operantly conditioned. Thus, although this distinction holds in the more traditional conditioning studies, it is not without its limitations. At least at the conceptual level the primary difference between the two is in the nature of the associations or connections formed by the conditioning procedures. Classical conditioning is best understood as a method of stimulus substitution in which one of the stimuli activates a specific reflex pathway. Operant conditioning is a method of regulating nonreflexive behavior by selecting any nonreflexive movement and increasing its frequency by reinforcement. *Motivation*, on this interpretation, refers only to those internal processes associated with operant behavior—that is, with behavior not incorporated into innate reflex arcs.

Biological Drives

The notion of a biological *drive* has often been advanced to account for motivation. According to *drive reduction* theories of

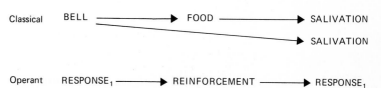

Figure 5–2 In classical conditioning the effective stimulus precedes the response. In operant conditioning the stimulus that comes to alter the probability of the response follows it (the response).

homeostasis

motivation the presence of physiological imbalances results in aversive sensations which the animal's (motivated) behavior is able to terminate. States of hunger are illustrative. For example, the animal deprived of food undergoes a variety of physiological changes including alterations of blood chemistry, changes in the rate of gastric secretions, changes in heart rate and respiration. As hunger proceeds, the internal metabolic mechanisms can no longer maintain equilibrium (*homeostasis*). These mechanisms, particularly the endocrine glands, respond in such a way as to alter the chemistry of circulating blood which, as it passes through the brain, selectively activates centers governing behavior. Glucose, for example, appears to have a selective effect on sites in the hypothalamus which, as we shall see, is intimately associated with eating and drinking. Similarly, sexually motivated behavior can be induced or diminished by varying the quantity of hormones normally produced by the ovaries or testes.

centralist vs. peripheralist theories

During the early decades of the present century there was much debate over whether biological drives originated in the peripheral physiology of the organism and then led to activation of brain mechanisms or whether the latter controlled the former. There were those who defended the *centralist* position on motivation and others who defended the *peripheralist* theory. All sorts of clever experiments were performed in behalf of each view. It was shown, for example, that if a canula was inserted into the pharynx, such that all food swallowed by the animal passed out of the body before ever getting to the stomach, the animal would not eat indefinitely—that is, something other than the *peripheral* cue of gastric distension was controlling eating.

What a half-century of research has established is that motivational regulatory mechanisms are not an *either-or* affair but the result of elaborate feedback connections between peripheral and central processes. Taking only endocrine functions as an example, it is known that the secretions of both the anterior and the posterior regions of the pituitary gland are directly regulated by the hypothalamus, and that the hypothalamus is activated by agents carried in the general blood supply to the brain, including agents whose concentrations are determined by secretions of the pituitary gland. The pituitary gland is also called the *hypophysis* and so we often speak of the *hypothalamic-hypophyseal system* in describing the feedback mechanisms. The problem with such a term, however, is that it suggests all the relevant work is done exclusively within the cranium. The more complete picture is sketched in Figure 5–3 which illustrates the functional interdependence among peripheral, hypothalamic, and hypophyseal mechanisms.

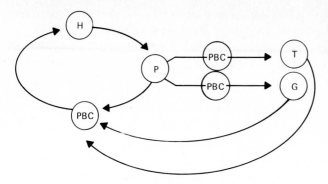

Figure 5–3 A schematic illustration of feedback controls involving the hypothalamus (H), the pituitary gland (P), and the peripheral blood chemistry (PBC). The influence of the pituitary secretions on those of the thyroid (T), as they affect PBC, and the gonads (G) is also indicated.

Pleasure and Pain Areas

Tied to the notion of a drive is the thesis that behavior is somehow designed to minimize the suffering and increase the pleasurable sensations of the organism. This *pleasure principle* has a long past in philosophy as well as a firm place in the common understandings of the layperson. It has been put on a scientific foundation in recent decades by the discovery of certain regions of the brain which organisms will work to stimulate; and by other regions of the brain which organisms will work to inhibit. It is now conventional to speak of these regions as *reward* and *punishment centers* even though the actual patterns of behavior are somewhat different from those emitted by the animal in attempting to obtain ordinary rewards (such as food) or to escape from ordinary punishments (such as shock).

The pioneering research in this area of self-stimulation of the brain was done by James Olds beginning in the early 1950s. He and his colleagues had actually set out to study sleep mechanisms in the rat, but owing to a fortunate misplacement of the stimulating electrode their attention was drawn to an even more interesting phenomenon. The rat, with an electrode thought to be implanted in the reticular formation, was placed in a box whose four corners were labeled A, B, C, and D. When the animal roamed to A, a weak stimulus was delivered through the electrode to what was in fact an area of the hypothalamus, not the reticular formation.

Olds was quick to notice the rat's tendency to remain in corner A while stimuli were applied. He then made the application of the stimulus contingent on the animal's going to a different portion of the box which, in a matter of minutes, the animal proceeded to do. What was apparent was that the animal was regulating its behavior in a way that would result in the administration of stimuli to its brain.

For the next twenty years, and until his accidental and

untimely death, Olds explored the "reward" and "punishment" systems of the brain of the rat, but with a technique for which he is now famous. He constructed caps that could be cemented to the rat's skull, with wires extending from a stimulus source to the electrodes buried in the brain. By pressing the lever in a Skinner box, the rat was able to deliver weak electrical stimuli to any region fed by an electrode. Olds ultimately turned to *microelectrodes*, having discovered that the larger electrodes yielded occasionally indefinite and confusing results.

Perhaps the most reliable finding to emerge from the research by Olds and now many others is that experimental animals will work to deliver weak signals to regions of the hypothalamus. It is somewhat paradoxical that one of the more effective hypothalamic regions is the same one that results in eating (to be discussed below) rather than in satiation. That is, what is rewarding to the rat is the stimulation of an area more akin to hunger than to satiety. Further research with microelectrodes indicates that the hypothalamic nuclei can be distinguished in terms of their rewarding effects, and that different nuclei are associated with eating and with (apparent) pleasure.

In still other studies it has been shown that the form of behavior elicited by stimulation of the brain depends in part on the external rewards available to the animal. If, for example, food, water, and a sexually receptive female are all present, the rat receiving hypothalamic stimulation will turn first to food, then to water, and finally to the female. If, however, the food is removed, the rat will turn to drinking and then to sexual activity. But the central point is that direct stimulation of the brain can produce behavior that is strikingly similar to what is observed in the naturally motivated animal. When stimuli are confined to the dorsal and more anterior nuclei of the hypothalamus, the animal seems to press the bar specifically for brain stimulation and not as a substitute for food, drink, or sex. That such behavior is extremely difficult to extinguish, that it is often difficult to *shape* (for example, having it occur at low rates), and that it tends to be of an insatiable variety can only raise questions about how *natural* a source of motivation direct brain stimulation is. But the effect is reliable and dramatic and has influenced the psychobiological perspective on the nature of motivation. The experimental arrangement for such studies is illustrated in Figure 5–4.

The pharmacological correlates of these findings have been the subject of much recent study. It now seems clear that those drugs that cause the release of brain catacholamines tend to enhance self-stimulation behavior. Those that diminish the supply of catacholamines are known to inhibit self-stimulation

Figure 5–4 Experimental arrangement for studying electrical self-stimulation of the brain. A small helmet is secured to the skull of the animal and provides a stable foundation for the implanted electrodes. An appropriate response, such as the pressing of a lever, results in the delivery of a controllable quantity of current to the region of the brain receiving the implanted electrode.

behavior. Both *norepinephrine* and *dopamine* appear therefore to be necessary for the maintainance of the self-stimulation effects.

Hypothalamic Lesions

hunger and thirst

More specific than such states as reward and punishment are the mechanisms directly related to the food- and liquid-consuming behavior of the organism. Hunger and thirst are unconditionally motivating conditions whose neural controls must shed light on the entire question of motivation. It is now known that the nuclei of the *hypothalamus* are at the center of that overall system that regulates consummatory behavior. The nuclei of greatest importance here are the *lateral* nuclei and the *ventromedial* nuclei. Stimulation of the lateral hypothalamic nuclei results in prolonged fits of eating leading to a doubling of the animal's normal weight. This condition of *hyperphagia* lasts throughout the period of stimulation, even to the point of rupturing the stomach lining. Destruction of the lateral hypothalamic nuclei leads to *aphagia* where, in the absence of intervention, the animal soon dies of starvation even though food is readily available. The rule in such cases of aphagia is that the animal also refuses to drink (*adipsia*), soon becoming pathologically dehydrated. This complex of aphagic and adipsic symptoms is called the *lateral hypothalamic syndrome.* Stimulation of the ventromedial nuclei of the hypothalamus will produce a cessation of eating on the part of a normal animal that has been deprived of food. They function as something of a satiety center which, under normal conditions, will inhibit lateral hypothalamic mechanisms.

If one were to consider only the earliest studies of the effects of hypothalamic lesions or stimulation on eating and drinking, the quick conclusion that would be reached is that a definite center of motivation had now been discovered. Further research, however, has created a far less coherent picture. It is now known, for example, that lesions in the lateral hypothalamus are followed very quickly by the development of pathologic changes in gastric tissues of the animal. There is a resulting change in the entire metabolic physiology of the organism—a change capable of producing considerable loss of weight. If animals are placed on stringent diets before surgery such that, at the time of surgery, they are only 75 percent or 80 percent as heavy as normal, there is a great reduction in the severity of the lateral hypothalamic syndrome *and* a markedly lower incidence of gastric pathology.

It is also important to realize that the lateral hypothalamic syndrome can be overcome by careful and attentive care of the postoperative animal. The animal can be weaned back to health (to normal eating and drinking) even though the hypothalamic nuclei are, of course, lost forever. What such findings indicate is that the concept of a motivational "center" is something of an oversimplification in that it fails to convey not only the *feedback* "loops within loops" characteristic of all developed nervous systems but also the compensatory capacities of the system. There is no question but that consummatory *behavior* displays great dependence upon the functions of the hypothalamus. But from the mere fact of eating or noneating it is hazardous to make inferences regarding "motivation." Eating and drinking are the consequences of numerous, complex, and interconnected factors which include but are surely not limited to blood chemistry, sensitivity of taste receptors, blood pressure and viscosity, degree of gastric distension, autonomic influences on digestive function, activity in various brain sites, the palatability of available food and liquid, olfactory functions, sensory-motor coupling—the list could be expanded to several pages. How these factors combine to create a sense of hunger or thirst—to create that pattern of sensation and feelings we ordinarily identify with the *motive* to eat and drink—remains a mystery. The classic *gourmand* eats excessively not because he or she is always hungry but because of the pleasure associated with the taste of delicacies. That such consummatory behavior is motivated is clear, but it is equally clear that hunger per se is not the motive. And the religious ascetic, who will eat no more than is necessary to sustain life, is said to perform a *sacrifice* when not responding to the feeling of hunger. Were there no hunger there would be no sacrifice at all. Behaviorally the ascetic could be described as *hypophagic,* but here the behavior would scarcely address the nature of the actual *motive.*

Lesion Studies

The success of the technique of surgical ablation (Chapter 2) in studies of basic sensory and motor functions quite naturally encouraged many to believe that the same method would reveal the so-called centers of the brain in which learning takes place. The strategy would be straightforward. Perform specific operations on various target sites, destroying specific regions, and record the effects these lesions have on the animal's ability to learn various tasks.

This was the approach adopted by Karl Lashley (Chapter 1) and exhaustively employed by him for some thirty years. But as early as 1929, in his *Brain Mechanisms and Intelligence,* Lashley was forced to doubt the very concept of *localization of function* in regard to learning and memory.

As applied to sensory and motor systems, the concept had been experimentally confirmed by dozens of experimenters in hundreds of studies and by numerous and reliable findings from neurological and neurosurgical clinics. Tumors and other forms of lesion in occipital cortex were known to result in varying degrees of blindness. The same relationships had long since been established in audition, motor coordination, speech, and the "skin" senses (touch, pressure, temperature, pain). Thus, by 1929, although much work obviously remained to be done, there seemed little reason to doubt that complex psychological functions such as learning would also come to be identified with specific regions and nuclei of the brain.

the search for the engram   Taking this general view as something of a scientific hypothesis, we can translate it into the broad question that guided most of Lashley's research: "What specific region of the brain is necessary if an animal is to be able to learn?" What three decades of careful research forced Lashley to answer was, in a word, "None!" Let us now see what led to this surprising conclusion.

If an animal, a rat, for example, is required to respond to one of two visual cues in order to obtain food—say by jumping toward a card on which an "X" is printed but not toward one on which an "O" appears—the rat will learn this discrimination quite easily. Lashley knew, intuitively we might suppose, that even simple learning of this sort must involve something more complicated than the mere coupling of sensory and motor events. He was convinced that the traditional associationistic theories were simplistic. In one series of experiments, rats were required to learn the discrimination with one eye covered, a procedure that did not retard learning in any way. Once the animals performed errorlessly, Lashley removed the patch from the covered eye and placed it over the eye that had been uncovered during initial learning. The rats, of course, continued to perform perfectly, indicating that whatever is involved in learning, it surely is not simply the formation of "associative bonds" between *specific* sensory pathways and specific motor fibers. A rat that has learned to jump toward the "X" with the right eye blocked will continue to jump toward the "X" when this eye is opened and the left eye is blocked. Thus, any theory of learning requiring a bond between, for example, fibers in the left optic nerve and specific fibers originating in the motor cortex is simply wrong.

It was equally clear that the motor side of traditional associationism did not conform to the facts. It is possible to induce a reversible paralysis in an animal by compressing but not cutting one of the spinal motor nerves. If, for example, the motor nerves at cervical levels C_5–C_8 are compressed on the left side, the left forelimb (in humans, the left arm) will be completely paralyzed since efferent impulses will not travel from the cord out to the muscles of the limb. This, however, is a reversible paralysis, the animal (or human) regaining normal movement in a matter of days or weeks.

If, under these conditions, an animal (such as a rat, dog, or monkey) is trained to respond to a specific stimulus with a manual movement by the unaffected limb, learning proceeds normally. Once learning has been established, the animal is then exposed to the procedure of spinal nerve compression on the normal side. Now the limb that was involved in the original learning is paralyzed, and we wait for the originally paralyzed limb to return to normal function. Once it has, the animal is tested on the same task. What we find is that the limb whose motor discharges were utterly silent during initial learning now performs with the same agility and correctness once the paralysis has worn off.

Just as the blindfold experiment indicates that learning does not require the formation of specific sensory bonds, this one establishes that it also does not require the formation of specific motor bonds. What was clear to Lashley was that the process of learning is not merely the connecting of sensory and motor pathways but something in which the complexities of *cerebral* organization must participate. The question, then, was whether some form of *cerebral associationism* (such as that proposed by Pavlov) would provide the best explanation of the facts. Thus, Lashley turned to the brain itself, this time to determine if there were specific locations which, when surgically destroyed or disrupted, produced either incapacities to learn or the elimination of whatever it was that the animal had learned.

In numerous experiments, most of them with rats, Lashley systematically destroyed specific cortical regions, in some studies before training began and in other studies after learning had occurred. It came as no surprise that when specific sensory areas (for example, striate cortex) were surgically removed the animal was unable to learn to discriminate between two stimuli. Blind animals cannot learn visual discriminations! But what Lashley was looking for was a region which was necessary not for sensitivity but for learning itself, a *learning center*. And it was just this that he never found. In his famous article, "In Search of the Engram," he arrived at the droll conclusion, after years of study, that learning "...is simply impossible!" His point, of course, was that since no specific structure in the brain was doing the learning—and since it is only as a result of the brain that learning can occur—one is forced by the very logic of the case to conclude that learning is impossible.

equipotentiality and mass action

More seriously, however, Lashley reached two general conclusions which he judged to be warranted by the data. They take the form of principles now thoroughly associated with his name: the principle of *equipotentiality* and the principle of *mass action*. Briefly stated, the first of these asserts that *all* areas of the cerebral cortex are equally essential to the process of learning. The removal of any *one* of these areas may produce deficits, but the animal's inevitable recovery from such deficits indicates that some other area has come to take over the function. Lashley's notion was not that every discernible region of the brain is the same or works the same as every other area, but that most, if not all, of the cerebral mass contains cells and networks that can perform operations normally carried out by a part of the whole. With respect to such complex processes as those of learning and memory, Lashley concluded that the *cortex functions as a whole*, that is, that *mass action* is the guiding principle.

As important as his experimental and conceptual contributions have been, however, Lashley was not to have the last word on the issue of localization of function. His research was largely confined to *cortical* lesions, and it has since been demonstrated that any number of *subcortical* sites significantly influence learning and memory also (Chapter 6). Even at the level of cortical organization there is some evidence supporting the view that *frontal cortex* is specifically involved in those learning tasks that require short-term memory and both the spatial and the temporal patterning of responses. It is important to keep in mind that the experimenter's choice of learning tasks will determine the conclusions reached about the role of the brain in learning. Lashley himself had shown that even massive lesions would produce only negligible effects on the animal's ability to learn a simple maze, but would make the learning of a complex maze nearly impossible.

delayed alternation

The importance of the frontal cortex in learning has been demonstrated through the use of what is called a *delayed alternation* task. In the usual configuration, the animal (monkey) is presented with two boxes or food wells covered by lids. Food reward is under only one of the lids on a given trial, and is always under the other lid on the next trial. Thus, in order to receive a reward on every trial, the monkey must alternate between left box and right box choices on a trial-by-trial basis. The task becomes a *delayed* alternation task by introducing various intervals of time between successive trials. The normal monkey has no trouble with such a task even when the intervals are quite long. Monkeys having undergone destruction or removal of frontal cortex (bilaterally), however, will begin to display deficits even at intervals as brief as ten or twenty seconds. And even when they display no deficit early in the training process, they generally never acquire the rate of success of normal monkeys even after hundreds or thousands of trials.

The same frontal lobe damage that interferes with the learning of delayed alternation has somewhat similar effects on human patients. Moreover, both chimpanzees and human patients, following surgical destruction of *prefrontal cortex* (in prefrontal lobotomies in humans, for example) display a marked reduction in emotionality. It is difficult, therefore, to take even the most reliable lesion effects as establishing a specific *learning* function in the frontal and prefrontal cortex. That is, it is not easy to separate motivational, attentional, emotional and cognitive functions when a surgical procedure is known to have some effect on all of them.

Lesion studies have been used effectively in the study of mechanisms of memory and will be reviewed in the next chapter. The relationship between learning and memory is, of course, an intimate one, and so we have every right to take those findings regarding memory mechanisms as also pertinent to the processes of learning. We would not at this point, therefore, conclude that lesion studies have turned up nothing—quite the contrary—but we are inclined to think that Lashley may have been close to the truth of the matter, even if not for the right reasons.

The facts that drove Lashley to his conclusions were (a) the inability to find a specific region of cortex necessary for learning to occur and (b) the nearly complete recovery of learning functions in animals that were subjected to extensive cortical destruction. Viewed in a certain light, both findings challenge the concept of *localized* learning functions within the cerebral cortex. When we add to this Lashley's observation that the magnitude of the deficit is determined chiefly by the *amount* of cortex removed, we have still another reason to doubt the localization hypothesis.

conceptual issues   As we noted at the beginning of this chapter, labels are often necessary but they are sometimes also deceiving. In applying the label "learning" we may be tempted to think of the process itself as unitary simply because we have chosen to identify it with a single word. But let us turn to a purely biological process in order to appreciate the danger of this temptation. Suppose we name each and every chemical event that results in the breakdown of ingested food "digestion." Then, systematically, we eliminate salivation and observe the effects on the final products of digestion. Next we remove the stomach and connect the pharynx directly to the head of the small intestine, repeating our examination of the products of digestion. We then cut out different lengths of small intestine and then remove it entirely; we could then do likewise with the large intestine. It should be clear that, in performing these surgical procedures sequentially—or, if we use different animals, performing only one of these procedures on a given animal—we may well reach the conclusion that *digestion* does not occur in any place at all! That is, the animal without salivary glands will still produce (partially) digested food, as will an animal lacking a stomach *or* a portion of small intestine *or* even all small intestine, etc.

Like digestion, learning is a process that depends on a great many independent and interdependent functions: sensory, motor, attentional, memorial, motivational, and emotional. It was out of respect for this fact that Lashley coined the term *mass action*. But perhaps the better alternative is to think of learning not as a specific function in its own right—and one requiring the activity of the entire mass of brain—but as the *word* we use for just these multifunctional processes that lead to systematic changes in the animal's adaptive mechanisms. On this view, learning is akin to a *change of state*. In other words, learning is comparable to a radio going from an "off" mode to an "on" mode of operation, where it would make no sense at all to ask "*Where* is the radio on?" If we look at each note recorded on a musical score, we will find a *sonata* in none of them. A sonata is not a single note but the *word* applied to an integrated pattern of notes conforming to certain principles of harmony and played in a certain "time." Lashley could not find the engram in part because an engram is a code for a specific entity, and *learning* is not an entity.

This becomes all the more obvious when we observe human patients with cortical lesions. When such lesions are highly localized, they are commonly associated with specific deficits. The patient may suffer from diminished visual sensitivity or from an impoverishment of movement or, as we shall see in Chapter 8, from one or another form of linguistic abnormality. But the highly localized lesion does not result in so general a deficit as the utter inability to learn *anything*. Some "frontal lobe" patients have been found to display symptoms not unlike those experimentally created in the chimpanzee; for example, difficulty with complex visual discriminations and with delayed alternation tasks. But the visual areas of the cerebral cortex in both species do send projections to frontal cortex and this fact alone makes it less than surprising to find some visual perceptual problems associated with frontal lobe syndromes.

Other features of the human frontal lobe syndrome often include the inability to process symbolic (such as verbal, pictorial, or diagrammatic) information, but even here we would be ill-advised to consider the deficits as *learning* deficits. The functions affected are of an interpretive rather than an adaptive nature and, in fact, the patient may display perfectly normal abilities in all sorts of nonsymbolic learning tasks. The frontal lobe patient may be extremely "disoriented," unable to give accurate answers to such questions as "What time do you think it is?" or "How long have you been in this hospital?" or "Has the doctor seen you today?" or "What time is supper served?" or "Where are you now?" And the same patient may often find it difficult to maintain attention or shift it from one problem to another. Typically, however, such a patient only exhibits bona fide deficits in learning when the underlying brain pathology is extensive. Thus, the human clinical population tends to favor Lashley's *mass action* thesis and tends strongly to challenge a strict localization theory of learning.

Although the literature is not entirely consistent, there is evidence reported of learning in the *decorticate* animal. Even more consistent are those studies in which classical conditioning has been achieved in "spinal" animals—that is animals whose brains have been surgically disconnected from the spinal cord. The fact that some learning is possible in decorticate animals or in "spinal" animals cannot, of course, be taken as evidence against the role of the cerebral cortex in learning. In both cases only the most rudimentary forms of behavioral adjustment are observed. What such findings do suggest, however, is that learning, as a *process* by which populations of neural cells come to be organized in their outputs, may be possible at every level of neural organization. Accordingly, the complexity of the observed learning may be determined chiefly by the complexity—rather than the location—of the neural interconnections engaged by the learning task. Species with little or no cortical mass are able to learn and, as Lashley showed, species with developed cerebral masses will continue to learn even when substantial fractions of these masses have been destroyed. The most severe deficits are associated with the greatest *amount* of destruction. It is this degree of invasion that is able to interrupt what is normally an immensely complex pattern of anatomical organization.

Once learning is accepted as the word we use to summarize a wide variety of different but organized functions, the confusion and inconsistencies of the lesion studies are less vexing. The usual sign or measure of learning is a change in the frequency of a given response or a chain of interdependent responses such as those involved in playing the piano, driving a car, or hitting a ball with a bat. Because such responses lend themselves to relatively simple methods of observation and measurement, there is a tendency to think that learning itself is no more than what we have actually observed or measured.

But let us consider just one of these examples, hitting a ball with a bat. The separate (but finally integrated) tasks the nervous system must complete if the learner is to become more proficient are far too numerous to cite here. We mention just a few of them in order to alert the reader to the range and the number of processes that must be accounted for if this form of learning is to be understood at the neurophysiological level: (a) detection of the pitched ball against a complex background, (b) the processing of velocity and acceleration data in order to anticipate the position of the ball at t_w, where t_w is the time-window within which the bat *can* make contact with the ball, (c) sensing and compensating for the weight of the bat and exerting force in such a way as to match the bat's velocity and acceleration to the dynamics of the ball's trajectory, and (d) maintaining a steady focus on the ball while using the position sense to keep constant account of the position of the *unseen* bat.

It should be clear even from so abbreviated a list that when we say "John has learned how to hit the ball", the *learning* we refer to entails hundreds or thousands of adjustments by John's sensory, motor, attentional, motivational, and integrative systems. Thus, to look for a *place* in the cerebral cortex where this learning has occurred is like looking for a "baseball playing center" in the brain. Again, it is not that *learning* is going on everywhere in the brain but that learning is no more than all the coordinated events occurring throughout the brain when complex chains of behavior are formed. A lesion that disrupts the coordination or that eliminates one of the vital links in the chain (for example, visual perception) will necessarily retard or prevent learning, but not because it has disrupted a "learning center."

The available data indicate that in those species with developed cerebral hemispheres learning depends on *general* cerebral function. There is also evidence indicating a somewhat more special role in learning for *frontal* cortex and for *association* cortex but, again, in general, and not in terms of some specific population of cells within either frontal or association cortex. Lashley's concept of mass action was, perhaps, overstated in degree but it seems to be the right kind of concept with which to interpret studies of learning based on the lesion method.

Behavior Genetic Findings

Early in this chapter we introduced the concept of *heritability* (h^2). We have also noted that mechanisms of behavioral adjustment are common throughout the animal kingdom and are displayed by organisms having only the slightest neural equipment. As we ascend the phylogenetic series in our psychobiological studies we find a most suggestive tendency: The complexity of new problems organisms can come to solve with practice increases along with increases in the complexity of the organism's nervous system. The most relevant term in all of this is *complexity*. Isolated neurons are pretty much the same wherever they occur, whether in one animal, in one species, or among entirely different species. Indeed, even the total number of neurons is a less than faithful guide to predicting the range of learned adjustments of which a given species might be capable. The most significant variable is the complexity of neuronal interconnections. And, since these interconnections are made possible by the chemistry of the synapse and by the microscopic anatomy of the participating neural cells, there is good reason to expect that hereditary mechanisms are directly involved.

An active branch of modern psychobiology is that of *behavior genetic analysis*. Its chief research method is that of *selective breeding* coupled with traditional measures of such psychological functions as learning, memory, and emotionality. Through selective breeding, the behavioral geneticist is able to achieve ever more homogeneous genotypes in successive (and

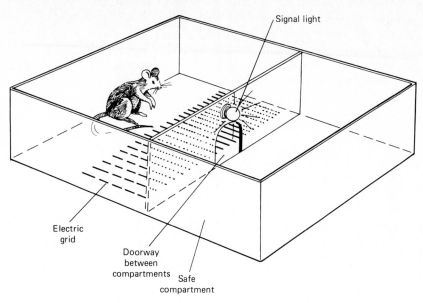

Signal light

Electric
grid

Doorway
between
compartments   Safe
compartment

Figure 5–5 A "shuttle box" for the study of avoidance conditioning.

heritability of learning

inbred) strains and determine the effects on one or another aspect of behavior.

A review of one series of experiments* is sufficient to illustrate the methods and to introduce the important concepts and implications arising out of such work. The research involves *avoidance conditioning* and employs a "shuttle-box" such as that depicted in Figure 5–5. The floor of one of the two compartments is wired such that the mouse can be shocked while standing in this compartment. To avoid the shock the mouse must run through the door joining the two compartments together. There are many variations on this procedure. A typical one has both compartments electrified and both equipped with sources of sound or light. When the mouse is in one compartment and the light comes on, shock will follow in some number of seconds. To avoid the shock the mouse must run to the adjacent compartment. Entering this one *before* the light is present will lead to shock.

What this configuration permits is a convenient measure of learning. The measure is simply the number of shocks endured by the animal before it learns how to avoid them. The shock cue can be made quite complex. For example, a green light may signal an impending shock only when it is the second of three sequentially lit stimuli. Thus, the sequence red-red-green or

*We depend here on the excellent article by Daniel Bovet, et al., "Genetic Aspects of Learning and Memory in Mice," *Science*, 1969, *163*:139–149.

green-red-green must not be responded to, whereas the sequence red-green-red must be.

If mice are chosen from a common strain and paced through this sort of avoidance conditioning, there is usually considerable variation displayed in the speed with which the different mice learn to avoid shock. In five sessions of one hundred trials each, a given mouse may come to avoid shock nearly perfectly whereas another might do no better than 10 percent. If, however, the most successful male and female mice are mated, the mice in the next generation are both better avoiders and more similar in their performance. In Figure 5–6 we illustrate changes in learning (expressed as percentage of successful avoidance responses) in successive generations of inbred mice. The parent generation (indicated as 0) yielded an avoidance rate during the final one hundred trials of about 15 percent. The first generation (I) resulting from inbreeding is observed to achieve a 60 percent rate of success. By the third generation (III), the success rate is nearly 90 percent.

Research of this kind is not always easy to interpret. We might argue, for example, that it is not *learning capacity* that is being genetically manipulated but something else; for example, the mouse's sensitivity to shock or attentiveness, or general level of activity. But such alternatives bring us back to our previous discussion of learning itself. Once we eliminate such properties as sensitivity, attention, and general activity, what is left of learning? What behavior genetic analysis has shown is that we can selectively breed for those characteristics traditionally defined as learning and, when measured, traditionally taken to be measures of learning. We do not know, of course, how the breeding specifically alters the microscopic anatomy of the

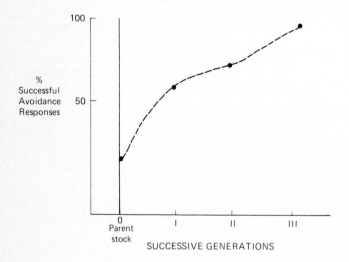

Figure 5–6 Heritability and learning. Illustrated here are the effects of successive inbreeding of a strain of rats on the learning of an avoidance response.

animal's nervous system, nor can the findings now be explained according to the principles of molecular biology. What we do know, however, is that a systematic change in the basic genetic composition will result in systematic changes in the basic physiology and biochemistry of the cells, including the neural cells. Learning, however defined, requires the propagation of neural impulses, their transmission across synapses, their activation of other ensembles of cells. Genetic manipulations leading to changes in the quantity or quality of transmitters or in the quantity of axonal or dendritic branches certainly are to be expected to influence learning.

Environmental Enrichment and the Brain

The genetic makeup of the organism is not, however, something that operates in isolation. Every phenotype is the expression of a complex interaction between genetic and environmental properties. Animals deprived of patterned visual stimulation from birth will come to have irreversible perceptual disturbances and will display degenerative processes throughout the visual system. Thus, no matter how healthy the animal's genetic endowment may be, a nurturing environment is essential to the normal development and normal functioning of the nervous system.

In recent decades, psychobiologists have studied the effects of extreme environmental variations on a number of chemical and physical features of the nervous system. Numerous experiments have all tended toward the same conclusion. A perceptually impoverished environment in which the developing animal has few opportunities for activity reliably produces anatomical and physiological abnormalities in the nervous system. The environmentally impoverished animal has, on average, a less massive brain, cortical neurons relatively poor in their arborization, and reduced concentrations of neural transmitters such as acetylcholine. Animals reared in enriched environments display just the opposite effects. Their brains weigh more and their cerebral hemispheres are thicker. Their cortical neurons are richer in spines and their brain extracts reveal far greater amounts of acetylcholinesterase. Quite simply, they have *better brains* anatomically and physiologically, and they adjust their behavior to novel and demanding situations more readily than their impoverished relatives. It is also known that when a given neural cell is denied its neighbors—that is, when those neighboring cells that make synaptic contact with it are destroyed—

the cell itself degenerates (*transneural degeneration*). Thus, conditions that significantly reduce activity anywhere in the nervous system can come to have widespread consequences. Like muscle, brains must be active, and not only during the period of most rapid development. Both the onset and severity of senility are rare among those who were intellectually involved throughout their adult years.

Psychobiological Theories of Learning

As with all areas of psychobiology, there is a nagging absence of theoretical integrations in the area of learning. As we have seen, Lashley's work made the older (Pavlovian) associationistic theories implausible. These associationistic theories have been rescued somewhat in revised form by D.O. Hebb (Chapter 1) who proposed in 1949 that learning is the result of the formation of *cell assemblies*. At the core of his theory is the notion that practice or repeated stimulation establishes a *reverberatory* electrical circuit among the neural units initially activated. With continued stimulation (or stimulation distributed over relatively short periods of time) the circuit comes to include greater and greater numbers of participating units. Hebb also proposed, long before there was confirmatory evidence, that changes in the synaptic space might be the structural mechanism of learning. These notions will be taken up in the next chapter and are cited here only to indicate that some form of associationistic theory may prove to be compatible with at least some of the facts of learning. But the facts have already outstripped the theoretical options. For now, we must be content to acknowledge a number of suggestive *correlations* which, though reliable, have yet to be converted into a coherent psychobiological theory of learning.

potentiation

It is well known, for example, that short bursts of stimulation delivered to certain *presynaptic* neurons can lead to long trains of *postsynaptic* firing, the phenomenon of *potentiation*. In this we have at the neural level something analogous to one of the properties of learning; namely, a long-term pattern of responding following a relatively brief period of repetitive stimulation. Some have even speculated that the phenomenon of potentiation is quite like the "reverberatory circuits" proposed by Hebb. In this connection, it is worth noting that potentiation is rather prominent in nuclei otherwise implicated in associative learning, for example nuclei of the hippocampus. The bearing these and related findings have on the mechanisms of memory is examined in the next chapter. Here we need only note that we are now in possession of a large number of basic neurophysiological facts—facts arising from studies of single units and small neural networks—that offer some hint as to what some of the mechanisms associated with learning may be. The phenomena of learning are so varied, however, that it seems very likely that more than one kind of mechanism is involved.

It may be, for example, that the more rudimentary forms of associative learning, such as that produced by classical conditioning, will prove to be mediated primarily by growth of the synaptic terminals. More complex associative learning may require the establishment of intracerebral pathways that functionally connect different sensory systems. Those forms of cognitive learning in which verbal and other symbolic elements are manipulated may depend on the activation of various cortical modules (Chapter 3) and the formation of patterned responding by them.

The psychological specialties most concerned with learning have yet to arrive at a settled *taxonomy of learning*. There are only general and not precise statements as to the complexity of various learning tasks. We think of some as purely associative (for example, conditioned reflexes) and others as clearly cognitive (for example, chess playing) but we do not yet have quantitative criteria universally applied in scaling the complexity or severity or degree of learning involved in studies of behavioral adaptation.

There was some enthusiasm for a time created by developments in the information sciences. It was hoped that the measure of information, the "bit", would be readily applicable not only to studies of human information-processing but to

information theory

studies of human and animal learning. The bit (*binary digit*) is the unit of information in the same way that the inch is the unit of length. An event is *informative* to the extent that it permits a choice or otherwise signals alternative outcomes. In the simplest setting, only two possible outcomes exist and, when one of them occurs, *one bit* of information is transmitted. The "heads-tails" outcomes of tossed coins are illustrative.

Technically, the number of bits of information transmitted by an event is computed according to the general equation

$$I = \log_2 (1/p)$$

where I is *information* (in bits), p is the a priori probability of the event, and $\log_2$ is, of course, the logarithm in the base 2 system. When a coin is tossed, the a priori probability that it will land head-up is 0.50, which is also the a priori probability that it will land tail-up. The information transmitted when either of these two equiprobable events occurs is, therefore

$$I = \log_2 (1/0.50)$$
$$I = \log_2 (2)$$
$$I = 1 \text{ bit}$$

As the number of possible outcomes increases from 2 to 4, to 8 to 16, and so on, the information transmitted by any one of the events when it occurs is 1, 2, 3, 4, and so on.

This metric has been employed only sporadically in psychological research. We know, for example, that human reaction time increases in nearly linear fashion as the information load (measured in bits) is increased. In a one bit discrimination task, reaction time is fastest, becoming systematically slower as the observer must process additional bits before responding. But there has been very little application of this approach to the area of animal learning and only slightly more to the area of human learning. We noted earlier that Lashley obtained his most pronounced effects when the surgically treated rats were required to learn a complex maze. Complexity in such studies generally refers to the total number of turns that must be made for the animal to "solve" the maze. We can say, therefore, that Lashley's rats displayed the consequences of surgery most clearly as the information load was increased.

Moving to the rigors of chess, we discover that the information load associated with a given move may be extremely great. A bishop that can be moved to any one of eight boxes will, in the circumstance, carry a three bit load. At the same time each of five pawns carries a one bit load and all the other pieces taken one at a time carry loads of one bit or more. But the entire chessboard at a given point in the game may contain thousands of possibilities which then must be multiplied greatly once one of the players also begins to process the sorts of countermoves the other player may make. Thus, if, as Lashley punned, learning is simply impossible, mastering the game of chess should be simply inconceivable!

Yet, when skilled players are asked, they all agree that they seldom if ever actually catalog the possible separate moves available to them and to their partners. Rather, they come to "see the board"; that is, they recognize *patterns of possibilities* and not individual pieces. What they are doing (or striving to do) is *decrease* the processing burdens by forming a *strategy*. Once the latter is formed, the moves of the individual pieces is virtually determined. How this is learned remains a mystery, but it is certainly not an associative process only, if at all. It is one of those Gestalt-like activities of the mind that would seem to resist the sort of quantification common in the information sciences. Needless to say, it is also the sort of activity that has successfully resisted all of the theories of learning psychology has advanced and psychobiology has employed.

Summary

Successful adaptation requires systematic changes in behavior under conditions of environmental alterations. All forms of animal life display such adaptive capacities. Unicellular organisms engage in *tropistic* behavior, a stereotyped whole-body response to specific classes of stimuli such as light, heat, and gravity. But with the appearance phylogenetically of bona fide nervous systems comes more flexible and intricate modes of adaptation. Through *reflex* mechanisms adaptive behavior can be confined to parts of the body and through *instinctual* mechanisms adaptive behavior can manipulate the external environment itself.

What is similar among tropisms, reflexes, and instincts is their relative independence of the need for practice, reinforcement, and trial and error. Within limits, all three modes of adaptation appear in full-blown form once the organism has attained the necessary maturity. This is not to say that tropistic, reflexive, and instinctual adaptations cannot be influenced by various environmental conditions. Animals can be trained to inhibit certain reflex responses and to cease engaging in instinctual behavior. But the basis upon which these latter effects are brought about is not itself either a reflexive or instinctual basis.

The class of behavioral adaptations with which psychobiology is most concerned is that which is called *learned behavior*. The chief experimental approach to the subject was for many years that of ablative surgery. Lashley's failure to find the engram indicated that, unlike basic sensory and motor functions, learning itself was not *centered* in the cerebral cortex, but was the result of general functions (the *mass action*) of the brain. To the ablative technique has been added direct electrical stimulation and self-stimulation methods. These have indicated the presence of somewhat more localized centers of reward and punishment within the brain. There are also now pharmacological studies supplementing these and tending toward the conclusion that the mechanisms of reward and punishment are of a chemical nature.

Although the accumulation of data has gone on at an accelerating rate, there remains the problem of theoretical integration. There is as yet no general theory able to embrace what is known from studies of behavior-genetics, ablative surgery, and psychopharmacology. There also is no generally adopted *taxonomy of learning*, nor is there wide agreement on the methods by which to distinguish *learning* from what are thought to be the different processes of attention, motivation, and emotion.

There is growing confidence that the anatomy and physiology of synapses will provide an explanation of at least rudimentary forms of associative learning. Conditions that lead to acquired behavioral adaptations are known to produce systematic changes in the size of synaptic terminals and in the quantity of synaptic transmitters. Environmental enrichment and deprivation have been shown to have marked effects at the neuronal level. There is, therefore, a genuine psychobiology of learning, but it is still in a very early stage of development, particularly conceptual development.

Suggested Readings

Neuronal Correlates of Adaptive Behavior

1. G. Horn and R. Hinde (eds.), *Short Term Changes in Neural Activity and Behavior*, Cambridge University Press, London, 1970.
2. M. Ito and J. Olds, Unit activity during self-stimulation behavior, *Journal of Neurophysiology*, 1971, *34*:263–273.
3. C. Blakemore and D. Mitchell, Environmental modification of the visual cortex and the neural basis of learning and memory, *Nature*, 1973, *241*:467–468.

Biochemical Correlates of Learning

1. B. Agranoff, *Biochemistry of Learning Processes* in L. Jaenicke (ed.), *Biochemistry of Sensory Functions*, Springer-Verlag, Berlin, 1974.
2. H. Hyden, Biochemical changes accompanying learning, in, G. Quarton, T. Melnechuk, and F. Schmitt (eds.), *The Neurosciences, A Study Program*, Rockefeller University Press, New York, 1967.

Psychobiology and Learning—General

1. M. Rosenzweig and E. Bennett (eds.), *Neural Mechanisms of Learning and Memory*, MIT Press, Cambridge, 1976.
2. K. Pribram, *Languages of the Brain*, Prentice-Hall, New Jersey, 1971.
3. D. Stein and J. Rosen (eds.), *Learning and Memory*, Macmillan, New York, 1974.

Learning and Motivation

1. E. Stellar, The physiology of motivation. *Psychological Review*, 1954, *61*:5–22.

2. P. Teitelbaum and A. Epstein, The lateral hypothalamic syndrome: Recovery of feeding and drinking after lateral hypothalamic lesions, *Psychological Review*, 1962, *69:*74–90.
3. J. Olds, The central nervous system and the reinforcement of behavior, *American Psychologist*, 1969, *24:*114–132.
4. L. Stein, Norepinephrine reward pathways: Role in self-stimulation, memory consolidation, and schizophrenia, in J. Cole and T. Sonderegger (eds.), *Nebraska Symposium on Motivation*, University of Nebraska Press, Lincoln, 1975.
5. E. Valenstein, V. Cox, and J. Kakolewski, Reexamination of the role of the hypothalamus in motivation, *Psychological Review*, 1970, *77:*16–31.

Learning and Attention

1. P. Bach-y-Rita, *Brain Mechanisms in Sensory Substitution*, Academic Press, New York, 1972.
2. J. Sprague, W. Chambers, and E. Stellar, Attentive, affective, and adaptive behavior in the cat, *Science*, 1961, *133:*165–173.
3. J. Tecce, Contingent negative variation (CNV) and psychological processes in man, *Psychological Bulletin*, 1972, *77:*73–108.

Heritability and Learning

1. J. Hirsch, *Behavior Genetic Analysis*, McGraw Hill, New York, 1967.
2. D. Robinson (ed.), *Heredity and Achievement.* Oxford University Press, New York, 1970.

6 Learning and Memory

Introduction

There is, perhaps, no issue in psychobiology of as great intrinsic interest and excitement as the mechanisms by which learning occurs. How does our brain actually record the information—that is, what are the plastic neural mechanisms—that underlie behavioral plasticity? Is there a single kind of memory or are there multiple kinds? Where is memory actually located in the brain? These are some of the questions motivating research in the field of the psychobiology of memory. Memory research, however interesting, is immensely complicated by a number of problems specific to it. The physiological basis of memory is microscopic according to all students of the field, and given the extreme complexity of the mammalian nervous system and the several levels of reductionistic representation, it has proven to be extremely difficult to link the microscopic mechanism with the molar outcome. Even in the simplest "model" invertebrate preparation, we can at best examine simultaneously the action of only a very few synapses. It is for these reasons that the microscopic psychobiology of memory is usually studied indirectly. We examine variable activity of some electrical signal; we observe molar behavior, or the effects of some chemical agent on behavior. Only a minority of the reports of research in this field deal with the microscopic actuality of memory itself. Even less common are studies comparing the processes of behavior with the neural substrates under identical conditions.

Compelling evidence of the neurophysiological mechanisms underlying the storage of memory is therefore rare. Most reported studies of the psychobiology of memory deal with changes in behavior of individual neurons, of indirect electrical

231

indicators like the electroencephalogram, or of the entire organism. It is for these reasons that it is almost impossible to talk about memory without spending most of our time talking about learning—the process through which memories are established. To do so, however, requires precise definition of both of these terms. This is the purpose of the following paragraphs.

In virtually all animals behavior is characterized by change and adaptation to the environment. Not all of this behavioral plasticity, of course, is due to learning. As we noted in the previous chapter, adaptation may occur as a result of the maturation and growth of the organisms in ways that are totally directed by its genetic heritage, independent of experience. To assert this, however, is to "finesse" the answer to one of the great questions of human intellectual history "What is (are) the cause(s) of behavioral change?" "Is it learning or the result of that innate genetic heritage with which the organism is endowed at the moment of conception?" This controversy—the nature-nurture or heredity-environment issue—has transfixed human attention for centuries. Even today emotionally loaded controversy over this complex issue poisons some of our political, scientific, and social life at the same time that cooler heads are studying the problem in the laboratory. To understand exactly what is at the root of this great conundrum, it is necessary to define, as precisely as possible, some of the terms used in its formulation. Clearly, not every one of the words means the same thing to everybody. Moreover, the various words tend often to change their meaning as new empirical observations exert their influence on our points of view.

In this chapter, we will concentrate on the effects of the experiential interaction between the organism and the environment on behavioral change. It is in that context alone that a relatively satisfactory definition of what is meant by learning and memory can be generated. The only way to evaluate a *memory* is in terms of its relationship to some previous experiential anchor. We note that *learning* is traditionally defined as a change in behavior caused by past experiences. But this is insufficient; to confine learning to the domain within which we would feel intuitively comfortable, certain very similar and analogous effects must be excluded. That is, learning must be distinguished from other experientially induced behavioral changes that are not instances of learning. Some of these imitators of "true" learning are fatigue, adaptation, and maturation. These often mimic learning very closely but are best understood as arising from processes quite different from those that appear to govern learning and memory.

In the following section we will set forth the criteria now widely adopted in distinguishing learning from these other phenomena. We will then proceed to a somewhat general discussion of psychobiological correlates of learning and memory before beginning a detailed and critical review of research and theory addressed to memory mechanisms. Thus, the first part of this chapter is intended to supplement the material presented in Chapter 5 and to introduce dimensions of learning and memory that go beyond the "behavioral adjustments" examined in Chapter 5. The concluding part of this chapter is then devoted to specific hypotheses advanced by psychobiology to explain the most current evidence arising from studies of memory.

Criteria of Learning

It is again necessary to underscore the sometimes arbitrary distinctions made between learned and unlearned patterns of behavioral adjustment. The patterns in question all come from the same organism and the often too rigid barriers erected between some of its adjustments and others are erected *by us*. It thus becomes especially important to know the grounds on which such distinctions are based.

Plasticity

A pattern of behavioral adjustment is said to be *learned* when the frequency of its occurrence can be systematically modified by environmental manipulations.

Nontransmissibility

Behavioral adjustments, like all measurable characteristics of the organism, are *phenotypes* whose heritability can be measured. Such adjustments are said to be *learned* when their frequency of occurrence in the parental strain has no effect on the frequency of their occurrence in subsequent generations.

Nonmaturational

In all developed species organisms are able to do many things late in development that they cannot do in infancy. Some patterns of adjustment, therefore, come into being almost exclusively as a function of age. When such patterns can be explained in purely maturational terms, they are said to be *unlearned.* Learned adjustments, therefore, involve behavior that cannot be predicted merely by knowing the maturational stage of development of the behaving organism.

Selective Reversibility

This criterion is a refinement of the criterion of plasticity and is designed to permit distinctions between learned behavioral adjustments and such processes as *fatigue, sensitization,* and *habituation.* Responses emitted at a high rate and without intervals of rest soon become progressively less frequent. Repeatedly elicited reflexes are illustrative. Such changes in the frequency of behavior are not evidence of learning because they cannot be selectively reversed. There is, for example, no way to *increase* the frequency of repeatedly elicited reflexes during the chain of elicitations except by introducing periods of rest. Thus, when the rate of responding to a stimulus is governed entirely by the rate of stimulation and the duration of rest intervals, the frequency changes in question are said to be unlearned. Reduced rates of responding caused exclusively by frequent elicitations without rest are referred to as *habituation.* There are also conditions under which rates of responding can be increased, however, but where such increases are also treated as unlearned. Certain neurons, for example, will display a disproportionate increase in the initiation of impulses after just a few rapid stimulations. This increase in response rate is called *sensitization.* Again, however, the increase is not selectively reversible by training.

Stimulus Substitution

The phenomena of fatigue, habituation, and sensitivity fail as evidence of learning in still another way. The conditions of stimulation leading to these phenomena cannot be replaced by qualitatively different conditions. That is, we cannot *substitute* different stimuli, reliably paired with habituating or sensitizing stimuli, and obtain the same effects. With learned patterns of adjustment the organism responds to stimuli in a systematic manner where such stimuli initially have no systematic effect on the organism's behavior.

We can illustrate the application of these criteria to a specific form of behavioral adjustment by reviewing *habituation* studies of the simple organism *Aplysia* sketched in Figure 6–1. Repeated stimulation of the siphon is soon accompanied by a reduction in the speed and the number of contractions of the gills. Here we have an instance of *habituation.* After a rest period, the response returns and, if an intense stimulus is then

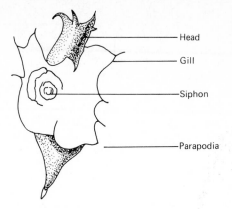

Figure 6–1 A sketch of *Aplysia*. The animal's gills are contracted for defense when stimuli are delivered to the siphon or the surface of the body.

Head

Gill

Siphon

Parapodia

applied to a different region of the body, full contractions occur. Thus there is a *dishabituation* effect. Both of these effects have been shown to depend on excitatory and inhibitory synaptic mechanisms. Habituation appears to be the result of a *depression* of the synapse of the motor neuron activating the gills and dishabituation the result of presynaptic excitatory influences originating centrally in the primitive nervous system of *Aplysia*. However, of the five criteria of learning the findings from studies of *Aplysia* can only be said to satisfy the plasticity criterion. That is, the rate of gill withdrawing responses can be decreased (habituated) and increased (dishabituation) by the application of certain stimuli. But the responses are not contingent on training, cannot be elicited by initially neutral stimuli reliably paired with the effective (tactile) stimuli, are common to all *Aplysia* that are fully mature, and cannot be *selectively* reversed independently of fatigue. We return to *Aplysia* on pp. 254–256.

A Model of Learning

Let us bridge the gap separating *Aplysia* from human behavior and borrow from the previous chapter something that is clearly learned; namely, hitting a baseball with a bat. Success here comes only after prolonged periods of practice and requires an exquisite integration of sensory and motor processes. Figure 6–2 is a block diagram of an extremely simplified model by which to keep track of the different factors involved when someone is a proficient batter. It is the model that will guide us through the researched facts on learning and those processes on which learning clearly depends. The reader should keep in mind, however, that it is far easier to draw and label a box than it is to

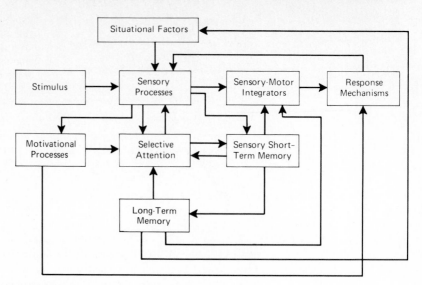

Figure 6–2 A simplified model of learning.

find out just what goes on in such boxes—in actual *brains* where in fact there are no boxes. Figure 6–2, therefore, is not a *theory* designed to explain learning but a description of a number of steps or stages probably involved in most instances of learning.

At the level of gross behavior all we see when we watch the skillful batter hit the ball is a pair of events—the movement of the ball toward the batter and the movement of the bat toward the ball. Between these events, however, a number of highly specific processes and mechanisms must be engaged. The batter, for example, knows what is expected of him on the basis of past learning and experience. A person brought to the ballpark from some distant planet and having no knowledge of baseball would have no idea of what the *situation* was. That is, although such a person might have keen senses and see everything the batter sees, these purely sensory events would not add up to a *situation* calling for actions of a certain type. The batter's knowledge of the situation is depicted in Figure 6–2 by the connection between *long-term memory* and that complex constellation of stimuli referred to as *situational factors*. These factors arrive at the sensory mechanisms by which they come to influence what has been labeled as *motivational processes*. Suppose, for example, that just as the pitcher releases the ball the umpire calls "Time out," meaning that at that instant the game is suspended. The batter, in response to this change in the situation, now relaxes those muscles which had been readied for response; he takes his eye off the ball and steps away from the batter's spot. The model in Figure 6–2 has the full range of sensory information channeled into those processes that regulate the motivational level of the batter and has the effects of these processes channeled into the mechanisms for *selective attention*. Note that the words "Time out" would have no meaning to someone who was not aware of the rules of the game or whose vocabulary did not contain such items. Again, it is on the basis of past learning (long-term memory) that the words come to have their effects on behavior. They come to alter the attention of the batter who is now able to direct his senses elsewhere. This is indicated by the connection between *selective attention* and *sensory processes*.

With the game resumed, the pitcher again releases the ball which again is tracked carefully by the batter's eyes. The information is changing continuously in that the retinal size of the ball increases continuously as it approaches the batter. Its velocity also changes continuously. This flow of continuously changing information must be integrated with the batter's response mechanisms so that the bat is brought to just the right place at just the right time. In any very short interval during the flight of the ball the batter would be able to locate its position very accurately. But *after* the ball has completed its flight the batter would not be nearly as accurate in retracing its history of motion. In other words, there are *short-term memory* mechanisms which provide moment-to-moment feedback to the sensory-motor integrators but which do not retain the trajectory information indefinitely. There must, however, also be *long-term memory* inputs delivered to the integrators to account for the fact that long experience improves the batter's performance.

Let us turn now to the process of short-term memory, the necessary preprocessing of information that will come to be present in the organism's long-term behavioral functions.

Short-Term Memory

erasure, decay, and interference

It is now clear that the nervous system includes "buffer" or short-term forms of memory which can be demonstrated in studies of healthy human subjects. For example, if we expose an observer to a brief presentation of a word (DOG) followed immediately by a number (47) and instruct the subject to begin counting backward by 3s as soon as the number appears, we can prevent the subject from rehearsing or thinking about the word. The object of such a study is not to see how quickly the subject can count backward (although our instructions would lead the subject to believe otherwise) but to learn the interval over which the subject can still recall the flashed word. Using one trial per subject and letting each subject count backward for different amounts of time we are able to interrupt the counting after a desired interval and ask each subject what word was presented before the first number was flashed.

When studies like this are completed it is found that there is virtually no recall whatever of the initial word when the subject is asked for it 20 or 30 seconds after it was presented. In counting backward as rapidly as possible, the subject is unable to review or rehearse the word—a word that would be easily identified were it simply flashed and followed by no other task.

The results of this are summarized in Figure 6–3. Note how quickly the *recall* decays over time. After less than a minute there is no evidence of any memory of the word. What such findings indicate is that material must be rehearsed in order to be stored permanently and that, in the absence of such reinforcement, it undergoes a more or less continuous *decay*, soon reaching a zero level, which can be taken as the equivalent of complete *erasure*.

The same kind of process can be illustrated in many ways. Suppose, for example, subjects are given brief (20 milliseconds) exposures to an array of letters

J   B   L   R   W   ⟨K⟩   F

Ordinarily after so brief an exposure the average subject can recall only two or three letters in the array. However, if a ring is placed over the position occupied by one of the letters during a test of recall coming, say, 100 milliseconds after the initial presentation, the average subject is able to state which letter *cued retrieval* had occupied that position. Here we have an example of *cued* retrieval which permits us to tap the short-term memory banks by inserting a locator cue. If a ring is placed over one of the positions *minutes* or even *seconds* later, the subject is no better at recalling the letter than he is when no locator cue is present at

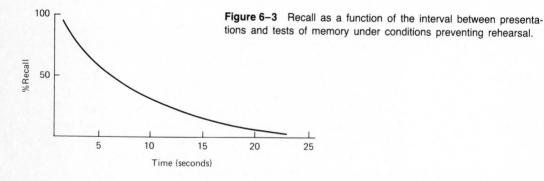

Figure 6–3 Recall as a function of the interval between presentations and tests of memory under conditions preventing rehearsal.

all. Clearly, then, the cue is working on a temporary storage process with time contants in the fraction-of-a-second range.

It would not be too misleading to propose that there are two sharply defined processes governing our ability to recall information or past experiences. The terms "short-term" and "long-term" are intended to distinguish between periods of time *during* which recent events can be erased and periods of time *after* which such erasure is at most partial and nonselective. Indeed, in most cases our inability to recall what was clearly in long-term memory is not the result of erasure but of *interference* produced by more significant or more recently acquired information.

The psychology of memory, as with all fertile realms of inquiry, now enjoys a wide range of theoretical controversies and experimental findings. It is not our purpose here to review either, but to take what seem to be the more firmly established principles and to examine their possible physiological foundations. For our purposes, therefore, the earliest stage of "short-term memory" is taken to mean only the following:

1. Memory of stimuli and events occurring no more than several minutes prior to tests of recall.
2. Memory which when disrupted results in a total loss of recall no matter how long a retention period or recovery period lasts.
3. Memory that is tied primarily to the physical rather than the symbolic properties of stimuli and that can therefore be disrupted by physically similar competing stimuli.

The behavioral adaptations most directly tied to such short-term processes are those controlled by classical and operant conditioning and related forms of associational learning. In classical conditioning the interval between the conditioned stimulus (CS) and the unconditioned stimulus (UCS) must be quite brief if the former is to acquire the eliciting powers of the latter. Similarly, in operant conditioning it is necessary for the reinforcer to be temporally close to the response that procures it. And in both forms of conditioning the relevant aspects of the stimulus are physical rather than cognitive. Note, however, that neither form of conditioning remains at the level of short-term memory throughout the conditioning sessions. The pairing of *bell* and *food* in classical conditioning must be closely spaced in time, but the conditioned animal, placed back in the harness after a two- or three-day rest, will salivate to the bell on its first presentation. And the same is true of the operantly conditioned animal returned to the test chamber after even a prolonged absence. According to the model that has guided us throughout this chapter these facts are to be understood as the result of interactions between short-term and long-term memory processes. It is in the very course of conditioning that the contents of short-term memory are transferred to more permanent modes of storage such that the conditioning survives over long periods of nonreinforcement. What the model predicts, however, is that such long-term storage can be prevented if, during the earliest phases of conditioning, measures are taken to disrupt the transfer or erase the contents of the *buffer* store.

Psychobiological studies of short-term memory are numerous and varied. The common strategy is to identify neural events closely following those environmental and behavioral events that characterize associational models of learning. The neural events studied to date include recordings from single units, macroelectrode recordings from large populations of cells, alterations in the gross EEG record during conditioning, surgical destruction or removal of areas of the brain thought to be important to the short-term memory function, electrical or chemical disruptions of brain function at various points during the conditioning process, and examination of the brains of human patients displaying short-term memory deficits. Several of the more suggestive findings may now be summarized.

Electroconvulsive Shock (ECS)

avoidance conditioning

If experimental animals are exposed to a simple conditioning procedure such as shock avoidance, it generally takes only a small number of trials before the presentation of a signaling stimulus reliably results in the conditioned response—for example, running away from the shock source, jumping a hurdle, and so on. It is possible, however, to throw the animals into a general convulsive seizure by clipping electrodes to each ear and passing current through the skull. In such cases the seizures are followed by a period of coma from which the animals recover completely. Figure 6–4 shows the effects of ECS on the development of conditioned avoidance. In the absence of ECS the animal will typically perform the correct avoidance response at least 80 percent of the time which is just what the ECS-treated animal does when there is a long interval between an avoidance trial and the delivery of ECS. When the interval is brief, however, the animal's performance drops to 10 percent or less.

Similar effects can be obtained from animals receiving ECS even under the influence of anesthesia indicating that it is not the aversive or possibly painful consequences of ECS that

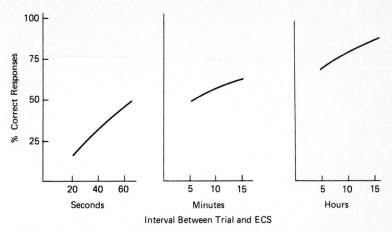

Figure 6–4 The effects of various intervals between trials and ECS on the acquisition of a conditioned-avoidance response. The greatest effect is obtained during the first minute following the trial.

consolidation

disrupt behavior. The usual interpretation is that the formation of associations initially involves a short-term memory process and that disruptions of the electrical activity of the brain during this process prevents the *consolidation* of such associations into a more permanent form of memory. Human patients receiving electroshock therapy for depression also display an amnesia for events just preceding the shock, although their recall of more distant events is unaffected. It is also likely that such amnesias require the induction of *cortical* seizures since the amnesic effects are not observed when seizures are induced in spinal or subcortical structures.

Neuroelectric Correlates

CNV

Many studies have indicated reliable EEG and evoked response correlates of learning. One reliable correlate is the *contingent negative variation* (CNV) observed in EEG traces during the formation of a learned association. As the number of training trials proceeds, those on which a relevant cue is presented result in a deflection of the EEG baseline in the direction of the increased negativity as is shown in Figure 6–5. Here a signal to remind the observer to perform a task (such as pressing a key) leads not only to a sensory evoked response to the signal but to a baseline shift in the entire trace. Given its time constants, the CNV may be more properly considered as a correlate of short-term memory except for the fact that it grows in amplitude over a long run of trials. We will discuss CNV further in Chapter 8.

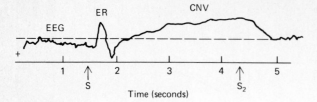

Figure 6–5 The time course of the contingent negative variations. The background EEG gives way to an evoked response (ER) triggered by a cue stimulus (S) which also signals that a response is required from the observer. The baseline shift in the negative ($-$) direction is *contingent* on this sort of signal tied to a specific response or some learned association. A second stimulus (S_2) that signals the end of the task is followed by the quick recovery of baseline activity and the termination of the CNV.

Frontal Lobe Syndrome

Both human patients with lesions in the frontal lobes and experimental animals with surgically destroyed frontal lobes display a variety of short-term memory deficits. Prominent among these is a confusion of the temporal order of sequential events observed by the human patient and a failure in *delayed response* tasks by experimental animals. The frontal-lobe animal will have trouble finding a peanut hidden under one of three cups even though the animal watched it being hidden just seconds earlier. The frontal-lobe syndrome, however, also produces a less attentive animal such that the effects on delayed response learning may be the result of interfering with the attentional memory loops sketched earlier in Figure 6–2. Actually, both attentional and mnemonic functions are probably performed in frontal cortex. Recently studies have been made of the electrical activity of individual cortical neurons in the frontal lobe of the monkey during delayed response learning. It seems that there are at least seven different functional types of neuron involved in tasks of this sort. One type displays increased activity when the hidden object (food) is concealed but decreased activity when it is suddenly exposed. Here we have a neuron type that is more active during the attentional phase of learning but inhibited once the target is discovered. The hypothesis supported by such findings is that specific cells are involved in the storage of information during a delay interval and that the destruction of such cells is at the expense of short-term memory.

Neuronal Conditioning

Perhaps the most direct evidence in support of the thesis that conditioning is mediated by neuronal mechanisms comes from research in which the electrical activity of single neurons in the

single unit studies

brain can be conditioned. Recent research has indicated that single neurons can be both classically and operantly conditioned. One version of the eye-blink reflex is illustrative of the former. If the bridge of a cat's nose is struck lightly both eyes blink. Preceding each blow with a "click" soon establishes a (classically) conditioned eye-blink response. It is now known that in the course of this conditioning individual neurons in the motor system controlling the eye-blink undergo systematic changes in their electrical properties, and that these changes come to be elicited by the "click." In other words, the individual neurons, initially unresponsive to the conditioned stimulus ("click"), come to respond to it in the course of classical conditioning. In still other studies a kind of *biofeedback approach* succeeds in increasing or decreasing the firing rates of individual neurons. If, for example, food is delivered to the animal only when the firing rate of a given neuron increases there occurs a systematic increase in the firing rate! The firing rates of the same neuron can thus be regulated in both directions by the systematic application of rewards.

What all of these studies have in common is the discovery of neuroelectric and neurochemical correlates of performance over relatively short temporal intervals. Note, however, that the ECS animal that fails to perform the avoidance response still knows where to find food, still grooms itself, still engages in normal mating behavior, and still performs well on tasks learned days or weeks earlier. The classical or operant conditioning of single units requires that the interval between conditioned stimulus and unconditioned stimulus or between the neural response and the contingent reward be very brief, surely no more than ten or twenty seconds. And the frontal-lobe patient who has so much difficulty untangling the order of a rapidly presented sequence of events has no difficulty ordering those events that are separated by days or weeks or years. At least at the grossest level of analysis, therefore, we are permitted to speak of a *short-term* set of processes distinct from those long-term processes on which our permanent or nearly permanent memories are based.

Long-Term Memory

It is with long-term memory that the term "learning" is conventionally associated and it is to long-term memory that we turn when we seek to understand most of the animal's acquired behavioral adjustments. In fact the behavioral functions are so utterly intertwined that the words "learning" and "memory" are very often confused. What, after all, do we mean by *learning* if not the ability of the animal to string past experiences together in such a way as to accomplish the same task in less time and with fewer errors? But genuine differences exist. The patient suffering from a total amnesia—the patient who does not know his or her name, the names or identities of near relatives, the location of his or her residence, the type of work in which he was engaged for years—is still able to learn new habits and acquire new information. Thus, although learning and memory are functionally interwoven in the life of every advanced species, they are also partially separate processes in that at least some memories can be lost while the ability to learn remains unimpaired.

The most obvious difference between a normal and an amnesic patient is not in their respective abilities as learners. Everything we learn about the amnesic can be learned by the patient. The problem is that the patient now knows these facts just as we do. At the most general level, we can talk about two kinds of knowledge—knowledge by *description* and knowledge by *direct acquaintance*. The former is illustrated by the knowledge we have of a city we've never visited when it is described to us by a friend. The latter is illustrated by the knowledge we have after we ourselves have visited the city. In this sense each person knows his or her own pains and feelings and experiences by direct acquaintance, whereas the pains, feelings, experiences and so on, of others is known only by (their) descriptions. In the case of amnesia the patient's knowledge of his or her own life is a kind of *knowledge by description*. To tell an amnesic the facts of his or her personal life is, for all practical purposes, to be speaking about someone else. What the patient cannot do is tie all these facts to a continuing *personal* history, a personal narrative. To use an informative if unscientific term, the amnesic cannot tie the facts to his or her own *self*.

agnosia and apraxia

There are less profound amnesias than this which result in the selective loss of what may be called cognitive and motor memories. Visual *agnosias*, for example, involve the inability to recognize common objects although they are clearly visible. For example a man might be shown a key and asked what it is. He struggles to find the right word but cannot. If asked "Do you know what this is?" he might nod affirmatively. However, once the key is placed in his hand he immediately says "Key." Here we have a visual interpretive deficit but not a sensory loss. The patient's visual sensitivity is normal. His deficit is the result of being unable to connect a current perception with the long-term memory of objects and their functions. On the motor side we discover similar deficits known as *apraxias*. One common form is the so-called "dressing apraxia." The patient may appear to be normal in all respects—that is, his conversation and general bearing are unremarkable, his senses keen, and his movements agile. But if he is handed a jacket and asked to put it on he simply cannot perform the sequence of steps required. He fumbles with the jacket the way the agnosic fumbles in search of the right word. Again we have the failure to connect a current perception with long-term *motor* memories of objects and their uses.

The agnosias and apraxias have been reliably found in patient's with lesions in *association cortex*. There is, however, little by way of strict localization. A lesion in one patient that results in agnosia may, in another, be correlated with aphasia. In the majority of cases, the agnosias and apraxias result from diseases in the *dominant* hemisphere (nearly always the *left* hemisphere, even in left-handed persons). But agnosias also result from lesions in parietal, occipital, and temporal cortex. It should be noted in this connection that none of these cortical regions, except the temporal lobe, is generally implicated in learning and long-term memory as these processes are ordinarily studied using nonhuman animals and surgical destructions. The point here is that *memory* is one of those pervasive functions that enters into nearly all modes of behavioral adaptation and that expresses itself in a great variety of ways. Properly understood, it is a word we use to represent a large constellation of processes that enable the animal or human to revive the past for the purpose of dealing with the present. To have a memory of specific things does not imply that each memory is a specific thing. To say, for example, that one's memory of *chair* is stored in the brain is not to say that a chair is in the brain! At the most general level it is to say only that those neuroelectric and neurochemical processes associated with the initial learning of what "chair" is can, at a later time, be revived or reconstructed, and that by *memory* we are only referring to the revival or reconstruction of these processes. It is not even proper to speak of these processes as somehow containing the memory but as constituting the *sufficient conditions* for the past to be recalled. But let us leave this important and complex issue until a later section and focus here on the *learning* part of the learning-memory complex. Under the heading of long-term memory we can include those forms of learning that involve prolonged exposure to relevant environmental conditions and that only become apparent after a significant number of training trials.

Effects of Environmental Enrichment

It is now clear from an immense amount of research conducted over the past thirty years that learning and environmental enrichment change the brain, as we noted in the previous chapter. This is one of the least controversial claims offered by the science of psychobiology. Conclusions arising out of this research, and noted briefly in Chapter 5, are these:

Dendritic Spines

At the level of neuronal cells, it is now known that conditions of environmental enrichment as well as prolonged involvement in learning tasks result in a significant increase in the number of spine-like growths on certain dendrites, particularly the apical dendrites of cortical pyramidal cells. Animals reared in darkness may have 50 percent fewer spines per segment of cortex than normally reared litter mates. Even more specific are the effects of conditioning in that a learning task results in a greater proliferation of spines than does mere activity or environmental exposure. Finally, comparisons of the neuronal spines in pyramidal cells from normal and from retarded human beings indicate that the latter are less numerous and of a more fragile shape. We return to this on pp. 259–264.

Biochemistry

Litter mates separated into groups exposed either to conditions of isolation or conditions of environmental complexity display significant differences in brain chemistry. Most relevant is the much higher ratio of ACh to AChE in the enriched sample. Moreover, rats genetically bred for maze brightness (that is, rats inbred for their ability to solve mazes) display a much higher ACh/AChE ratio than maze dull rats. Thus, not only does the behavioral phenotype display heritability but so too does the biochemical phenotype for one important transmitter.

Biochemical Depressants

Certain drugs such as puromycin are known to inhibit the formation of brain proteins. Administration of these substances *before* training does not appear to affect acquisition of conditioned responses. But when the administration of the drug covers the period from minutes to about an hour following the training there are pronounced effects on the recently acquired behavior. Where ECS seems to operate primarily in the range of seconds and minutes, the biochemical agents are most effective in the half-hour to hour range. This suggests that the earliest memory coding (the genuinely *short-term* coding) is electrical and that it is followed by a longer-term *intermediate memory* process in which chemical modes of consolidation predominate. We shall expand on this later.

Data from Lesion Studies

Many hundreds of experiments have been performed on a variety of species involving the learning of many types of tasks following the destruction of one or of some combination of cortical and subcortical regions of the subjects' brain. The major conclusion warranted by all this research,as noted in Chapter 5, is a negative one. There is no specific region of the brain uniquely associated with long-term memory or the forms of learning that depend on it. Lesions in visual cortex will, of course, impair the learning of visual discriminations, but there is no *general* learning deficit produced. Obviously, an animal whose visual perception is destroyed or severely impaired will do poorly on visual discrimination learning tasks. The failure to find a memory engram in a specific place in the brain has been matched by the failure to find a "learning place" in the brain. What does seem clear, however, is the connection between large areas of the cerebral cortex—particularly the prefrontal, frontal, and temporal lobes—and a number of *cognitive* functions involved in complex learning. Lesions in prefrontal cortex in the monkey, for example, will produce great deficits in a number of complex tasks such as *discrimination reversal*. This type of task requires the animal to learn one discrimination (choosing a vertical as opposed to a horizontal stimulus), but to reverse the choice after each successful response. Bilateral lesions in the human hippocampus have been found to produce deficits in the ability to learn names and places of recent origin in the patient's experience. The problem seems to be one of transferring short-term memory contents into long-term storage, although the bilaterally hippocampectomized monkey is far less impaired than the human patient in this respect. The specific effects in both cases, however, are complicated by age differences, sex differences, and the nature of the task.

It should be obvious that this entire area of research and theory is conceptually troubled, though factually rich and growing. If some added degree of order is to be attained, we must constantly return to matters of definition, classification, and explanation. Let us step back, therefore, and examine the phenomena of memory once again, beginning with a deeper analysis of the variety of phenomena considered as different kinds of memory.

A Taxonomy of Memory

We will now proceed to classify memories. A particularly useful criterion for classifying memories is a temporal one based upon the period of persistence of the trace. This is an important conceptual step forward from the operational definitions presented earlier. This criterion has the dual advantages of being independent of the particular procedures by means of which the memory was established, while at the same time providing a powerful means of conceptualizing what constitutes the physiological and anatomical equivalents of memory. The basic idea, often attributed to Donald Hebb (Chapter 1), is that there exist different kinds of memories (and the implication is often drawn that these represent different neural mechanisms) that persist for different durations. Regardless of how the memory is established, the neural mechanisms underlying several different kinds of briefly lasting memories are assumed to be more alike (and perhaps identical to each other) than they are like the mechanisms that underlie long-term traces.

It was Hebb who originally suggested there were two distinct kinds of memory—one of which persists for a very brief period (*short-term memory*) and one that is permanent or at least very long lasting (*long-term memory*). He also suggested that the

four modes of memory

briefly persisting or transient memory is designed for the temporary storage of information. It can be loaded very quickly but the information thus stored must be transformed (*consolidated*) to the more permanent kind of long-term memory for longer term storage to avoid being lost. More elaborate models of learning involving three or four kinds of memory of varying persistence have been forthcoming. The original idea of a duplex memory evolved into a quadriplex version. In Table 6–1 we review one such model consisting of four different kinds of memory. The *sensory store* or *register* serves as a very brief and transient form of memory that holds information for very brief periods, up to only a half-second or so. The contents of this sensory register decay so quickly that unless the stored information is transferred in that brief period of time to the next stage, which is *short-term memory*, the information recorded in the sensory register will be lost. Short-term memory is presumed to persist for only about 20 seconds before it too decays. Some

TABLE 6–1 The Properties of the Four Kinds of Memory

	Storage System			
	Sensory Memory	Short-term Memory	Intermediate-term Memory	Long-term Memory
Capacity	Limited by amount transmitted by receptor	The 7 ± 2 of the memory span	Very large (no adequate estimate)	Very large (no adequate estimate)
Duration	Fractions of a second	Several seconds	Several minutes to several years	May be permanent
Entry into storage	Automatic with perception	Verbal recoding	Rehearsal	Overlearning
Organization	Reflects physical stimuli	Temporal sequence	Semantic and relational	?
Accessibility of traces	Limited only by speed of read out	Very rapid access	Relatively slow	Very rapid access
Types of information	Sensory	Verbal (at least)	All	All
Types of forgetting	Decay and erasure	New information replaces old	Interference: retroactive and proactive inhibition	May be none

Source: R.R. Ervin and T.R. Anders, *The Neurosciences: Second Study Program,* 1970.

investigators believe that there is also a distinguishable *intermediate-term memory* that has it own special properties and in which information may persist for periods that vary from several minutes to years. Finally, all agree that there is a *long-term memory* capability of the nervous system in which information may persist for the lifetime of the organism.

Table 6–1 summarizes many important features of the system of memories that we have been discussing. We have already mentioned that the main distinguishing features among the various memories is the duration over which the information may be maintained. But another feature that distinguishes the various kinds of memories from each other is the capacity of each. George Sperling, in a now classic paper, made it clear that the sensory store has an enormous capacity. It seems to store virtually everything in pictographic form. However, this image fades so quickly in most people that very little of it can be read out before the image has faded. Sperling's point is that the sensory store can hold much more information than can the short-term store. The short-term memory is known to possess a very limited capacity. In fact, the limited capacity of the short-term memory was the topic of what may be one of the most cited papers of the modern psychological literature, "The Magical

Number 7 Plus or Minus Two: Some Limits on Our Capacity for Processing Information," written by George Miller. There are no really good estimates of the capacity of the intermediate or long-term memories, on the other hand, but the suggestion is that they have very large capacities, indeed, and some psychologists have even suggested that they may somehow store *all* of the information which has come through our senses during our entire lifetime.

This then brings us finally to two questions most relevant to the topic of this chapter: "What is memory?" and "Where does it occur?"

The first question concerns the actual physiological and anatomical change that occurs in the nervous system corresponding to memory. The actual physical change underlying memory has been referred to as the engram. There have been a large number of theories concerning the nature of the engram over the years, but only one has lasted. Most researchers in the field are now convinced that it must be accounted for in terms of changes in the *efficiency or conductivity of synaptic junctions*. We shall elaborate greatly on this point in the following sections of this chapter.

The answer to the second question, given in Chapter 5, can also be repeated at this point; it is also accepted nearly universally. A host of experiments attest to the fact that memory is not localized in any particular place within the nervous system but is distributed throughout the nervous system.

memory and the synapse The notion that memory is intimately involved in synaptic function is a plausible hypothesis—indeed the *most* plausible hypothesis given what we know of brain physiology. Only a few alternative theories have been proposed that run counter to this hypothesis and they have not gained broad acceptance in the scientific community. One notable alternative raised some years ago was that information was stored in the coded sequences in the molecules of the nervous system in a way that is comparable to the way the genetic code is stored in the sequence of bases in a molecule of deoxyribonucleic acid (DNA) in the nucleus of a cell. This hypothesis (proposed in one form or another since the nineteenth century) asserts that the act of learning in some way codes information about the experience into a string of chemicals making up a macromolecule. Specifically the modern theory suggests that RNA is the coded memory molecule. This hypothesis failed to gain sufficient empirical support over the years and has been rejected by most of the scientific community. However, it is very important to remember that this does not necessarily mean that RNA is not involved in learning. In fact, we now know that RNA is intimately involved in the construction of some of the same proteins that also seem to be important in determining synaptic conductivity. The most current view is that these molecules are not the engram actually storing information about experiences, but rather are involved in the growth of new synapses.

Other neuroscientists have from time to time proposed other mechanisms for the engram that depend on functions of parts of the neuron other than synapses. Some have suggested, for example, that the nonsynaptic neural membranes may change their properties, or that neurons may even be generated or be destroyed as a result of experience. However, all such mechanisms seem not to provide the flexibility or immediate responsivity displayed by the synapse. More speculative ideas involving the actual storage of information in glial cells or some putative interaction between glia and neurons do not enjoy many adherents in today's scientific community.

In sum, the synaptic hypothesis is the *only* one that has plausibility and vitality today. But it must be acknowledged that even this very plausible idea is virtually without direct empirical support. To the contrary, the chain of logic implicating the synapses as the *sine qua non* of memory and learning is quite indirect. The synapse is the place in the nervous system in which changes can occur. There are a number of pieces of evidence indicating the existence of both short- and long-term synaptic effects, and the concept of a synaptically mediated memory is otherwise consistent with what we believe to be the other relationships between mental (and/or behavioral) phenomena and the state of a neural network. Most psychobiologists agree, therefore, that the only plausible way the neural network could change is by means of variations in the conductivity or effectiveness of the interconnections between neurons—that is, as a result of *synaptic plasticity*. However, no one has even seen a synapse change its function or grow in any way that can be linked specifically to complex human learning. Even in simple invertebrate model preparations, it is difficult to link specific synaptic changes with the simple conditioning procedures that are typically used in studies of this sort. In short, the synaptic hypothesis is nearly universally accepted, but on the most indirect basis. The best argument for this particular theory of the engram is that there simply seems to be no compelling alternative.

Let's delve a little more deeply into the possible role of synaptic plasticity at this point as a preview of our more detailed discussion later in the chapter. There must be two kinds of synaptic *plasticity* corresponding to the two main kinds of memory, short-term and long-term. First, one kind of synaptic plasticity must itself be transient. For example, repeated use of a synapse may temporarily increase the probability that a

synaptic plasticity

low level signal will pass through the junction but this altered probability must last for only a brief period of time. Such a temporary *potentiation* of synaptic action is probably associated with some transient change in the presynaptic or postsynaptic membrane. Signals would thus temporarily reverberate through a network because of the short-term fluctuations in synaptic conductivity. These brief periods of enhanced effectiveness would correspond to the sensory storage or short-term memory durations. On the other hand, some synaptic changes must be more persistent, in fact permanent. Such a synaptic change is more likely to involve synaptic growth, the generation of new interconnections, or other changes in the membrane that would last as long as the organism is alive. Such persistent synaptic changes would be required to explain intermediate- and long-term memory. The next section examines these possibilities.

We have already considered where the engram is stored. No experiment has ever demonstrated a particular locus in the brain that, if removed, destroys all memory of all past experience. Similarly, many different brain regions have been shown to be altered by experience. As a result of such findings, it is now agreed by psychobiologists that almost any region of the central nervous system may be involved in the storage of information. Other studies, which are discussed in detail later in this chapter, have shown that even particular memories are probably not localized in the brain. The effects of experience always seem to be distributed throughout large portions of the brain. There are many adaptive advantages to a *distributed memory* of this sort. Localized injury or destruction of neurons would not significantly reduce the quality of the stored memory if parts or copies were deposited in widely dispersed regions of the brain.

There is another consideration, however. Even though it seems quite likely some engrams actually are stored throughout the brain, there is another context in which some degree of functional localization of learning processes can be observed. Many regions of the brain are known to be involved in controlling and regulating learning, even if they are not the actual local repositories of the engram. Stimulation or ablation of regions like the frontal or inferotemporal cerebral lobes, the hippocampus, the amygdala, and the septal nucleus (locations in the brain that are also, as we have seen, intimately involved in emotions and motivations) do seem to influence particular kinds of learning. However, because these regions are often involved in processes that regulate the internal environment, and because learning is greatly affected by these internal environments, it is not at all clear what the meaning is of, for example, an experiment in which a hippocampal lesion is shown to reduce the ability of an organism to perform a particular task over long periods of time. Has the experimenter actually discovered a center that controls learning or simply altered the motivational level of the organism? It is exceedingly difficult to select from among the alternatives roles that might be played by any brain center, as we noted in Chapter 5. Even sensory and motor lesions affect learning, but few psychobiologists would assert that these regions are the specific locus of the engram.

The overall conclusion we draw from the data now available is that no single center uniquely is responsible for generating or storing memories. At the very least, multiple regions of the brain, interconnected in complex inhibitory and excitatory manners and strongly interacting with each other are involved in all forms of learning.

In the following sections of this chapter we will consider in detail the findings that provide us with insights and answers concerning the psychobiology of memory. Specifically we will consider possible synaptic changes associated with memory— consolidation, and localization of memory processes.

Possible Synaptic Changes Associated with Memory

As we have asserted, the only plausible and comprehensive explanation of memory is based on changes in synaptic conductivity as a result of experiences. Given the temporal dimension along which we classified memory, it has already been made clear that we will have to consider different kinds of synaptic changes to accommodate the different kinds of memory. While all four (sensory storage, short-term, intermediate-term and long-term) do not require individual mechanisms, at least one transient and one permanent synaptic effect are required to begin to make sense of any synaptic theory of molar learning.

Sensory storage seems not to be a synaptic effect, it should be noted. Most researchers in the field now believe that this very brief *iconic* storage is actually mediated by the receptors themselves. It is absolutely clear that the other three kinds of memory must be *central* and *synaptic*. In this section we consider some of the neurophysiological data supportive of the synaptic hypothesis of the engram. First we discuss transient synaptic changes and then the more permanent changes.

Transient Synaptic Changes

Because the nervous systems of vertebrates are extremely complicated and constructed from very small and highly interconnected and idiosyncratic neurons, psychobiologists have often turned to the simpler nervous systems of invertebrates to study neural interaction and synaptic plasticity. Even in these simple animals, however, it is not possible to observe synaptic activity directly as the creatures undergo some more or less natural learning experiences. Therefore, highly artificial stimuli usually have to be substituted for the normal ones the animal might encounter in its usual life. For example, repetitive electrical stimuli often are used to test or alter synaptic conductivity. It is also difficult in such experimental situations to observe directly the changes accruing at the particularly involved synapse. All that can be done is to observe the changes in the responses of neurons that are *probably* connected to the synapses under study.

Invertebrate nervous systems have other advantages, however, that overcome these difficulties. They are relatively simple; investigators confront only a few dozen neurons in some neural networks rather than the tens of thousands or millions in a mammalian system that seems to be performing an analogous function. Furthermore, the neurons in an invertebrate nervous system are not only very large but their arrangement and placement are also highly repetitive from one preparation to the next. This allows the psychobiologist more directly to study the function of a single neuron in an invertebrate ganglion. A considerable amount of attention has been paid to neuron L10 in the sea hare's (*Aplysia*) nervous system (shown in Figure 6–1). Because of the anatomical constancy from one animal to the next, the researcher can be assured that this same cell will be in exactly the same place in each and every specimen. If there is a similar kind of order, anatomical stability, and repetitiveness in the mammalian nervous system, it has not yet become apparent to researchers.

Let us now consider a typical experiment on *Aplysia* that is

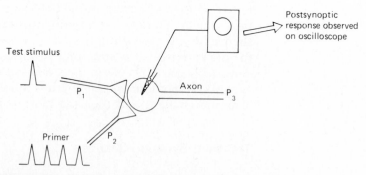

Figure 6–6 A sample preparation of neurons from the abdominal ganglion of Aplysia arranged to demonstrate heterosynaptic facilitation.

suggestive of the kind of synaptic mechanism that could account for short-term memory. (In no sense should it be assumed that this is the only explanation of short-term memory—but this experiment at least illustrates one possible way in which a neuron could exhibit a transient storage capability.) Assume that the Aplysia's nervous system has been dissected free and three neurons laid out as shown diagrammatically in Figure 6–6. Two presynaptic neurons labeled P_1 and P_2 feed into a single postsynaptic neuron labeled P_3. To test its operation, presynaptic neuron P_1 is stimulated with a weak electrical stimulus. Under ordinary conditions, such a stimulus produces only a small postsynaptic graded potential in P_3. This weak stimulus is referred to as the *test stimulus*. Next in this experiment the investigators strongly stimulate P_2 with a brief train of electrical shocks referred to as the *priming stimulus*. The effect of the priming stimulus is to produce a very large response in P_3. The next step is the critical one. It not only produces the unusual effect, but also acts to model the learning process in higher animals. If the test and priming stimuli are presented simultaneously for about a minute, subsequent presentations of a single test stimulus without the priming stimulus will produce a postsynaptic graded response in P_3 that is far larger than the test stimulus could have produced prior to its being paired with the priming train. This increase in effectiveness persists for prolonged periods of time as shown in Figure 6–7.

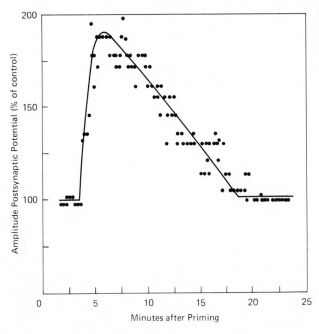

Figure 6–7 The results of the heterosynaptic facilitation experiment. (Redrawn from Kandel, E.R. and Tauc, L., *Journal of Physiology*, 1965, 181:1–27.)

The point of this demonstration is that the facilitation of the effect of the single test stimulus to P_1 is the result of transient changes that almost certainly occurred at the synapse between P_1 and P_3. It could hardly be otherwise since there was no evidence the presynaptic neuron through which the test stimulus was conducted was affected in any way by the priming stimulus and P_2 is not connected to P_1. Nor was there any change in the presynaptic response—only the postsynaptic graded potential was enlarged.

heterosynaptic facilitation

Because two different synapses (the one between the P_1 and P_3 and the one between P_2 and P_3) are involved, this improvement in synaptic effectiveness has been designated as *heterosynaptic facilitation*. We should note that heterosynaptic facilitation in this invertebrate has many superficial similarities with classical conditioning in mammals. In both cases a previously weakly effective stimulus has acquired a high level of effectiveness by virtue of pairing with a stimulus that is initially strongly effective. However, no one believes they are exactly the same thing or that one is the exact neural mechanism of the other.

Heterosynaptic facilitation is only one of many different ways to demonstrate changes in synaptic effectiveness resulting from experience. Another process often observed in mammalian nervous systems is called *post-tetanic potentiation*. In this case the system is conceptually much simpler. Figure 6–8 shows the experimental arrangement required to demonstrate post-tetantic potentiation. A single presynaptic neuron feeds into a single postsynaptic neuron. Typically this process is demonstrated in the vertebrate spinal cord. The experimental procedure involves the repeated stimulation of the single presynaptic neuron with a train of electrical stimuli. This is referred to as a *tetanic stimulus train* (so named by the classic physiologists, since such stimuli often produce a sustained muscular contrac-

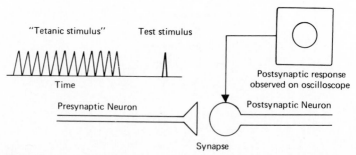

Figure 6–8 The experimental arrangement to demonstrate post-tetanic potentiation.

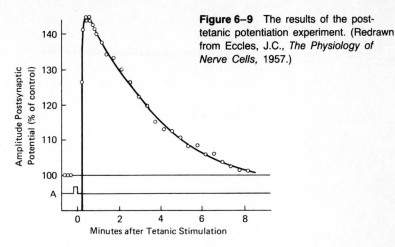

Figure 6–9 The results of the post-tetanic potentiation experiment. (Redrawn from Eccles, J.C., *The Physiology of Nerve Cells*, 1957.)

tion—tetanus). Figure 6–9 shows the effects on the amplitude of a postsynaptic potential when a single test stimulus is presented to the presynaptic neuron at various times following the tetanic stimulus. This *potentiation* (enlargement) of the response may last for several minutes and does not occur in the absence of an interposed synapse. Here again we observe a change in synaptic efficiency that has properties analogous to those that would be required to produce short-term memory. Repeated stimulation enhances the response strength, but only temporarily. After a period of time, the memory fades away leaving no trace of the potentiating stimulus. Interestingly enough, this occurs after a duration roughly the same as the duration of short-term memory. Once again, this is not to say that post-tetanic-potentiation *is* short-term memory but only that there exist mechanisms in the vertebrate nervous system with approximately the correct temporal properties.

The important fact in the context of the present discussion is that the transient potentiation effect also must be localized in the synapse: No comparable charge can be discerned in the axons of the presynaptic neuron. On the axon the effect of excessive (tetanic) stimulation is only fatigue and response decrement.

It is, however, not at all clear what the actual changes are that account for the increase in synaptic effectiveness when one observes post-tetanic potentiation. It is possible that changes may have occurred on the presynaptic side of the synapse. There may be an increased tendency to emit the particular synaptic transmitter substance required by this particular junction as a result of the repeated activation. One presynaptic change, however, that quite certainly is not a plausible explanation of either an increased excitatory or inhibitory effect is depletion of the available chemical transmitter substance. The actual amount of transmitter chemical used by the synapse even when it is heavily activated is much, much less than the amount stored in the presynaptic regions. Furthermore, the metabolic processes occurring in the region of the synapse are efficient enough to replenish the small amount of transmitter substance used virtually as fast as it is depleted.

On the other hand, a more likely explanation seems to be a drastic change in the sensitivity of the receptor sites on the postsynaptic membrane. The protein molecules that constitute these postsynaptic receptor sites are likely candidates to mediate the change in synaptic conductivity since they do change drastically as a result of excess activation. The postsynaptic receptor sites may be temporarily sensitized or desensitized by extraordinarily high levels of neural activity, or they may be desensitized by the accumulation of various breakdown products.

However, it is important to reiterate that all of this story is still speculative—we simply do not know what structural or chemical change is occurring at the synapses that account for their change in conductivity. Nevertheless, the confirmed existence of transient synaptic changes such as post-tetanic potentiation and heterosynaptic facilitation makes it clear that short-term physiological processes do exist at synapses. These can play the role of the engram, guiding and channeling reverberative neural activity for brief periods of time in a way corresponding to short-term memory. Such synaptic changes are capable of temporarily reorganizing the state of a neural network for a brief period of time. Such modified networks could easily allow signals that would otherwise be too short to recirculate or reverberate and thus preserve a trace of what has gone on before—in other words, to serve as a temporary or short-term memory.

Permanent Synaptic Changes

It is unarguable that transient changes in synaptic conductivity are very poor candidates to encode the long term memories that last a lifetime. The random errors to which such a circulating system of neural responses would be susceptible would (and probably do) quickly degrade the short-term engram. Thus these transient memories would fade away in a few minutes after the termination of the stimulus conditions that initiated them. Circulating or reverberatory patterns of neural activity based on such temporary changes such as post-tetanic potentiation or some similar process, susceptible to random influences and errors, would quickly become lost in the confusion of any subsequently induced neural activity. The changes underlying long-term memories, therefore, must be "punched" into the nervous system in a much more stable way that would allow stored information to remain intact and recallable over the lifetime of the organism.

structural synaptic changes

There is a well-accepted set of hypotheses concerning the nature of the long lasting engram that is also based on synaptic changes. These hypotheses incorporate concepts of synaptic growth and change that are of a much more permanent nature than those seemingly involved in short-term storage. Indeed, an extraordinarily wide variety of such changes has been suggested from time to time, in spite of the fact that no such mechanism has even been directly linked to the learning process. For example, actual physical enlargement of existing synaptic terminals has been observed, and many experiments now have reported the actual physical birth and growth of new junctions under conditions that are comparable to learning situations. It is at this point that the macromolecules regulating and encoding protein production in the cell do begin to play a reasonable and plausible role—reason and plausibility being absent from the concept that information was literally stored in the sequence of nucleotides in RNA, for example.

Obviously, to establish any theory relating synaptic growth and long-term memory, it would be necessary to show that experience can actually alter synaptic structure in a way that is sufficient to account for learning. Although it is virtually impossible to link such changes directly with behavioral changes, an increasing number of studies have shown that there are physiological, chemical, and anatomical changes in synaptic structure as a function of controlled experience.

A particularly useful preparation for demonstrating structural changes in synapses utilizes the pyramidal cells of the cerebral cortex. This type of neuron is covered with a very large number of synaptic *spines*. The density of spines on a pyramidal neuron has proven to be a highly useful indicator of *experience-generated* synaptic growth. Rats brought up in an enriched environment have a larger number of dendritic spines on most parts of the pyramid cells. Similarly the weight of the cortex in general and the visual cortex in particular may be enhanced by as much as 6 percent.

Dendritic spines on pyramidal cells in the regions of the brain receiving inputs from an intact eye are found to be much more plentiful than the spines on similar cells in the cortical regions that were deprived of their inputs by enucleation of the other eye. Indeed, not only are there distinct differences in the number of spines on the two sides of the brain, but individual spines also vary in their respective shapes. Spines on the side of the brain innervated by the intact eye are broader in shape than those on the side innervated by the eye that is removed.

The growth or engorgement of spines on a pyramidal neuron could affect synaptic conduction in a number of different ways. An actual physical increase in the number of spines could increase conductivity by providing more opportunities for a single presynaptic neuron to activate a postsynaptic neuron. It could also bring many new neurons into a circuit than had previously been present. Physical swelling of spines, however, could accomplish the same effect by reducing the electrical resistance or providing an increased area through which could pass increased amounts of transmitter substance. In the microscopic domain being considered here, the *shape* of the spine is obviously an important factor in determining the functional efficiency of a given synapse. Differences in synaptic efficiency mean organizational differences in the neural network.

neural sprouting

Electrical stimulation is another kind of experience that can also be used to induce changes in the neuroanatomy of the nervous system. Studies have shown that there is considerable sprouting of neuronal filaments, as well as increases in the spine count, on the side of the brain opposite the side to which repetitive electrical stimuli are applied. On the stimulated side, however, there are relatively few new neuronal sprouts.

The fact that additional spine and filament sprouting only occurs on the side of the brain *opposite* to the stimulated side can be interpreted to mean that growth of neural tissues (synapse and fibers) depends on the selective activation of some synapses in some way and is not just produced by neural activity per se. The neurons on the stimulated side of the brain were being directly stimulated; they did not grow. The neurons on the opposite side of the brain were being stimulated through at least one synaptic junction; they did grow as a result of the experience. Perhaps, we may conclude, synaptic activity is itself a necessary precursor of the increase in synaptic count, size, shape, or conductivity, or of synaptic growth in general.

The important point is that use itself is not sufficient to induce either synaptic plasticity or learning. There is a law of molar behavior that also makes this same point—*The law of effect*. This molar psychological law asserts that some reinforcement or validation is necessary for learning to take place. It is conceivable that the neural correlate of *effect* is *synaptic activity*. If this is so, synaptic activity and memory are tied together even more intimately than previously thought.*

Consolidation

We have now considered some neural mechanisms that could plausibly account for short-term and long-term memories. The transient neural activity that lasts for only a few minutes at most, however, must in some way be converted into the more permanent structural changes if long lasting engrams are to be produced. This transformation from short-term memory to long-term memory, the process called *consolidation,* seems to involve either physical growth of existing synaptic junctions or the creation of new ones. Other less plausible theories of long-term synaptic change (such as the selective destruction of synapses existing at birth, the creation of entire new neurons, or the direct involvement of glia as storage media) have been suggested but none of these alternatives has yet gained the support of psychobiologists. Admittedly, we still have no compelling evidence of any neural code of long-term memory, but it does seem to many that growth and sprouting of synaptic membranes is the most likely way in which transient engrams become consolidated into permanent ones.

It is at this point that the macromolecules involved in genetic storage also become plausibly and reasonably involved in the memory storage process. While the idea that memory actually is stored in the nucleotide sequences of RNA molecules no longer has many adherents, it does seem clear that RNA is involved in some way in consolidation. The most plausible involvement is in terms of synaptic growth. Growth of synapses means growth of membranes and membranes do consist in part of proteins. Proteins also probably make up all of the various receptor sites *the role of RNA* and channels on the neuronal membrane. Protein growth, as modern chemical genetics has taught us, is regulated by RNA, and, as we shall see, many experiments demonstrate the presence of RNA metabolites and changes in RNA constituents during learning.

The classic experiment showing the influence of experience on RNA chemistry was carried out by Hydén. He took advantage of the fact that rats have the same kind of crossed over motor

---

*We do not wish to take sides formally in the long debate regarding the necessity of reinforcement for learning. In the present context we use the term "reinforcement" in a way that is broader than orthodox behaviorists would sanction.

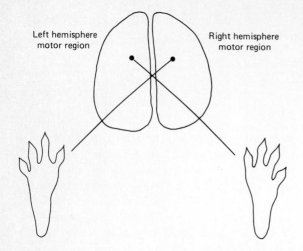

Left hemisphere motor region

Right hemisphere motor region

Figure 6–10 The crossed arrangement of the rat's brain and the rat's paws. The motor regions control the paws on the opposite sides of the body.

nervous system that humans do. That is, the left paw (and hand) is controlled by motor regions on the right side of the brain and vice versa, as shown in Figure 6–10. Hydén trained his rats to constantly use their left paws, assuming the right side of the brain would thereby be more highly activated than the left side. When biochemical assays of the brain tissue on both sides of the brain were made, it was found that the four RNA bases (adenine, guanine, cytosine, and uracil) occurred in significantly different proportions on the trained and untrained side. The shift in concentrations of A, G, C, and U, respectively, is shown in Table 6–2. The significance of this experiment is not that those changed proportions of the four bases are memory. It is not even likely that the motor regions Hydén chemically assayed were the actual sites of the engram produced by the training period. What this experiment does say is that experience affects the

TABLE 6–2   Shifts in the Concentration of the Four RNA Bases in the Rat's Brain as a Function of Experience

	Control Mean	Learning Mean	Change in Percent
Adenine	18.4 ± .48	20.1 ± .11	+ 9.2
Guanine	26.5 ± .64	28.7 ± .90	+ 8.3
Cytosine	36.8 ± .97	31.5 ± .75	− 14.4
Uracil	18.3 ± .48	19.6 ± .56	+ 7.1
$\dfrac{A + G}{C + U}$	0.81 ± .27	.95 ± .35	+17.3
$\dfrac{G + C}{A + U}$	1.72 ± 0.54	1.51 ± 0.26	+12.2

Source: H. Hydén in K.H. Pribram and D.C. Broadbent, *Biology of Memory*, 1970.

chemical structure of the brain and particularly it affects the proportions of the chemicals that make up RNA.

Other studies have further strengthened the claim that the genetic chemicals associated with the growth of new protein are involved intimately in some way in the consolidation process. Specifically, chemicals known to block the production of new protein also block the consolidation of short-term into long-term memory. For example, goldfish placed in an avoidance training situation (in which the animals must learn to move across a barrier to avoid a painful electric shock) learn this task very quickly and also retain this memory for prolonged periods of time under normal conditions. They can be retested weeks later and display considerable savings. The engram produced by the training is obviously transferred into long-term memory. But if puromycin, an antibiotic that inhibits protein formation, is injected into the fishes' brains one and one half hours after training, the fish remember very little about the training when tested three hours later. Their short-term memory has faded, but is not replaced with long-term memory. They must be retrained virtually from scratch in order to learn to avoid the painful electrical shock when placed back in the test apparatus.

The inference that can be drawn from such findings is that new protein formation—the process specifically inhibited by puromycin—is specifically involved in consolidation and that ipso facto consolidation is in some intimate way associated with protein synthesis. This is the message that comes from the fact that a protein inhibitor like puromycin also inhibits learning. But we also can assert something about the temporal course of the process. Puromycin injection is not always effective. It must be injected at a particular time to produce its inhibitory effect. There does seem, therefore, to be a *critical period*, a particular point in time, at which certain essential processes take place. The entire consolidation process took about three hours. The critical point occurred at about the midpoint of that period.

The goldfish originally learned to avoid the electrical shock. The injection of the puromycin resulted in a lack of retention of this learned skill, presumably because the short-term memory faded and the puromycin prevented that information from being consolidated into some more permanent form of long-term memory. The skill, once learned, was forgotten. This kind of forgetting as a result of some intervention that occurred after the original learning is referred to as *retrograde amnesia*. Retrograde amnesia can occur in many other types of learning situations, as noted in Chapter 5, and always seems to be closely related to the consolidation process we have just outlined. Retrograde amnesia also occurs in humans following electroconvulsive shock (ECS) therapy. Similar studies have

retrograde amnesia

been done with drugs of one kind or another and reports of trauma induced retrograde amnesia are legion. Experiments and anecdotes like these support the idea that there is a critical period of time following training during which consolidation occurs.

We have discussed in this section microscopic evidence of experience-induced growth and chemical evidence of RNA constituent changes as a result of the injection of protein inhibitors or the administration of electrical shock. All these findings are associated in some way with growth and those chemicals that mediate the new protein production. This is the proper context to interpret the role of the genetic molecules in memory—not to *store* information as had once been suggested— but to guide and control *growth* of new synaptic tissue. It is the changing pattern of synaptic interconnection that is so closely associated with memory, not the pattern of the atoms in molecular DNA or RNA.

In concluding this discussion of possible synaptic bases of the engram, we should recall again that both short-term and long-term synaptic changes seem to occur only when there is some kind of effect or *reinforcement*. Exactly what reinforcement is can be quite variable from one situation to another, but many psychologists think memories cannot be created unless the act performed is adaptive for the organism in some way or another. This is the general import of the *law of effect*. At the synaptic level, it may be that reinforcement or effect is actually embodied in the form of synaptic activation.

We do not know what it is about synaptic activation, as opposed to axonal activation, that specifically mediates the storage of the engram; however, we may speculate that it concerns the fact that synaptic transmitter substances themselves may not only be effective in inducing activity in postsynaptic tissues, but also in stimulating growth in those same postsynaptic regions.

Localization of Memory Processes (Again)

It is possible to ask the next question "Where do these structural changes stimulated by experience—these engrams— occur in the brain?" As possible as it is to ask this question, the fact is that the question may be a bad one and the answer somewhat surprising. Recall the earlier discussions of the research and theories of Karl Lashley. Lashley's findings were among the earliest indications that many areas of the brain, not just particular regions, were capable of storing memories and that no highly localized and specialized storage regions existed for many kinds of learning.

In recent years, additional experiments have been reported that provided further support for the concept of distributed engrams. A research group headed by the late James Olds, for example, used single cell action potentials to make this same point. Olds and his colleagues inserted a large number of electrodes sensitive to single cell action potentials into the brains of a group of rats. These electrodes picked up bursts of spike action potentials. The latency between the presentation of a conditioned stimulus and the response of this burst of action potentials was used as the criterion measure of learning. If the latency became progressively shorter as the training trials were sequentially presented, then Olds' group asserted that "learning" had occurred in the region of the brain from which this neural activity was recorded.

neuronal spikes and conditioning

Olds and his group looked for locations in the rat's brain containing neurons that responded with bursts of spike action potentials with latencies shorter than 20 milliseconds. These units were considered either to have been modified by the conditioning procedure or to reflect directly the activity of regions that had been so modified. The results obtained by this group turned out to be highly supportive of Lashley's lesion experiments. Olds' group found that there were no major regions of the brain that did not contain at least some of these short latency bursting neurons. From the brain stem to the cortex, virtually every major subdivision of the brain contained at least some nuclei that had contained neurons displaying this indication of short latency cellular plasticity. If, as Olds postulated, these short latency responses are in fact valid signs of learning, then we too must conclude that the effects of learning are widely distributed throughout major areas of the brain.

Lashley's and Olds' experiments have provided strong evidence that the engram is not localized in any particular part of the brain. Considering the very large number of different kinds of learning that have been identified, however, it is not too surprising to learn that many different regions of the brain seem to be specifically involved in learning in one way or another even if they are not the locus of the engram itself. In fact, if one looks back over the history of research in the psychobiology of learning, one finds that virtually all regions of the central nervous system have been shown to be involved in learning and memory at one time or another. Some of these regions may be the site of some physiological or anatomical change that corresponds to the engram. But other regions are now known to be involved in learning in quite a different way—rather than as the locus of the engram, they are believed to regulate the *establishment* of the engram or to affect the retrieval of information from the stored engram.

We shall next consider some of the neural regions that have been shown to be involved in learning in one way or another and seek to determine their specific role. The temporal and frontal regions of the cortex, the hippocampus, and several other regions of the limbic system in particular seem to be among the most important regions studied so far. Let us now consider some of these regions and their putative role in learning and memory, beginning with the spinal cord.

The Spinal Cord and Classical Conditioning

When one considers that even the simplest animals—protozoans—have been "taught" something even if it is only a simple evasive response, it is at first glance surprising that there has been so much difficulty in establishing that the much more complex mammalian spinal cord is capable of learning. Of course, there are many difficulties involved in this research, not the least of which is simply keeping a spinal animal alive. But this can be done by artificially respirating the spinal animal. However, other technical difficulties also arise in this type of experiment. What may seem to be small differences in procedure can also produce quite different results and, in some cases, even diametrically opposed conclusions. The classic studies in this field were carried out by Shurrager and Culler and by Kellogg in the 1940s. Shurrager and Culler classically conditioned acute spinal cats (that is, animals that had had their spinal cord transected just prior to conditioning) and used excised muscle preparations in their attempts to demonstrate spinal classical conditioning. In this situation, Shurrager and Culler were able to demonstrate what most psychobiologists now agree is unequivocal evidence that the spinal animal is able to learn to avoid a noxious stimulus. They concluded, therefore, that the isolated spinal cord was capable of recording an engram. Kellogg, on the other hand, used chronic preparations (that is, animals that had their spinal cord transected well before the experiment and allowed to recover as much as possible). Kellogg, to the contrary, was able to find no evidence of classical conditioning in the spinal animal after many trials. He concluded the spinal cord could not establish engrams therefore.

Recent research on this problem tends to support the positive results obtained by Shurrager and Culler. Classical conditioning of spinal animals has been demonstrated by a number of

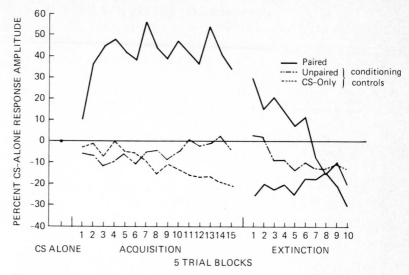

Figure 6–11 A demonstration of classical conditioning in the spinal animal. (Redrawn from Patterson, M.M., Cegavske, C.G., and Thompson, R.F., *Journal of Comparative and Physiological Psychology*, 1973, 84:88–97.)

investigators (see Figure 6–11 for a typical set of findings) and instrumental conditioning has been demonstrated as well. Furthermore, convincing work has been done to show that the spinal cord is capable of habituation and sensitization. The spinal rat does habituate withdrawal responses to repeated stimulation with electrical shock. Whatever the mechanism is that is responsible for the flexion of the muscle, it becomes less likely to respond to a stimulus after that stimulus has been presented repeatedly. Yet, the process is clearly not one of simple fatigue. The same muscle group could be induced to respond at its original strength if the stimulus was placed at some different location on the rat's skin. Figure 6–12 shows the

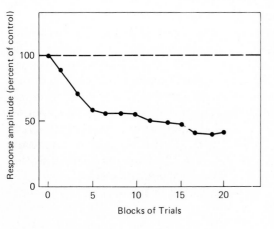

Figure 6–12 A demonstration of habituation in the spinal animal, (Redrawn from Thompson, R.F., and Spencer, W.A., *Psychological Review*, 1966, 73:16–43.)

course of the habituation observed in one experiment over the course of many hundreds of stimulations.

Clearly the spinal cord is capable of some kinds of "retention." Classical and instrumental conditioning, as well as habituation (and its converse, sensitization) have all been observed in preparations that could only involve spinal neuron and synaptic plasticity. Although we do not depend on our spinal cords for very many kinds of memory storage, this evidence is important in adding further support to the hypothesis that memories of previous experience can be recorded virtually any place in the nervous system. The ability to store information introduced by previous experience, in other words, is a general property of all nervous tissue; it is this factor that conceptually links the work on spinal conditioning to Lashley's and Olds' work.

The Hippocampus

One of the brain regions of greatest interest in recent years with regard to the regulation of learning, is the *hippocampus*. The hippocampus is a portion of the cortex located on the underside and interior edge of the cerebral hemisphere. It is also considered to be an active participant in the functions of and a key part of the limbic system. As we shall see in Chapter 7, the limbic system is also closely associated with motivational and emotional states.

One approach to studying the effects of the hippocampus on learning is to carry out some standard tests of learning before and after an operation that produces a lesion in this region. For example maze learning ability is severely inhibited following a hippocampal lesion but an animal's ability to learn to avoid a shock may actually improve after such lesions. The effect of a hippocampal lesion, therefore, seems to depend very much on the particular task facing the animal.

It is, however, not at all clear on the basis of lesion studies exactly what the role of the hippocampus is in the memory process. The issue is muddied because the same lesion has many other measurable influences beyond interference with memory. A hippocampal animal is much more active and distractable and seems to have much poorer control over its motor responses than does a normal animal. The hippocampus is, after all, a part of the limbic system and thus deeply involved in motivational and emotional behavior as well as learning. The question therefore is "Does the hippocampal animal perform less well because memory is directly affected or because of interference with other internal processes?" This is not an easy question to answer. The intact hippocampus seems to produce a generalized quieting or inhibiting influence on many different aspects of brain and behavioral activity. A lesion there produces a disruption of this inhibition and an agitated, active, and easily distracted animal that learns less well. We have to look elsewhere for deeper insights into the specific role, if any, of the hippocampus in memory.

patients with hippocampal lesions

Human clinical and laboratory animal data suggest another role for the hippocampus in learning and memory. Patients with bilateral hippocampal lesions typically have a good memory of events that occurred long ago and do quite well on tests of short-term memory. However, they seem to have very poor memory of events that happened in the recent past following the time the lesion occurred. In extreme cases, this failure to transfer short-term memory to long-term memory can be complicated by a reduced ability to retrieve what can otherwise be shown to be existing memories. Such a disease state has been well known for years; it is called *Korsakoff's syndrome.*

The suggestion that emerges from this serious medical condition is that the hippocampus is involved in some way in the processes underlying the *consolidation* of short-term memory into long-term memory. Bilateral hippocampal lesions in animals also seem to produce retrograde amnesia of a kind comparable to that observed in Korsakoff's syndrome. Closely related to this decrement of consolidation following injury to the hippocampus is the fact that retrograde amnesia can be produced by electrical stimulation of this same region in both animals and humans. However, in other instances electrical activation of the hippocampus in the period *following* learning can actually lead to an enhancement of retention. Presumably the timing is critical—at certain points in time hippocampal stimulation disrupts memory consolidation, while at other times such stimulation enhances consolidation. However, there are such substantial differences between the effects of hippocampal lesions in animals and humans that any glib assertion of the specific role of this important center in human behavior must be utterly speculative.

In sum, the functions of the hippocampus encompass several different behavioral effects. But there is some order in this variety. The general quieting role of the hippocampus is such that a lesioned animal is less likely to be in a state that is conducive to learning. In particular, it seems that such an animal is much less likely to transfer successfully short-term memories for recent events into more persistent memories. In humans, a similar tendency can be observed, with clinical syndromes displaying very similar properties.

Another general conclusion to which we can come is that the hippocampus, by means of what are yet inexplicable processes, regulates and controls the consolidation of short-term memories into long-term memories. There is, however, no evidence to support the suggestion that the engram is actually *stored* in the hippocampus. At the most, it is a regulator of learning, and at the least, it is a region that regulates the general motivational and emotional status of the animal in a way that has only indirect influences on learning.

The Amygdala

Another region of the cerebrum that has been shown to affect learning is the *amygdala*, also a portion of the limbic system. Animals with lesions in the amygdala display general behavior partially similar to those with hippocampal lesions. Amygdalectomized animals are much more passive than normal. It seems, therefore, that the amygdala (and perhaps also the septal regions) are activators of behavior rather than inhibitors or quieters. Lesions of the amygdala affect learning in various ways. Like animals with hippocampal lesions, the exact effect seems to depend upon the specific nature of the task. Consolidation also seems to be influenced by amygdaloid lesions; retrograde amnesia is also produced by electrical stimulation of this region as well as the septal nucleus. Alas, the effect of electrical stimulation of the amygdala seems to depend on the nature of the task and the experimental condition even more than hippocampal effects do. For example, the magnitude of an aversive electrical shock (2 ma versus 15 ma) can actually reverse the outcome of an experiment to determine the effect of amygdaloid electrical stimulation. Low aversive shock levels result in enhanced learning. On the other hand, if the aversive shock level is high, then learning is inhibited.

Clearly the amygdala is deeply involved in memory, as well as arousal, but the complexities of its interactions with other nuclei are still inscrutable. The full story of the amygdala is yet to be understood.

The Frontal Lobes

Another important cortical region that has clearly been implicated in memory is the *frontal cortex*. Many kinds of learning, particularly those involving time or those involving the sequencing of a series of responses are substantially disrupted by frontal lobe lesions. In the case of the frontal lobes, their involvement in learning seems to be best described by the phrase, *time binding*. Animals (and humans) with frontal lobe damage seem to have great difficulty in any task that involves linking together the serial steps in a chain of behaviors. The classic human syndrome following frontal lobe injury usually involves a reduced ability to make plans and to lead an "ordered and well organized life." The tragic accident of Phineas Gage (see Figure 6–13) is the most famous case in point. Humans with frontal lesions far less serious than Gage's tend to perseverate in their behavior once it is begun; that is, to remain locked into a single point in time. Frontal patients also have difficulty following instructions. Frontal lobe lesions, in general, seem to affect the sequencing of serial steps.

Thus the frontal lobe seems to play a major role in helping the learner to link together various stages in a learning trial as well as to sequence well-learned activity. Frontal lesions have other effects on behavior that also may influence memory, however. For example, frontal animals (like those with hippocampal lesions) are much more active and distractable than normal. They also seem to have poorer motivational control. These

time binding

Figure 6–13 What happened to Phineas Gage? An accidental explosion caused a crowbar to pass upwards from his face and through his brain. He lived for many years and, in most respects, quite normally. There was, however, evidence of diminished motivation and judgment.

factors too may be important in interfering with performance. Indeed, a wide variety of other types of deficits have been discovered in frontal animals beyond the delayed response deficits discussed in Chapter 5. Such animals do poorly in matching to sample, learning to avoid shocks, and in maze learning. The very generality and breadth of these difficulties make sense only in terms of a region that produces an overall deficit in time binding.

Thus, modern psychobiological research has shown that there are many regions of the nervous system, from the spinal cord to the cerebral cortex, in which some influence on learning and memory can be demonstrated. Obviously learning and memory, like all other mental processes, involve sensory, motor, motivational, associational, and even emotional mechanisms. In order to learn, all parts of the organism's system must be operating in a coherent manner. Bilateral ablation of the inferotemporal cortex, for example, seriously impedes tasks that require visual discrimination and memory. Visual discriminations in general, however, also are affected by lesions in many regions of the brain. Thus, psychobiologists no longer, as did some earlier investigators, assert that the hippocampus or the frontal lobes are the specific site of the engram for short-term memory, visual or otherwise. Rather, current theoreticians tend to accept the idea that the nervous system as a whole is capable of information storage and the environment, both internal and external, must provide an overall situation conducive to learning. If the motivational state or the ability to maintain linkages from one moment to the next is less than optimum, or if the animal cannot discriminate forms, then learning is inhibited.

We conclude this section on the localization of memory processes by acknowledging that the prospect of localizing the engram remains poor in the light of these studies. Though there are many regions that influence learning, none of them seems to be the actual site of the engram. Whatever it is, the engram appears to be distributed throughout the brain.

Statistical and Holographic Codes

In this chapter we have concentrated on the physiological basis of learning and memory in higher animals. We must acknowledge that there still is no way to say with total assurance what exactly the engram is or where it may be located. Nevertheless, an extraordinary situation exists in this field today. In spite of the absence of a solid empirical foundation there is a curious agreement concerning the physiological and anatomical basis of memory. In spite of many different theoretical statements, upon examination we see that there is relatively little disagreement among them. Some theories emphasize what all of the synapses are doing *on the average* rather than what each is doing in particular. Any single synapse plays only a small role in the specification of an engram, according to this point of view, and its role may easily be replaced if it dies or "forgets." E. Roy John raises the possibility that different synapses may store the same information at different points in time at least for brief periods of time. The neural networks that represent remembered information may, therefore, vary from time to time and never be exactly alike. Yet we may still be able to remember perfectly well as long as the average *state* of the network remains approximately the same.

John's statistical theory of memory implies that it may be possible for a single synapse to serve different functions at different times just as a single memory function may be encoded by different synaptic junctions from time to time. How difficult it would be, we must now begin to appreciate, in this ever changing, distributed, and only statistically stable situation to find the particular engram associated with a particular memory in any but the simplest nervous systems.

A second important idea—the idea of interference patterns among those statistical states—was introduced by Karl Pribram. Pribram has suggested an answer to the riddle of how microscopic changes in synaptic conductivity distributed throughout the brain could interact to produce a global memory. His hypothesis is that waves of neural activity are generated and that these waves interfere with each other in a way that is comparable, but not of course physically identical, to the interaction of light waves in the three-dimensional photographic technique called optical holography. Holographic images share many features with memory processes. Like the engram, they appear to be distributed throughout the film. Holograms also follow a law of mass action very much like the one reported by Lashley; if one breaks up a holographic plate, the resolution of the remaining image depends upon how big a piece of the film remains intact. Holographic images, thus, are not stored in any particular place on the film, but rather each point in the reconstructed image is stored throughout the film. If you destroy portions of the film, you do not find any single place whose destruction destroys the entire image. Rather the projected image simply becomes less and less sharp in direct proportion to the mass of the film that is destroyed.

Pribram, on the basis of the many similarities between the hologram and memory, proposes that memory is stored in the brain in a similar fashion. He does not suggest, of course, that there are actually optical holograms in the head but rather that the interference of light is *analogous* (that is, it can be modeled by the same mathematics) to the interference of the patterns of neuroelectrical activity in the brain.

It is important to appreciate that even though Pribram's and John's theories are couched in different languages—one uses the terms of statistics and the other that of the optical holography—they are compatible. John tells us that *averages* are important in the representation of memory; Pribram tells us that *interferences*, perhaps among averages of neural activity, are equally important in linking together the isolated elements of the engram. Both speak to the way that the global pattern emerges from the microscopic detail of neuronal and synaptic organization.

Summary

Now that we have considered these two important hypotheses and the data presented earlier in this chapter, we are in a position to summarize the general theory of memory that has wide currency today. Any modern global theory of memory must be generally supported by the available data, but at the same time, such a theory must extend beyond the data. What we offer is, of necessity therefore, somewhat speculative, but as we have noted previously, there is a surprisingly wide base of agreement concerning the main points of the theory.

Memory, as has been suggested on the basis of behavioral data, is a multiple stage process. The best way to organize these stages is along a temporal dimension. Specifically memories are classified as *short-*, *intermediate-*, or *long-term* on the basis of the persistence of the memory. *Sensory memory* with very large pictorial capacity, exhibits the briefest duration of all—the memory lasts for less than a second. Short-term memories with very modest capacities—best estimated as "seven plus or minus two" items, chunks, or units—fade in ten or twenty seconds, while intermediate- and long-term memories seem to persist for many years, if not the lifetime of the organism. The latter two forms of memory—intermediate-and long-term memories—appear to have immeasurably large capacities.

Virtually all portions of the central nervous system have now been shown to be able to act in some way as the repository of some kind of memory, including the spinal cord. Furthermore, in most situations the engram that represents the actual physical change in neuronal structure and/or arrangement seems to be distributed throughout the brain. Many animal studies have shown that a *law of mass action* holds for a wide variety of learning tasks. The degree of memory impairment is a function of the amount of tissue removed, not where it is located. Most human clinical data are at least suggestively supportive of this same principle. Patients typically do not lose specific memories when their brains are injured, but seem rather to lose control of memory processes. Many parts of the brain are thus *equipotential* in terms of their ability to store memory.

However, different portions of the brain are involved in learning and memory in ways that may transcend the physical storage of the engram. For a vertebrate to learn anything apparently requires the participation of all of the brain. The sensory, motor, integrative, motivational, and emotional centers are necessary and all seem to be involved to a greater or lesser degree. Interference with the normal function of any of the regions associated with these processes can usually be shown to interfere with some aspect of learning. At the cellular level, it seems almost certain that the site of the physiological change corresponding to memory can be nothing other than the *synapse*. No other portion of the neuron has the *plasticity* and flexibility of the synapse or plays such a key role in the organization of the great neural networks. However, it is essential for the reader to remember the caveat presented several times previously in this chapter—though widely accepted the synaptic hypothesis is supported by only the flimsiest empirical foundation.

Thus, the important idea is that synaptic conductivity is the prime cause of the reorganization of the neural net. Though we do not know anything about the specific sites of the neuronal network that corresponds to internal mental activity, we do know something about the mechanisms that probably account for plasticity in synapses. Like the two kinds of memory, both short and long lasting plastic changes in the nervous system have been identified. Short-term synaptic changes usually last for only a few minutes and are exemplified by such processes as *heterosynaptic facilitation* or *post-tetanic potentiation*. The main effect of transient changes is—most probably—temporarily to vary the pattern of circulating neural impulses. A number of data attest to the fact that these transient engrams must subsequently be transformed into more permanent changes in synaptic structure if they are to survive and be "remembered." This transformation from short-term to long-term memory is called *consolidation*. The involvement of RNA and protein synthesis in a variety of experiments, as well as microscopic evidence, suggests that consolidation actually is embodied in the physical growth of new or enlargement of old synapses. Consolidation may also be interfered with by enhancing or interfering with the activity of a number of brain nuclei, particularly those within the limbic system. At the cellular level consolidation seems to require transsynaptic activation; simple use is ineffective in producing the growth of permanant engrams. At the molar level this requirement of transsynaptic activation goes under the name of the *law of effect*. In other words, something is learned only to the extent it is meaningfully reinforced; use alone is insufficient for learning to take place.

In conclusion, the study of the biological basis of learning and memory is a highly active field in today's psychobiological laboratories. Much progress is being made in understanding how neurons can adapt to experience. However, the difficulty of the problem should not be underestimated. There may be a Nobel prize in there somewhere, but it is going to take a great deal of effort and some nonnegligible amount of genius to crack open this incredibly difficult problem.

When (or if) it is solved, the solution will incorporate processes that go beyond memory itself. For tied to memory—at least to significant human memories—are the complex processes of attention, motivation, emotion, and personality. It is to the latter two that we now turn.

Suggested Readings

Adaptive Mechanisms at the Level of Single Units
1. E.R. Kandel and L. Tauc, Mechanism of prolonged heterosynaptic facilitation, *Nature*, 1964,*202*:145–147.
2. E.R. Kandel, An invertebrate system for the cellular analysis of simple behaviors and their modifications, in F. Schmitt and F. Worden (eds.), *The Neurosciences: Third Study Program*, MIT Press, Cambridge, 1974.

Phenomena and Data of Memory
1. J. Adams, *Learning and Memory: An Introduction*, Dorsey Press, Homewood, IL, 1976.
2. W. Kintsch, *Learning, Memory, and Conceptual Processes*, John Wiley, New York, 1970.
3. Sperling, G. The information available in brief visual presentations. *Psychological Monographs:* General and Applied. 1960, *74*, 1–29.

4. Miller, G.A. The magical number 7, ± 2. Some limits on our capacity for processing information. *Psychological Review*, 1956, *63*, 81–97.
5. Neisser, U. *Cognitive Psychology*. New York, Appleton Century Crofts, 1967.

Biochemical Correlates of Memory
1. J. Deutsch, The physiological basis of memory, *Annual Review of Psychology*, 1969, *20*:85–104.
2. G. Ungar (ed.), *Molecular Mechanisms in Learning and Memory*, Plenum Press, New York, 1970.

Chemical Interference with Memory Consolidation
1. R. Barraco and L. Stettner, Antibiotics and memory, *Psychological Bulletin*, 1976, *83*: 242–302.
2. M. Hamburg, Retrograde amnesia produced by intraperitoneal injection of physostigmine, *Science*, 1967, *156*:973–974.
3. J. Flexner, L. Flexner, and E. Stellar, Memory in mice as affected by intracerebral puromycin, *Science*, 1963, *141*:57–59.

Electroconvulsive Shock (ECS) and Amnesia
1. C. Duncan, The retroactive effect of electroshock on learning, *Journal of Comparative and Physiological Psychology*, 1949, *42*:32–44.
2. W. Hudspeth and L. Gerbrandt. Electroconvulsive shock: Conflict, consolidation, and neuroanatomical functions, *Psychological Bulletin*, 1965, *63*:377–383.

Electrophysiological Correlates of Memory
1. E. John, *Mechanism of Memory*, Academic Press, New York, 1967.
2. E. John, Switchboard vs. statistical theories of learning and memory, *Science*, 1972, *177*:850–864.

Memory "Transfer"
1. J. McConnell, Memory transfer through cannibalism in planarians, *Journal of Neuropsychiatry*, 1962, *3*:542–548.
2. Consult the special issue of *Science* devoted to the topic of *memory transfer:* 1966, *153*.

7 Emotion, Personality, and Psychopathology

Introduction

In the two preceding chapters we have explored some of the ways in which organisms adapt to environmental variations. We have emphasized the acquisition and the retention of new modes of adaptation and have discussed the neural mechanisms that serve learning and memory. In some respects, much of what we have considered in these two earlier chapters could, at least in principle, be achieved by a properly constructed and programmed robot. That is—again, at least in principle—we should be able to assemble a device that displays a high-fidelity simulation of the reflexive, instinctive, and acquired behaviors of the advanced species and that mimics animal and human memory. This possibility has encouraged many to think of animals, including the human animal, as elaborate computational devices with flexible (adaptable) programming features.

Notions of this sort are not entirely new. As early as the seventeenth century Descartes would ask himself whether there was anything so uniquely human as to permit him to distinguish between human life and the very best simulation of it. The question is still alive and has now become even more pressing in light of the great technical advances in computer science, artificial intelligence, and automaton theory.

When the non-specialist is introduced to such possibilities, perhaps the most common reaction is first one of disbelief and then one of challenge. "Do computers have feelings?" "Does the computer have a personality?" "What computer needs psychotherapy?" The point of such questions is to underscore what most persons take to be the defining human attributes; not our ability to perform calculations or remember lists of words, but

279

our capacity for emotionality and that property of psychological uniqueness that is captured by the term *personality*.

This is not the place, of course, to settle or even to discuss, the immense issues raised by the evolving computer technologies. Philosophers have recently begun to explore such questions as whether or not computers have "rights" and should be protected by laws, whether the destruction of a "self-programmable" computer is morally equivalent to the killing of a rational being, and whether it is right to *own* (enslave?) such an entity. Note that what is important here is the need to reassess what we have traditionally meant by such terms as "persons," "rights," "murder," and the like. It may be that what is finally so special about the human race is its continuing willingness to doubt that it is so special. If, as the maxim says, necessity is the mother of invention, then doubt is the mother of wisdom. Our doubts about our own special status have always been excited by technical developments or scientific achievements. Descartes, for example, was moved to his "automaton" theory of animal behavior by the great advances in mechanical engineering during the sixteenth and early seventeenth centuries. A short time later, Newton's extraordinary discoveries led many to conclude that human actions are as naturally *determined* as are the motions of the planets. And today, with the development of computers, we are again tempted to think of ourselves as just another type of material organization, not fundamentally different from other adaptable, problem-solving, information processing "devices." As such devices come to simulate more and more of what we have always taken to be our unique *rational* capacities, there is a tendency to discover the essence of our humanity in our emotional characteristics, in our "personalities."

Even if computers had never been invented, however, there would still be a strong challenge to the view that our emotions make us special. Long before Darwinian theory, observers had recorded the striking similarities between human and animal forms of emotionality. Aristotle, for example, was content to explain the emotions as the result of a condition of the body and was fully aware of the range of emotionality displayed by any number of nonhuman species. Evolutionary theory neither invented nor confirmed this point of view (for a theory *confirms* nothing) but it did provide it with a larger organized context. In the struggle for survival, both the animal and the species as a whole must adapt. The required adaptations may involve little more than changes in coloration or diet or may require elaborate chains of behavior. The animal must flee from danger and fight for its turf. It must be attracted to mates and must nurture and protect its offspring. To succeed in these regards the animal cannot rely on rational calculations—of which it may be utterly incapable—but must be impelled by internal commands, by *feelings*. Among the advanced species, therefore, the capacity for fear, anger, affection, sexuality, and a wide range of pains and pleasures is as essential as learning and memory. On the Darwinian account, emotionality is but another of the adaptive processes, no more special than the rest.

James-Lange theory   Nearly a century ago the great American psychologist William James carried this line of reasoning even further in what has come to be known as the *James-Lange theory of emotion*. It was James's view that the advanced species, as is the case with many of the less advanced species, are *equipped natively* (we would say *genetically*) to react to threatening environments. The sensory apparatus registers the relevant features of the environment and thereupon triggers the appropriate (adaptive) responses. It is, however, in the *sensory* consequences of these responses that the causes of emotion are to be found. The usual summary of the James-Lange position takes this form: We see a bear in the forest, we run, and *then* we become frightened. The point here is that the emotion of fear is no more than that collection of sensations associated with the sight of the bear and the initiation of flight. On this account, the cause of the emotion is the behavior, and not vice versa.

After a century of research and theory we find few psychobiologists who would subscribe either to Darwin's specific formulations or to the James-Lange theory. What has survived of the older views is the emphasis on *adaptation* and *function*. The psychobiologist approaches the issues of emotion, personality, and psychopathology within a broad Darwinian and Jamesian context. Accordingly, the central questions take this form "What physiological and biochemical processes are associated with the expression of emotional behavior?" "What function is served by such behavior in the animal's overall adaptive capacity?" "What biological (and, more specifically, *neurological*) alterations are sufficient to alter this capacity?" And in human beings who display seriously maladaptive behavior "What physiological and biochemical correlates can be reliably found?"

In this chapter we review the relevant findings arising out of this perspective. As we shall see, there are formidable problems of definition and methodology and, in some instances, ethical problems as well.

The Emotions and Stress

As with so many of psychology's major subjects the emotions are something we all know about but would have a difficult time defining or describing to anyone not already familiar with them.

At a general level, we acknowledge that emotions differ both in *quality* (fear, love, or anger) and in *intensity* (displeasure, anger, or rage). We also know that, at least in some persons or at certain times in the lives of most persons, a given emotion may have a very long duration—note, for example, *chronic* anxiety. Finally, emotional feelings interact or blend. Thus, danger or adventure of a certain sort can give rise to a mixture of fear and pleasure just as music can produce a blend of joy and anxiety.

visceral correlates

We know also that, unlike other sensations, emotional feelings have uniquely *visceral* counterparts, which are often expressed in ordinary speech "I was so disappointed that I became sick to my stomach," "At the end of the love-affair, they were both heartbroken," "I was so nervous I couldn't swallow," "He was so embarrassed that his face turned crimson-red," "His fear made him cold all over." These commonplace descriptions have a firm empirical foundation in laboratory studies of emotion. It is the case, for example, that those circumstances that produce changes in emotional feelings or in (seemingly) emotional behavior on the part of nonhuman animals also have significant effects on the *autonomic nervous system* (ANS) which controls blood vessels, cardiac muscle, and the smooth muscles of the viscera. We have already discussed the *sympathetic* and *parasympathetic* branches of the ANS in Chapter 3 and have seen how ANS activity can affect the pupils of the eyes, the production of tears, salivation, heart rate, and so on. The ANS richly supplies the visceral organs with their nerve supplies and is activated by nearly all situations in which some form of emotionality results. In large measure the ANS is controlled by nuclei in the *brain stem* and these, in turn, are under the influence of the hypothalamus and of that feedback system involving the hypothalamus and the pituitary gland (*hypophysis*). The block diagram given in Figure 7–1 provides a sketch of these relationships.

pituitary influences

The pituitary gland is something of the *master gland* of the *endocrine* system. Its activity is carefully regulated by the hypothalamus. Indeed, it is because of the intimate relationship between these structures that the two are best thought of as comprising a *hypothalamic-hypophyseal system*. The pituitary gland, for example, consists of a pair of distinct glands—an anterior one called the *adenohypophysis* and a posterior one called the *neurohypophysis*. The hormones secreted by the latter regulate the kidneys, the lactation of females occasioned by the birth of offspring, the muscles of the uterus, and the muscles of blood vessels. But these very hormones are not produced by the pituitary gland, they are only stored and secreted by it. They are produced in the hypothalamus and are passed into the pituitary gland by nerve processes originating in the hypothalamus. The

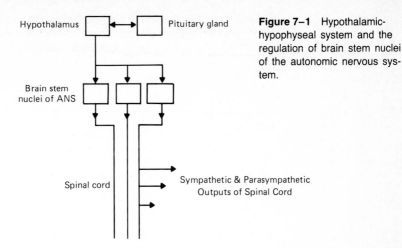

Figure 7–1 Hypothalamic-hypophyseal system and the regulation of brain stem nuclei of the autonomic nervous system.

anterior pituitary gland (*adenohypophysis*) does manufacture its own hormones but their secretion is controlled by signals delivered in the blood supply from the hypothalamus. The endocrine glands and their chief products are summarized in Table 7–1. This system is so intimately tied to the body's *stress reactions* and adjustments that it is invariably engaged in emotion-producing situations.

Stressful and emotional situations, which engage both the ANS and the endocrine system, generally produce physiological symptoms available to external measurement. We mention here just a few of the many measures that change when organisms are placed under emotionally significant conditions: Heart rate, blood pressure, muscle tension, pupil diameter, body temperature, electrical resistance of the skin (the so-called *galvanic skin reflex*), blood sugar concentration, salivation, perspiration, white cell (leucocyte) count in the blood, breathing depth and rate, skin color (pallor), oxygen consumption. All of these are relatively easy to measure. The galvanic skin reflex (GSR) for example is highly correlated with subjective reports of anxiety or fear. Under stress, both human beings and animals display increased numbers of white blood cells, increased (but shallow) respiration, a paleness of the skin surface, a drop in blood pressure in the periphery (cold fingers and toes), a dryness of the mouth, a cessation of normal digestive processes, and an increase in the production of urine. Prolonged stress results in gastrointestinal ulcerations, hair loss, and general metabolic failures, which can end in the death of an animal.

These general autonomic and endocrinological effects, though pronounced, do not faithfully discriminate between different qualities or even intensities of emotion. Most of the changes, for example, that attend *exhilaration* are quite similar in states of

TABLE 7–1 The Endocrine Glands, Secretions and Functions

Gland	Secretion	General Effects
Pituitary		
Anterior	Growth-hormone	Promotes musculo-skeletal development
	Thyrotrophic hormone	Controls release of thyroid hormones
	ACTH (adrenocortical trophic hormone)	Controls hormone release from cortex of adrenal glands
	Gonadotrophic hormones	Stimulates gonadal cells into production of sex hormones
	Prolactin	Stimulates lactation
Posterior	Oxytocin + hormones causing water retention	Regulates drainage of kidneys
	Vasopressin	Regulates muscles of blood vessels
Adrenal		
Medulla (core)	Epinephrine	Stimulates ANS
Cortex	Aldosterone and Cortisol	Steroid production to promote healing, stress-resistance, and so on
Thyroid	Thyroxine	Controls general metabolism
Parathyroid	Parathormone	Salt and water metabolism
Gonads	Estrogen and progesterone in the female; testosterone in the male	Controls copulatory functions
Pancreas	Insulin	Regulation of sugar metabolism

anger, just as many of the signs of *anxiety* are present in patients complaining of *depression.* Part of the problem is definitional. In other words one person's slight depression is another person's awareness of life's ironies. Tied to this is the ever present problem of individual differences. But apart from differences in persons and differences in the way words are used—or shall we say in addition to these—there is the extremely constricted nature of the laboratory as a setting within which to study human stresses and emotions. Take the case where a person is sorely grieved by the death of a loved one or abidingly angry with a thoughtless neighbor or enduringly happy in a relationship. Here we have three "textbook" emotions; sadness, anger, and joy. How are these to be simulated or stimulated in a laboratory? The bulk of research on human stress, at least as it has been conducted in laboratories, has made use of such stressors as mild shock, loud sounds, and the like. Such stimuli may be stressful but they scarcely induce either the kind or the intensity or the duration of stress endured by persons in the course of actual life.

emotion and stress

The strategy adopted to compensate for this has been to study psychiatric patients or other persons complaining of intense and prolonged states of agitation or stress. By and large these studies have confirmed research on normal laboratory subjects. That is, the chronically anxious or fearful patient displays many of the gross physiological signs elicited from normal subjects under conditions of acute stress. But in this case it is not clear that agreement is especially useful. Since we already know that there is very little in common between the effects of, say, mild electrical shock and, say, a life-long and paralyzing fear of heights or of other persons, any measure that suggests comparability is suspect on its face. To choose one example, we might note the frequently reported finding that schizophrenic patients display "high arousal" in their EEG tracings, and relatively little "alpha" activity. In Figure 7–2 we can compare a record displaying alpha rhythms (8–13 cycles per second and of high amplitude) with one that lacks these and displays what would be considered "high arousal." The trace in A is what one ordinarily obtains from a normal subject, quietly relaxed but awake, and not engaged in any sort of demanding task. The trace shown as B would be obtained from the same subject if a loud noise were introduced or if the subject were called upon to solve a complex problem in mathematics. What the trace in B does not distinguish is a case of intense attention and a case of sudden stimulation. Similarly, from the fact that schizophrenics

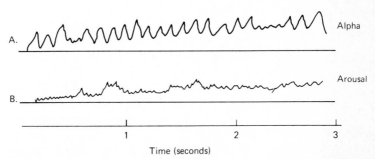

Figure 7–2 Illustration of EEG alpha rhythm in trace A and its absence in trace B.

tend to have EEG traces such as that given in B, no one would conclude they were doing math problems!

If all we consider is whether a stimulating state of affairs imposes burdens on the body's regulatory mechanisms—and if we call every such state of affairs *stressful*—then every emotion, including the most positive ones, must be classified as a stress. Note, therefore, that there is not a perfect correspondence between stress as psychologically recorded by the individual and stress as physiologically recorded by that same individual's body. Whether the psychological state is one of anger or rage or joy or contentment or envy or depression or love, the body pays a price and this price can be measured in the form of gross changes in the autonomic and endocrine mechanisms. The resulting findings are of unarguable value to our attempts to understand physiological adaptations to stress, but are less than entirely useful to the study of emotion. Stress attends all of our emotions but defines none of them.

Limbic Emotions—Fight, Flight, and Sex

There is still a lively debate on the question of just which emotions are *primary*. Some have thought of emotions the way science understands colors—that is, as a small set of primaries, which, by interaction, can give rise to a nearly continuous range of different feelings (hues). Indeed, the poets have sensed an even more direct relationship, giving us "torrents of red rage," "vernal (green) tranquility," and "cold blue eyes." Without taking the color model too literally, psychologists have attempted to partition all emotions into a few core emotions. Perhaps the most popular set has been that of *anger, fear, joy,* and *sadness*. Thus, excitement would be formed from the combination of fear and joy, anxiety from fear and sadness, and envy from anger and fear. This clearly is a game anyone can play, so we will stop here and turn the combinatorial possibilities over to the reader. In order to move on, however, we will have to take for granted that this same reader knows what we mean, at least generally, by the terms anger, fear, and pleasure. Whether anxiety is a weaker form of fear or an entirely different emotion, or whether joy is an intense form of pleasure or something utterly unique is the sort of question we cannot and at present need not begin to answer.

behavioral correlates

Once we leave the confident realm of our own personal feelings we face the difficult task of determining how to tell that any other person or any animal experiences emotions of any kind at all. The natural inclination, in dealing with fellow human beings, is to take for granted that, when someone says something like "I'm very depressed today," that person has the same sort of feeling we would have were we to say the same thing. There really is no foolproof way of establishing this—anymore than we can establish anyone else even has a mind. But at the level of common sense and common observation it is useful to make such inferences and it is almost impossible to get through social life without them.

But aside from what others actually say, we also take notice of how they behave. If a friend dropped by, smiling from ear to ear and humming a pleasant melody, and casually announced that he was having an absolutely unbearable toothache, we would conclude either that he was kidding or lying or insane. Thus, with those who can actually tell us about their emotions we expect at least a loose correspondence between their feelings and their general behavior. This is not to say that one might not "conquer his fear" and display iron stiffness in the face of danger, or that lovers might not seek affection by feigning hurt feelings or that actors will not convince us of feelings they do not really harbor. Rather, it is to acknowledge that in the ordinary course of things our behavior does reveal the more intense of our emotions and that when it doesn't we have a right to be suspected. By the same token, and through the same inferential process, we are generally confident that a dog is "happy" when its tail is wagging, when it rushes to us, licks at our hand and face, runs around us in circles, and makes brief yelping sounds. The same dog, now quivering in the corner, its tail between its hind legs, its nose dry and eyes half-shut, is likely to be judged as "frightened," at least when these signs reliably follow threats of punishment. On the same basis we make inferences about the emotions of other human beings; we tend to defend attributions of emotion to nonhuman animals on a *behavioral* basis. Logic here is overruled by the twin forces of common sense and utility. And it is just as common for neural scientists—after acknowledging that we can never actually *know* how animals "feel"—to proceed to describe love, anger, fear and anxiety as these are (apparently) experienced by rats, cats, dogs, and monkeys. Even in choosing more neutral terms (for example, "mothering," "flight," "fight," "procreative behavior") the scientific language is not entirely stripped of anthropomorphic colorations, since even these terms sugest intentions on the part of the animal and an awareness of means-ends relationships. Few of us doubt such characteristics, but it is important to appreciate their purely hypothetical status, their "metaphysical" nonscientific status. With these warnings duly noted we can turn to the question of the relationship between brain activity and those organized patterns of behavior that suggest states of emotionality.

It was in the 1930s that the anatomist Papez first proposed to explain emotionality according to the organization and inter-action of structures lying below and surrounded by the cerebral cortex. The *Papez circuit,* as it is called, involves the structures of the limbic system and their projections. Nearly a half-century of anatomical and physiological research has demonstrated that the system itself is far more complicated than had been supposed. It is difficult to diagram or even to sketch because of the richness of the interactions among its major structures. But a hint of this complexity can be obtained from Figure 7–3 and its legend, repeated from Chapter 3. Here we discover the principal components of the limbic system and just a few of the feedback circuits involved.

Not shown in this figure are the median forebrain bundle and important pathways joining septum, hypothalamus, and brain stem. It runs roughly in the plane 7-8-5 and is a principal part of the reward system discussed in Chapter 5. Referring to the limbic structures in Figure 7–3 we can now briefly review the forms of emotional behavior known to be correlated with their activation.

Rage and Aggression

Stimulation of the lateral regions of the hypothalamus of experimental animals reliably results in expressions of rage. The cat will hiss, bear its claws, and attack nearby objects,

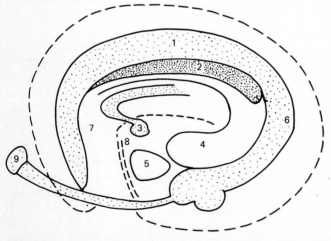

Legend

1. Cingulate gyrus
2. Corpus callosum
3. Mammillary body (of hypothalamus)
4. Head of hippocampus
5. Amygdala
6. Presubiculum
7. Region of septum
8. Column of fornix shown here near amygdala
9. Olfactory bulb

Figure 7–3 Highly simplified sketch of major structures of the limbic system. The dashed lines mark off the surrounding *neocortex* and indicate the location of its temporal lobe. Consult the legend for the names of the structures. The limbic structures in the figure are 1, 3, 4, 5, 6, 7, 8, and portions of 10. There are extensive projections from 5 to both 7 and 3; from 4 to both 3 and 8; and from 3 to the *anterior thalamus* and thereupon to 1.

including the experimenter. By using even more confined stimuli, experimenters have been able to divide hypothalamic rage into (a) somewhat wild and violent behavior and (b) more deliberate predatory behavior which results in the killing of prey. In areas surrounding the hypothalmus stimulation often gives rise to a form of "sham rage." Here the animal (cat) will hiss, bear its claws, and otherwise display signs of anger, but will not direct an attack at specific and threatening objects. Often the difference between violent attack and careful stalking can be produced by stimulating the same region of the hypothalamus but with signals of different intensity.

Klüver-Bucy syndrome

It is now clear that the rage-initiating regions of the hypothalamus can be inhibited by influences from both the septum and the amygdala. Highly agitated animals become remarkably docile when the amygdaloid complex is stimulated. One of the earliest studies suggesting such effects involved the removal of the temporal lobes of monkeys (bilateral temporal *lobectomies*). After a postoperative period of recovery the animals displayed a variety of symptoms: (1) extreme docility, (2) hypersexuality, and (3) a condition called *hypermetamorphosis*, which refers to their need to experience familiar items repeatedly in order to determine whether such items were edible. These symptoms collectively are known as the *Klüver–Bucy syndrome*. Only after these pioneering studies was it learned that the amygdala, which is buried within the temporal cortex, was directly responsible for the docility resulting from surgery. The amygdalectomized animal is gentle, will surrender its place in the normal dominance hierarchy of the colony, and will display few if any of the signs ordinarily produced by hypothalamic stimulation.

Sexual Behavior

Again, the hypothalamus has been directly implicated in the control of sexuality in lower organisms. In a number of species it has been possible to trigger copulation merely by delivering electrical signals to nuclei of the hypothalamus or by directly stimulating these same nuclei with sex hormones. Surgical destruction of the same nuclei results in sexually inactive animals. The same effects are produced by castration of male animals and in the ovariectomized female, indicating a close relationship between limbic and hormonal mechanisms of sexuality. The picture, however, is a complicated one. Any number of genital reflexes (including erection of the penis) survives even in animals with high spinal transections which eliminate direct control by the brain. It is also known that the same reflexes often survive destruction of brain regions (for example, medial preoptic region) which are necessary for integrated, copulatory behavior. It should also be noted that the literature in clinical neurology offers some evidence of human sexual disturbances associated with limbic tumors, but as of now any attempt to equate studies of animal and human sexuality would be extremely speculative.

Overview of "Limbic" Emotions

Although the current picture is a cluttered one, certain generalizations do come out of the most recent decade of research. In the advanced species the central nervous system can be partitioned into a number of broad and overlapping functions; for example, signal detection, sensory-motor coordination, and behavioral adjustments central to the survival of the organism and the species. In previous chapters we have examined the processes of perception, learning, and memory and have noted the special part played in these processes by cerebral cortex and spinal cord, by thalamus and various sensory relay structures, by reticular formation. Once we move beyond perception, learning and memory and into that arena in which the most basic organismic drives operate, the limbic system emerges as a uniquely significant collection of structures. Its normal functioning appears to be essential to patterns of self-defense, procreation, and organized behavior within a social complex. It is not, however, an independent system, but one that interacts thoroughly with hypothalamic mechanisms, with the hypothalamic-hypophyseal hormonal systems, and with the major sensory and motor nuclei of the nervous system. In the advanced species it is also partly regulated by descending cortical influences and by those conditions ordinarily placed under the categories of *learning* and *memory*. From these basics, the leap to the subject of human *personality* is long and perilous and one that can only be attempted after due cautions are taken into account.

Personality

One of the principal obstacles to a developed psychobiology of *personality* is the continuing inability of psychiatrists and psychologists to establish just what is meant by the term. We all have a general notion or intuitive sense of the meaning of the word, but neither of these is sufficient for truly scientific purposes.

humoral theories

At least since the time of the ancient Greek physicians many have subscribed to the view that each person has a unique collection of feelings, attitudes, and inclinations capable of surviving all sorts of experiences and serving to identify him or her as a certain *type* of person. The school of medicine thought to have been founded by Hippocrates considered these personality "types" to be a reflection of the person's biological constitution and especially that part of the constitution controlled by certain chemical *humors*. Galen, in the second century A.D., adopted a similar theory which continued to be authoritative until well into the seventeenth century. Persons were thought to be *"phlegmatic"* or *"bilious"* or *"sanguine"* because of a relative abundance of one sort of humor and a relative deficiency of another. We can consult Ben Jonson to learn how the Elizabethans thought of the humors. In his *Every Man Out of His Humour*, he states the theory thus:

Some one peculiar quality Doth so possess a man, that it doth draw all his affects, his spirits, and his powers, In their confluctions, all to run one way.

Jonson's understanding is consistent with both the ancient and the modern views. Personality is thought of as the overall aspect of our makeup that imprints our perception, our feelings, and our actions with a distinct stamp. This is not to say that learning plays no part nor to suggest that discipline and habit will not permit a person to control one or another of his or her "affects, spirits and powers". Rather, it is to underscore both the common and the scientific evidence standing behind the claim that persons, in their psychological attributes, fall into roughly distinguishable categories or types. When we describe someone now as phlegmatic, meaning somewhat passive and not easily aroused, we no longer attribute this characteristic to one of four or five basic humors, nor do we think that every bilious person has a troubled liver. But like the ancients and Galen and Jonson we do imply that these are relatively permanent characteristics of the person and are not likely to be eliminated by anything short of brain damage.

conceptual problems

All of this may be said to be the common and even the technical meaning of the term *personality*, but once we move beyond this sweeping generality the number and the intensity of theoretical disagreements increase rapidly. "How many "types" of personality are there?" "When may a personality be said to be normal, or healthy, or diseased?" "At what age does the person first display a basic personality and what are the relative contributions of heredity and experience?" "How is personality to be measured and what evidence is to be taken as valid?" "What, indeed, are the criteria of validity?" "Is personality an ensemble of purely emotional attributes or does it also reflect the perceptual or intellectual or motivational characteristics of the person?" "Can valid inferences regarding personality be drawn from behavior alone?" "Does personality change with age, across cultures, throughout history, and so on, or are there only alterations in the manner by which it expresses itself?"

None of these questions has been fully or finally answered in such a way as to eliminate controversy among professionals. Because of this, what may be called "the psychobiology of personality" is steeped in conceptual and methodological difficulties. One cannot rationally choose a method of investigation until one has settled on just what it is that is worthy of investigation. In this respect, the psychobiologist is largely at the mercy of specialists in psychiatry and clinical psychology whose theories and studies of personality provide the only context in which psychobiological research can proceed.

Beyond the problems of classification and definition, there are other difficulties that beset research on the biological basis of personality. Virtually all such research can be broadly divided into two classes: studies of animals and studies of humans. The former typically employ surgical procedures or pharmacological administrations or electrical stimulations in attempts to alter what would appear to be the emotional states of the organism. The latter use not only these methods but also interviews, psychological tests and the person's introspective reports of feelings. With these basic paradigms it then becomes possible to observe the effects of drugs or conditioning or further surgery or stimulation on such emotional or affective attributes.

We have already noted in the earlier pages of this chapter the general findings emerging from animal studies of this sort. The question remains, however, whether these same findings can be properly included under the heading, "personality." This, after all, is a term ordinarily designed to cover the most subtle and pervasive factors influencing human perceptions, judgments, and feelings. It is *not* confined to properties of observable behavior. We can, for example, describe a personality as *intropunatively* hostile meaning that the person's hostility is directed inwardly such that he is himself the object of it. The point is that "personality" refers not so much to a set of specific stimulus-response chains or connections but to what can only be imprecisely called a "view of the world" or a "view of oneself in relation to the world." This at least is the sense in which clinicians use the term and it is just this that raises some doubts about the usefulness of research on lower organisms. (Does a white rat have "a view of itself in relation to the world?" And if so, how would we know?)

Problems of a different kind arise when research is confined to studies of psychiatric patients. Ethical considerations properly but severely constrict the range of purely experimental treatments or measurements to which such patients can be exposed, even with their own consent. Typically it is only the most severe and intractable cases that are chosen for research since those who are deriving benefits from traditional modes of therapy are not switched from traditional modes to experimental ones. It is all too common, therefore, for patients who are included in such studies to be drawn from groups having relatively long histories of institutional care.

In addition to their specific problems such patients often display what has been called the *institutionalization syndrome,* a set of behavioral and perceptual attributes apparently tailored to meet the unique demands of institutional settings. Often their diets, general hygiene, habits of exercise and rest, and overall health are not representative of the noninstitutionalized population or even of psychiatric populations treated on an outpatient basis.

In this connection it is worth noting the growing literature devoted to the *interaction* between environmental and pharmacological variables in the determination of drug effects. If, for example, mice are divided into groups of "isolates" and "aggregates"—members of the former housed in isolation and those of the latter housed with mates—the two groups will display entirely different metabolic reactions to such psychoactive agents as barbiturates, amphetamines, and lithium salts. Such effects are illustrated in Figure 7–4 which compares the reflex inhibition produced by barbiturates on mice living either alone

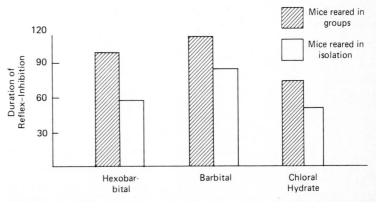

Figure 7–4 Differential effects of barbiturates on animals living in isolated vs. grouped conditions. The effect is measured as *minutes* during which the fighting reflex is inhibited after administration of the drug.

or in groups. Similar isolation effects have been reported in studies of schizophrenic patients receiving depressant drugs.

We see, then, that the relationship between a given chemical and some measure or index of personality is not always a straightforward one. It can be affected by the environmental context within which the animal (or person) and the drug are functioning and by a host of other factors often beyond the experimenter's powers to control or even observe.

Psychopathology and Normalcy

If the very concept of personality is ambiguous then notions of a "diseased" or "normal" personality cannot be expected to be entirely clear. In contemporary psychology and psychiatry the emphasis is on *adjustment* and the persons are said to suffer disturbances of personality when unable to meet the demands and obligations of ordinary life. But note that even the concept of adjustment is not without its own ambiguities and arbitrariness. That people cannot or will not adjust to a certain situation may make them *abnormal* in a purely statistical respect; i.e., their behavior departs from the norm as this norm is statistically established. But the genius, the martyr, and the hero are also "abnormal" in this merely statistical way, although one would be ill advised to take all such instances of "abnormality" as evidence of *disease*. The same must be said in the case of criminal actions. There is, to be sure, a certain justification for thinking of those who commit frequent or violent crimes as "insane" but this alone does not establish that a "disease" is responsible.

relativistic notions   It has sometimes been argued that the concept of *disease* is an arbitrary one not only within psychiatric or psychological circles but within medicine at large. There are, for example, environments in which a tendency toward diabetes might actually be of benefit and other environments in which the salt retention associated with hypertensive heart disease would also be of value. According to this relativistic view, the term "disease" is to be understood as incorporating not only a collection of physiological or medical facts but also the characteristics of the overall environment in which the person is expected to function. For example, sickle-cell anemia is a disease, but it is uncommonly frequent among African tribesmen who, because of this condition, enjoy protection against far more devastating diseases carried by local insects.

The relativistic view has much to recommend it, at least in theory, but it does not apply as readily to psychiatric notions of disease as it does to scientific or medical concepts of disease. There is no controversy within medicine as to whether a given condition—diabetes, hypertension, or sickle-cell anemia—represents a life-threatening condition in the limiting case. Even where such a condition might improve the chances of the sufferer in some specific context, there is general agreement that the condition itself reflects the *failure* of the body to perform a life-preserving function or to serve the long-term interests of the species as a whole. Moreover, within the scientific and medical specialities there is general agreement at least on just what counts as evidence for or against the claim that there is a disease process. But on questions of "mental disease" we find no such agreement. "Where does commitment end and obsession begin?" "At what point is a fear a *phobia*?" "Where is the line to be drawn so that we might separate conviction and deep belief from *"delusions"*? "What is the difference between shyness and *pathological* shyness?" And "When is depression a sign of *psychotic* depression?"

Questions of this sort have received no final and widely accepted answers from clinical psychologists and psychiatrists. If a single standard is operative it seems to be that pertaining to a patient's likelihood of doing serious harm either through direct action or neglect. This is the standard most frequently adopted when the decision is made to hospitalize and classify someone as *psychotic*. A different standard is invoked when the decision involves only the administration of psychotherapy to voluntary patients. Such patients, presenting no imminent danger to themselves or others, but apparently incapable of functioning usefully and to their own satisfaction are classified as one or another variety of *neurotic*. Perhaps the most general distinction made between psychotic and neurotic conditions is based upon the extent to which the patient makes regular and coherent contact with "reality." Thus, not only are the psychotic symptoms usually far more severe and dangerous than those associated with neurosis, but they seem to be unrelated to the actual (real) world in which the patients find themselves. The neurotic, therefore, may be described as someone who overreacts or underreacts to the actual facts of life and general surroundings, whereas the psychotic's reactions are to events and conditions of his or her own manufacture. Again, these are mere generalities and are framed in a language at least once removed from the kind of vocabulary needed by genuinely scientific approaches. With these limitations in mind, however, we can summarize the common diagnostic categories employed

neurosis and psychosis

in studies and treatments of the disturbed personality. The summary is given in Table 7–2.

Psychobiology does not have a settled position on each and every one of the entries in Table 7–2, in part for the reasons just discussed. Where the disturbances of personality are extreme, the agreement among clinicians is greater and it is with these disturbances and this degree of agreement that the psychobiologist is able to undertake useful research. With respect to this research it is worth pointing out here what may be taken as the broad perspective adopted by the neural sciences in the matter of "mental illness." Within the neural sciences, and particularly within psychobiology, it is *not* assumed that

TABLE 7–2   Major Categories of Personality Disturbances

General Category	Type	Variety	Chief Symptoms
Psychosis	Schizophrenia	Catatonia	Sensory and motor withdrawal; unresponsive to stimuli or persons; totally passive
		Hebephrenia	Childishness and infantile modes of behavior
		Paranoid	Delusions and hallucinations; suspiciousness; claims of a grandiose or persecutory nature
		Simplex	Physical retreat; hermit-like withdrawal from life
	Manic-depressive		Swings from manic to depressive states, the latter often accompanied by suicidal tendencies
	Paranoia		Delusions generally without hallucinations; adoption of different self-identities but, unlike paranoid schizophrenic, able to conform realistically to the terms and nature of the otherwise false identities
	Involutional Melancholia		"Benign psychosis," "menopausal psychosis"; severe depression that often disappears after the "change of life"
Neurosis	Phobia		Intense and unnatural fears of heights, open spaces, water, travel, and so on, coupled with paralyzing anxieties
	Obsessive-Compulsive		Attention nearly completely engaged by a single thought or worry; behavior nearly completely occupied by some ritual or mechanical habit
	Hysteria		Sensory or motor deficits unrelated to physiological disease; emotionality that is intense but unfounded
	Mania		Uncommon exhilaration or excitement tied to the commission of socially condemned actions including criminal actions
	Multiple Personality		"Three Faces of Eve"; the presence of more than one otherwise integrated personality

every form and sign of "mental illness" is evidence of a diseased brain! Indeed, the psychobiologist is under no obligation to agree with the diagnoses and classifications prevailing in psychiatry and clinical psychology. Instead, research in this field uses such diagnoses and classifications merely as ways of dividing a sample of experimental subjects into groupings for the purpose of determining if some reliable biochemical or physiological finding correlates with the groupings themselves.

Stated in the simplest terms, the psychobiologist's strategy is something like this: First, here we have a number of subjects who have been given the label schizophrenic or manic-depressive on the basis of interviews and psychological tests. Is there something about the biochemistry or physiology of their nervous systems that would result in their being classified as "abnormal" on purely *physical* grounds? Second, if there is something of this nature, can we press on further to determine whether it is merely a *correlate* of the (alleged) mental illness or, in fact, the kind of physical abnormality that might be plausibly taken as a *causal* factor?

Psychopathology and Heritability

Some twenty years ago, in his presidential address to the American Psychological Association, Paul Meehl made this observation

Suppose that you were required to write down a procedure for selecting an individual from the population who would be diagnosed as schizophrenic by a psychiatric staff; you have to wager $1000 on being right; you may not include in your selection procedure any behavioral fact....What would you write down? So far as I have been able to ascertain, there is only one thing you could write down that would give you a better than even chance of winning such a bet—namely, 'Find an individual X who has a schizophrenic twin.*

This claim, which was based upon research, continues to be confirmed by studies of mental patients and their family histories. Statistically significant degrees of *heritability* (h^2) have been found for the major classifications of psychosis and for those neurotic disturbances characterized by intense anxiety. The most common procedure involves the administration of such tests as the MMPI (Minnesota Multiphasic Personality Inventory) which allows the separate scoring of dispositions

*P. Meehl. *American Psychologist*, 1962, *12*:827.

toward *dependency, hypochondriasis, schizophrenia, depression, social introversion,* and a number of other traits. Scores on such tests are then examined in the context of the degree of genetic relatedness of those taking the tests.

The overarching question, of course, is whether monozygotic twins yield significantly more comparable test scores than those obtained from dizygotic twins, more distant relatives, and unrelated persons. In a crude way, the issue of environmental similarity is "controlled" by comparing, for example, the correlations obtained from identical twins reared together with the correlations obtained from fraternal twins or siblings also reared together—the assumption being that the environments are no more similar in the former case than in the latter. But studies also include monozygotic twins (*MZ*) reared apart from an early age with fraternal twins and nontwins reared either together or apart.

The major conclusion arising out of a half-century of research of this kind is that severe mental disturbances do display significant heritability, as do less severe *inclinations* toward mental disturbance. To the extent that "personality" is measurable in any manner it is but one more *phenotype* whose heritability can be computed, at least in principle. But it is important to understand that a high degree of heritability (h^2) does not indicate that the trait in question is insensitive to the environment. Heritability refers to the portion of the total *variance* displayed by a phenotype attributable to additive genetic influences. It does *not* refer to the average value of the phenotype. To discover, then, that "psychosis" is highly heritable is to learn that the chief source of the *variance* displayed by a population (somehow) phenotypically "psychotic" is hereditary. This fact still leaves an undetermined amount of room for environmental factors to influence the *average* phenotypic value, although it constricts the room for environmental factors to influence the *variance*.

What is important, however, about the reliable finding that major personality categories do display significant values of (h^2) is that it reinforces the assumption that individual differences in personality may be explained in biochemical-physiological terms. And at least to this extent it attaches greater credibility and relevance to the mountains of data we now have from physiological studies of "psychotics," "neurotics," and "normal" personalities. As long as so much arbitrariness surrounds the use of these terms, it is advisable to place them within quotation marks, if only occasionally and as a reminder. However, persons are assigned to such categories on the basis of observations and measurements, and we can take these seriously even as we continue to debate the meaning of labels.

Psychoparmacology

The location of the actual psychoneural equivalent of either mind in general or emotional personality in particular is, of course, not known. Personality, however, like any other mental process, ultimately must be attributed not to nuclei and macroscopic centers but to the states of the great networks of neurons which make up the brain. Since we have already alluded to the difficulties of such a network strategy, it is obvious that no immediate solution to the problem of the physiological basis of personality lies in that direction.

Another way to approach the psychobiology of personality and the psychopathologies is to consider the effects of chemicals on these mental states. There are many drugs that affect mental states and their effects can be extraordinary and diverse, ranging from mild relief of pain to the generation of artificial psychotic disturbances that are totally disruptive of any kind of a normal life.

synaptic mechanisms

As diverse as the psychological drugs and their effects are, there is a common conceptual thread that ties virtually the entire research area together. By far the larger proportion of the drugs that are ingested or injected from external sources, as well as the hormones secreted by the endocrine glands of the body itself, seem to exert their psychological influence by virtue of their ability to alter synaptic action and interaction. This psychopharmacological conclusion is entirely consistent with the general outlook that mental states are equivalents of the interconnectivity pattern of neural nets and that the states of these networks are determined by the synaptic junctions rather than by the neurons themselves.

The reader is forewarned not to lose sight of the fact that psychopharmacology is an *atheoretical* approach. We know nothing of the details of chemical effects on neuronal network interactions. The reason that a particular chemical seems to act specifically on a particular nucleus of the brain is that different nuclei contain different proportions of different kinds of synapses. Dopamine, noradrenaline, GABA, acetylcholine synapses, for example, are distributed in different ways throughout the brain as exemplified in Figure 7–5. A drug may affect personality by activating or inactivating a particular nucleus of the brain, but it does so by virtue of its impact on the chemistry of a particular type of synapse located in a particular region rather than by a precise modulation of individual synapses in some great neural net.

The best classification of the drugs and chemicals that affect

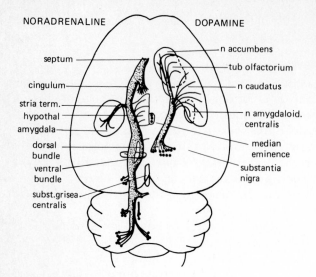

NORADRENALINE   DOPAMINE

septum

cingulum

stria term.
hypothal
amygdala

dorsal
bundle
ventral
bundle

subst.grisea
centralis

n accumbens

tub olfactorium

n caudatus

n amygdaloid.
centralis

median
eminence

substantia
nigra

Figure 7–5. A dorsal view of the rat brain displaying the organization of the noradrenaline and the dopamine synaptic-transmitter systems. (Redrawn from Ungerstedt, U. *Acta Physiolgica Scandinavica*, 1971, *82*, Suppl. 367: 1–48.)

personality is one proposed by Richard Thompson. He divides psychologically active drugs into five different categories. Let us consider each of them in turn, give some examples, and generally consider how each seems to work.

Depressants: Sedatives and Hypnotics

Sedatives are defined as drugs that produce a general quieting or calming effect; *hypnotics* are drugs that produce sleep. The borderline between the two is, of course, fuzzy because calming, drowziness, and sleep are probably just different points on a continuous dimension describing the arousal level. Overdoses of calming substances produce drowziness and a susceptibility to sleep that are indistinguishable from the effects of hypnotics. Alcohol and phenobarbital are examples of sedatives that easily cross over the borderline between these two states as the dosage is increased. As common as these drugs are the action of neither alcohol nor barbiturates is very well understood. Some authorities have speculated that alcohol works by selectively deactivating the ARAS, thus leading to a lower level of arousal,* drowsiness, and then sleep. In small doses, alcohol is thought to be a mild stimulant, but whatever stimulating effects alcohol may have are probably indirect, resulting from the inhibition of some inhibitory center. There is no doubt among current workers that this drug is primarily a neural depressant.

alcohol and barbiturates

*The ARAS (ascending reticular arousal system) is discussed in detail in pp. 330–336.

The action of the barbiturates is equally poorly understood, but it has also been suggested that they tend to deactivate the brain perhaps by virtue of their specific action on acetylcholine transmission in cholinergic synapses. Since cholinergic synapses are widely distributed throughout the brain, barbiturates are thought to exert their influence, whatever it is, very generally throughout the nervous system.

Stimulants

amphetamines

Stimulants are drugs that excite or activate. These are the drugs that lead to enhanced levels of arousal and wakefulness. Sample stimulants include nicotine, caffeine, and amphetamines. Again, despite the widespread use of caffeine, very little is known about its pharmacological action beyond the suspicion that it may represent, in part at least, one exception to the general rule that psychoactive drugs work on synaptic junctions. *Caffeine* is known to stimulate the vascular system. But the question is "Is this a secondary effect or a primary one?" Does caffeine mainly exert its influence because of its effect on the circulatory system, perhaps influencing muscles and neurons with some metabolite, the amount of which is enhanced by the increased flow of blood? Or, to the contrary, does it also have a direct neurological result that only indirectly influences the vascular system?

Nicotine, on the other hand, does seem to have a very specific effect on cholinergic synapses. This drug is known to actually enhance the action of acetylcholine at some types of synaptic receptors. *Amphetamines* also seem to work in a similar manner, but in their case their enhanced action is on *catecholaminergic* (those using norepinehrine as the transmitter substance) synapses.

Anesthetics, Analgesics, and Paralytics

Anesthetics are defined as drugs that produce a loss of sensory experience. In extreme cases, such as in general anesthetics, there is also a loss of consciousness. Local anesthetics, however, can limit sensory inputs (from a single region of the skin, for example), while leaving the rest of the nervous system totally functional and the patient fully awake. *Analgesics* act specifically to reduce pain, but in ways and by means of mechanisms that still pose the greatest of mysteries to psychobiologists. Aspirin (acetylsalicylic acid) for example, is one of the most effective and safest analgesics known, and yet its action on the nervous system remains a matter of almost complete mystery. *Paralytics*, the third subclass of this category, on the other hand, act specifically to inhibit muscular activity. Since paralytics do not inhibit sensory functions, they should never be used in place of anesthetics. Any experimental animal that is immobilized by curare, a strong paralytic, would suffer enormously even though it is incapable of emitting any of the motor responses indicative of pain.

The physiological basis of the action of anesthetics, analgesics, and paralytics, unlike the depressants and stimulants, is fairly well known and is quite different in each case. Local anesthetics such as procaine (and cocaine in low doses) undoubtedly work by blocking nervous transmission in the long axons. General anesthetics, such as ether and chloroform, on the other hand, produce a generalized inhibition of the central nervous system, particularly the higher levels where consciousness is presumably mediated. Curare, it is now well established, acts to block the transmission from neurons to motor units at the neuromuscular junctions by reversibly blocking the acetylcholine receptors on the motor units as we have noted. Derivatives of opium can be either analgesics or general anesthetics, depending on the dosage. Opiates are known to work through the mechanism of very specialized receptors in the central nervous system. The existence of such specialized receptors suggests that natural opiates (or opiate-like substances) exist within the body (since one would be hard pressed to explain how the receptors have evolved if the substances did not exist naturally). Such sub-

endorphins

stances, called *endorphins*, have been detected widely scattered throughout the central nervous system.

Psychogenetics

Psychogenetic drugs are those that produce symptoms of mental illness, extremely disturbing altered states of personality that push individuals beyond the limits of socially acceptable behavior. Within this category are some of the most frequently abused "dopes" that have afflicted society for centuries. In addition to

psychotomimetic agents

opium derivatives, like heroin, a large number of other substances such as *psilocybin* from mushrooms, the *ergot fungus* from spoiled rye, and *marijuana* from the plant *Cannabis sativa* as well as a wide variety of articifial substances (for example, lysergic acid diethylamide, LSD) can produce psychotic-like states. Drugs such as these have become a major social problem around the world in recent years. It is important to remember, however, that there is nothing new about this problem, even if it does seem that at least in some western societies, the abuse of psychogenetic drugs is at an all time high. The ergot fungus was such a scourge in the days before proper food storage (in particular of grains). Although we know that the ergot fungus tends to block serotonin receptors, the action in the nervous system of such other drugs as marijuana and heroin remains virtually unknown. There is no doubt that they work, but how is still a great puzzle.

Psychotherapeutics

Just as there are drugs that create psychotic symptoms by interfering with the normal metabolism of synapses, there are other drugs that seem to interfere with the interferences caused by preexisting abnormal conditions within the nervous system. These drugs have the happy property, therefore, of providing some amelioration of some of the most terrible afflictions of human history—the mental disorders. Some psychotherapeutics act merely to reduce anxiety and thus provide a mild therapeutic effect for the less severe neuroses. Others have the ability to lift patients from the deepest pits of self-destructive depression or to lower them from the heights of mania. Once again, we are dealing with the still mysterious way in which these personality variables are associated with brain states, and it is only in rarest instances that we have any inkling of the physiological basis of the action of psychotherapeutics.

Psychotherapeutics are among our most important drugs and judicious use of them in recent years has been instrumental in greatly reducing the proportion of our population incarcerated in mental hospitals. Less than 25 percent of the peak population of mental institutions in the 1950s is now hospitalized across the United States. This is a remarkable and dramatic social development. In spite of this social achievement, and the undisputed psychiatric effectiveness of these psychologically active drugs, their exact action still remains obscure. Even though we know something about the chemistry of the action of specific drugs on general classes of synapses, we know virtually nothing about how these modifications of synaptic conductivity influence the psychological processes.

transmitter systems

What we have learned is that the drugs seem to work on specific proteins of the central nervous system and that the basis for their selective action is the chemical differences among the transmitter systems used by various regions. To understand this process better, it is necessary to appreciate that various nuclei and centers of the brain differ chemically as well as anatomically. Indeed certain anatomical systems of the brain can be defined in terms of the particular transmitter substance that is predominantly used in their constituent parts. For example, a *serotonin* based system is concentrated in the raphe nuclei of the brain stem and a *dopamine* system is also known to exist involving the substantia nigra and the basal ganglia of the cerebral hemispheres. We also know about a *noradrenaline* system involving the amygdala and the septal nuclei. (The dopamine and noradrenaline systems were shown in Figure 7–5, a top view of the rat's brain.) On the other hand, it is not likely that there is a distinct acetylcholine (the most familiar neurotransmitter) system. Cholinergic synapses are found widely distributed throughout the central and peripheral nervous systems, a fact that may account for their early discovery.

These are but examples, however, and there certainly must be many other specific transmitter systems. There are many other neurotransmitters that have already been identified in brain tissue.

What we have been talking about so far in this section are the general biochemical mechanisms of synaptic activity and about the practical applicability of psychotherapeutics to the solution of social and personal mental health problems—those aberrations of personality and consciousness that we see often these days. We should not delude ourselves, however, into thinking we now possess any deeper understanding into the direct action of drugs on minds than did our remote preliterate predecessors who smoked hashish, popped mushrooms, dazed themselves on poppy extracts, or tranquilized themselves with various roots. What we have done is to establish a more or less general correlational relationship between certain drugs and chemicals and certain personality and conscious states. There does seem to be something especially significant about the relationship between manic-depressive psychosis and what are called the biogenic amines and between schizophrenia and dopamine, but these associations do not constitute the kind of specific cause-and-effect relationship that really satisfies the inquiring scientific mind searching for an explanation beyond mere description and correlation. As useful and practical as this field of research has been, it has done little to help us unravel the fundamental perplexity of the mind/body problem.

A similar conclusion can be drawn about hormones, the natural products of our endocrine system that have also been shown to have powerful effects on our personality and other aspects of our behavior. Hormones can regulate such specific behaviors as feeding and sex as well as mimic some of the generalized mental effects observed in studies of the psychoac-

hormonal effects

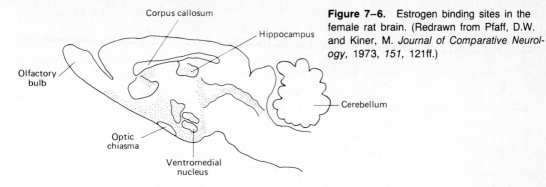

Corpus callosum
Hippocampus
Olfactory bulb
Optic chiasma
Ventromedial nucleus
Cerebellum

Figure 7–6. Estrogen binding sites in the female rat brain. (Redrawn from Pfaff, D.W. and Kiner, M. *Journal of Comparative Neurology*, 1973, *151*, 121ff.)

tive drugs. Removal of the gonads can alter such highly specific activities as the progression of behavioral steps in reproductive activity in rats. Both male and female mating behavior is disrupted by castration of their respective gonads. Yet these specific steps in sexual activity can be reorganized if androgens or estrogens are injected into an animal.

Hormones are also known to produce direct effects on the brain most probably through exactly the same type of synaptic mechanisms we have just discussed. These influences on synaptic conductivity are in addition to their many other well-known influences on growth and metabolism. For example, Figure 7–6 shows the points in the rat's brain where estrogen is known to bind.

Psychosurgery

If our ignorance of the basic mechanisms underlying drug effects on personality is deep, our understanding of the effects of an even more drastic intrusion—surgical intervention—into the brain/mind system is abysmal! The therapeutic use of neurosurgery for the purposes of altering behavior or relieving psychiatric conditions is called *psychosurgery*. The reader should carefully note the distinction between psychosurgery as just defined and the more general term *neurosurgery*. Neurosurgery includes any surgery on the nervous system. For example, some neurosurgery involves procedures specifically intended to cure conditions such as epilepsy and Parkinsonism or to repair damage to peripheral nerves. These interventions, however, are only indirectly related to psychology. The logic and the theory underlying this kind of neurosurgery are well understood and highly developed.

Psychosurgery, on the other hand, is based on a theoretical foundation of knowledge of brain/mind relationships that is flimsy at best. To put it baldly, the foundation idea behind the application of surgery to cure psychiatric problems is that a specific lesion introduced into a particular place in the nervous system will selectively alter personality and mental states in a positive way, producing only minimal side effects.

From what we have already learned in this book the reader should appreciate that this implies a state of knowledge about the localization of psychological functions that is hardly justified by contemporary scientific evidence. We do not know where personality, aggression, or any of the other psychological constructs developed over the years reside in the brain. Indeed, there is substantial evidence that *none* of these psychological processes resides in any particular place. Rather, current theory holds that all major psychological processes are represented by neural mechanisms that are widely distributed throughout the brain. We have also seen how the various brain nuclei most heavily involved in mental processes do not operate in isolation—they are almost always heavily interconnected in both excitatory and inhibitory fashions. In this regard we have also seen the emergence of a consensus that no single nucleus totally accounts for any particular mental process, and no particular mental function is uniquely localized in any particular part of the brain.

The bottom line of these complexities of neuroanatomy and psychoneural equivalence is that we do not know where in the brain such subtle behavioral and mental traits as anger, depression, violence, or for that matter even pain, are to be found. In light of this understandable ignorance (resulting from the tremendous complexity of the brain) most psychosurgical therapies designed to modify behavior or mood are based on heuristic, trial and error, or sometimes imaginative and fanciful theoretical foundations. A history of medicine in which traumatic brain injuries have been shown to affect some kind of behavior (the classic case was the observation that Phineas Gage's frontal lobe lesion—see Figure 6–13—seemed to lessen his managerial skills and personal drive) or analogies from what had been observed in animal laboratories is often almost anecdotal justification for the most drastic of psychosurgical operations.

However incomplete may be the theory behind the placement of a particular lesion in a particular place in the brain, psychosurgery does seem to work in some cases. Suffering human beings have been freed from physical and mental pain by operations in what appears to be a nontrivial portion of the cases in which psychosurgery has been attempted. There is nevertheless extensive disagreement over the degree to which patients are helped and the damage that is done to other aspects of their mental life by this drastic therapy. The reasons for this disagreement are not difficult to discern. No two situations are ever exactly alike when one is dealing with human psychosurgical cases. Data, therefore, are always of less high quality in such studies than in situations in which the brains of animals with well-controlled genetic backgrounds and precisely defined lesions can be manipulated. Furthermore, the effects one wishes to measure following such surgery are sometimes subtle psychological processes that are often not adequately defined or precisely measurable. It is not as if one is dealing with the size of the visual field or the weight of the brain. To the contrary, subjective states are being evaluated that may themselves be even more elusive than the neural structures that mediate these processes. In sum, the problem of psychosurgery is extreme from a purely technical basis.

However, that is not the full extent of the difficulties involved in this controversial field of therapy. Ethical issues abound when one considers that for the most part the brain tissue that is surgically removed is not pathological in any observable way. What does this mean in the context of the medical oath forbidding surgeons to cut healthy tissue? Furthermore, in these days of informed consent, what can one assume about the validity of the consent of a patient so severely handicapped as to require this most drastic kind of surgical intervention?

Obviously we are dealing here with problems of social, legal, and philosophical complexity which rival the complexity of the psychobiological relationship itself. For the interested reader who would like to know more there is no better source than the two books on the topic written by Elliott Valenstein (see "Suggested Readings"). In the remainder of this section we shall concentrate more on the psychobiological issues surrounding this controversial field of brain/mind surgery.

The surgical treatment of the brain to alleviate psychiatric disorders in modern times (surprisingly, psychosurgery had been attempted even in prehistoric times) was first reported in the late nineteenth century. However, modern enthusiasm for psychosurgical procedures appropriately dates from the work of Egas Moniz in Portugal starting about 1935. Moniz, who won the Nobel prize in medicine in 1949 for this work, was specifically influenced by the earlier work of psychobiologists who showed personality changes in monkeys following prefrontal lobotomies. Anecdotal medical reports of cases like that of Phineas Gage must also have influenced Moniz.

Nevertheless, the idea that artificial lesions of the frontal lobes could improve mental states and behavior took root in a number of different institutions around the world. In subsequent years a wide variety of surgical techniques were developed specifically to produce lesions in the frontal lobes. These procedures included the insertion of knives (leucotomes) through the temples, the top of the head, and the forehead. The "ultimate" development of this surgical artform was the transorbital procedure proposed by the American Walter Freeman in 1948. (Freeman and his colleague James Watts were the authors of what was then clearly the most influential book in the history of psychosurgery in 1942.) The transorbital procedure involved the penetration of a thin icepick-like surgical knife into the frontal lobe by passing it up above the orb of the eye and through the thin bone at the back of the eyesocket. This procedure was technically quite simple, so much so that it was often carried out in a surgeon's office under only local anesthesia.

After mixed results with frontal lobe operations and following new research developments in psychobiology, particularly those which showed the limbic system to be deeply involved in motivational and emotional responses, additional neural centers became the targets of psychosurgeons. New technical developments also made it possible to aim at smaller and deeper nuclei. Stereotaxic instruments and atlases became available which allowed surgeons to probe at such small regions as specific subnuclei of the hypothalamus. Freezing, radioactivity, suction, and other innovations in producing lesions substituted for the surgeon's knife; and fluoroscopic X-ray techniques allowed the surgeon to observe at least the shadows of the instruments inside the patient's skull. Each was chosen primarily on the basis of preliminary research carried out on animals.

Table 7–3 tabulates the brain sites, and also the psychological conditions for which these sites are lesioned in the hopes of therapeutic relief. This table, therefore, represents a contemporary *theory* of brain localization of psychological processes in humans according to the best insights, intuitions, and evidence obtained by those working in this field of mind/brain relationships. No area of psychobiology need be as explicit in presenting its conceptual model nor required to put its theoretical "cards on the table" so openly as have the psychosurgeons.

Because of the limited and confused empirical basis for the theory underlying psychosurgery and because of the many

Watts and Freeman

psychosurgical sites

TABLE 7-3

Diagnostic Label	Total Number of Patients	Frontal Lobe Procedure	Cingulum	Amygdala	Thalamas	Hypothalamus	Multiple Target Sites	Midbrain	Brain Stimulation
Aggression	35			12(34.3%)		4(11.4%)	19(54.3%)		
Neurotic depression	136	9(6.6%)	127(93.4%)						
Psychotic depression	11		11(100.0%)						
Fear and anxiety	4	3(75.0%)	1(25.0%)						
Obsessive-compulsive neurosis	37	9(24.3%)	25(67.6%)				3(8.1%)		
Schizo-affective disorders	7	7(100.0%)							
Schizophrenia and other psychoses	80		32(40.0%)				47(58.8%)		1(1.2%)
Drug addiction and alcoholism	14	1(7.1%)	13(92.9%)						
Pain	379	17(4.5%)	177(46.7%)		120(31.7%)		25(6.6%)	8(2.1%)	32(8.4%)
Psychopathic behavior	6				6(100.0%)				
"Emotional illness"	9		1(11.1%)				8(88.9%)		
"Agitated states of the aged"	2	2(100.0%)							
Involutional melancholia	1		1(100.0%)						
Epilepsy with psychiatric disorders	45			45(100.0%)					

ethical and legal questions, the use of surgery to treat psychiatric problems has tended to wane since 1965. Today, though we know more about the biology of the brain and mind than ever before, the ethical issues involved in this medical approach to psychoses have reduced the frequency of psychosurgery while at the same time they have raised the level of controversy.

Perhaps this final topic illustrates better than any other something very germane to the overall message of this book. Psychobiology is a *highly* relevant and important discipline. It may indeed be the center of scientific excitement during the coming century just as physics was in the first half and biochemistry was in the second half of this one. Psychobiology is not simpy an esoteric field, of interest to but a few ivory tower laboratory scientists or philosophers; this science is central to many difficult and immediately relevant aspects of human existence. The questions that are raised about the efficacy and the ethics of psychosurgery are but instances of the most important questions of our own meaning and being. The important thing is that we are learning answers to some of them.

Summary

To the findings just discussed *thousands* of others could easily be added. Drugs of one sort or another have been cited as effective in the treatment of juvenile delinquency, acute depression, hostility, loss of sexuality, loss of affect (*anhedonia*), manic and depressive phases of psychosis, paranoid delusions, chronic anxiety, insomnia, criminal violence, alcoholism, and drug addiction. It is now safe to say that, for almost any specific expression of a "personality" characteristic, there is a known drug identified as significantly affecting either its frequency, its intensity, or both.

However, when we attempt to integrate these findings into a general physiological *theory* of personality—and include in our attempt the related findings from surgical and genetic investigations—the pieces do not fit in any satisfactory way. The crucial studies must, by the very nature of the issue, be studies of *human* personality, but these remain at the level of correlations—for example, "feelings of hostility" as a function of how much of a particular drug the patient has received. And even the thick book of correlations is not entirely reassuring since we now know that the effects of drugs can be powerfully affected by the expectations of the recipient, by the recipient's underlying "personality," and by the behavior of others as witnessed by the recipient.

It may be, and much of the available evidence suggests as much, that a given personality "type" is also a given neurochemical "type," but it would be surprising if this relationship held in any but the most obvious pathological conditions. In this connection it is important to remember that a biochemical imbalance that seems to result in a disturbed personality does not establish that the personality, itself, *is* biochemical. To take a trivial case, we know that a person whose supply of oxygen is cut off will soon become unconscious, but we would hardly infer from this that consciousness *is* oxygen or is no more than an expression of the presence of oxygen.

That this issue will be with us for a very long season seems to be guaranteed even as we acknowledge the extraordinary advances that have been made in the basic sciences of genetics, biochemistry, and neuroanatomy. The problem now is less one of identifying the anatomical and chemical pathways of the nervous system than of establishing a reliable and valid taxonomy of personality. As we have proposed throughout this chapter there is more to personality than episodes of anger or affection or fear or depression. At present, the level of biochemical and anatomical analysis has already outstripped the level of psychological analysis. As long as this is so, a *psychobiology of personality* will remain incomplete.

Taking fear, aggression, and sexuality as basic emotional dispositions, we have seen that the structures of the limbic system are uniquely involved. Coordinated patterns of flight, fighting, and copulation can be elicited from a variety of species through the technique of limbic stimulation or limbic surgery. By and large such techniques produce effects that closely mimic the behavior of animals in the natural setting. Some of the effects can be produced by appropriate manipulations of the endocrine and autonomic systems which are functionally tied to limbic structures chiefly through the hypothalamic-hypophyseal system. At a more fundamental level the effects appear to be regulated by the brain's biogenic amine (norepinephrine, serotinin, dopamine) systems which infiltrate the limbic complex and hypothalamus.

The relationship between these basic emotional dispositions and *personality* is neither direct nor simple. Surgical and chemical approaches to mental illness have provided results that are uneven, to say the least, and that shed little if any light on the relationship between brain and personality. Studies of the heritability of certain psychiatric disturbances offer evidence of a biochemical basis for certain extreme varieties of psychopathology; a basis indirectly confirmed by research in psychopharmacology and neurochemistry. The bearing all this has on the larger question of the physiological basis of personality remains an open question.

Suggested Readings

Psychobiology and the Emotions

1. A. Ax, The physiological differentiation between fear and anger in humans, *Psychosomatic Medicine*, 1953, *15:* 433–442.
2. P. Fried, Septum and behavior: A review. *Psychological Bulletin*, 1972, *78:* 292–310.
3. L. Levi (ed.), *Emotions: Their Parameters and Measurement*, Raven Press, New York, 1975.
4. K. Moyer, *The Psychobiology of Aggression*, Harper & Row, New York, 1976.

Biochemical Aspects of Emotion and Personality

1. J. Barchas and E. Usdin (eds.), *Serotonin and Behavior*, Academic Press, New York, 1970.
2. J. Cooper, F. Bloom, and R. Roth, *The Biochemical Basis of Neuropharmacology*, Oxford University Press, New York, 1970.
3. E. Usdin and S. Snyder (eds.), *Frontiers in Catecholamine Research*, Pergamon Press, New York, 1973.
4. H. E. Himwich (ed.), *Biochemistry, Schizophrenia, and Affective Illnesses*, Williams & Wilkins, New York, 1970.
5. B. Ho and W. McIsaac (eds.), *Brain Chemistry and Mental Disease*, Plenum Press, New York, 1971.
6. M. Lipton, A. DiMascio, and K. Killiam (eds.), *Psychopharmacology: A Generation of Progress*, Raven Press, New York, 1978.

Neural and Neuroelectric Correlates of Emotion & Personality

1. D. Benson and D. Blumer (eds.), *Psychiatric Aspects of Neurologic Disease*, Grune & Stratton, New York, 1975.
2. M. Buchsbaum, F. Goodwin, D. Murphy, and G. Borge, AER in affective disorders. *American Journal of Psychiatry*, 1971, *128:* 19–25.
3. P. Flor-Henry, Lateralized temporal-limbic dysfunction and psychopathology, *Annals of the New York Academy of Science*, 1976, *280:* 777–795.

Psychosurgery

1. R. Heath, Electrical self-stimulation of the brain of man, *American Journal of Psychiatry*, 1963, *120:* 571–577.
2. Mark and F. Ervin, *Violence and the Brain*, Harper & Row, New York, 1970.
3. E. S. Valenstein, *The Psychosurgery Debate*, Freeman, San Francisco, 1980.
4. E. S. Valenstein, *Brain Control*, Wiley, New York, 1973.

8 Consciousness, Language, and Thought

Introduction

We concern ourselves in this chapter with *the* most perplexing and difficult areas of psychobiology. The topics discussed here are exceptionally refractory for many reasons. There are the usual technical questions, such as "What regions of the brain are involved in language or logical thinking?" But apart from these there are profound difficulties of definition and conceptualization. What, for example, are we actually referring to when we use the word "consciousness"? What is the nature of the relationship between language and thought? What, indeed, does the word "thinking" mean?

consciousness   We have noted that three centuries ago Descartes wondered whether one might be able to distinguish between a well-designed automaton and a sentient organism. About one hundred years ago scientists began to conclude that such distinctions might actually be made impossible once technology had progressed sufficiently far. Even today there is no universally accepted set of criteria by which to distinguish consciousness from an elaborate (though totally mechanical) computer simulation. This is not to say that the "intelligence" attained by the better computer simulations is of a very high order. It does, however, suggest that very similar kinds of behavior (outputs) can be generated by machinery as different as nervous systems and computers. The "conscious" brain and the "unconscious" computer can and do accomplish the same tasks. And since we remain confused as to the essential nature of consciousness, we cannot judge finally whether the two are actually operating according to entirely different principles. What is available to us

313

at the level of common sense is a definition of consciousness arising out of our own *intrapersonal* experience, our own sense of our individual consciousness or *self-consciousness*. But this is a treacherous datum upon which to attempt to base a science, if only because of the total circularity of this definition of the consciousness.

behavioristic challenges

It was not long ago that such problems of definition and the limits placed on *intrapersonal* validation led psychology to reject the study of these internal states entirely. John Watson's behavioristic rebellion was against the introspective "mentalism" of the 1920s and 1930s. The intellectual descendent of this rebellion—the neobehavioristic stimulus-response psychology which dominated behavioral science in the 1950s and 1960s—rejected the scientific goal of studying consciousness, language, and thought altogether. In their place overt behavior and, even more specifically, behavioral change (that is, learning) were substituted as *the* appropriate subject matter of psychological science. During this behavioristic period psychobiology became a secondary aspect of this science. What sense did a quest for the solution of the mind/body problem make if the concept of mind had been rejected by the parent science?

the mind restored

In recent years, however, there has been a resurgence of interest in consciousness and related mental states as legitimate topics of psychological and psychobiological study. This resurgence of interest in ideas, once popular, then rejected, and now rejuvenated, is not really based on any fundamental conceptual breakthroughs, but rather on the reemergence of an appreciation that behavior is but a sign or an indicator of the psychological states that exist within organisms. Psychology is no longer the science of behavior; it is, once again a science of mind. A perspective has been reestablished that asserts that these implicit psychological or mental states and processes, and not overt behavior, are the true subject matter of psychological science. This renewed acceptance of concepts like consciousness, thought, attention, sleep, and even such complex states as intelligence and personality as valid targets of research has also given rise to a willingness to consider these mental variables in terms of their physiological correlates.

Herein lies one of the most important aspects of our thinking about thinking from an analytical or reductionistic point of view. If one were either to speculate at an abstract level concerning the psychobiological equivalent of consciousness or to extrapolate from what is known of neural representation, we believe that one will be tempted to conclude that consciousness itself is as much a function of the state of some appropriately large neural network as is any other mental experience.

The neural network associated with consciousness is undoubtedly both enormous and distributed throughout many regions of the brain. It is also, in a way that is totally devastating to hopes of a completely neuroreductionistic explanation of consciousness, extremely complex. It is probably beyond the grasp of a complete physiological analysis. We are, therefore, left with only certain indirect and global physiological measures to use as indicators of mental states.

The electroencephalogram (EEG), for example, is a useful tool for studying mental states because it appears to vary in a lawful manner with changes in the state of consciousness and thought and as a result of manipulations of those portions of the brain (for example, the ascending reticular system, ARAS) that are particularly involved in the maintenance of conscious awareness. But it must be appreciated that such molar electrophysiological indicators, though correlated, are not the direct equivalents or the *psychoneural equivalents of mind* in any precise sense of "equivalents". They are only signs or indicators of those deeper levels of neural organization that do represent mental processes. When psychobiologists measure a gross brain potential with the electroencephalogram, they are looking at a signal that may be concurrent with consciousness, but is *not* consciousness itself. The recorded voltage is no more consciousness than the electrical signal that might be recorded from the liver during some associated autonomic activity! Indeed it is possible to find many nonneural responses (for example, the electrical conductivity of the skin, the GSR or galvanic skin reflex) that are also good indicators of the state of consciousness or attention or arousal at any moment.

The caveat against casually identifying electrical signals with the mind (even when the signals come from the brain) must be kept in focus as we proceed through this chapter. It is an empirical fact that in many instances even brain signals can be *dissociated* from the conscious states with which they normally covary. This means that the correlation between these signals and mental states is less than perfect and that the two are not *equivalent* in the formal sense. In other words, the two measures, consciousness and brain signal, may only be generated by common processes. One is not the necessary and sufficient substrate of the other.

What then is consciousness that we might study its physiological equivalents? It is possible, in fact all too easy, to put a string of words together (and it may be a long string indeed since many volumes have been confined solely to this very issue) to answer this question. However, in the final analysis we are usually forced to turn to a common sense answer based on personal experience. If one claims to have been "asleep", we can appreciate what "asleep" means only because of our own experience. There is nothing *behaviorally* unique about sleep that rigorously defines this state. Unconsciousness, after all, can be behaviorally simulated without an actual loss of consciousness. There are some physiological changes that are highly correlated with the absence of consciousness, but as we said previously, they are at best signs and it is not at all certain exactly what they mean.

As difficult as it is to define, consciousness is even more difficult to measure. What dimension does one use to determine the degree or magnitude of attention being directed toward a stimulus? Obviously any impersonal (public) measure of conscious states must be indirect. Thought is elusive. Nothing emphasizes this better than the fact that the main characteristic of such a brain/mind correlate as the electroencephalogram is the disappearance of regular electrical signals as the mind becomes active.

Thus, we must conclude, even as we begin this chapter, that there are enormous problems of definition and measurement in the field of the psychobiology of consciousness. Many of the approaches to the problem depend on techniques of the most tenuous logical and technical validity and on the most elusive concepts in any science. The paucity of reliable data is startling in light of the intense popular interest in consciousness. But proper science appreciates its limits and hesitates (for responsible enough reasons) to speculate where feckless "pop" psychologies fearlessly plunge ahead. When scientific techniques are applied to the problems of consciousness, as for example in the study of hypnosis or drug influences, there is usually an atheoretic tone to the empirical data being accumulated; *correlation* rather than *explanation* reigns supreme. How often we describe the effects of some drug in a way that is devoid of any appreciation of what it is actually doing to alter the state of the great neural networks underlying consciousness! It is usually the case that nothing is said about possible mechanisms other than a pro forma assertion that these psychoactive drugs are more likely to work at synaptic junctions or on the transmitter chemistry of a class of widely distributed neurons than on any other part of the neuron.

The reader proceeding into this chapter should keep these extraordinary conceptual difficulties in mind and remain appropriately skeptical as psychobiological correlates are presented. There is, for example, no known reason that we should sleep (there are other forms of rest) and we have no idea of what sleep is. But a superficial identification of sleep with certain electroencephalographic recordings can give us a false sense that we actually know what is going on. There are some things we can measure but not fully understand, and this is surely the case with consciousness, thought, and language. What joins these topics together is that consciousness and thought deal with self-awareness, one's appreciation of one's own "mental state." And language, of course, is the most effective behavioral expression of this state. Thus, as elusive and poorly understood as these terms may be, they are at the very root of the essence of humanity and of the science of psychology as well. What we offer in this chapter can achieve no more than a characterization of the state of the science in regard to content and approach. Specifically, we now consider the psychobiological approaches to *selective attention, sleep and arousal,* and *language.*

Selective Attention

It is not uncommon for a man conversing in a crowded and noisy room to stop suddenly as he hears his own name mentioned by someone in another group; or for the soundly sleeping woman to be instantly aroused by the soft sobs of her child; or for the busily active dog to come to a complete halt with the first scent of its master. In each of these cases we have complex interactions taking place between sensory processes and the mechanisms of *selective attention.* In daily life the senses are bathed in environmental stimuli, only a fraction of which may be directly related to immediate or long-range needs and interests.

The importance of selective attention can be illustrated this way. Let us take human reaction time, at its fastest, to be on the order of 150 milliseconds, which is a measure therefore of our response capacities. Keeping the arithmetic simple, let us reduce this to 100 milliseconds and say that our "output systems" for voluntary actions can generate discrete behavioral events at the rate of 10 per second. However, when we turn to the "input systems"—in this case the retina and its associated fibers—a radically different set of numbers must be dealt with. The retina's 130 million receptors can each undergo decomposition of its pigment in far less than a second. If the retina were taken to be a mosaic of functionally separate processors, it would be able to perform 130 million "yes-no" operations in one second. This is a highly idealized number since the receptors do not operate with complete independence and it is not possible to stimulate all of them one at a time. Still, there are about one million fibers in the optic nerve, each able to carry a number of impulses in one second. Again, therefore, we find an input processing capability far in excess of the response capacity of the reacting observer. Quite simply, the behavior of the organism cannot keep pace with the sensory capabilities.

From a purely evolutionary point of view there would be nothing gained by an organism able to respond to every possible discrimination made at the level of the receptors. The necessary machinery would be enormously cumbersome to say the least. Survival depends on the ability to react to *relevant* environmental events—those that bear directly on nutrition, shelter, safety, procreation, and the like. It is through selective attention that the organism is able to confine processing to just these relevant features of the environment. With respect to human observers, we use the term *selective attention* to refer to those processes by which limited information-processing powers are allocated to specific portions of the total stimulating environment.

attention as filtering

It is obvious that we have very few thoughts simultaneously present in awareness. Subjectively, most of us would agree that we can probably "think" only one thought at a given time. There is room for dispute here, but even the most committed "multiple-thought" theorists would surely limit the number of simultaneous thoughts to two or three items at most. Some active process keeps this number low.

Attention, we see, is analogous to *filtering* in that it involves the relatively easier passage of certain signals (sensations or thoughts) and the attenuation or elimination of others. The filters that are ordinarily used in audio equipment are constructed out of materials that respond differently to different incoming frequencies. When a speaker is said to give a flat response over the audible spectrum, it means that the speaker's response is indifferent to frequencies in the range, 20 to 20,000 H_z, but that its response falls off sharply below and above this range.

Devices of this sort are *fixed filters* in that their responses are designed to be constant over time. Roughly speaking, sense organs are also fixed filters in that they are "tuned" to a fixed range of effective stimuli. The frog, for example, whose mission in life does not go much beyond the capture of flies and the making of other frogs, has a fixed filter designed to detect fly-like objects.

But in the advanced species the task of selective attention is accomplished by filtering processes that develop over the course of an entire life's experiences. The advanced species *learn to attend*. Moreover, the most current theories of selective attention take into account the fact that perceptual filtering involves a process of attenuation rather than the outright and inflexible rejection of stimuli. To this extent, even the analogy of a filter fails to respect the subtle manner in which developed nervous systems operate on incoming signals. It is through such subtlety that we find variations in the degree of our conscious awareness of the elements in the immediate environment.

channel capacity

It would appear that an observer is only able to use what psychologists now believe is primarily a *single channel* of consciousness. People perform very poorly when asked to do two things at the same time, such as listen to different simultaneously presented messages (one to each ear), or search a list for two different kinds of item. Somehow, from among all of the stimuli impinging on us, we are able to select only one set for processing at a given moment and by a single channel of consciousness.

A number of investigators have attempted to define attention more precisely and, remarkably, in light of the empirical and conceptual difficulties, a certain consensus seems to be emerging. Many now agree that attention has three distinct aspects. The first aspect is *receptivity*, whereby attention regulates the degree to which the organisms will respond to stimuli in general. The second aspect is *selectivity*, where attention determines to which part of the manifold of incident stimuli the organism will respond. The final aspect is *effort;* attention, on this account, involves a conscious, willful effort to focus and concentrate on a specific stimulus.

Make no mistake. There are many uncertainties and difficulties left when one considers attention and consciousness even from such a near-consensus point of view. We cannot always be sure for example what a word like "willful" implies.

The study of attention has led to a unique approach to the problem that displays considerable depth and comprehensiveness. The main electrophysiological technique that has been used is the averaged *evoked brain potential* (EBP)* described in Chapter 2. The EBP, however, comes in many different versions. We have already been introduced to the idea of a primary sensory evoked potential recorded most readily over the primary projection region for that modality. However, other kinds of averaged EBPs can be obtained that are especially useful in the study of attention. The *contingent negative variation*

CNV and expectancy

(CNV), for example, is recorded from the vertex (top) of the skull. The CNV is a long, slow negative-going wave that occurs in situations in which the observer is warned by a signal to expect something to happen. If the observer is told, for example, to ignore the warning tone (the warning tone is the stimulus that would have produced the CNV if it had had significance, that is, if the subject had been told to expect something to

*The acronyms EBP, AER (average evoked response) and ER (evoked response) are used interchangeably.

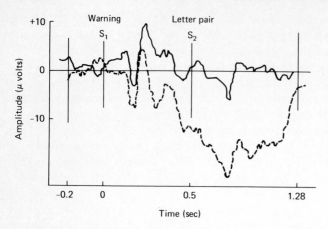

Figure 8–1 An example of the effect on the CNV as a function of the instructions given to the observer. The solid line depicts a condition in which the observer is told to ignore the warning and not respond to a word pair stimulus. The dotted line depicts a condition in which the subject is told to use the warning to get ready and respond to the word pair. (Redrawn from Posner, M. in Gazzaniga, M. and Blakemore, C., eds., *Handbook of Psychobiology*, 1975.)

happen following the warning tone), the CNV does not occur. Many experiments show this large variation in the magnitude of the CNV as a function of the instructions to the observer.

Figure 8–1 is an example of this effect. The dotted line shows the response that occurs when the observer is told to use the warning signal (which evoked the CNV) as a cue to get set for a subsequent letter-matching task. The solid line shows the absence of the CNV in a situation in which the observer was told to ignore the warning signal. Clearly the *significance of the cue* and its relation to the attentive state of the observer are important variables in determining the magnitude of the CNV.

But is the converse also true? "Is the CNV, in some special way, especially associated with the mental state we call attention?" Here the logic of the argument is not so clear. It is entirely possible that the CNV is an epiphenomenon of some sort only indirectly linked to attention. It may be that it is more closely associated with some kind of motor orienting response (perking up the ears or fixating on a target) or some equally nonequivalent neurophysiological aspect of the attentive state.

The more conventional EBP recorded from the (sensory) specific projection areas has also been shown to be affected by the subject's state of attention. Early experiments reported that particular components of the EBP were enhanced if the observer paid attention to the stimulus and were attenuated by inattention. Figure 8–2 illustrates this effect. In recent years this general finding has been confirmed using more sophisticated and involved experimental designs. For example, we can measure evoked brain potentials in response to a given stimulus, such as a flash of light or click of sound, while the observer is engaged in a task that demands full attention. For example, the subject might receive tape-recorded messages through one earphone and "clicks" through the other. On some

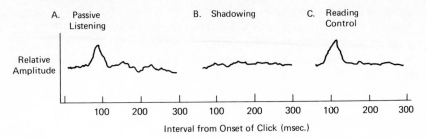

Figure 8–2 Auditory evoked responses during passive listening, "shadowing," and a control condition. Note that the principle component of the brain's response is eliminated under conditions requiring the observer's attention.

divided attention

trials, the subject is instructed to repeat exactly what is contained in the message and to do so in such a way as to reduce the lag between the recorded message and the subject's repetition of it. Such tasks are called *shadowing* tasks because they require the subject to "shadow" the recorded message, that is, to duplicate it in nearly simultaneous fashion. In Figure 8–2 we can see the difference between brain responses to "clicks" when the subject is only listening to a superimposed message and brain responses to the same "clicks" when the subject is actively *shadowing* the message. In the latter case, the major components of the auditory evoked response are virtually eliminated. Under the condition labeled "control" in Figure 8–2 the subject is called upon to read a passage from a text while the clicks are being presented. Note that the auditory evoked response is largely unaffected. In other words, mere vocalization does not eliminate the auditory evoked response nor does the passive listening to a recorded message. It is only when the subject's attention is actively engaged by the recorded message that the brain's response to an extraneous signal is attenuated. And, under this condition, the subject after a run of 50–100 such clicks, when asked if any were heard and, if so, how many, typically reports having heard none.

There are, however, a number of problems concerning the meaning of these data that have continued to raise controversy. There will always remain some residual doubt concerning whether the attention-enhanced EBP is created by the *specific* act of attending to the stimulus or by virtue of some *general* arousal that would affect many other aspects of the brain and somatic responses equally well. In other words, is the effect of attention one of enhancing the EBP or is it mediated by a generally heightened level of arousal in many aspects of the body's physiology?

In extreme conditions of attentiveness, for example, when the observer is asked to shadow or echo a verbal message (presented through one earphone) while at the same time being stimulated with a repetitive simple tone through the other, the EBP to the tone may be completely obliterated. One technical problem in using this signal as an indicator of a mental state is that the EBP is discernible in the random electronic and physiological noise in which it is embedded only after tens of repetitive trails during which the repetitive stimulus components are averaged out of the spontaneous noise. Just how, then, does one maintain a constant state of attention for the several minutes that may be required to collect data sufficient for averaging? There are various methodological approaches to reducing the severity of such problems, but when all is said and done it would be too simplistic to take EBP signals as the neural equivalent of the attentive state.

attention and peripheral "gating"

Another problem concerning these brain signs of attention concerns their physiological origins. In general two different theoretical approaches have dominated recent thinking concerning the biological basis of these signals. The first theory, emphasizing *peripheral gating*, was originally proposed by Hernandez-Peon, Scherrer, and Jouvet in 1956. These neurophysiologists believed that the diminishment in the central EBP response was due to an actual reduction in the strength of the signal being communicated along peripheral nerves. They believed this diminishment to be a result of inhibiting centrifugal signals (those traveling outward from the central nervous system) when the experimental animal (a cat) was distracted by a mouse in the cage. The centrifugal signals, it was proposed, reduced the sensitivity of the receptors themselves; and, indeed, centrifugal synapses that could regulate sensitivity are known to exist at the base of auditory hair cells. The basic idea of the peripheralist theory, therefore, is that the brain potential decreases in amplitude because the peripheral mechanism sends out a smaller signal. This reduction is a result of central control, but that is a secondary point—the main point is that the primary effect is peripheral.

An opposite point of view has been expressed by other investigators unable to replicate this peripheral attenuation of the auditory signal, even when there is clear evidence of a variation of the response of a cat's nervous system when its "attention" was distracted. Thus, some workers now support an alternative theory, to the effect that such attenuation, when it does occur, takes place chiefly within the central nervous system.

The problem is complex, of course, but it is clear that, whatever the exact neurophysiological basis of the attentive state, there also occurs, concomitant with it, a number of electrophysiological signals of which the EBP is only one. In

the orienting response

fact, there seem to be very few responsive physiological systems in the body that do not produce some correlated response when an attention attracting stimulus occurs. *Attention attracting* in this case is virtually synonymous with *novel.* An unusual, new, surprising, and unexpected stimulus introduced into the environment of virtually any organism can be shown to produce a constellation of behavioral and physiological responses collectively referred to as the *orienting response.* In mammals, including humans, the orienting reaction may include EEG changes; desynchronization has already been described as a result of thinking and also occurs as an outcome of the presentation of a novel stimulus.

There are many other responses observed during the orienting reaction that are not the immediate outcome of brain state changes in the same way as is the EEG. For example, the pupil typically dilates during the orienting reaction. Furthermore, both heart rate and respiration temporarily decrease. The popular notion of the heart stopping for a moment when one is startled is validated by electrocardiographic recordings during the orienting reaction. There is also a redistribution of blood to the head and away from the viscera and the limbs. Well-defined motor responses, of course, also occur. We literally *orient* in a physical manner with our shoulders, our hips, and our eyes to a surprise!

There are also other aspects of the orienting response presumably associated with attention, that involve the skin. For example, there is a prototypical increase in the electrical conductance of the skin that has been used for many years by psychobiologists as an indication of arousal and attention. Previously, as we noted, this response had been referred to as the galvanic skin response, or GSR (implying that it was a voltage change) but we now know that the actual electrical event is a change in resistance induced by changes in circulation and/or sweating in the capillaries of the skin. It is certain, however, that the skin conductance change is at best an epiphenomenon only distantly related to the neurophysiological changes that are of immediate importance in regulating shifts in attention. The GSR occurs because something else more directly useful happens (for example a constriction of the blood supply to the skin) not because the skin conductance itself changes. The popularity of the GSR in the last few decades is primarily based upon the fact that it is a convenient indicator, easily measured with standard electrical resistance measuring equipment. It is not the mind, however, nor is it likely to be ever a functionally adaptive, as opposed to an epiphenomenal, aspect of the orienting reaction.

Although this fact is obvious when we are dealing with the

skin, it is also thought provoking to appreciate that this caveat also applies to brain signals such as the EEG and the EBP. Are they the true psychoneural equivalents of the mental processes with which they correlate? Or are they, too, epiphenomenal in spite of the fact that the site of their physical origin is in the brain?

Arousal and Sleep

Conscious effortful attention is one aspect of arousal. The word attention refers, as we have noted, to the channeling or directing of mental capacities to particular aspects of the stimulus environment. There is, however, another direction from which the study of consciousness can be approached. This approach depends on the fact that gradiations or degrees of consciousness have been known for as long as humans have considered their own mental states. Each of us is aware of states of consciousness that are different in some way from states in which we find ourselves at other times. Most dramatically we spend many hours asleep, during which most of the time is spent at a very low level of arousal if not total unconsciousness. In other instances we are intensely aware—our consciousness may vary upward to situations in which the intensity of our awareness and levels of behavioral activity may be considered to be abnormal in a clinical sense.

Both wakefulness and sleep periods can be further subdivided into even finer categories. There is, however, no single dimension of the "depth" of consciousness. Stages of sleep, however, may arbitrarily be distinguished on the basis of associated motor behavior into periods of active sleep and quiet sleep, or (as is becoming extremely popular nowadays) into even finer

sleep and the EEG

gradations on the basis of differences in electroencephalographic recordings. Figure 8–3 shows one sample set of EEG recordings that has been used to identify the different stages of sleep. It is important to emphasize that it is likely that these discrete stages are arbitrary divisions on a continuum of variation and not sharply demarcated biological divisions.

Let us consider these discrete categories in more detail. Normal wakefulness is characterized by relatively low amplitude and relatively high frequency waves in the electroencephalogram. The dominant frequency, that is the major frequency component, in the normal waking electroencephalogram is about 10 Hz (cycles per second).

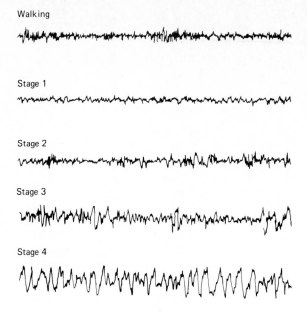

Walking

Stage 1

Stage 2

Stage 3

Stage 4

Figure 8–3 A set of EEGs associated with the various stages of sleep. REM sleep looks the same as Stage 1 sleep. (Redrawn from Hartmann, E., *The Biology of Dreaming*, 1967.)

REM sleep

As one sinks into deeper and deeper sleep, however, there is a progressive slowing of the dominant frequency of the EEG and an increase in the amplitude of the waves. This progressive increase in the amplitude is referred to as *synchronization*, and is assumed to be related to the concurrent or synchronized idling of larger numbers of neurons when the brain is inactive.

In very deep sleep, the EEG changes into a vastly different pattern distinguished by two particularly surprising features. First, the EEG suddenly returns to what appears to be a normal waking EEG, even though behaviorally the sleeper remains sound asleep. This electroencephalographic anomaly has led to the expression, *paradoxical sleep,* since the EEG reading looks like an "awake" reading, while the subject paradoxically is reported to be "asleep." Paradoxical sleep, however, has another name—*Stage 1 REM sleep*—which it has earned because of another curious feature; this kind of sleep is characterized by rapid movement of the eyes, or REM. These eye movements, which may occur as rapidly as once every second, are detected by use of the *electrooculogram,* a recording of a voltage picked up from electrodes on the temple and forehead. These electrodes respond to an electrical signal that changes as a function of the position of the eyes. Figure 8–4 shows a typical electrooculogram recorded from a sleeper in Stage 1 REM sleep.

Stage 1 REM, or paradoxical sleep, is cyclic during the night. It alternates with the other stages that are characterized as slow

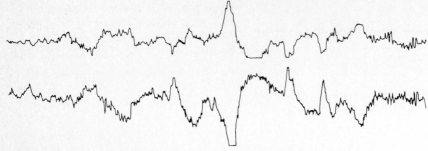

Figure 8–4 A typical electrooculogram obtained during Stage 1 REM sleep showing rapid eye movements. The upper curve is the record from the left eye and the lower is from the right eye. (Courtesy of Dr. Michael Feinberg of the University of Michigan.)

wave sleep on the basis of their typical EEG pattern. Figure 8–5 shows a sample of one evening's sleep schedule characterized according to the EEG patterns we have already mentioned. Note that there is a tendency for deep slow wave sleep to occur earlier in the evening and that Stage 1 REM sleep alternates throughout the evening with the other slow wave periods of sleep. Stage 1 REM sleep seems to be exceptionally important in doing whatever it is that sleep does. If a person is awakened every time upon entry into this stage of sleep, there is a progressively stronger tendency for the REM sleep periods to be prolonged when the subject goes back to sleep as well as a progressive need for sleep, the greater the period of REM sleep deprivation.

REM and dreaming

Stage 1 REM sleep has another relationship to consciousness that deserves special attention. In 1957 Dement and Kleitman, two pioneers in the study of sleep, discovered that dreaming seems to occur most often during the Stage 1 REM sleep. Although there is, of course, no direct way to know when a person is dreaming—eye and muscle movements are not neces-

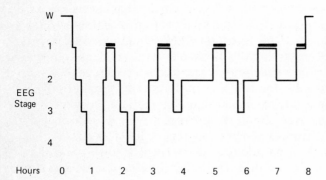

Figure 8–5 A sample sleep schedule showing the various stages through which one sleeper passed during the night. The heavy lines indicate periods of rapid eye movements and thus designate REM sleep. W indicates wakefulness. (Redrawn from Hartmann, E., *The Biology of Dreaming*, 1967.)

sary to dreaming—and thus this hypothesis of dreams during REM 1 sleep is somewhat equivocal, they did devise a scheme in which the relationship could be studied indirectly. To do this, Dement and Kleitman awakened sleepers during various stages of sleep and simply asked them if they had been dreaming. Sleepers awakened during Stage 1 REM sleep reported ten times as often that they had "just" been dreaming than when they were awakened during slow wave sleep. Similarly if sleepers were awakened at various periods of time following Stage 1 REM sleep periods, the longer the delay between the end of the REM sleep and the awakening, the fewer reports of dreaming were obtained.

Thus we have a long tradition of descriptive knowledge concerning sleep and its attendant psychological processes such as dreaming, and even its physiological correlates. However, this kind of knowledge provides no information concerning two much more important questions about sleep and arousal "What is sleep?" and "What are the physiological causes?" To answer these questions we have to turn to a different kind of research.

Surprisingly, though we have described and classified sleep stages, there is still no generally accepted answer to the fundamental question of the nature of sleep. Clearly the nervous system goes into a different state when it is "tired" than when it is "fresh" and a period of sleep allows recovery of normal function. But what do the words "tired" and "fresh" mean and what are the functions that recover? People deprived of sleep for extended periods of time may have heightened or reduced levels of activity, psychological manifestations ranging from personality change to hallucinatory experiences that are very close to what would have been called dreams if the persons had been asleep, and even certain physiological changes. The *need* for sleep is therefore unquestioned, and it is not too much to assume that its main role is to restore *something*.

But to restore what? That is the unanswered question blocking deep understanding of the sleep process. Whatever it is that sleep is or does seems to be deeply ingrained in the physiological mechanisms of virtually all vertebrates. (Even sharks, long supposed not to sleep—the myth was that they would sink if they did not keep moving since these fish are naturally negatively buoyant—have now been found sleeping on the floor of underwater caves.) *Circadian rhythms* (daily rhythms that do not depend on external cues, but rather on internal clocks) have been demonstrated in rats, even when they are blind.

It is also known that there are certain chemicals in the blood that do vary in their concentrations according to these circadian rhythms. Interestingly enough, many of these chemicals (such

circadian rhythms

as serotonin) are found in the pineal gland more so than in any other portion of the body. The interesting fact is that the pineal gland is a vestigeal reptilean eye—an eye that might have at an earlier time in evolutionary history been sensitive to the earth's daily cycle of light and dark.

Other hypotheses on the nature of sleep—for example, the idea that it is an adaption to the day-night cycle keeping us out of trouble when we cannot see, or reducing superfluous responses during a time during which they would be ineffective—avoid the question of what sleep is *nowadays* and why our need for it is still so great. It would be both surprising and unsatisfying if this powerful drive were no more than a vestige from the ages preceding the electric light or even the oil lamp!

Similarly, speculative theories that suggest that sleep is necessary only to help remetabolize the waste products accumulated during the wakeful state, quickly run afoul of the reduced need for sleep that occurs as people become older. Figure 8–6, for example, shows the gradual decline in both total sleep and REM sleep that is needed as people age. It seems a priori unlikely that the elderly are more able to tolerate or better metabolize the waste products of daily life than are younger people. Other more exotic explanations of sleep, for example those suggesting that it is necessary for the consolidation of long-term memories from short-term memories, also leave much to be desired in terms of the completeness of the postulated explanation, and probably reflect the currently popular scientific Zeitgeist in psychological research more than the biological facts of the matter.

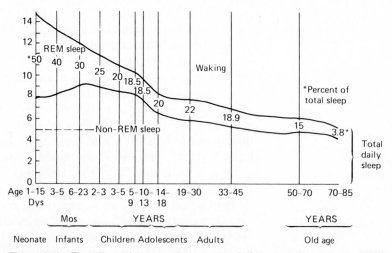

Figure 8–6 The effect of age on the amount of sleep and the amount of REM sleep required by humans. (Redrawn from Roffwarg, J.N., and Dement, W.C., in Webb, W.B., ed., *Sleep: An Experimental Approach*, 1968.)

It seems that we must accept the situation as it is; sleep remains a mystery—we simply do not yet know what it is or what it accomplishes. There are no obvious metabolic or genetic roles played by this mysterious process; at least they are not as evident as those that exist for other forms of behavior (some of which are also quite periodic) such as eating and sex. Nevertheless there is no question that the need for sleep can be as powerful a motivation in human behavior as these other drives are.

Even though the function and nature of sleep remain obscure, we are learning something about the main neural centers involved in the control of arousal and wakefulness. Before we consider some of the details, let us first advance a very important general principle. From what we have learned about the central nervous system and sleep, it is now almost certain that wakefulness, arousal, and consciousness are processes that are driven and controlled by activating systems low in the brain stem. Consciousness may be the psychoneural equivalent of cerebral cortical activity, but the most powerful regulatory mechanisms affecting the level of that consciousness are subcortical. That is to say, sleep would be the natural state of the cerebrum if it were not activated by a flow of activating stimuli from lower centers.

subcortical processes

Research leading to the conclusion that subcortical mechanisms regulate arousal began about forty years ago when Bremer studied the relationship between the integrity of the brain stem and behavioral and physiological indicators of arousal in cats. Bremer first cut the cerebral hemispheres free from the brain stem by surgically transecting the nervous system just below the thalamus and hypothalmus and between the superior and interior colliculi, as shown in Figure 8–7. This transection of the nervous system cut off all sensory input from the spinal cord and inputs from all of the cranial nerves with the

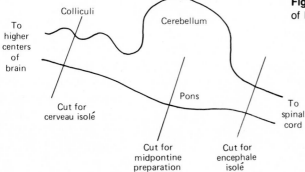

Figure 8–7 A diagram defining the various kinds of brain transections.

exception of the olfactory and optic nerves. Animals with this drastic insult to their nervous system do survive for as long as three months; however, they immediately sink into a coma and exhibit all of the characteristics of a profoundly *unaroused* state, both behaviorally and in the resulting high amplitude and low frequency synchronized EEG. This preparation was called the *cerveau isolé* by Bremer.

The second step in Bremer's study was to make a somewhat different surgical preparation. This preparation was denoted the *encephale isolé*. This isolated brain state was achieved by cutting the central nervous system at the intersection between the medulla and the spinal cord. Here , too, the animals, though paralyzed, survived, but in a way that indicated that they were able to fall asleep and reawaken in synchrony with the normal circadian cycle. This level of brain isolation is also shown in Figure 8–7.

Although Bremer originally attributed the difference in the behavior and EEG of the *encephale isolé* preparation to the differing degree of sensory input, we now appreciate that the true implication of this study is that there is something *in the brain stem* itself that is actually necessary for the maintenance of the aroused state. To determine what it is, other investigators have repeated Bremer's basic experiment, but have instead transected the brain stem about halfway between the locus of the *cerveau isolé* and *encephale isolé* cuts. This preparation is termed a *midpontine transection* and is also shown in Figure 8–7. Midpontine animals have the same sensory inputs as the cerveau isolé animals—everything except olfaction and vision is cut off—yet they are quite awake, in fact, they are virtually insomniac almost all of the time. Thus sensory input along the primary pathways does not seem to be the essential influence on the arousal level of the cat. Some other region of the upper brain stem located between the midpontine and *cerveau isolé* transection levels is specifically implicated in arousal. As we shall also see, the output of some regions below the midpontine cut—the *raphe nuclei*—seem to be necessary to produce sleep. This may account for the insomnia of the midpontine animal.

In more recent studies other experimenters have identified the specific region below the midpontine transection controlling sleep. It is the ascending reticular activating system (ARAS), a core of very diffuse and widely branching neurons in this portion of the brain stem. Figure 8–8 shows one of these large diffuse reticular neurons with its typical forest of dendritic arborizations. The outcome of this tangle of heavily interconnected fibers is to distribute sensory signals to all parts of the cerebral cortex, as shown in Figure 8–9. As was demonstrated thirty

ascending reticular activating system (ARAS)

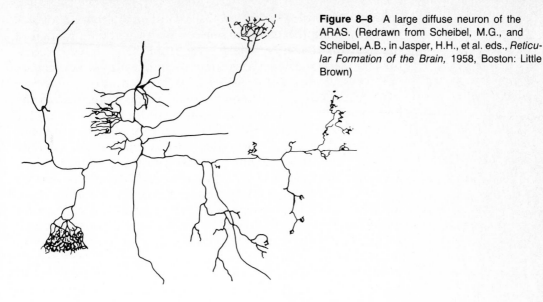

Figure 8–8 A large diffuse neuron of the ARAS. (Redrawn from Scheibel, M.G., and Scheibel, A.B., in Jasper, H.H., et al. eds., *Reticular Formation of the Brain*, 1958, Boston: Little Brown)

years ago by Moruzzi and Magoun, electrical stimulation of the midbrain reticular formation produces a state of chronic wakefulness in an otherwise normal animal. Other investigators have shown that if this particular region is destroyed then the lesioned animal sinks into the classic coma of the *cerveau isolé* preparation, even though other regions of the brain stem and other sensory pathways remain intact.

Parts of the reticular system are now referred to as the *ascending reticular activating system* (ARAS) to emphasize the very important role this region of the brain stem plays in arousal and consciousness. But, how does the ARAS work? The answer to this question probably can be best understood in the

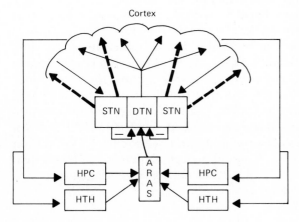

Figure 8–9 Ascending reticulur arousal system (ARAS) activates the diffuse thalamic projections (DTN) which broadly affect cortical excitability. The specific thalamo-cortical projection system (STN) activates restricted and specialized regions of the cortex. The STN pass inhibitory influences to DTN. Note also pathways from cortex to STN and from cortex to both hippocampus (HPC) and hypothalamus (HTH), each of which sends projections to ARAS.

context of the role that the ARAS plays as an alternative sensory pathway. Like the primary sensory pathways, the function of the ARAS is to convey information from the peripheral receptors to the central nervous system. Unlike the other sensory pathways, however, the ARAS is not specific to a particular sensory modality in terms of its inputs nor does it project to any highly localized or particular primary projection region on the cerebral cortex. The ARAS receives sensory inputs from virtually all of the sensory modalities (it is *multimodal*, in other words), then integrates these inputs into a generalized neural response, and finally distributes these neural signals to what we believe to be virtually all portions of the cerebral cortex. These distributed signals, in some way that admittedly we do not yet understand, drive the brain into an aroused, attentive, conscious state. This aroused state is absent when the signals from the ARAS are not present.

This explanation is what gives meaning to the results of Bremer's neurosurgical experiments in which the brain stem was transected at various levels. Those cuts that deleted ARAS pathways to the cerebrum always reduced the state of arousal of the animal to coma-like levels. Those that did not interrupt ARAS pathways spared the normal sleep-wakefulness cycles. Furthermore, any interventions that increased activity in the ARAS (for example, electrical stimulation and/or natural sensory stimulation) produced aroused, often even insomniac, animals. Interventions such as the *cerveau isolé* operation, on the other hand, produce comas.

The ARAS makes extensive synaptic contact with the *internal* thalamic nuclei—those nuclei that project diffusely to the cerebral cortex. (*Specific* projections to the cortex originate in the *lateral* thalamic nuclei.) The evidence now suggests that these two systems stand in a somewhat antagonistic relationship. Repetitive stimulation of thalamic nuclei results in the *recruitment* of cortical activity but this can be inhibited by the simultaneous activation of the reticular formation. A balance it seems, must be struck between arousal and selective attention. The highly aroused animal may be as insensitive to specific stimuli as a weakly aroused one. What is required is a method of controlling the arousing functions of the ascending reticular activating system (ARAS) so that specific sensations (mediated by the specific thalamocortical pathways) can reach the appropriate cortical centers. In typical feedback fashion, this control is exercised both by the thalamus and by the cortex itself in that reticular activity can be modulated by thalamic and by cortical influences. Figure 8–9 illustrates the sort of feedback loop able to perform these functions.

In summary, all experiments support the idea that the ARAS is an arousal center. With an intact reticular system, the animal is awake; if the ARAS is surgically interrupted, or when it is inactive, the animal sleeps. The association is extremely tight and allows us to conclude with considerable assurance that the ARAS is probably the main and immediate source of the neural signals that produce arousal and wakefulness. This does not mean, however, that they are the locus of the psychoneural equivalent of arousal and wakefulness. That role is probably better reserved for the great nuclei of the cerebral cortex.

Next we must ask what specifically do the ARAS signals have to do to the cortex to maintain an aroused state. To this question, we have only the vaguest and most speculative answers. We do know that both a primary projection pathway and the ARAS pathway must be simultaneously active for conscious perceptual experience to exist in any modality. One test of this idea was based on the fact that the EBP signals produced by the primary pathways and the ARAS are also distinguishable from each other when they are averaged from the background EEG "noise." The signals from the primary pathways (somatosensory, visual, and auditory) are highly localized on the skull over the regions of the brain known to be the primary projection regions (see Chapter 3). The primary pathway signals occur very promptly after the stimuli, usually in the first 50 milliseconds. The signals produced by the ARAS pathway, however, are delayed very much and occur only 100 milliseconds or more (typically 300 milliseconds) following the stimulus. They are also diffusely distributed across the skull, a fact in agreement with what we know about the anatomy of the ARAS.

If one places a subject in an experimental situation as shown in Figure 8–10 in which an electrical stimulus is applied to the ulnar nerve at the wrist and the averaged EBP is recorded from the skull, the responses produced in both the primary sensory pathway and in the ARAS can be obtained. An analysis of the similarities and differences between the two components of the response can help at least to suggest their respective roles. Figure 8–11 shows the recordings taken from two electrode positions for two states of the observer—asleep and awake. When the recording electrode is placed over the contralateral (that is, on the side of the body opposite that to which the stimulus is applied) somatosensory cortex and the subject is awake, the "typical" response occurs—there is a large and immediate primary component observed that is followed by a delayed component of longer wavelength and greater ampli- tude. The reason that the primary response is larger here than

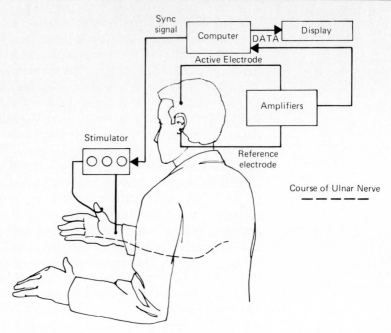

Figure 8–10 The experimental arrangement to record evoked potentials from the brain when the ulnar nerve is stimulated electrically.

on the ipsilateral side is that the somatosensory system is crossed; signals from the left side of the body are mainly transmitted to the right half of the cerebrum and vice versa.

If, on the other hand, the electrode is placed on the opposite side of the scalp—the ipsilateral side—only the nonspecific and much delayed ARAS signal is observed. The effect of electrode position thus is defined. But what about the other variable, the level of arousal as defined by the sleep-wakefulness alternatives? What we see in this case is that if the observer is allowed to go to sleep, the signal recorded from the contralateral electrode shows a remarkable change. The specific component presumably reflecting the activity of the primary projection pathways remains virtually intact. However, the widely distributed, long-lasting component presumably reflecting the activity of the ARAS pathway is diminished greatly in magnitude. The recording electrode on the same side of the body as the stimulating electrode displays a comparable change. Now both the primary projection signal and the ARAS signal are gone, and the EBP is virtually flat.

The implication of this finding is straightforward and entirely *consciousness of* consistent with what we have learned from the brain transection studies previously discussed. For consciousness to occur (in this case this means for *awareness of a stimulus* to occur) it is

consciousness of stimulation

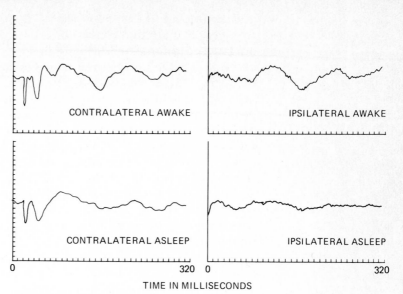

CONTRALATERAL AWAKE

IPSILATERAL AWAKE

CONTRALATERAL ASLEEP

IPSILATERAL ASLEEP

0   320   0   320

TIME IN MILLISECONDS

Figure 8–11 Evoked brain potentials from two skull locations for sleep and awake states. (Redrawn from Uttal, W.R., *Annals of the New York Academy of Sciences*, 1964, 112:60–81.)

necessary for both a signal from a specific receptor and a generalized activation signal from the ARAS to be present. Consciousness does not occur in the absence of ARAS activation, even when the primary sensory signal is successfully transmitted to the cortex. We believe this means that activation of the primary projection region is *not* the psychoneural equivalent of perception!*

Thus the ARAS, true to its name, acts to enhance and excite consciousness. We saw earlier however, that the ARAS does not function completely in solitude to regulate and maintain arousal and regulate sleep. In support of this assertion we note reports that there is a certain amount of recovery of wakefulness after massive lesions of the ARAS which initially produced a comatose animal. Some other source of activating signals thus must be substitutable for the lost ARAS signals after a period of recovery.

Although we know virtually nothing about the locus of this recovery of wakefulness, a number of investigators have demonstrated that the arousal level of an animal can be highly modified by the ablation or stimulation of many other regions of the brain in addition to the ARAS. The hypothalamus (not surprising, considering its role in so many other motivational

---

*The effects of direct stimulation of primary projection regions must be understood in different terms, however.

and emotional states) also seems to be particularly deeply involved. Stimulation of the posterior hypothalamus produces an aroused animal while a somnolent state is produced by anterior hypothalamic stimulation. Furthermore, stimulation of the medial thalamus also inhibits arousal. Regions lower in the brain stem are also known in which stimulation or ablation may produce alterations in sleep and wakefulness. These include regions in the medulla and the pons, in particular. The several regions of the pons known as the *raphe nuclei* seem also to be directly involved in sleep and arousal. Jouvet showed that the specific contribution of the raphe nuclei is to deactivate the animal and thus to allow sleep. The fraction of time an animal with lesions in the raphe nuclei spends in Stages 1, 2, 3, or 4 *slow-wave deep sleep* declines in proportion to the amount of this region destroyed.

Even more effective in controlling arousal, however, is stimulation or ablation of various regions of the cerebral cortex itself. Thus, behavioral correlates of enhanced arousal occur when the frontal lobes are damaged. A similar activation occurs when the hippocampus is lesioned. It has been suggested, moreover, that there are broad regions on the floor of the cerebral hemispheres that are important in permitting sleep. Not too surprisingly, many of these regions are also either part of, or closely related to, the limbic system. Many other regions of this important regulatory system also seem to be involved in the cycling of sleep and wakefulness.

The general conclusion to be drawn from these data (even accepting the fact that we really know relatively little about the metabolic significance of sleep) is that sleep and arousal, like most other mental states, seem to be controlled by very complex networks of neural nuclei. No single center is both necessary and sufficient for maintaining either sleep or an aroused state. Many different nuclei contribute to the regulation of these states; some nuclei inhibit, other excite. It is, however, a *balance* among many such antagonistic centers that determines whether we are asleep or awake.

Language

René Descartes in the seventeenth century was perhaps the first philosopher to ask whether a machine could be made so skillfully and could so faithfully mimic human actions as to be indistinguishable from a human being. This question has remained a lively one in philosophy ever since, and was raised to new heights several decades ago with the advent of computers able to perform complex "intellectual" operations.

Turing machines

Thus, by 1950, the British logician A.M. Turing would argue that machines able to accomplish the same tasks once thought only humanly possible should be accorded the same cognitive status as humans.

Descartes, however, would never agree with Turing if they had been contemporaries. Descartes reasoned that there would always be a core of genuinely human attributes that no conceivable machine would duplicate. No machine would ever attain the *idea* of a supernatural being; no machine would ever engage in abstract mathematical reasoning; and no machine would ever display a *creative* use of language. Before dismissing these conclusions as nothing more than evidence of ignorance— as conclusions Descartes himself would abandon if he knew what we now know—we should pause to note the grounds on which he based them. Recall that Descartes only raised the issue because he had already been convinced that a very wide range of human endeavors could be matched by machines, *automatons*. He could find no reason in principle why, for example, a machine could not be constructed so as to respond in a discriminating way to specific stimuli and even improve in its performance with practice. What we would now take to be rudimentary forms of perception and behavior were fully included in Descartes' automaton theory, and this was one reason why he viewed all nonhuman animals as automatons. In fact, from this very view we begin to appreciate how much of perception and behavior Descartes was willing to explain in exclusively mechanistic terms. He was as aware as we are of the extraordinary abilities of animals—their learning, memory, sensitivity, emotionality, and instinctive capacities. Thus, in his confidence that these characteristics could be built into mindless robots, Descartes showed himself to be a defender of a radically mechanistic psychology. But his radicalism did not go to the full limit, for he exempted from the mechanistic realm three characteristics. The idea of God, the abstractions of mathematics, and the creative use of language would forever be unavailable to any entity lacking a *soul*, whether the entity was a manufactured machine or an animal.

Descartes' dualism

We will not go into the details of Descartes' analysis of this issue but we will sketch his argument briefly. What these three characteristics have in common is that they do not refer to possible objects of sensation. The *idea* of a supreme being is not an idea that could possibly arise out of purely sensory experiences for all such experiences include the idea of *limits*. Similarly, mathematical propositions are the gift of reason, not sensation, and lead to conclusions that are both certain and necessary—but *experience* produces nothing that is either certain or necessary. Thus, a creature (or device) limited to sensory modes of knowledge could deal effectively only with the material environment and could have no awareness of (rational) principles. Lacking these, however, the device could not possibly use language *creatively*. It might come to associate names with things or to mimic certain sounds, but it would never frame original ideas linguistically since it would never have such ideas. What Descartes seems to have had in mind is the claim that such a device could only do what it was told (or programmed) to do.

But all of this was handed down by a philosopher more than three centuries ago when no one even guessed at how developed science and engineering would become. For a moment, therefore, let us set aside Descartes' so-called biases and approach the subject of language as if it were just one more psychological process to be explored in the laboratory and the clinic and for which we must find the physiological basis. Just as we reserve the right to disagree with Descartes' notion that animals are automatons, we can also disagree with his more fundamental claim that human beings represent an absolutely unique class.

If we adopt this approach, at least for the moment, we begin to note that on first inspection the subject of *language* appears to present the neural sciences with no special or unique problems. Like perception, learning, memory, and so on, the term seems to refer to a specific process presumably tied to identifiable processes and regions of the brain. The strategy followed in studies of these other psychological processes should be appropriate here also—that is, find regions of the brain whose destruction eliminates language, find pathways essential to the production of language, follow the evolutionary development of language mechanisms from the level of primitive vocalization to adult human speech, and search for chemical and neural codes by which external events and things become translated into linguistic elements. Then, when these are done, we would be left with the task of bringing the entire process under the more general process called *learning*. After all, people *learn* language and come to display it in just the same behavioral ways that they display other complex psychological characteristics such as emotion, memory, and even personality.

language as behavior

But now let us pause to ask whether this perspective actually does justice to language. Is it the case, for example, that *language*—as opposed to speech or vocalizations—is a *behavioral* event best understood as something that has been *learned*? A person with severed vocal chords may be unable to speak, but we surely do not conclude that he has lost "language." And on the view that language is no more than the acquisition of complex chains of behavior there are simply too many facts tending to refute it. Children all over the world begin to display grammatical speech at very nearly the same age, despite the fact that child rearing and educational practices vary immensely. Children raised by mute parents and then placed within a linguistically nurturing environment come to possess linguistic competence far more quickly than an associative process would allow. Moreover, parents notoriously ignore grammar and proceed to reward or punish the *content* of children's speech, but grammar nonetheless comes to be the defining feature of this speech from a very early time. Then, too, every linguistically competent member of a society can comprehend and articulate a virtually *infinite* number of gramatically correct sentences only a relatively few of which were ever heard before. In all these respects *language simply does not "behave" like behavior.*

But what of the fact that monkeys and apes can be taught sign language? Does this not indicate that Descartes was wrong and that human language, no matter how rich and complex, can be shared by nonhuman organisms? Here again such questions entail a theory of language that is limited to the point of being wrong. It is true that nonhuman primates have been trained to emit sequences of gestures which, when assembled, can be taken as a kind of "sentence" expressive of a need: "Don...give Lana milk...give Lana ball." But all such sequences, no matter how long, are easily classified as chains of discriminative responses not unlike those acquired by rats and even pigeons. There is surely no difficulty, for example, in getting a pigeon to peck sequentially at a circle, a square, an oval, a star, and a cross where

Circle	=	Don
Square	=	Give
Oval	=	Pigeon
Star	=	More
Cross	=	Seed

In such cases the alleged "sentence" is, in fact, something *we* construct from the sequential responding of the bird. We can arrange the contingencies of reinforcement in such a way that every chain of behavior must begin with a response to the circle and then to the square. We can then tie whatever pigeons will otherwise work for (food, water, warmth, and so on) to a particular symbol and sit back as the bird unfolds any number of "sentences."

denoting and connoting functions

As amusing and instructive as such demonstrations may be, they do not address the phenomenon of *language*. First, language as it always appears and has appeared in human communities is comprised not only of *denotative* elements but also and more significantly of *connotative* elements. The former refer to specific objects and classes of objects (apples, sticks, edibles, traffic lights, or proper names). Thus, for each term of denotation there is an empirical counterpart or *referent*. But the connotation or *meaning* of linguistic elements refers not to a thing or empirical item at all. We cannot point to "justice" or "theft" or "mercy" or a legal "right" or a "noble cause." When we say that in Euclid's geometry parallel lines never intersect, or that in Riemann's geometry parallel lines intersect at two loci, or that if the major premise and minor premise of a syllogism are true, then the conclusion is *necessarily* true we are not referring to any objective or sensible entity or thing. No one attempts to prove that Euclidean parallels never intersect by drawing such lines! Moreover, even if we were to begin to draw them, and were to continue for years, we could only conclude that they "probably" will not intersect. According to the theorem, however, they certainly and necessarily will never intersect because nonintersection is part of the definition of Euclidean parallel lines.

Even in the case of "theft," the term refers not to some observable action but to a complex relationship involving concepts of ownership and legality. A theft is not merely the taking of something but the *wrongful* taking of what *belongs to* another. The italicized words here do not denote an object but convey a meaning. To the extent that this is what Descartes had in mind when he referred to "the creative use of language," it is important to note that no nonhuman animal has ever been shown to comprehend or employ the connotative elements of language. And to this same extent, it remains quite proper to assert that, at least as of now, only human beings are *known* to engage in language. What is important about this distinction, apart from its continuing relevance to philosophical questions, is that it permits us to examine the neuropsychology of *language* as a subject fundamentally different from what may be called the neuropsychology of *speech*.

Speech and Brain Localization

From the standpoint of clinical neurology it probably makes better sense to discuss *disorders of symbolic communication* than to attempt to identify a single and narrow pattern of deficits functionally tied to a specific structure or region of the brain. It was in the last century that Broca identified a region of the brain which, when diseased, resulted in the patient's inability to
Broca's area
communicate verbally. This region, named *Broca's area*, was for a time considered *the* "speech center." It is now quite clear, however, that matters are not this simple. Figure 8–12 presents

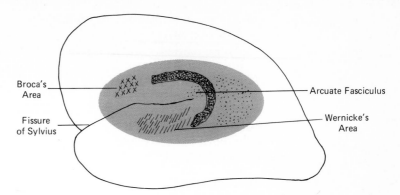

Figure 8–12 Lateral view of the left hemisphere indicating areas associated with linguistic deficits. The *arcuate fasciculus* is a band of fibers running from Broca's area back to the angular gyrus. The entire region within which disturbances have been uncovered is shaded.

a sketch of the *dominant hemisphere* (nearly always the left hemisphere) and indicates the relatively wide area with which language disturbances have been clinically associated.

Disorders of Symbolic Communication

The communicative disorders can take a variety of forms even in the same patient. Characteristic ones are given below.

Dysarthria. With dysarthria there is a lack or deficit in *articulation.* The patient can understand the speech of others but cannot articulate his or her own. This deficit can be produced in a variety of ways, such as lesions in the corticospinal pathway or the cerebellar pathway associated with the muscles of speech, Parkinsonism, cerebellar lesions, and muscle-wasting diseases.

Dysphasia. Dysphasia, which takes many forms, refers not merely to the ability to articulate but to express and comprehend speech as a *symbolic* mode of communication. Where the loss is complete, the condition is known as *aphasia.* The two major categories of dysphasia (or aphasia) are the *expressive* and the *receptive.* The former refers to an inability to initiate coherent and meaningful speech; the latter to the inability to follow it with comprehension. Many patients display a mixture of expressive and receptive dysphasia. In *Broca's dysphasia* (or Broca's aphasia) speech is either greatly reduced or entirely lacking. Where there is some speech production it is halting, "telegraphic," often grunt-like. The *Wernicke's syndrome* patient emits quick and reasonably well formed verbalizations which, however, are meaningless.

Dyslexia. Dyslexia, refers to deficits in reading and in the recognition of visually presented verbal material. One form of dyslexia, called "word blindness", results in the complete inability to recognize written words or letters or even colors. Lesions in the occipitotemporal gyrus on the dominant (left) side can produce this deficit.

Dysgraphia. A person who has dysgraphia is unable to write coherently. The disorder may even result in the person's writing of nonwords (*paragraphia*) or pure nonsense.

Dyscalculia. Again, lesions in the dominant hemisphere, in the region of the angular gyrus, can result in dyscalculia. The patient is unable to manipulate or deal with mathematical symbols or to perform rudimentary calculations.

Apraxia. What the patient who has apraxia cannot do, apparently, is organize movements in space, that is, recognize his or her own activities within the spatial domain. Lesions in the *parietal lobe* of the dominant hemisphere have been known to produce apraxias. For example confusion might occur in performance of intended movements, such as putting on a jacket or pouring something into a cup.

Agnosia. The term agnosia refers generically to a variety of deficits in which failure of recognition is the chief symptom. In the visual agnosias, for example, the patient with normal visual sensitivity will fail to recognize such common items as keys, magazines, and articles of clothing. In the auditory agnosias patients cannot recognize popular melodies and may not even be able to follow a conversation. Lesions in the dominant side parietal cortex and parieto-occipital cortex may result in agnosia.

To begin to appreciate the complex interconnections associated with such disturbances we should examine Figure 8–13 which is a block diagram illustrating several of the crucial pathways involved in language. *Heschl's gyrus* is the primary auditory area of the human cerebral cortex. Recall that Broca's and Wernicke's areas are bridged by the *arcuate fasciculus*, which lies within the cortex underneath the *angular gyrus* in its most caudal projection. Recall also that the "strip" of motor cortex runs from the midline down to a point near the fissure of Sylvius and that, from vertex to base, it controls movements from foot to head. Thus, the motor cortex in the region of Broca's area, Wernicke's area and Heschl's gyrus is the region associated with lips, tongue, larynx, and the facial muscles— that is with the anatomy necessary for the production of articulate speech.

In light of these arrangements, we can speculate on the major pathways implicated in communicative disturbances noted earlier. It must be emphasized, however, that this is speculation, since the details of the anatomy of symbolic communication have yet to be worked out in any convincing manner. The following illustrations therefore should be taken as suggestive, not as determinative.

1. *Receptive Dysphasia.* Persons who have this disorder cannot understand the spoken word or the meaning of otherwise meaningful sounds. We have in this case a form of *auditory agnosia.* The representation of these sounds in the cerebral cortex will be located in the primary auditory area (Heschl's gyrus). The *comprehension* of these sounds will depend on the proper projection of information from Heschl's gyrus to Wernicke's area and the proper "processing" of the information within Wernicke's area. Thus, the major (suspected) circuit in cases of auditory agnosia is *7-to-2* as shown in Figure 8–13. That the problem is nearly invariably in 2 (rather than 7) is indicated by the presence of normal auditory sensitivity in patients with auditory agnosias. Ordinarily one would expect definite hearing losses when Heschl's gyrus is diseased.

2. *"Word Blindness."* The patient who has no comprehension of written words or symbols often displays a disease process in the circuit indicated as *6-to-5* in Figure 8–13. The primary visual cortex does not project directly to the angular gyrus but indirectly through the *primary visual association areas.* The angular gyrus, in turn, projects to Wernicke's area. It appears to be the case that the angular gyrus is necessary for the integration of auditory and visual information and that its inputs to Wernicke's area are essential to the recognition

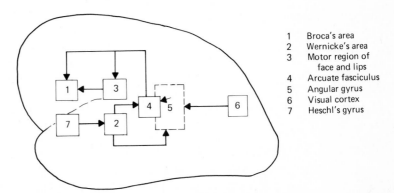

1	Broca's area
2	Wernicke's area
3	Motor region of face and lips
4	Arcuate fasciculus
5	Angular gyrus
6	Visual cortex
7	Heschl's gyrus

Figure 8–13 Schematic diagram of several pathways involved in symbolic communication, roughly imposed on the outline of the dominant hemisphere.

of visually presented symbolic material. Thus, the more complete circuit associated with "word blindness" and severe dyslexias would run from *6-to-5-to-2-to-1* in Figure 8–13.

3. *Expressive Dysphasia.* Suppose now that we have a patient who cannot recite written material. He or she may be able to generate coherent sentences, but cannot verbalize visual information. Here we have a more complicated circuit, beginning at 6 and then involving the angular gyrus, Wernicke's area and Broca's area; *6-to-5-to-2-to-1* in Figure 8–13, with the 2-to-1 connection made via the arcuate fasciculus *(4)*.

Language and Cerebral Dominance

As we have already noted, in the vast majority of persons the left hemisphere is dominant both with respect to handedness and linguistic functions. The human nervous system possesses sufficient plasticity, at least early in life, for these latter functions to be taken over by the right hemisphere when the left one has become severely incapacitated. And there are also instances of mixed cerebral dominance—of *ambidextrous* hemispheres—as well as right-hemisphere dominance. But the general rule is that of left-hemisphere dominance in the matter of linguistic function. The chief source of evidence here is the extremely reliable correlation between linguistic deficits and left-hemisphere lesions, and the nearly complete survival of linguistic functions in cases of right-hemisphere lesions.

symbolic functions

The picture is far less clear, however, when we examine symbolic cognitive functions in general, and not just linguistic functions. Both clinical and experimental evidence has established the significant and often essential role of the right hemisphere in the recognition and proper employment of a wide variety of sensory cues. What we refer to here is not the patient's sensitivity as such, for it is no surprise that damage to the sensory cortex on the right side will result in reduced or eliminated sensations on the left side of the body. Rather, we refer to the integration of sensory data from two or more sensory channels and the ability to use this integrated information *cognitively*. Thus, a man who has a lesion in the right parietal cortex may fail to comprehend that the arm or hand he is looking at is *his;* he may not be aware of the passive displacement of one of his own limbs; he may display unfamiliarity toward an otherwise familiar scene; he is likely to be unable to identify common objects placed in his right hand but unavailable for visual inspection (the condition of *astereognosis*).

The regions of the brain typically involved in deficits of this kind are the *association areas* of the cerebral cortex; the areas that are connected *within* one of the hemispheres and that individually serve a variety of sensory processes. The *visual* or *striate cortex*, for example, is concentrated in the occipital poles of the two hemispheres and damage to it reliably results in diminished or even the total loss of visual sensations. But a relatively large area of cortex, extending from the lateral margins of the occipital region to the posterior surface of the temporal and the parietal lobes, is involved in the processes of visual recognition, comprehension, and integration. This somewhat scattered and not clearly demarcated region is the *visual association area* of the cortex. And there are analogous association areas in each hemisphere for touch and for auditory functions. Lesions in the auditory association cortex, for example, may leave an animal quite normal in its ability to distinguish between two tones of different frequency, but unable to distinguish between two series of tones or a single series in which notes are presented at different rates. The deficit, then, is not sensory per se but one of integration.

When it comes, however, to those forms of comprehension or cognition that involve genuinely linguistic functions we must examine not simply the association areas within one of the hemispheres but the lines of communication from one hemisphere to the other. Let us set certain complexities aside for the moment and assume as factual that language is chiefly dependent on the left hemisphere, more specifically, on those regions of the left hemisphere identified as Broca's area, Wernicke's area, the arcuate fasciculus, and the angular gyrus. Now let us suppose that a person has an object, say a sheet of paper, placed in his left hand but is blindfolded so that he cannot see the paper. Without any difficulty, and based solely on the tactile cues, the person quickly reports, "paper" when asked to identify the object. Figure 8–14 presents a schematic

Association Cortex

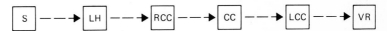

Figure 8–14 A simple pathway involved in the *verbal* identification of a common object by the left hand. Here the stimulus (S) is delivered to the left hand and becomes represented in the right cerebral cortex (RCC) which permits sensation and even recognition but not verbal identification. Coded information is then passed through the *corpus callosum* (CC) to the left cerebral cortex (LCC) whose language areas are involved in the verbal response (VR). LH refers to left-hand.

diagram of the principal channels of communication that appear to be essential to performance of this kind.

corpus callosum

The *corpus callosum* is the major commissure joining the two hemispheres. It is also the largest tract in the nervous system, with some two hundred million fibers in it. It is not, however, the only pathway by which the two hemispheres can be functionally connected. There are also two lesser tracts, the *anterior* and the *posterior commissures,* as well as the *massa intermedia* which is a tract joining the two thalami, each of which projects to the cerebral cortex on the same side. Thus, information processed in the left thalamus can be propagated to the right thalamus via the massa intermedia and thence to the right hemisphere. However, the cortical-cortical connections are those made possible by the corpus callosum and the anterior and posterior commissures.

Only in the past two decades, through imaginative research and several striking clinical findings, have the functions of these commissural connections been uncovered. The most important initial discovery, made by Roger Sperry at the California Institute of Technology, was that animals whose commissural fibers had been surgically cut were remarkably unaffected in their ordinary sensory and motor performance. The *commissurotomized* animal moved with the same agility, solved problems, was just as alert and attentive as a "normal" animal. But if the same animal—a cat, for example—has one eye covered while learning a simple visual discrimination and then, during later tests has this eye uncovered and the previously covered eye uncovered, there is virtually no evidence of the previous learning. It is as if what the left eye saw during learning (and the right eye did not see) is now completely unavailable to the animal.

Figure 8–15 is a sketch of the projection of the visual pathways from retina to cerebral cortex. Note that rays of light are refracted by the lens in such a way that an object seen in the periphery of the left eye is projected onto the *nasal* region of the left retina, whereas an object seen in the nasal area of the left eye is projected onto the *temporal* region of the left retina. The fibers of the optic nerve originating in the nasal regions of each retina cross at the optic chiasma and project to the visual cortex on the opposite side. The fibers that originate in the temporal regions of each retina, however, do not cross in the optic chiasma and thus they project to the visual cortex on the same side. If, for example, an object is held at arm's length just in front of the nose (in the nasal *visual* field) its rays will be refracted in such a way that its image will fall on the temporal *retinal* fields of both eyes. Accordingly, the optic nerve fibers of

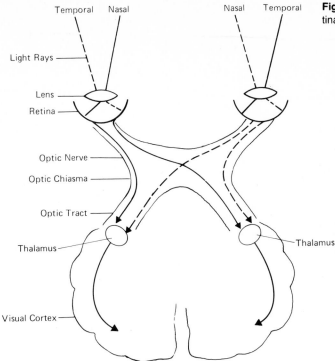

Figure 8–15 Neural projections from retina to visual cortex.

the left eye will process the information to the left visual cortex (by way of several relay stations) while the fibers of the right eye will project the information to the right visual cortex.

Let us now take a case where the object is held at arm's length by the left hand and at an eccentricity of about 45° to the left. If the observer now looks straight ahead, the object will appear in the temporal field of the left eye and the nasal field of the right eye. With this arrangement, the object will project upon the nasal retina of the left eye and the temporal retina of the right eye. Thus, it will be the right visual cortex that receives the information processed by both eyes. In the usual case, both hemispheres receive information from each retina. In fact, since the foveal and perifoveal regions of either eye project nearly equally to both hemispheres, both of the hemispheres are activated even when one eye is closed, as long as the observer's fovea is stimulated.

If, however, the observer examines an object with only one eye and if the object falls not on the fovea but onto either the nasal or the temporal regions of the retina, then only one hemisphere will receive direct projections from the viewing eye. In the ordinary case, this poses no problem since the visual cortex in

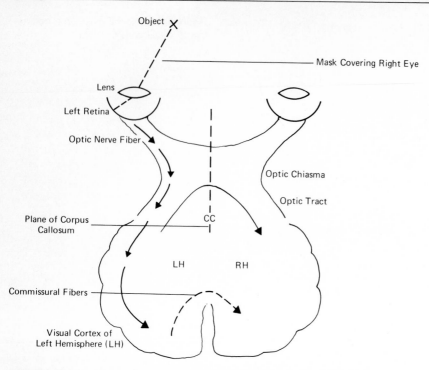

Figure 8–16 The object (x) is in the nasal visual field of the left eye while the right eye is covered. The object is projected onto the left temporal retina whose fibers project back into the left hemisphere. Although the right hemisphere is not directly activated under these conditions, it is indirectly activated by commissural fibers in the *corpus callosum* (CC) joining the two hemispheres.

one hemisphere communicates to the visual cortex in the other hemisphere by way of the major commissures. This is illustrated in Figure 8–16. Here we see an object falling on the temporal retina of the left eye. The excited pathways are all in the left hemisphere and terminate in the visual cortex of that hemisphere. But additional circuits are then involved, bringing information from the left hemisphere to the right hemisphere by way of commissural fibers.

It is now possible to give a partial explanation of the inability of the *commissurotomized* animal's failure to "remember" what had been learned during left-eye learning when later tested under conditions of right-eye viewing. The information that had been (somehow) coded in the left hemisphere could not be transferred to the right because the commissurotomy had eliminated all interhemispheric channels of communication. To speak loosely, we might say that the right hemisphere remained "ignorant" throughout the time that the left hemisphere was being "instructed."

Language and the Commissurotomized Human Patient

We are now in a position to turn to one of the most dramatic sets of findings in psychobiology. There are certain forms of epilepsy caused by the spontaneous and erratic "firing" of cortical cells in a localized region of the brain. As long as the "misfire" is confined to one hemisphere, the patient is not thrown into seizure. However, if a "mirror focus" develops in the other hemisphere a generalized seizure occurs. Thus, to prevent such dangerous and debilitating seizures, it is necessary to prevent the spread of erratic electrical discharges to the other hemisphere. In many cases this can be achieved chemically but some cases have been shown to be entirely resistant to available drugs. Based on the fact that the commissurotomized animal is normal in all outward respects—and on the additional fact that a "mirror focus" can only be brought about through the commissural connections between hemispheres—the decision was made to treat this form of epilepsy surgically by cutting all the commissural bands joining the two hemispheres. As a result of this surgery, which has succeeded in its purely therapeutic aims, we now have a modest but extremely suggestive literature on *split-brain man.*

As might have been expected from the years of research on lower organisms, the commissurotomized human patient appears quite normal. There is no significant alteration in intellect, personality, perception, motor coordination, emotionality, or speech. The patient quickly recognizes friends and relatives, learns and remembers with as much competence as was displayed preoperatively, reads and writes normally, and converses in an easy and a coherent manner.

When more subtle and refined tests are employed, however, the effects of commissurotomies are seen to be quite striking. It should be underscored here that not every commissurotomized patient displays precisely the same pattern of symptoms and that even the more reliable early findings have come under challenge as better methods of investigation have evolved. It is something of a misnomer, therefore, to speak of *the* "split-brain" patient for, in important respects, no two of them are entirely alike. Nevertheless, there is a sufficient comparability in some of the symptoms to permit the following summary of typical postoperative effects.

1. The patient has no difficulty locating and pointing to a region of the body which has been stimulated, provided the hand on

the same side does the pointing. Typically, however, the patient cannot point with his left hand to that part of the right side of his body which has been stimulated, and vice versa. However, after a longer period of recovery (two months or so) there is usually significant improvement in this sort of cross-localization task.

2. It is commonly the case that *verbal* accounts of stimuli applied to various regions of the body are poor or absent when the stimulation is delivered to the left side.

3. A patient allowed to manipulate an object is able to find that object when it is mixed in with others as long as the hand doing the searching was the one which had initially held the object. Intermanual performance, however, is generally degraded.

4. When visual stimuli are presented in such a way as to be confined to the right visual field (thus projecting only to the right hemisphere), the patient does not give a verbal report of them. If, for example, the patient is presented with an apple visually, but only in a way that confines the projection to the right hemisphere, and an orange that is confined in its projection to the left hemisphere, the patient will report only "orange" and will select an orange manually when asked to pick out with his hand the object he sees. The patient is also unable to write the name of objects projected to the right hemisphere while having no difficulty writing the names of those projected to the left hemisphere.

5. Verbalizations pertinent to any feature of the environment are either absent or utterly incoherent when that feature is confined to right-hemisphere processing. Although it is no longer warranted to speak of the right hemisphere as "mute," the evidence clearly indicates reduced verbal function.

6. As an information-processor, the right hemisphere works adequately or even normally with spatial and (to a degree) numerical data but is significantly impoverished with respect to verbal recognition, registration, and production.

As we have said, although these six generalizations are closely supported by the facts emerging from more than a decade of research on "split-brain" patients, each of them must be offered with some qualification. Commissurotomies are not performed on entirely normal brains but only on those that have suffered a history of seizures and powerful medications. The postoperative patient has been altered by the surgery and only in time will we discover the extent to which the alteration calls for new and different modes of communication with the patient; new and different modes of rehabilitation which might partially compensate for the hemispheric disconnection.

But with these and related qualifications stated, we are still entitled to take the findings as reaffirming the well-documented "dominance" theory of language and the unique role of left-hemisphere functions in all modes of symbolic communication based on language. Research on the commissurotomized patient has made an even stronger case for the century-old claim that language functions are lateralized in the brain—the claim with which we now associate such names as Broca and Wernicke.

Language, "Self", and the "Deconnection Syndrome"

It was not long after the appearance of the first articles on the "split-brain" patient that scientists and philosophers began to speculate on what they took to be the larger implications. Additional data provided sparks to the fuels of speculation. One male patient, for example, was shown portrait photographs of a number of persons, all of them strangers except one—a photograph of the patient himself. With the presentations limited to right-hemisphere projection, the patient was still able to recognize himself and even to respond in a whimsically negative way when asked to evaluate the person in the picture. The conclusion was that this patient's right hemisphere had a degree of "self-consciousness"—a conclusion offered to challenge what was already becoming the official view that the "self" was (somehow) "in" the left hemisphere.

Let us briefly review how the question of *self* or *selfhood* arises from the findings. In all cases studied to date the "split-brain" patient is found responding differently to information projected to different hemispheres. Based on how the material is assembled and on the task required of the patient, it is even possible to have the patient negate claims regarding right-hemisphere processing that have been affirmed in regard to left-hemisphere processing. The patient, that is, seems to be of "two minds" and therefore, at least on the usual construal, might be thought of as being *two persons*! Thus we find some claiming that only the dominant hemisphere has a "self" or that there is a different "self" in each hemisphere or (more radically) that each brain harbors two persons.

But the time comes when we must put fun aside and turn to a sober account of the facts and to logically coherent interpretations of the facts. We have already noted in earlier chapters any number of conditions under which normal observers will be of "two minds." Consider, for example, studies of *cued retrieval* in which the observer is presented very briefly with an array of letters. In a single and brief (20 millisecond) presentation, the observer can recall only two or three of the six (or more) letters in the array. However, if a ring is placed over the location occupied by one of the letters, and if this ring is imposed on that location within about 50 milliseconds of the termination of the array, the observer is now able to report which letter had occupied that location. We can say that without cued retrieval the observer *denied* (forgot, failed to report, or refused to affirm) more than half the letters but with cued retrieval he declared (recalled, noticed, and affirmed) their presence. Is this observer to be taken as evidence of two *selves*?

There is another traditional psychobiology study that gets at the same issue. If one brief flash is followed in 10 milliseconds, or even 50 milliseconds, by a larger and more intense flash, the observer fails to report the first one; that is the first flash undergoes *backward masking* by the second one. But instead of requiring a verbal report, let us have the observer press a reaction time key as soon as any flash is seen. Under these conditions, if only the second (masking) flash is seen, reaction times should be displaced by an amount equal to the sum of the duration of the first flash and the interval between the end of the first flash and the onset of the second. Say, for example, that the first flash is 30 milliseconds in duration and the second comes on 50 milliseconds after the first has gone off. If only the second flash is processed by the observer, his reaction time should be on the average 80 milliseconds slower than it is when only the second flash is presented. The fact, however, is that reaction time is just as fast in response to the first ("unseen") flash when a masking flash follows as it is when only the first flash is presented. Here we have an observer responding to a flash that is (using verbal report data) not seen. *Two selves? Two minds?*

Much of the confusion aroused by the "split-brain" research is a confusion of terms and the product of more imagination than discernment. Let us remain mindful that a hemisphere—left or right—is an ensemble of cells, not *selves*, and that if no single cell can be plausibly thought of as a "self" then no number of the same kind of cell can be. If all the bowls of sugar are entirely lacking in salt, we will not get salt by increasing the number and complexity of the arrangements of the sugar bowls. The problem of "emergence," which is taken up briefly in the concluding chapter, is a vexing one, indeed. In light of it, however, it doesn't make sense to speak of a hemisphere having or housing or knowing a "self", even if it might make sense to speak of a hemisphere as being one of the necessary conditions whereby we have or know about *our* selves.

self and self-identity   It is also important to distinguish the different meanings that attach to the terms "self," "self-identity," and "personal identity." A totally amnesic patient will not be able to tell us anything factual about his or her past. The patient may, that is, be entirely ignorant of his or her own identity and may be said, therefore, to lack a *self-identity*. We, however, may have very many personal facts about the amnesic, culled from school records, family accounts, employment history, and so on. That is, we may know who the patient is even though he or she does not. In this case, we would say that the patient has a *personal identity* but not a *self-identity*. But in still other cases neither we nor the patient may know anything about him or her such that we would say the patient has neither personal identity nor self-identity. Yet, even in this case the patient knows *that* he or she is even though the patient cannot answer the question "Who are you?" There is, then, a *self* even where there is no self-identity or personal identity. To refer to the commissurotomized patient, therefore, as one whose right hemisphere has no "self" is not right or wrong—it is simply incoherent.

Summary

This chapter has dealt with three issues that were collected under the rubric of consciousness, language, and thought. We dealt with conscious attention, sleep and arousal, and language. The analysis of each of these topics is fraught with enormous complexities and difficulties. Problems of measurement and definition abound. The single theme that ties all of this material together is that it all deals with the highest level of mental processes—thought—those normal and abnormal mental states that are most precious to each of us in defining the nature of our own beings.

The social and ethical significance of these matters is so great that we frequently have found ourselves wandering away from the specifically technical details with which this book is concerned mainly to consider some of the deep social and philosophical implications this science offers to human life. Yet in spite of this importance, we must accept the fact that this field is perhaps the fuzziest one in a scientific sense with which we have dealt. It has often been difficult to express formally exactly what it is that we mean by such a concept as "attention" even though it is intuitively obvious to each of us what the difference may be between attending to something and not doing so. In the absence of good theory, we have been forced to concentrate on the effects of various technical manipulations and neuroanatomic details on mental states. Often we have been able to describe the nature of some relationship without understanding exactly what is going on in any informing way. Nevertheless, there are certain general principles, which are at least made more plausible as a result of some of our discussions.

An important general message is conveyed by the surgical work on arousal, attention, and language. That message is that the brain is made up of a very large number of nuclei or centers, many of which strongly interact with each other to represent any psychological state. *There is no single center in the brain for any single psychological function.* Processes as complex as mental responses almost certainly must be influenced by vast regions and multiple nuclei of the brain to at least some degree. On the other hand, the partial success that ablation studies of arousal or language (to take two important examples) have had makes it clear that the brain is not perfectly homogeneous either. The brain is differentiated to some degree, but we should not expect to find places that are each totally responsible for sleep, or aggression, or unhappiness should we make the strategic error of looking for them. It is a far better approximation to reality to assume that these responses arise as a result of the overall activity of the brain than to assume that they are highly localized.

Much clinical evidence has accumulated over the past century correlating specific language disturbances with specific pathological states in the dominant (usually left) hemisphere. The cerebral anatomy involved in language is rather diffuse, and even more so when those areas of association cortex are included to account for intersensory linguistic functions. Chief among the areas associated with language are *Broca's* and *Wernicke's areas,* the *arcuate fasciculus,* and the *angular gyrus.*

The special role of the dominant hemisphere in language has been further elaborated by studies of patients whose interhemispheric (commissural) connections have been surgically destroyed. The major deficit resulting from this procedure is the inability or the reduced ability to assign words or meanings to objects and events projected to the nondominant hemisphere. Attempts to extend these findings to the more metaphysical realms of "self-consciousness" have been unconvincing and largely incoherent.

The relationship between language and thought is widely acknowledged as an intimate one. Psychobiology's inability to provide a rigorous and scientific account of language itself imposes severe constraints on its ability to deal with the phenomena of thought and cognition in general. What is now available are numerous correlations with which to connect certain cognitive and intellectual disturbances with lesions in a number of cerebral locations. (But the mechanisms of grammatically regulated discourse are unknown as are those processes by which language takes on its connotative properties.)

This then, is the state of psychobiology as we see it. In the next chapter we try to sum up the most important themes arising from this vast body of scientific research.

Suggested Readings

States of Arousal and Consciousness
1. J. Delafresnaye (ed.), *Brain Mechanism and Consciousness*, Basil Blackwell, Oxford, 1954.
2. B. Libet, W. Alberts, E. Wright, and B. Feinstein, Responses of human somatosensory cortex to stimuli below threshold for conscious sensation, *Science*, 1967, *158:*1597–1600.
3. H. Magoun, *The Waking Brain*, Charles C. Thomas, Springfield, IL, 1963.
4. K. Pribram and D. McGuinness, Arousal, activation, and effort in the control of attention, *Psychological Review*, 1975, *82:*116–149.
5. E. Murray, *Sleep, Dreams, and Arousal*, Appleton-Century-Crofts, New York, 1965.

Neural Science and the Nature of Consciousness
1. J. Eccles, *The Human Psyche*, Springer, New York, 1980.
2. G. Globus, G. Maxwell, and I. Savodnik (eds.), *Consciousness and the Brain*, Plenum, New York, 1976.
3. K. Popper and J. Eccles, *The Self and Its Brain*, Springer, Berlin, 1977.
4. D.N. Robinson, *Systems of Modern Psychology: A Critical Sketch*, Columbia, New York, 1979.
5. W.R. Uttal, *The Psychobiology of Mind.* Earlbaum, Hillside, NJ, 1978.

"Split-Brain" Patients and Animals
1. M. Gazzaniga, *The Bisected Brain*, Appleton-Century-Crofts, New York, 1970.
2. R. Sperry, Split-brain approach to learning problems, In, J. Eccles (Ed.), *Brain and Conscious Experience.* Springer-Verlag, New York, 1966.
3. D. N. Robinson, What sort of persons are hemispheres? Another look at the 'split-brain' main, *British Journal for the Philosophy of Science*, 1976, *27:* 73–78.

Brain Mechanisms and Language
1. N. Geschwind, The organization of language and the brain, *Science*, 1970, *170:* 940–944.
2. W. Penfield and L. Roberts, *Speech and Brain Mechanisms*, Princeton University Press, New Jersey, 1959.
3. E. Lenneberg, *Biological Foundations of Language*, Wiley, New York, 1967.

9 Twenty Questions for an Evolving Psychobiology

We have now devoted many pages to the facts, methods, and controversies that give modern psychobiology its content and its character. But the careful and properly unconvinced reader will have many questions. These questions will be partly philosophical, partly scientific. At their root, they will seek to determine how much of the traditional subject matter of psychology can be absorbed by psychobiology.

To honor the reader's nagging doubts and to give greater focus to them, we conclude this book with a game of "Twenty Questions"—but, in this case, a profoundly serious version of the game. Important subjects produce more than twenty questions of course. The truly important subject sets no limits on the number of relevant questions that can be brought to bear on it. Thus, the following questions are designed to raise still others and, in the process, perhaps settle a few. But far from closing off future debate, these twenty questions and the answers are meant to convey the *spirit* of psychobiology, the attitudes and working hypotheses adopted by those who have created the subject and by those who continue to nurture it. The active research scientist must, of course, keep these and related questions in a safe place far enough away from the equipment and the data so as not to interfere with the very purpose of experimentation. But these questions should also be close enough to the work so that the *conceptual* foundations of the discipline are never forgotten. We conclude, then, with a review of the issues that gave rise to psychobiology and that continue to animate it if only in its most sober moments. *These questions and answers are designed to be provocative and to make certain points.* The positions taken here should not be attributed to either author but to many unnamed scientists whose experi-

357

ments and theories have created the psychobiological perspective.

Question 1. It seems quite clear, in the light of the work that has been done in philosophy of mind, that the "solution" to the age-old mind/body problem simply cannot come from science. After all, most of the traditional philosophical positions regarding this problem can be reconciled to nearly any finding the neural sciences might come up with. Yet, if the mind/body problem is, in a way, *the* problem, and if it is immune to the methods and facts of science, what long-term goal remains for psychobiology?

Answer 1. The idea that the solution to the mind/body problem cannot come from science itself is debatable. It is by no means clear or obvious that the premise that science is not the way to a solution is valid. That is, it is at least conceivable that the solution to the mind/body problem might come from science (given our state of ignorance today and the time over which man may have to work on it). It is, of course, also possible that the problem is truly insoluble using any conceivable scientific paradigm. Even then, however, the obstacles to its solution may not exist for the reasons suggested in this question. Rather, the fundamental limits on how much we can learn about the relationship between brain and mind may arise simply from the complexity of the problem; it just may be that the brain is too complex a structure to be analyzed by either another brain or any other brain-like device invented by the brain. The number of interconnections that exist among neurons of the brain are only current estimates, of course, but it is clear that the count is very large. At least some scientists in this field believe the mathematics of the possible combinations (combinatorics) may be beyond calculation in any practical sense. One sage has suggested that problems of the type posed by the neural network of the brain, but of much smaller magnitude, may require for their analysis a computer consisting of as many elements as there are basic particles in the universe operating for as long as the universe has existed!

Thus, we do not even know the answer to the deeper question (are the mind and brain analyzable by science?) raised in the formulation of this question. It is possible that science may solve the mind/body problem, and it is possible that it may not. What is being suggested here is that any barrier to a solution that may be encountered could turn out to be a simple, practical matter (that is, computability) totally understandable within the context of science rather than of metaphysics.

Furthermore, the second premise of this question (traditional philosophies are reconcilable with any neuroscientific finding) may also be questioned. There is no innate inconsistency of any traditional mind/body philosophy with any finding of modern *neuroscience* only if one does not include the psychobiological implications of those data—that is, only if one ignores what the data say about the mind/body problem. Indeed, there are very clear assertions concerning the nature of the relationship between the brain and body and the mind and soul implicit, if not explicit, in most of the philosophical positions that are sometimes quite antagonistic to basic psychobiological premises. For example, most of the dualisms of the past explicitly specify that the mind and the brain are two different levels of reality that only passively interact, if at all. *Psychobiology*, on the other hand, is a theoretical expression of a materialistic monism that actually asserts casual relationships between the two domains. Psychobiology, as opposed to most other areas of neuroscience, invokes relational data and concepts that are quite inconsistent with traditional philosophies.

Thus, there are many long-term goals in psychobiology, not the least of which is to determine the limits of this science and the nature of those causal relationships. The question posed here raises issues that are still moot.

Question 2. Related to the first question, the next one is more specific. It has been argued, with some success, that mental events and states are radically different from purely natural or material events in the external world. Whereas the latter lend themselves to what is called a *causal* explanation, the former are only intelligibly explained in the language of *reasons*. To ask, for example, why someone voted for one candidate instead of another is not to inquire into the neuromuscular mechanisms involved in pushing down one lever instead of another. Rather, it is to inquire into the reasons (or *motives* or *aims* or even *preferences*) but by any such word these reasons do not follow either the logic or the sequence of *causal* events. Wherever there is a cause in nature, an effect follows. But there can be reasons for acting that are not followed by actions. Now, if significant human actions require *reasons* and explanations and if science—including psychobiology—can only develop *causal* explanations, does it not follow that psychobiological explanations will always be insufficient and generally beside the point?

Answer 2. Whatever success an argument espousing a *radical* difference between mental and external physical events may have depends entirely on the connotation of the word radical. There certainly are differences between *intrapersonally* (or mental) and *interpersonally* (or behavioral) observable events and they can be quite radical in one sense of the word. However, these differences may not be so radical as to represent two different kinds of reality as is so often suggested by dualistically oriented philosophers. It has been argued, also with some success, that both mental and external events are as natural and material as are the motions of physical objects. That is, mind and motion are both *activities* of physical objects. At the very least, close examination of experimental methodology and physical reality seems to make it clear that the problems faced by students of mind are no different than those faced by physicists and astronomers. In other words, the difficulties faced by psychologists may be no different in kind from those faced by these other scientists, just more complex.

The problem of obscure causality is not uniquely faced by psychologists. In many physical problems the causal links are so complex or so numerous that it is also necessary to use statistical methods to estimate the outcome. Physicists studying gas laws, as one striking example, do exactly what psychologists do (in principle); both scientists study the molar behavior of the mechanism in which they are interested. The point is that one must be exceedingly careful not to confuse differences in methods, required because of the number of variables involved, with differences in the fundamental nature of reality. It is all too easy to misread into events influenced by myriad causes a different kind of reality than that underlying events influenced by a small number of causal forces.

The use of the words motives, aims, reasons, or preferences in this question is an example of this kind of fallacy. The argument can be made that these terms are statistical concepts which describe processes that do not seem to follow "simple causation" only because the number of influencing variables is so great that we cannot discern the causal relationships. Such processes only *seem* to violate the logic or sequence of causality. The more we learn about mental states and processes, the more we appreciate that though the psychologist's subject matter is more complex, it is no different in kind from any other real, material system with more obvious causal relations. Psychobiological explanations may currently be, and indeed are likely to be for the foreseeable future, incomplete but they are not "beside the point." Rather, they are the very best explanations of the matters for which they are the *intended* medium of explanation. This does not mean that all problems of the human condition are likely to be solved by psychobiology; no science can make that promise. But if the question at hand is the mind/body problem, then this is the science of choice and all that we can glean in the way of answers to these difficult problems is as much to the point as anything can be.

Question 3. Those who have followed the recent decades of psychobiological research can only be awed by the growth and the power of its methods and techniques of investigation. Yet, when all is said and done, we still have no more than *correlations*. If one agrees that the trademark of a developed science is the possession of general laws—laws that go beyond mere correlations—might not one continue to doubt the scientific status of psychobiology?

Answer 3. Again, the issue here seems to be complicated by definitions of words. While some of the terms used in this question (such as correlation and law) may seem to be *denoting* different *things*, they may, in fact, only be *connoting* different *points of view*. Many scientists and philosophers of science would argue that all science is correlative and that the only difference between an apparent law and a measured correlation is the degree of certainty that appertains to one or the other. Thus, once again, the arbitrary dichotomization of what is really a continuum has led to a conceptual mis-construal. What we really have in any experimental science is a system of relationships, some of which are very tight and virtually always result in situations in which a change in the independent variable leads to a related change in a dependent variable and others of which we have less certainty that such changes will concurrently occur. But nothing is absolutely certain, no sequence totally impossible; some changes are more probable, while others are less so.

The point is that, if pressed, one would have a difficult time distinguishing a precise line of demarcation between what one might call a correlation and what one might wish to call a law. Even the best of laws fails once in a while (otherwise they would not be laws but identities) and even the most unlikely occurrences sometimes occur one after the other (for reasons that we may refer to ex post facto as coincidence) falsely implying that they are causally related.

In short, the science of psychobiology is in no greater danger of being invalidated because the relationships it observes are statistical and correlational, or occur with lower probability than in any other science. Every science has the same problem, and when the number of involved variables gets large, the degree of correlation between input and output usually drops off, whether it is the study of the human mind or the movement of billiard balls.

Question 4. There seems to be a kind of question begging involved in applying the same methods of measurement to species whose nervous systems are radically different and whose psychological characteristics are also radically different. Isn't it likely that neural systems across species seem to "be alike" merely because very limited methods have failed to uncover the differences? Since we know, for example, that rats cannot do what people can do, what should we make out of the fact that their mechanisms seem to be essentially identical?

Answer 4. The nervous system of each species differs in many ways from those of other species. That fact is well-established by neuroanatomical and neurophysiological work. Both at a gross level and at a microscopic level, it takes no great degree of sophistication to tell that something is different when the brains of even those animals that are close together on the phylogenetic tree are compared. On the other hand, similarities also exist, some of which are relevant to psychological comparisons and some of which are not. It is a fact that all neurons operate on the basis of a sodium-potassium-chloride chemistry (probably resulting from our common evolutionary heritage). It is also a fact that the brains of most higher animals are characterizable by some general gross anatomical similarities when compared. Brains are generally encephalized and bilaterally symmetrical, possess input and output channels, and so on.

All of this is as close to truth as any science can bring us. The point is, however, that this is not the point. These chemical and anatomical bodies of knowledge may not be the essence of the relationship between mind and brain. What is the essence of, and thus the basis of the best response to this query, may lie in the way in which the individual neurons are connected together. However similar two brains may appear at the gross level, at the level of cellular interconnections there may be a vast difference; and the modern view is that this is the level at which things really matter.

Thus the question posed here has to be dissected into several issues. First, although assuredly rats cannot do everything that people can do, they do many things that people do. This subset of activities is reasonably consistent with the observed subset of human neural mechanisms that are known to exist in the rat's nervous system. The mental life of a rat is not as rich as that of a human, but neither are the neural connections nor even the simple mass of brain tissue. The brains are only superficially "identical." Is there really such a discrepancy between mind and behavior and neurophysiological findings, as implied by this question?

Question 5. Whether synapses are excitatory or inhibitory appears to be determined genetically, as is the general anatomy of the nervous system. Shouldn't this lead one to expect much greater uniformity in the behavior of organisms that one actually finds?

Answer 5. There is no particular reason that even a very strong genetic determination of the polarity of synaptification or even of the general nature of their distribution should strongly predetermine the specific nature of behavior or mind. A widely accepted notion in psychobiology today is that it is the *detailed* arrangement of the network of neurons that is a necessary and sufficient equivalent of mental processes, not the particular polarity of individual components. Either an excitatory or an inhibitory synapse could be used to perform any function if appropriately connected in some network. Similarly, as was noted earlier, the general gross anatomy or the location of the neurons of the nervous system is of little consequence. It has been recently shown that a few normally functioning human beings (students at some of Britain's most prestigious universities) possessed terribly deformed brains. Because of a condition known as hydrocephalus (high fluid pressures in the ventricles of the brain), the cerebral hemispheres are sometimes smashed flat against the interior of the skull. The cerebrum appears as only a flattened sheet in CAT scans. In spite of this gross neural deformity, these students suffered no measurable behavioral or mental effects, and the condition, discovered for other reasons, came as quite a surprise. The reason for the innocuousness of the terrible anatomical pathology is that the aspect of the brain that is critical for mind is the detailed network of interconnections of the neurons of the brain. Thus, even though the overall shape of the brain was greatly deformed, the essential aspect—the network organization— remained relatively constant, and normal mentation (that is, the thought process) was maintained.

The point is that neither gross anatomy nor the nature of individual neurons is very important in the determination of mind. Thus, even though they are genetically predetermined, their relative unimportance makes this question a false issue. Both experiential and environmental forces act to produce detailed network states that are responsible for the acknowledged differences in human mentation and behavior. These differences are well within the range of the genetically determined similarities that do characterize our species.

Question 6. Much debate occurs about the *evolution* of nervous systems and changes in the mass of brains over the eons. But neurons seem to be very much the same wherever they are found, suggesting that this evolutionary process involved no more than an increase in their number and in their interconnectedness. What is often implied is that the psychological properties missing in a single neuron can somehow come into being with two or twenty or twenty million neurons. However, if a given property—call it X—is nowhere to be found in items of a certain kind—call them Y—then it would seem that no number of Ys will ever yield X. Suppose, for argument's sake, that neurons were actually composed of proteins and water. If neither the protein nor the water possesses, say, consciousness, motivaton, feelings, and so on, then the mere addition of still more protein and water cannot supply these. Why, then, do psychobiologists continue to hold the conviction that psychological processes and attributes are the result of anatomical complexity?

Answer 6. The answer to this question is a continuation of the answer to the previous one. What is missing, it seems, from the implicit premises of these questions is the set of concepts that has been bestowed on us by modern communication and information science. It is very important for the reader to appreciate that the mind does not emerge as a result of the specific *chemistry* of the components from which the brain is built. The precursor sciences of psychology and psychobiology are not chemistry and physics, but are rather the sciences that are involved with the communication and processing of information. In other words, *it does not matter what neurons are made of; what does matter is the way they are connected together.*

Some current psychobiological and philosophical thinking about this problem asserts that mind would appear if elements of any kind were appropriately interconnected, as long as they were capable of executing the same logical functions. A list of suitable logical elements includes neurons, relays, large scale integrated circuits, and potentially many other such elements as long as the new element is logically equivalent to a neuron. The only problem is a practical one,—the difficulty to artificially gather together enough of the mechanical elements to simulate the biological network.

Although computers, at least in the current form, are not good models of the brain, they at least provide a metaphor of what we are asserting. Modern digital computers can be (and have been) constructed from mechanical parts (relays), vacuum tubes, discrete transistors, and integrated circuits in their brief history. Each successive one of these technologies allows certain practical advantages to be obtained, but, *in principle*, there is little difference between the modern large-scale integrated (LSI) "chip" computer and the relay computer beyond such practicalities as speed of operation. So too, logical engines equivalent to brains could, in principle, be constructed with a wide variety of technologies.

Given this context, let us turn to the two specific questions incorporated into Question 6. First, let's consider the issue of how mind might emerge from insentient matter like protein and water. This process is close to what philosophers refer to when they use the term *emergence*. Admittedly, a serious criticism may be made that the emergence of truly *new* properties from combination of elements that do not exhibit those properties would be a very "peculiar" event. This criticism can be countered, however, by noting that it is "peculiar" in the preinformation revolution context only. Certainly, modern information scientists could say that properties not previously evident can and do occur as a result of combination, even though an older, obsolescent philosophy would require that "something" be added to account for emerged properties. To the proponents of this new view, combination itself is the "thing" that is added. Nothing new has really been added; only a quantitative factor has allowed previously unexpressed properties to become manifest.

The modern view of emergence is that through combinations, therefore, the most unexpected "emergent" properties of an ensemble could, in fact, be predicted if one knows all of the properties of the elements of that ensemble. The difficulty is that some of the properties of the elements—what they will do when they are in combination with others—cannot be made explicit until they are actually combined.

In this modern context, steeped as it is in the information processing thought of the last thirty years, emergence thus takes on quite a new look. Suitable arrangement of simple parts is all that is needed to account for complex processes. According to this view, water and protein need not themselves have mental properties for adequately large ensembles of these materials to exhibit such complex phenomena as thought. Indeed, the *existence proof* of the validity of the hypothesis that emergence of new properties does occur when "adequately large numbers are combined" exists within the confines of each of our skulls.

The important conclusion is that the nature of the elements in isolation is quite incidental. To persevere to the contrary produces a misleading strategy *if* one wants to know about mind. The chemistry of neurons is but a metabolic substrate, setting limits on how the network will operate, but not explaining how it does all the wonderful things it does. Anything on the list of possible components mentioned previously could do as well, in principle. Therefore, the absence of mentation in water, protein, silicon, glass, or anything else is nothing but a red herring in the mind/body problem. In sum, one should not commit the fallacy of misconstruing an ensemble of elements as being qualitatively different from the elements themselves; there may only be a quantitative difference.

Now let us consider the other question embedded in this double-barreled query. Neurons are very much alike wherever they are found in the human nervous system or in any nervous system. Indeed, the best explanation of this finding is that they have a common evolutionary heritage. It is true that evolution, in a general sense, accounts for "an increase in their number and interconnectedness." But this "increase" is not a triviality, as suggested by the words "no more than" in this query. Rather, this variation in the information processing capacity of a brain is none other than the essence of the matter, and the only possible basis of our understanding of how, in principle, mind emerges from the properties of microscopic neurons. This principle holds, even if we do not and perhaps cannot know the complete "wiring" diagrams in detail.

In sum, this question is based on the underlying premise that the individual neuron is the key to the mind, and one modern view asserts that this is not the case. To repeat the central idea, it is the *arrangement* of the parts, not the *nature* of the parts, that is the critical component in any solution to this wondrous problem.

Question 7. From the fact that sensory coding takes nearly the same form across the various species, is it proper to conclude that these different species have very much the same experiences? Does a dog see a tree?

Answer 7. Sensory coding takes nearly the same form, not only across species, but also from one modality to another in the human being. Amplitude and quality are not dissimilarly encoded in the various senses; yet there are vast differences in the way in which we interpret these codes. This, then, brings us to the important point. Since the codes we are considering here are those of the communication pathways prior to the central "interpretation" of those messages, the nature of the codes is virtually irrelevant to final mental experience. At that level, some other encoding scheme becomes relevant. Even there, however, the nature of the code is not critical. The fact that an electrical response occurs in a particular part of the brain is sufficient to allow a different kind of interpretation to be made of what may appear to be very similar codes.

In this context, it seems likely that what an animal perceives is determined not by the code, but rather by the dimensions of the situation that would make for a meaningful response. Context, for example, can drastically change a percept. It has been shown that exactly the same "peripheral" neural code for chromatic wavelength can be interpreted in various ways depending on the surround. *Peripheral* codes, therefore, do not uniquely define a percept. Therefore, the answer to the first part of this question has to be "No!"—It is not proper to draw the conclusion suggested. However, this does not mean that it is not actually so. Does a dog see a tree? While there is no way to definitely answer this question (any more than one can find out what another human being sees), it seems plausible that any animal's experience of a spatial arrangement on its retina is probably pretty much like that of any other. This answer, of course, finesses a host of relevant questions concerning the consciousness of the animal and what the word "perceive" might mean to an automaton, for which we also have few answers.

Question 8. Here and in other chapters it is noted that different methods produce results which are not always in agreement. How does one decide which method to trust? If, for example, the most available method for studying coding is electrophysiology, but if the coding itself is actually accomplished chemically (or structurally), will our theories of coding not finally be expressions more of our methods than of the process itself?

Answer 8. The thrust of this question is incontestable. It is entirely true that different methods produce different results, that these results do not always agree, and that the methods often influence theoretical explanations. However, this uncertainty must be appreciated for what it is. Science is not a mechanical process; rather, it works on the basis of hunches and arguments for which there are usually several sides. One chooses among these arguments by means of the same criteria used in resolving other disagreements—simplicity, consistency with other data, predispositions, and even elegance of the concept. It is a rare (and usually trivial) instance in which a controversy is completely resolved by means of a single experiment. In those cases in which it is, more often than not, the sudden resolution is the result of the opening of a new observational door by the invention of some novel tool that provides data that is more directly related to the controversy than previous data had been.

In this context we must appreciate that our theories are always the result of our methods (just as our experimental data are the result of our theories). Sometimes the particular data that are available misleads us into believing that we know more than we do, but there is also a practical side to this issue that must not be overlooked. One must not reject what data and methodology one does possess in favor of some hypothetical and nonextant alternative. Furthermore, methods constantly improve and bring us closer and closer to whatever it is we are studying. Our theories thus become less speculative, and less influenced by method, and more a reflection of the biology of the situation. But one cannot deny the intent of this question. Methods do limit perspective even as they open new windows. We must always try to keep this in mind as we evaluate new theories.

Another aspect of this question concerns the emphasis on electrophysiology as opposed to chemistry. It is probably the case that neither single-cell neurophysiology nor biochemistry is the essential level of analysis. As has been suggested elsewhere, it is the interconnectedness that is the critical variable. Our science certainly has been "misled" by the availability of both the chemical and microelectrode methodologies, as suggested by this question. Neither one is the "correct" methodology in the context set here.

Question 9. Psychobiology, like other divisions of modern psychology, stresses the important role of *behavior*. This is quite understandable since research depends on the ability to measure observable phenomena. Nevertheless, every person knows that many of the most significant aspects of personal "psychology" never rise to the public surface of behavior. Many thoughts, hopes, dreams, and feelings often remain entirely private and they may be far more significant to us than anything revealed by our measurable actions. It would seem, therefore, that a psychobiological science confined only to behavioral correlates would miss or officially ignore what are arguably the most significant psychological properties we have. Is this so?

Answer 9. Yes, this is so!

Question 10. Much attention has been given to the definition of learning and to ways of distinguishing between learning and such processes as habituation, sensitization, reflexes, and instincts. However, the actual anatomy, physiology, and biochemistry are the same, no matter what we *call* the process. Why, then, should the "higher" species be able to learn whereas lower members of the kingdom cannot, even though the basic equipment is the same in nearly all cases?

Answer 10. Learning is a highly specific term used to denote particular kinds of behavioral changes that eventuate as a result of experience and that are not attributable to fatigue or any other metabolic-like process. In humans there is a restricted class of information processing phenomena that meet these criteria and which have been of interest for years. For these reasons "learning" is considered to be a distinct biological process. A strong argument can be made that, in fact, the anatomy, physiology, and biochemistry of this process are not the same as most of the other learning-like adaptive processes. But this does not necessarily mean that learning is different in principle from those simpler processes. As complexity of the "basic equipment" increases, so too does the complexity of the adaptive processes executed.

The problem is common in psychology. Are the mental states we have defined different from other related processes in principle or only in magnitude? However, such a problem is also common in any field in which taxonomic classifications are being made and thus may be considered to be a general feature of any application of the scientific method.

The answer to the specific question about learning in "higher" species then becomes obvious. Greater adaptive flexibility up to and including what we consider to be the most elaborate features of human learning become progressively more available as the nervous system becomes more complex. That is why we can learn some things that a frog cannot.

Question 11. When learning is said (and shown) to be dependent on such processes as attention and emotion, one gets the distinct impression that something uniquely nonbiological is referred to, but is disguised in the scientific language of "process." We can agree, can we not, that it makes no sense to speak of a neuron as *attentive* or *emotional*? But then it must also not make sense to speak of two neurons or five million neurons in this way. Why not, therefore, come right out and say that learning requires that the animal or the person be *personally interested* in the task or the outcome? And, having said it this way, why not go on to appreciate that this *personal* involvement is simply inexplicable in terms of neurons, synapses, and circuits?

Answer 11. Here again, the concept of combinatorial emergence (that is, complex properties emerge when simpler elements are combined) helps to clarify and elucidate this fundamental issue. We would all agree that it makes no sense to speak of a neuron as attentive or emotional (even though some perceptual psychobiologists seem to be making the same absurd judgment when they say that individual neurons account for perceptual phenomena). However, this does not mean that it is equally nonsensical to speak of a large ensemble of neurons as exhibiting these molar properties. In fact, it is obviously the case that they do! Large neural networks (for example, our brain) do demonstrate just these properties. Unless one is willing to accept a nonphysiological origin of these real psychological processes, then given that individual neurons cannot, it is *only* the combination of neurons into networks that can account for these wonderful, though as yet, unexplained phenomena. What would be "uniquely nonbiological" would be any assertion that these emotions arose in some other nonneural way. Emotions are quite as biological as any other bodily process, but they are properties of ensembles, not elements. The words personal, emotional, and attentive are simply molar or statistical terms that denote our experience of these ensemble properties. In fact, one can argue that these terms denote exactly the same *things* as does a lexicon of words like network, state, and average neural interconnectedness.

Question 12. The research on memory "molecules" and memory "codes" is all very interesting, but has it explained *my* memory? When I recall having been to a foreign city or having dined at a fine restaurant, I don't recall molecules or codes; I recall the events themselves. Again, it makes no sense to speak of molecules as having memories or of neurons "recalling" the past. It only makes sense to speak of a *conscious* recollection. It may be proper, therefore, to say that, of all the places one might keep one's memories, one happens to keep them in the *brain*, but it is scarcely proper to say that the *brain* (or any other large organ) has memories. It would be like saying that, when a person records the memorable events of life in a diary, it is the diary that remembers the events! Must we not, therefore, make a distinction between the psychobiology of *coding* (or storage) and the psychobiology of *memory*?

Answer 12. To be very candid, we all must admit that psychobiology has not yet explained the memory process. However, to assert as a fact that we remember the experience and not the molecules or codes only muddies the issues. It is a general property of the human mind that it is aware only of the *outcomes* of neural processes and not the neural *processes* or mechanisms that account for those outcomes. We *see* color; we do not experience trichromatic (or other) neural codes. Somehow we put together a rational story from the neural information that comes in, but the details of the language in which that information is encoded are not experienced themselves.

It makes sense to speak of conscious recollection if one is interested in the molar mental state. It makes equally good sense to speak about the possible means by which information may be stored in the brain (the engram) if that is the target of one's interest. Most of the confusion here occurs because we tend to mix up the vocabulary describing the experience with the vocabulary describing the mechanism of storage. The word "memory" is used indiscriminantly and improperly in both contexts. Use of the separate words *engram* and *recollection* would greatly help to alleviate this problem. The brain stores engrams as changes in the normal state. Recollections are the experienced global outcomes of the changes in neural state that are produced, just as any other aspect of the mind is the outcome of some neural network state. The problem posed in this question about the diary arises from exactly the same source; a pun on one word, *remember*, with two meanings. The book remembers, in the sense that it *stores* symbols; the mind remembers, in the sense that it is an interpretation of those stored symbols.

The question of why memories are stored in the brain, rather than in some other organ, is easily answered. Only in the brain is the degree of interconnectedness rich enough to account for the massive amount of information that must be stored. The other organs of the body that have been considered to be repositories of information—such as the heart or liver, have highly redundant cellular structures and thus could not provide the rich information–storage capacity required. Furthermore, unlike other kinds of cells, nonneural synaptic interconnections in the nervous system respond rapidly enough to allow the states of the great neural networks to be altered as rapidly as we encounter new experience. The other organs, cells, or molecules proposed as memory storage elements are neither fast enough nor informationally rich enough. Speed and capacity are the properties that place the mind in the brain rather than in the liver.

Question 13. Granted that different mechanisms serve the different functions of long-term and short-term storage, what is it in the *environmental* event that determines whether it will be permanently stored? It cannot be a matter merely of biological or "Darwinian" significance, for we often recall for very long periods of time events that seem to have no biological consequence at all.

Answer 13. We really are not sure yet, as with so many other important problems in psychobiology, how experiences become part of long-term memory. There are some theories that assert that the information capacity of the brain is so great that *all* experience is actually consolidated into long-term memory. (If so, obviously not all of that information is actually available all of the time. Our scores on examinations and our forgetfulness with "lost" telephone numbers make that assertion irrefutable.) Other theorists, however, assume that some specific event or condition is required to store events in long-term memory. Possible alternatives include simple repetition or rehearsal, attentiveness, ecological significance, and most interestingly (in the context set here), the activation of at least one intermediary synapse. Responses within a single neuron do not seem to produce engram-like changes in that neuron.

The problem of Darwinian significance is so closely tied up with those stimulus factors that determine to what we will attend and what we will ignore, that it is extremely difficult to differentiate among the factors that influence long-term retention. On the other hand, it is also difficult to determine whether any event has *no* biological significance. No one yet seems to have been able to unravel this knot.

Question 14. The relationship between heredity and personality is a striking one, particularly with respect to psychopathology. This would lead one to suspect that specific neurochemical agents, themselves understandable in terms of genetic coding, are at the core of mental illness and of personality itself. But we also know of many instances of successful therapy and of the ability of a wholesome environment to restore sound mental functions. How can these environmental events alter something as apparently ingrained as the genetically established neurochemistry of the brain?

Answer 14. In essence, this is the nature-nurture question posed from the point of view of a genetic determinist. The answer to this question must be framed as a reminder that complex properties like personality are the result of both our genetic heritage and the experiences we have had during our lifetime. Certainly our metabolic biochemistry influences behavioral processes and chemicals can alter behavior, but so does experience. The main point of this answer is that modern theory asserts that complex processes like personality are almost certainly the outcome of interactions between heredity and environment.

Geneticists distinguish between the *genotype* (the full gamut of possible attributes contained within the genetic code) and the *phenotype* (that smaller set of attributes that is actually expressed). Perhaps we all possess, to a greater or lesser degree, a saint or a sociopath within us. Clearly, however, there is some environmental influence selecting what proportions of a mix of these properties will emerge in our personalities. Simply put, we are not rigidly predetermined engines. Psychobiology no more makes that assertion than does social psychology. The plasticity of synapses allows for plasticity of personality just as for any other kind of learning; environment and experience can and do alter mental states; no aspect of mind is totally "ingrained" or fixed; molar plasticity arises out of synaptic plasticity. This does not mean, however, that a plastic synapse possesses personality; it also does not exclude personality being the outcome of an ensemble of plastic synapses.

Another aspect of this question is the possibility raised that "specific neurochemical agents...are at the core of mental illness and...." While we know that neurochemicals are effective agents, and that most of them exert this influence through their effect on synapses, we know nothing about what they do in detail to alter the neural nets that embody mental processes. Such chemicals are metabolic rather than informational agents, and are not in a theoretical sense at the core of the mind/body problem at all. Neurochemistry is, from the psychobiological point of view, more akin to a metabolic manipulator than an informational one. No one has ever altered specific thoughts with chemicals, only general states affecting an overall change in the function of the system.

Question 15. As any actor will tell you, behavior can disguise as much as reveal the emotions. On what basis does the psychobiologist defend the position that studies of behavior are indirect but valid approaches to the issue of *emotion*?

Answer 15. Like any other instrument, behavior does not totally reproduce the underlying states of which it is an indicator. It is fallible, it can be deceived, and it is incomplete. On the other hand, *interpersonally* communicated behavioral information is all that we have to tell us about *intrapersonal* experience. It is certainly true that actors and liars can deceive us, and so do faulty meters as Three-Mile-Island-type disasters so emphatically prove. We try to avoid this kind of deception by having other means of verification or redundant instruments. We try out our ideas on many people in many and varied situations and replicate experiments under various conditions. We develop hypotheses that are at least consistent within the framework of knowledge that we possess at the moment. We have no proof of the validity of any instrument—behavioral or otherwise—and few, if any, measures to even estimate the "precision" of behavior as an indicator of mind. There are no electronic lie detectors that could really work. Is there then any alternative to behavior if we are to study the mind?

Question 16. The evidence and arguments seem to be convincing that only human beings can properly be described as *linguistic*. This suggests that there is something equivalently unique about their "machinery," especially their brains. Is this not enough to raise grave reservations over the use of nonhuman nervous systems to attempt to understand human psychological processes in general?

Answer 16. Quite to the contrary; the evidence is not at all convincing that only human beings display linguistic behavior. This is one of the most vigorously researched and debated issues in contemporary psychobiology. Laboratories around the world are studying certain kinds of animal behavior to determine whether it is or is not "linguistic," the way in which the word is used here. Even beyond the uncertainty about the answer to this ongoing problem, we really do not have very good definitions of what is meant by the term "linguistic."

Nor is there any resolution about the uniqueness of human brain and its relation to linguistics. Some parts of the repertoire of skills that constitute what we generally agree is linguistic behavior are present in other animals—chimps do put symbols together in strings, macaws do make intelligible sounds, many other animals seem to communicate among themselves with acoustic patterns that have recognizable symbolic vocabularies. At least some parts of the neural mechanisms underlying language must, therefore, be common to many species, even if they are not fully linguistic in the way humans are.

The doubts expressed in this question seem to indicate a lack of acceptance of the concept that lower animals are part of a continuum that includes mankind. No one is asserting that all animals are men when they assert that men are animals. Nor is any psychobiologist asserting that nonhuman nervous systems are complete models of human nervous systems. What is being asserted is that there are some commonalities, and that these common features do provide a basis for a comparative psychobiology—a science whose goal is to determine the nature of and extent of those commonalities, not to prejudge the issue. By studying nervous systems at all phylogenetic levels, we are likely to begin to understand nervous systems in general, not human nervous systems in particular. To understand the human nervous system in all of its idiosyncratic grandeur, we must study the behavior, mind, and brain of humans.

Question 17. Although the word *language* generally connotes the way we go about having conversations and passing on information to others, the actual gifts of language go well beyond these social functions. It is, after all, on the basis of language that we engage in the *logic* of problem solving and come to develop entire systems of thought, not to mention such creations as art, law, morality, and politics. What is, in this context, especially interesting about these creations is that they often involve nonempirical and nonmaterial considerations. The *certainty* of syllogistic reasoning, for example, has no parallel in the world of matter or the world of perception; nor does the idea of a *just* act or that of a mathematical *point*. However, it seems that the entire argument of psychobiology is that *all* psychological attributes are the result of biological and chemical processes—processes which, themselves, are not *certain* or *just* or *abstract*. To put the question simply, how can mere "matter in motion" come to possess such nonempirical and utterly immaterial conceptions or, for this matter, conceptions of any kind whatever?

Answer 17. In 1936, A.M. Turing established a very important theorem in mathematics that is critical to providing even the beginning of an answer to this question. He asserted that any idea, no matter how complicated, could be represented by a simple mathematical notation (the binary number system). Thus, with as few as two digits (0 and 1), Turing said, any idea, even something like justice or logic, certainty or the idea of abstraction itself, could be "encoded." The logical error inherent in this question is that it concentrates on the physical aspects of the media with which the message is communicated, rather than its symbolic or informational aspects. For example, it is immaterial whether a television signal is communicated over a light pipe, a wire, or the air. These aspects describe the physical nature of the media conveying the signals. Indeed, does it matter to the viewer whether the signal was frequency, amplitude, or pulse modulated? The meaning conveyed by the signals can be reconstructed at the receiver from any of these transmission modes equally well if the receiver knows what to do.

The point is that it is the *message* that is encoded by the various *arrangements* of physical energy that is important in this context. However immaterial or nonempirical an idea is, it is that meaning of the symbols that is important in the nervous system. Abstract ideas can be represented by manipulations of symbols in a wide variety of physical media—this book being one case in point and the reality of thought executed by the brain being another. Both alphabetic characters and neuronal network states can encode the same information.

By the way, some would dispute the fact that language is necessary for all kinds of logical reasoning. Some problem-solving behavior seems to be language free (animals can solve problems), and some motor acts (driving) closely akin to problem solving on the part of humans can go on in what seems to be a nonlinguistic mode.

Question 18. Is there a *person* who must be assumed for the very idea of *personality* to have any meaning and, if so, is there a "psychobiology of the person" in the offing?

Answer 18. Personality is usually defined as the ensemble of responses that characterizes an individual organism's behavior. If that definition is acceptable, there must obviously be some kind of organism (or machine) to be so characterized. Thus, the concept of personality does seem to require reference to an actual, or at least postulated, entity to be meaningful, except in those cases where it is a class in a taxonomy of personality types and refers to a prototype rather than to any particular individual. Like any other idea, however, it may refer to a nonexistent individual—characters in novels have distinct personalities in spite of their lack of actual physical existence in physical space-time.

The problem in answering the second part of this question is that the complexity of the human mind is such that we are often required to study large samples in order to find out what the "typical individual" is like. The "typical individual," however, is an abstraction for whom we may reasonably expect to develop a psychobiological model. However, we do not have enough knowledge of all of the variables involved in personality to seriously expect that we will be able to successfully predict individual behavior at present. It can, for example, be shown that schizophrenics as a group exhibit a slower recovery time in their evoked brain potentials *on the average.* As solid as this empirical fact is, it does not allow one to say that a person with a slow recovery time *is* a schizophrenic. A psychobiology of the individual person, therefore, will remain elusive. For a wise model of the individual mind, we still tend to turn to students of the whole individual, more molarly oriented psychologists, philosophers, poets, novelists, and historians.

Question 19. You have made a strong case against psychosurgery. But suppose the psychosurgeon says "There are countless cases of wrecked lives for which psychotherapy has no solutions. Unless something is done for these persons, their days will be passed in institutions, behind bars, and in the absence of most of the pleasures that make human life worth living. If I think there is some chance to turn all of this around, am I not morally obliged to try?" What will your reply be?

Answer 19. It is difficult, indeed, to answer a question like this for which there exists strong arguments on both sides. On the one hand, the integrity of the human individual is nowhere more delicately sheltered than in the brain/mind. Some sad individuals might be helped, on the other hand. Obviously, there is no right solution to this dilemma. Perhaps the only ethical thing to do is to rely on the validity of the current social decision. At the present time, in general, our society has turned away from psychosurgery, paying more attention to the ethical arguments against psychosurgery and ignoring the practical ones. Some suffering inevitably is going to ensue from this decision. We have made a collective judgment that less misery is likely to result than if the opposite decision had been made. This may not be the "right" thing to do, but then there may be no "right" thing to do.

Question 20. With all the facts and methods now claimed by psychobiology, how do you account for the fact that this young science is without a single, coherent, explanatory *theory* to account for even one class of psychological phenomena?

Answer 20. The premise on which this question is based is totally incorrect! Who says there are no coherent explanatory theories in psychobiology? Quite the contrary, there is an abundance of them. Theories abound in virtually every area in this field—big theories, little theories, and medium-sized theories. Indeed, the meaning of every one of the measurements described in this book becomes intelligible only in terms of some kind of a theoretical statement. Theories of perception are particularly comprehensive and coherent. Psychological theories of motivational and emotional states exist in abundance. None of this is to say that any of these theories are correct or complete. This is a young science (in its modern form emphasizing experimental analysis) beset with horrendous problems of complexity and definition. There is, perhaps, no other area of modern science in which the problems are as difficult or the solutions less apparent at the present time. There are many fundamental questions that have not been answered. Questions remain concerning whether or not some of the issues can be resolved. Yet, it is surprising how much progress has been made, not only in a theoretical sense, but also in a practical one.

Psychobiology has all the potential of being *the* science of the twenty-first century. It may play the central role that physics and chemistry played in the twentieth century. Certainly there is no grander problem in human existence than the relationship between the brain and the mind. It is the epitome of all that humans seek and have sought throughout history to know of themselves and the world in which they live. Whatever the current difficulties, is there any more noble goal of the human endeavor?

Glossary*

Absolute Refractory Period the interval during which the active neuron is absolutely unresponsive to any other stimulus, no matter how intense. (121)

Adequate Stimulus the minimum stimulus capable of activating a sensory system or one of its components. (136)

Adipsia prolonged cessation of liquid-consumption resulting in severe dehydration. (211)

AER averaged evoked responses: See *evoked potentials*

Afferent refers to sensory fivers carrying information to the brain or spinal cord. (92)

Agnosia an interpretive failure (e.g., in vision, audition or touch) with no significant loss of sensitivity. (244; 342)

All-or-None Law the law describing the non-decremental amplitude of the conducted neural impulse (121)

Alpha Rhythm the dominant EEG amplitude and frequency (8–13 Hz.) of the relaxed, awake person in the absence of active mentation or disruptive or sudden stimulation. (285)

Analgesic a class of anesthetic agents but specifically affecting sensitivity to painful stimulation. (302)

Anesthetic any chemical agent that reliably reduces or eliminates sensitivity. (301)

Anterograde Degeneration the degeneration of regions of the neuron cut off from the metabolically active cell body. (46)

Anthropomorphism attributing human characteristics or psychological traits to non-human animals, usually on the basis of behavioral stimulants. (200)

Aphagia the cessation of eating for prolonged and ultimately fatal durations. (211)

*Numbers in parentheses are just some of the pages on which Glossary terms are discussed.

379

Aphasia expressive or receptive losses of vocal-language communication. (341)

Apraxia the inability to carry out an integrated series of actions, such as those involved in dressing oneself. (244; 342)

ARAS ascending reticular arousal (or activating) system; a multi-branching network of fibers extending through the brain stem and running through the core of the brain. (330–334)

Autonomic Nervous System (ANS) that part of the peripheral nervous system consisting of the sympathetic and parasympathetic branches and regulating major vegetative and stress-dependent functions of the body. (94–95)

Axon (or fiber); the filament-like projection from the soma of a neuron, along which neural impulses are conducted. (89)

Bell-Magendie Law the principle according to which the sensory and motor functions of the spinal cord are recognized as anatomically distinct. (12)

Binding Sites specific membrane regions (of, for example, receptor cells or neurons) to which specific substances have a special affinity. (see, for example, 305)

Bit binary digit; the unit of information. (225–226)

Blind Spot region on the retina from which the optic nerve arises and where there are no receptors and, therefore, no vision. (146)

Bodian Stain a stain that non-selectively visualizes cell bodies and myelinated axons. (53)

Brainstem the "stem" of structures—medulla, pons, and cerebellum—on which the cerebral mantle and sub-cortical structures rest. (103–104)

Broca's Area a region in the vicinity of the third frontal convolution on the dominant (left) hemisphere associated with the production of normal speech. (340–341)

CAT Scan computerized axial tomography; an X-ray technique allowing the visualization of entire cross-sections of the body and providing three-dimensional information. (48–50)

Central Nervous System (CNS) the brain retina, and spinal cord. (91)

Centrifugal as applied to fibers and pathways, those arising in the brain and projecting outward toward peripheral organs. (149)

Cerveau Isolé the surgical preparation that eliminates all spinal cord signals to the cerebrum and all cranial nerve signals (except those from the olfactory and optic nerves) to the cerebrum. (330)

Circadian Rhythms daily rhythmic fluctuations in gross metabolic activity regulated by internal clock-like mechanisms. (327)

CNV contingent negative variation; a negative shift in the baseline of the EEG reliably produced by stimuli that call for specific responses by the observer. (246)

Cochlear Microphonic the auditory receptor potential. (171)

Commissurotomy the surgical severing of commissural connections. (346)

Conditioning, Avoidance the procedure requiring a specific response, following a stimulus-cue, in order to avoid a painful or aversive stimulus. (21)

Conditioning, Classical or *Pavlovian;* the method by which initially ineffective or neutral stimuli come to have the reflex-eliciting properties of unconditioned stimuli. (206–207)

Conditioning, Operant or *Instrumental;* the method of increasing the frequency of certain behaviors through selective reinforcement. (206–207)

Corpus Callosum the band of some 200 million fibers joining the two cerebral hemispheres. (346)

Cytoarchitectonics an anatomical system by which regions of the brain are classified according to their dominant cell-types. (59)

Delayed Alternation a behavioral task requiring trial-by-trial alternations of responding but with a delay introduced between trials. (216)

Depolarization the partial or complete elimination of charge-differences across the membrane of a cell. (116)

Diopter the unit expressing the resolving power of a lens or optical system; measured as the reciprocal of focal length in meters. (146)

Dualism the philosophical position that accepts the separate and real existence of mental events or entities and thus requires, in an exhaustive account of the actual contents of reality, *both* mental and material entities. (6–7)

Dysarthia failure to articulate properly words and phrases. (341)

Dyscalculia failures in the performance of routine calculational tasks. (342)

Dyslexia deficits in the recognition and/or production of visually presented verbal material. (342)

EBP evoked brain potential; the electrical response of the brain to discrete stimuli. See also AER and *evoked potentials.* (319)

ECS electroconvulsive shock, typically resulting in a period of amensia. (240)

ECT Scan emission computed tomography computed from signals emitted by isotopes that have been introduced into the brain. (67)

EEG electroencephalogram; (recordings of) the constant, background electrical waves of activity recorded from the scalp and roughly correlated with varying degrees of consciousness and arousal. (324–327)

Efferent refers to motor fibers carrying signals from brain or spinal cord out to the muscle and glands of the body. (92)

Encephale Isolé the surgical preparation that severs the connection between brain and spinal cord. (330)

Endorphins naturally occurring opiate-like substances in the brain. (302)

Epiphenomenalism a dualistic solution to the mind/body problem which attributes all mental events and processes to functions of the nervous system. (8)

Equipotentiality the principle advanced by Karl Lashley to suggest that nearly any remaining region of the cerebral cortex can assume functions once controlled by surgically removed regions. (215)

Evoked Potentials also average evoked response (AER) or evoked brain potentials (EBP); the electrical potentials evoked from the brain by discrete stimuli and recordable either directly from the brain or from the scalp using computer-averaging techniques. (62)

Fiber see *axon*

Fink-Heimer stain a silver stain that marks degenerating axons. (46)

Forebrain the major division of the brain containing the cerebral hemispheres, the limbic system, basal ganglia, thalamus and hypothalamus. (103)

Freeze Fracturing a method for separating the most delicate structures of a cell, such as the sides of the neural membrane. (58)

Ganglion a collection of cell bodies in the peripheral nervous system. (91)

Generator Potential the receptor potential; a graded potential which, at a critical value, results in the initiation of action potentials. (160)

Genotype the genetic endowment of the individual (plant or animal) received from the parental strain. (201)

Golgi Stain a silver stain for visualizing entire neurons. (52)

Graded Potentials electrical potentials that vary in proportion to the intensity of applied stimuli and/or as a function of the distance from the site of stimulation. (125)

Gray Matter the gray-appearing regions of the nervous system consisting chiefly of unmyelinated short axons and cell bodies. (44)

GSR galvanic skin reflex, a change in the electrical conductivity of the skin often associated with stress. (315)

Habituation progressive decreases in response-strength resulting from successive and rapid elicitations of the response. (234)

Heritability the value (h^2) expressing the contribution of additive genetic factors to the total phenotypic variance displayed by a population. (202)

Heterosynaptic Facilitation enhanced responses of a postsynaptic unit resulting from the "priming" of presynaptic units. (256)

Hindbrain or brainstem; the division of the brain containing the pons, medulla, an cerebellum. (103)

Hologram the optical reconstruction of three-dimensional objects through interactions and interferences of wavefronts. (273)

Homeostasis the (theoretical) processes engaged by states of physiological "disequilibrium" and designed to restore "equilibrium". (208)

Hybrid a mixed genotype as regards a particular characteristic such as color or shape. (201)

Hypermetamorphosis part of the Klüver-Bucy Sundrome (*vide infra*); the need for excessive inspection of and stimulation by familiar objects (e.g., a screw or stick) to determine its general class (e.g., edible-non-edible). (289)

Hyperphagia abnormally high rates of food-ingestion. (211)

Hyperpolarization an increase in the degree of polarization caused by increasing the charge-differences across the cellular membrane. (116)

Hypnotic any chemical agent that reliably promotes sleep. (300)

Hypophysis pituitary gland. (208)

Identity Thesis an attempted solution to the mind/body problem based on the claim that mental events are not caused by processes in the brain but are, in fact, just these processes. The thesis finally collapses into a form of monistic materialism or an inadvertent dualism. (8)

Innate Releasing Mechanism the underlying physiological process triggered by specific stimuli and resulting in innate patterns of behavioral adjustment. (204)

Interactionism the variety of dualism (*vide surpa*) according to which mental events and physical events either exert mutual influences (two-way interactionism) or influences in one direction only; i.e., "mind over matter" but not vice versa or "matter over mind" but not vice versa. (7)

Internuncial a neuron connecting other neurons. (98)

Instinct an unlearned but organized and complex pattern of behavior typically associated with the survival and propagation of the species as a whole. (204)

Institutionalization Syndrome behavior and perceptions characteristic of persons living for prolonged periods in institutional or other confining settings. (293)

Korsakoff's Syndrome profound losses of general cognitive abilities coupled with severe memory deficits. (269)

Klüver-Bucy Syndrome the docility, hypersexuality and cognitive distortions resulting from surgical removal of the temporal lobes but tied more specifically to the amygdala and associated limbic structures. (289)

Lamarckian a discredited theory, named after the 19th Century naturalist, Lamarck, who proposed that the acquired characteristics of the parental strain were passed on to the offspring. (201)

Language the manipulation of both denotative and connotative symbols in conformity with grammatical rules (338–340)

Lateral Hypothalamic Syndrome the aphagia and adipsia produced by destruction of the lateral hypothalamic nuclei. (211–212)

Law of Effect the "law" according to which the probability of a response is determined by the reinforcements ("effects") previously brought about by that response. (264)

Limbic System a collection of highly integrated forebrain structures associated with emotionality, memory functions and motivation. (110–111)

Loyez Stain a stain with a special affinity for myelin. (55)

Mass Action the principle advanced by Karl Lashley according to which the cerebral cortex functions as an integrated whole in the control of complex psychological functions. (215)

Materialism, Monistic (or Radical) the metaphysical claim that the domain of reality is exhausted by material entities and that alleged "mental" events or entities are utterly fictitious. (8)

Mendelian Inheritance named after Gregor Mendel, the theory of discrete transmission of specific traits, such as the color, size and shape of offspring; the mode of inheritance occurring as a result of unitary and independent genes. (201)

Microelectrode a very small (typically a capillary-glass) electrode measuring only microns in thickness at its tip and able to penetrate single cells. (71–73)

Midbrain the major division of the brain containing the cerebral peduncles and the superior and inferior colliculi. (103)

Monozygotic Twins Twins sharing identical genotypes and arising from a single (mono-) zygote or fertilized ovum. (298)

Myelin the fatty sheath convering the axon. (89)

Nerve a collection of fibers running together in the peripheral nervous system. (91)

Neuron Doctrine the doctrine according to which the neuron is the anatomical unit of the nervous system and exists as a structurally unique entity. (18)

Neurosis a psychological disturbance generally involving abnormal degrees of anxiety and compulsive or obsessional characteristics but without hallucinations or delusions. (295–296)

Nissl Stain a stain used for the selective visualization of cell bodies. (53)

Node of Ranvier the break in the myelin sheath where the axonal membrane is exposed. (89)

Nucleus (a) as pertains to the central nervous system, a collection of cell bodies (91); (b) as pertains to individual neurons, the region of the cell body (soma) containing the genetic material controlling the metabolic functions of the cell. (89)

Ohm's Law the law relating current (I), voltage (E) and resistance (R) in an electrical circuit: $I = E/R$. (40)

Opponent-Process the physiological coding process in color vision; cells that either increase or decrease their rate of firing, relative to the baseline level of firing, depending on the wavelength of stimulating light. (180)

Papez Circuit the feedback circuit involving major structures of the limbic system and associated with emotionality. (288)

Parasympathetic Branch See *autonomic nervous system.*

Perikaryon see *soma.*

PET Scan positron emission tomography. (67)

Phantom Limb continued sensations "felt" in the place occupied by an amputated limb. (193)

Phasic Response one that occurs at the onset or termination of stimulation. (140)

Phenotype the measurable characteristics (physical and psychological) of the individual. (201)

Phrenology the mental "science" sired by Gall and based on the discredited thesis that psychological predispositions could be assessed by examination of the irregularities of the cranial bones. (13)

Polarization the condition resulting from an unequal distribution of electrical charge across a membrane or other barrier. (115)

Post-tetanic Potentiation potentiation (*vide infra*) produced by tetanic (bursts of pulses) stimulation of the presynaptic neuron. (256)

Potentiation the enhancement of prolonged activity in a postsynaptic cell by stimulations delivered to the presynaptic neuron. (224)

Psychoneuronal Equivalence the suggested euqivalence between a given psychological process or function and a given neurophysiological event or state. (315)

Psychophysical Parallelism the variety of dualism (*vide supra*) according to which mental and physical processes follow parallel time-courses but without any form of interaction between the two. (7)

Psychosis a severe psychological disturbance rupturing the patient's contact with reality and generally including hallucinatory and/or delusional elements. (295–296)

Psychosurgery any neurosurgery employed for the treatment of psychological conditions. (305–310)

Psychotomimetic chemical agents that lead to psychotic-like conditions. (302–303)

Reaction Range the theoretical range of phenotypic variations made possible by a given genotype. (202)

Receptive Field the total area of the visual field within which a stimulus will reliably evoke activity in the neuron. (189)

Receptor Potential See *generator potential.*

Reflex an unlearned and specific movement elicited by a stimulus, the response confined to specific organs or areas of the body. (203)

Reflex Arc a two-, three- or n-unit circuit containing sensory and motor neurons and mediating reflexive responses to stimuli. (97–99)

Relative Refractory Period the interval during which the active neuron is absolutely unresponsive to any other stimulus, no matter how intense. (121)

REM rapid eye-movement; a stage of sleep (REM sleep) reliably associated with periods of dreaming. (325)

Resting Membrane Potential the charge across the membrane, typically –70 mV., of the unstimulated neuron. (118)

Retrograde Amensia loss of memory resulting from trauma or injury occurring soon after original learning. (263)

Retrograde Degeneration degeneration of regions of the neuron between the cut portion and the cell body, often including the cell body. (46)

Saltatory Conduction the "skipping" or node-to-node conduction possible in myelinated axons. (121–122)

Sedative any chemical agent that reliably promotes calm and quietude. (300)

Sensitization progressive increases in the rate of neural responses produced by several rapid stimulations. (234)

Sodium Pump the metabolic process by which sodium ions are forcibly extruded from within the acon. (116)

Soma the body of the cell, also called the perikaryon, and containing the nucleus of the cell. (88–89)

Spike Action Potential the all-or-none wave of electrical activity that courses down the length of the axon; also the neural impulse. (118–119)

Stimulant any chemical agent that reliably increases periods of wakefulness and levels of arousal. (300)

Stimulus Substitution the theoretical term suggesting the manner in which conditioned stimuli come to have the reflex-eliciting properties of unconditioned stimuli. (207)

Sympathetic Branch See *autonomic nervous system.*

Synapse the space between the terminal branches of one neuron and either the soma or dendrites of the neighboring neuron. (90)

Synchronization a progressive increase of the amplitude of EEG waves during sleep. (325)

Time-Binding the capacity to organize sequences of behavior in time and in a future-oriented fashion; the capacity notably diminished by damage of the frontal cortex. (271)

Tonic Response one that occurs as long as the stimulus is applied. (140)

Tract a collection of fibers running together in the central nervous system. (91)

Transducer any device or mechanism receiving energy in one form and converting it to energy in a different form; e.g., the photoelectric transducer. (158)

Transmitters chemical substances released by the terminal vesicles of axons and capable of altering the polarization of postsynaptic neurons. (123)

Tropism a total and unlearned bodily orientation toward (positive) or away from (negative) a specific stimulus such as light or heat. (203)

Voltage Clamp the technique by which the neural cell's voltage is "clamped" or held constant while ionic movements are tracked during stimulation. (120)

Weber's Law the psychophysical law according to which, at the point of just-noticeable difference, the ratio of (a) the difference between a comparison stimulus and the standard stimulus to (b) the value of the standard is constant. (183)

Wernicke's Syndrome the emission of meaningless bursts of "telegraphic" speech, associated with lesions in Wernicke's area. (341)

White Matter regions of the nervous system whose appearance is determined by large tracts of myelinated fibers. (44)

Index